Social Identity

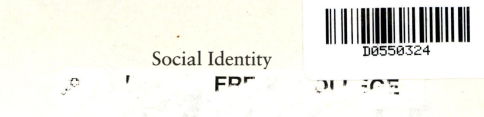

Social Identity
Context, Commitment, Content

Edited by

Naomi Ellemers, Russell Spears and Bertjan Doosje

Copyright © Blackwell Publishers Ltd 1999

First published 1999
Reprinted 2000

Blackwell Publishers Ltd
108 Cowley Road
Oxford OX4 1JF
UK

Blackwell Publishers Inc.
350 Main Street
Malden, Massachusetts 02148
USA

British Library Cataloguing in Publication Data

A CIP catalogue record for this book is available from the British Library.

Library of Congress Cataloging-in-Publication Data

Social identity: context, commitment, content / edited by Naomi
  Ellemers, Russell Spears, and Bertjan Doosje.
    p.   cm.
  Includes bibliographical references (p.) and index.
  ISBN 0–631–20690–6 (alk. paper). — ISBN 0–631–20691–4 (alk. paper)
    1. Group identity. 2. Social groups. 3. Intergroup relations.
  4. Social perception. 5. Context effects (Psychology).
  I. Ellemers, Naomi. II. Spears, Russell. III. Doosje, Bertjan.
  HM131.S58433 1999
  302.4—dc21   98-52221
                                                         CIP

Typeset in 10 on 12.5 pt Sabon
By Ace Filmsetting Ltd, Frome, Somerset
Printed in Great Britain by MPG Books Ltd, Bodmin, Cornwall

This book is printed on acid-free paper

Contents

Contributors

Manuela Barreto	Free University, Amsterdam, the Netherlands
Nyla R. Branscombe	University of Kansas, USA
Bertjan Doosje	University of Amsterdam, the Netherlands
Naomi Ellemers	Free University, Amsterdam (now at Leiden University, the Netherlands)
Dick de Gilder	University of Amsterdam, the Netherlands
Intse J. Hamstra	University of Amsterdam, the Netherlands
Jolanda Jetten	University of Amsterdam, the Netherlands (now at the University of Queensland, Brisbane, Australia)
Martin Lea	University of Manchester, United Kingdom
Antony S. R. Manstead	University of Amsterdam, the Netherlands
Jaap W. Ouwerkerk	Free University, Amsterdam, the Netherlands
Tom Postmes	University of Amsterdam, the Netherlands
Gün Semin	Free University, Amsterdam, the Netherlands
Heather J. Smith	Sonoma State University, USA
Russell Spears	University of Amsterdam, the Netherlands
John C. Turner	The Australian National University, Canberra, Australia
Daniël Wigboldus	University of Nijmegen, the Netherlands

Acknowledgements

Although the editors' names are printed in a particular order on the cover, this is not indicative of the relative input or importance of our contributions to this volume. As is the case with our joint journal papers, this book is the product of a genuinely collective effort and, in true social identity tradition, we have come to think of ourselves in terms of our common identity ('NABERU'), rather than as individual investigators. We have also seen the work reported here referred to as 'the Amsterdam school' of social identity research (although one of us – Naomi – has just moved to a position at Leiden), and this volume was designed to bring together the fruits of this collaboration conducted during the past five years. However, this group is clearly much bigger than ourselves: it extends to our (former) students as well as other colleagues in Amsterdam and around the world. They have all contributed in central ways to our thinking about social identity. We have profoundly enjoyed this inspiring and productive collaboration, and greatly appreciate the willingness of a large proportion of them to present their research in the different chapters in this volume.

A special word of thanks is due to John Turner, one of the 'founding fathers' of social identity theory and the progenitor of self-categorization theory. We are particularly delighted that he contributed a chapter to this volume, in which he looks back and reassesses social identity theory in view of recent empirical research and theoretical debates, as well as providing a vision of where it is going.

We would like to thank the University of Amsterdam, the Free University in Amsterdam, the Dutch research council (NWO), the European Commission and the Kurt Lewin Institute for supporting this research.

We also want to acknowledge the role of the people at Blackwell, without whom this volume would not have been written. Alison Mudditt commissioned the book and showed admirable faith in our project. Martin Davies and Alison Dunnett were equally enthusiastic and saw it through in its latter stages. We would like to thank them for their encouragement, efficiency and patience. Thanks also to Sarah Dancy who copy-edited the manuscript, to Ann Dean for doing the index and Henk Nieman who provided the cover picture. Our gratitude extends to all who have served in different ways to make this book come true.

Naomi Ellemers
Russell Spears
Bertjan Doosje

Introduction

NAOMI ELLEMERS, RUSSELL SPEARS AND
BERTJAN DOOSJE

This volume aims to provide an overview of recent developments in social identity theory, primarily (but not exclusively) from the research perspective of the editors and fellow contributors. Much of the research presented here has already been published in separate articles, but the scale and focus of primary publication in journals means that it has not always been possible to get an overview of a whole programme of research, integrated within the larger theoretical framework. This forum provides the opportunity to draw together the different strands of this programme, to reveal their common theoretical roots and its recurring themes. It also allows us to present ongoing research against the background of established work, providing the reader with insights into new empirical directions and theoretical developments. The work that is reviewed represents a distinctive empirical and theoretical approach to issues of social identity, which is the result of a long-term collaboration between the three editors, as well as our work with other contributors to the book. For want of a more meaningful social identity, this might be characterized as the 'Amsterdam School' of social identity research. The different chapters thus depart from a common theoretical perspective, and cover a broad range of different topics and theoretical issues, including perceptions of self and others, communication and social influence, and the behavioural consequences of these social identity processes.

In putting together these chapters, as is evident from the title of the volume, we have focused on three recurring themes, namely context, commitment and content. Even in the laboratory, where much of the research that is reviewed in this volume has been carried out, groups and group memberships derive their meaning from a particular social context. As has been argued extensively in self-categorization theory, people use groups to define their identity in relation to other relevant groups *in situ*. In other words, the nature of the salient intergroup comparison influences how people perceive themselves in relation to others. One important implication is that a primary goal is to derive and maintain a distinct social identity. Despite some apparent differences in emphasis, this represents a common meeting point for both social and self-categorization theories. We review empirical evidence, indicating that, in certain contexts, commitment to a distinctive identity may even override people's concern with deriving high status or positive self-esteem from their group membership. Some rather deterministic views of social identity theory might lead us to believe that the primary purpose of social identity is to feed individual esteem, but this rather reductionist reading strips the theory of its very social roots and *raison d'être*. As becomes clear from the earliest chapters of this volume, managing social identity is not just about running away from threat. Identity threat is not a single beast, but takes multiple forms, relating to context and group commitment. A social identity threat may not only dictate when the group's relative standing reflects negatively upon the individual, but also when the group cannot be meaningfully distinguished from other groups. Moreover, for those who embrace the group less enthusiastically than it does them, the fact that they cannot be meaningfully distinguished from their group may be yet another source of identity threat. Both the nature of these threats and our reactions to them are likely to be a product of the social context, the commitment to the group and the content of relevant norms and identities.

The relevant social context may not only pose a threat to identity, but can also impinge upon group members' possibilities of coping with it. Empirical research has accumulated to show that private convictions about the group's worth do not necessarily result in public displays of defensive responses (such as ingroup favouring biases). Instead, it seems that consensual views about the traits or abilities that characterize a particular group limit the extent to which its members feel free to claim that their group is superior. Hence, the comparative context – that is, the salience of particular outgroups as well as the question of how the ingroup compares to these other groups – determines which ingroup-enhancing responses seem reasonable without violating consensual definitions of social reality. Additionally, the social context in which these responses are expressed appears to be taken into account by group members. This implies that different coping strategies may be employed, depending on the audience that is likely to witness group members' responses to a threatened identity. If we accept that variations in the comparative and social context are likely to affect and modify the ways group members cope with identity threat, this raises the important question of whether standard research procedures can inform us of the variety of ways in which people actually think of and respond to their group membership, or whether they truly reflect how people cope with specific reality constraints.

A further way in which 'context' plays an important role in this volume is in terms of the different domains in which we have sought to investigate the theoretical ideas. Thus, while we think a valuable characteristic of our approach is our aim to understand central psychological processes by seeking to control key variables in experimental simulations, we also systematically combine and complement these results with observations of real groups in natural contexts. With this approach we achieve the experimental control that supports the internal validity of our argument and illustrates the external validity of our conclusions for applications to a range of real-world contexts (organizational, political and multicultural).

Turning to the second central variable, commitment, one of the main concerns throughout the volume is to show that, in line with Tajfel and Turner's original (1979) position, ingroup identification or group commitment should not merely be seen as an outcome variable, reflecting the relative attractiveness of one's group membership given the status quo. Instead, as is the explicit focus of self-categorization theory (Turner, 1987), whether or not people identify as members of a particular group affects the way they deal with that group membership. Importantly, group commitment not only predicts which kinds of inter- and intragroup relations people are likely to perceive as threatening, but it also determines the way they respond to such threat. More generally, a recurring theme in the research reviewed in this volume is that group commitment is an important indicator of other responses, and moderates group members' social perceptions as well as their behaviour on a range of different indicators.

While emphasizing that, given identical circumstances, people may differ in the extent to which they identify with their group, we are wary of reducing ingroup identification to an individual difference variable. Without trying to deny that there are such individual (or cross-cultural) differences in people's overall level of group attachment, in this volume we use the terms 'ingroup identification' or 'group commitment' to indicate the extent to which people feel attached to a specific group in a particular context. Thus, it is important to keep in mind that they may identify more strongly with one group than with another, or even feel more or less committed to the same group in different situations. While we feel that this approach does more justice to the theoretical richness of the concept, it also poses methodological problems. From an experimental point of view, it is difficult to deal with a variable that, at the same time, can be a dependent and an independent variable, can develop over time or change across contexts. In fact, perhaps it is this complexity that has prevented many other researchers from considering ingroup identification in this more dynamic way. Nevertheless, we acknowledge that group commitment can both reflect existing relations and determine the ways people try to change these relations, and think this is crucial to gaining better insights into the processes at hand.

When we distinguish between responses of high and low identifiers, the general pattern is that those who feel highly committed to their group are more inclined to protect their group's image and exert themselves on behalf of the group, while less committed group members are more likely to be concerned with their personal image and pursue individual goals. In this sense, it would seem that high identifiers show more solidarity compared to low identifiers, who in turn appear to be more 'opportunistic' in aligning with the group only when this serves to enhance their own personal identity. While we think this is an adequate characterization of the behavioural preferences displayed by people who differ with respect to their group commitment, we want to stress that this does not necessarily mean that the response tendencies of less committed group members are morally inferior or socially undesirable. In fact, for some groups, whose characteristic behavioural style implies a rejection of more general pro-social norms (e.g. soccer hooligans), the very fact that overall group commitment is relatively strong, so that group members feel compelled to behave in accordance with their group's norms, is the very cause of (in this case) the social problems associated with these groups. As we will see, people who identify weakly with their group are precisely those most likely to show remorse and repentance when the group's own moral standing is brought into question. Thus, it is important to keep in mind that strong group commitment, resulting in compliance with local group norms, is not necessarily beneficial to the greater social system and vice versa. This is a good example of how commitment can lead to diverging outcomes, either pro-social or anti-social, partly because of the perspective of the intergroup context (what is pro-social for the ingroup, may seem anti-social from an outgroup or even an interpersonal perspective), but also as a result of the divergent content of group identity guiding group behaviour.

This brings us to the third central topic in this volume, which we label with the term 'content'. Some critics of social identity theory have accused it of neglecting the issue of content. Perhaps the rejection of the generic norm explanation of the minimal group bias was seen by some to signal a neglect of normative content in behaviour. Critics have variously championed social representations and more discursive approaches as being more sensitive to an appreciation of the full rich-ness of the content of interaction and behaviour. However, we think that any abandonment of content in the social identity tradition is premature and mis-guided. If there is any truth to this, it reflects more an empirical omission rather than being theoretically grounded. Moreover, self-categorization theory has per-haps been much less vulnerable to this charge, as content of identity defines the very dimensions of social comparison that then feeds back into the content of our identity. Given that groups can and do hold divergent value systems, different expressive behaviours can denote a similar tendency to conform to group norms. Although generic social norms may have fallen from favour as explanatory de-vices, group behaviour may be guided by considerations that are specific to a particular group membership or social context. The power of group-specific norms is a theme that recurs through a number of chapters here.

In this way it becomes possible to account for seemingly inconsistent findings in the literature, by arguing, for instance, that for some groups displays of ingroup favouritism denote a concern with the group's well-being, while in other cases (e.g. for members of a religious group) an equal treatment of people with different group affiliations is in accordance with ingroup goals. In fact, even attitudes or behaviours that are not explicitly acknowledged as group values can be relevant sources of identity expression, as long as they are seen as typical or characteristic for members of a particular group, and guide the attitudes and behaviour of indi-vidual group members (even 'individualism', resulting in individualistic behav-iour, can be a group norm). Thus, when we allow for variations in attitudinal or behavioural content, it becomes possible to understand the common processes underlying a variety of expressions of the general tendency to behave in terms of one's group membership. Again, which of a range of possible attitudes or behaviours is seen as characteristic for a particular group will depend on the salient social context, while the extent to which individual group members feel compelled to display these characteristic behaviours may differ depending on how strongly they feel committed to the group.

This volume starts with a chapter by John Turner, which provides an up-to-date overview of the state of the art in social identity and self-categorization theories, dealing in turn with the main theoretical debates that have been addressed in empirical research. In contrast to 'single hypothesis' theories, the social identity approach is characterized by its theoretical richness and complexity. Indeed, since the original formulation of the theory in the 1970s (Tajfel, 1974; 1975; 1978a, b and c; Tajfel & Turner, 1979), empirical research in this area has yielded important insights that have led to substantial theoretical elaboration and refinement over the years. Thus, while many of our current insights can be traced to and were inspired by the initial foundations of the theory as they were originally laid down, our increasing understanding of the processes at hand reflects an ongoing theoretical development. One important implication is that the social identity approach can give rise to a variety of predictions specifying people's responses under different circumstances. At the same time, this complex and organic nature of the theory calls for a periodic reassessment of these theoretical developments in the light of recent empirical findings. John Turner gives an overview of the main issues that have recently been brought up in empirical research and illuminates how these relate to and extend the original foundations of the theory.

The next three chapters provide a more detailed review of the empirical work leading up to these theoretical developments, in so far as they are related to the three central themes in this volume. After an outline of a taxonomy of different social identity threats (Chapter 2: Branscombe, Ellemers, Spears & Doosje), the next two chapters are intended (amongst other things) to specify consequences of identity threat and identity salience more generally, for social perception (Chapter 3: Spears, Doosje & Ellemers) and intergroup behaviour (Chapter 4: Doosje, Ellemers & Spears). Then, three chapters examine how identity threat and/or group salience affect intergroup discrimination in outcome allocations (Chapter 5: Jetten, Spears & Manstead), strategic behavioural expressions (Chapter 6: Ellemers, Barreto & Spears) and linguistic biases in communication (Chapter 7: Wigboldus, Spears & Semin). Finally, we move to specific domains to illustrate the applied implications of our reasoning at the personal, organizational and societal level, by examining computer-mediated communication (Chapter 8: Postmes, Spears & Lea), performance in work groups (Chapter 9: Ouwerkerk, Ellemers & De Gilder), and collective deprivation (Chapter 10: Smith, Spears & Hamstra).

1

Some Current Issues in Research on Social Identity and Self-categorization Theories

John C. Turner

Introduction

Social identity and self-categorization theories embody a theoretical and research tradition which now stretches back over a quarter of a century to the beginning of the 1970s. In 1971 Tajfel and his colleagues (Tajfel, Flament, Billig & Bundy, 1971) published the results of their studies in the minimal group paradigm; and a year later Tajfel (1972a) published a chapter on social categorization in which he attempted to make sense of the minimal group data by invoking the concept of social identity and the hypothesis of a motive for positive social identity. Nevertheless, social identity theory proper only came into full shape in the mid-1970s, when the more complex elaborations of the theory which had been steadily developing (e.g., Tajfel, 1974; Turner, 1975) were put into a more systematic and detailed form (Tajfel, 1978a; Tajfel & Turner, 1979). By the late 1970s issues arising from social identity theory and research had helped to stimulate the ideas which subsequently became self-categorization theory (Turner, 1978a, 1982, 1985; see Turner & Oakes, 1989, for a summary of these issues). Self-categorization theory did not just resolve some issues relevant to social identity theory; it also represented a major expansion in the range of applicability of the social identity tradition, from intergroup relations and social conflict into the realm of group processes, stereotyping and social cognition. This process has continued, with social identity and self-categorization ideas also now being applied to the interrelationship of self-concept and personality and in fields other than mainstream social psychology (e.g., Turner & Onorato, 1999; Turner & Haslam, in press).

Social identity and self-categorization theories are, despite some confusion on this point, different theories, but there is no question that they rest on the same anti-reductionist metatheory (see Tajfel, 1972b; 1979; Turner, 1996a; Turner & Bourhis, 1996; Turner & Oakes, 1986, 1997) and invoke the same concept of social identity. Self-categorization theory is, as a matter of record, a continuation of the tradition begun by social identity theory, extending and elaborating its idea that social identity processes are fundamental to understanding collective behaviour. They are different theories, but they are allied and largely complementary, doing different jobs from the same broad social psychological perspective. It is for this reason that the term social identity theory is sometimes used (at a more inclusive level) to refer to both theories; this chapter will speak of the social identity perspective, approach or tradition to indicate both theories.

It is noteworthy, as this and other recent books testify (Abrams & Hogg, 1999; Brewer & Miller, 1996; Hogg & Abrams, 1993; Oakes, Haslam & Turner, 1994; Robinson, 1996; Spears, Oakes, Ellemers & Haslam, 1997; Tyler, Kramer & John, 1999; Worchel, Morales, Paez & Deschamps, 1998), that after some twenty-five or more years not only does social identity research continue unabated, but in fact it is being pursued more vigorously now than ever before. This is quite some feat for a theoretical perspective in social psychology. At the same time, the social identity perspective has always been relatively controversial in the sense that it has always had its share of critics. Because of the complexity of the ideas, it has always been subject to significant misunderstandings. On the one hand, there is a contemporary recognition of the quantity and quality of the research it has stimulated and of the freshness and novelty of the insights it offers into classic and contemporary problems in social psychology. On the other, there is a persistent claim amongst its critics (and even some of its friends) that the research has failed to support some of its key hypotheses and that there are significant conceptual flaws. At the same time as reviewers tell us that the tradition has major difficulties, its influence on current research continues to grow and is felt in ever more areas.

There is not space in one chapter to review twenty-five years' research, nor even would it be easy to review properly the work done in just any one area or on any one problem. The book as a whole will review much of the relevant work. This chapter will comment on what has been learned in a rather different way. It will summarize the perspective, and note briefly some of its most important and radical implications, at the same time responding to some of the main criticisms which have been levelled against it. There is no claim that the theories are 'finished and perfect'. This cannot be true of any scientific theory. Both still have room for conceptual development and such development is taking place. Both may ultimately be proved wrong, in the sense that they may be replaced by a different and better understanding of the relevant phenomena, but we shall not advance to a better understanding by rejecting ideas for the wrong reasons. The core insights of the social identity tradition will need to be assimilated in any future theorizing (just as the social identity perspective has absorbed the insights of the earlier group dynamics tradition), which means that we must be clear as to what they are. In many respects the business of elaborating and testing the social identity perspective has still really only just begun, even given the work that has been done, since the ideas have continued to develop year in and year out, preserving the vitality and relevance of the original vision.

The Social Identity Perspective

Social identity theory

The body of ideas that has become known as 'social identity theory' (a term coined by Turner & Brown, 1978, to simplify the various descriptions of the ideas that Tajfel employed) began as an attempt to explain intergroup discrimination in the 'minimal group paradigm' (Tajfel, 1972a; Turner, 1975, 1978b). In that paradigm Tajfel, Flament, Billig and Bundy (1971) found that the mere social categorization of people into distinct groups could produce intergroup behaviour in which subjects favoured ingroup over outgroup members (see Brewer, 1979; Turner, 1975, 1981; Turner & Bourhis, 1996). It appeared that the mere awareness of being in one group as opposed to another was sufficient under certain conditions to trigger processes of intergroup discrimination and competition. Tajfel (1972a) and Turner (1975) argued that the social categorization of subjects in this minimal paradigm created a social identity for them. The subjects accepted the assigned social category membership as a relevant self-definition in the situation. 'Social identity' was conceptualized as that aspect of a person's self-concept based on their group memberships; it was a person's definition of self in terms of some social group membership with the associated value connotations and emotional significance (e.g., a self-definition as 'us women' or 'we Americans').

It was argued that since people evaluated themselves under certain conditions in terms of their ingroup memberships, there was a psychological requirement inherent in social identification that relevant ingroups compare favourably with relevant outgroups. There was, in effect, a need for positive social identity, expressed through a desire to create, maintain or enhance the positively valued distinctiveness of ingroups compared to outgroups on relevant dimensions, and aroused under conditions where people defined and evaluated themselves in terms of their group memberships. Tajfel (e.g., 1979, p. 184) referred to this basic psychological analysis of a motivation for positive social identity producing a drive for ingroup superiority as the sequence of social categorization–social identity–social comparison–positive ingroup distinctiveness. The basic hypothesis here – which is at the psychological heart of the theory – is the notion that social comparisons between groups which are relevant to an evaluation of one's social identity produce pressures for intergroup differentiation to achieve a positive self-evaluation in terms of that identity (or 'collective self-esteem'; see Crocker & Luhtanen, 1990).

Many readings of the theory assume that this psychological analysis was the end of the story. In fact, it was only the beginning. The psychological analysis was then applied to the complexities of real-life intergroup relations in socially stratified societies (see Tajfel & Turner, 1979, for a summary). It was used to explore the psychological consequences for members of the different status positions of groups (e.g., high or low) and the perceived nature of intergroup status differences (e.g., secure or insecure) and to elaborate the different ways in which group members could and would react to the challenges posed to their social identities by their different locations in the social structure and their shared beliefs about the nature of the social structure.

Moreover, this was not a simple matter of arguing that low status group members would be more discriminatory or ethnocentric than high status group members, or that people would show more outgroup discrimination the more they identified with some ingroup. For Tajfel and Turner (1979) the character of intergroup attitudes and action is predicted by an interaction between the need for positive social identity and group members' collective definition, perception and understanding of the social structure of intergroup relationships (Turner, 1996b, 1996c). Thus, for example, depending on whether they perceived group boundaries as permeable or impermeable and status relationships as secure or insecure (stable and legitimate or unstable and illegitimate), low status group members might adopt a strategy of upward individual mobility or social creativity or a strategy of collective, ethnocentric, social competition. Similarly, high status group members might be highly discriminatory and ethnocentric under conditions where they saw their legitimate superiority as threatened by the low status group, but not where they perceived their superiority as illegitimate. Groups would adopt quite different strategies to achieve positive social identity (and ingroup bias or 'social competition' is only one of these strategies) as a function of an interaction between their status position (high or low), their beliefs about the nature of group boundaries, the intensity of ingroup identification and their collective ideologies and shared beliefs about the nature of the social system and intergroup differences of status, power and wealth. To suppose, therefore, as many researchers have done, that social identity theory holds that there should be simple correlations between ingroup bias in some real-world setting and degree of ingroup identification, or status position, or some measure of personal self-esteem, is seriously to misconstrue the theory.

Tajfel (1979) pointed out explicitly that social identity theory had three aspects, each of which was an indispensable part of the story. One was the psychological analysis of the cognitive-motivational processes producing a need for positive social identity. Another was the elaboration of this analysis in its application to real-world intergroup relations noted above. The third was the hypothesis of the 'interpersonal–intergroup continuum' (Tajfel, 1974, 1978a, ch. 2). Tajfel suggested that social behaviour varied along a continuum from interpersonal to intergroup. At the 'intergroup' extreme, all of the behaviour of two or more individuals towards each other is determined by their membership of different social groups or categories (i.e., by group affiliations and loyalties to the exclusion of individual characteristics and interpersonal relationships). The 'interpersonal' extreme refers to any social encounter in which all the interaction that takes place is determined by the personal relationships between the individuals and their individual characteristics (i.e., idiosyncratic personal qualities are the overriding causal influences). Tajfel used the interpersonal–intergroup continuum to explain when social identity processes are likely to come into operation and how social interaction differs qualitatively between the extremes. He argued that, as behaviour became more intergroup, attitudes to the outgroup within the ingroup tend to become more uniform and consensual and outgroup members tend to be seen more as homogeneous and undifferentiated members of their social category.

Shift along the continuum was a function of an interaction between psychological and social factors. Tajfel emphasized, in particular, the degree to which group members shared an ideology of 'individual mobility' or 'social change' and saw the social system as characterized by rigid and intense social stratification. He suggested that subjective and objective barriers to moving between groups, leading to the perceived impermeability of group boundaries, tended to be associated with a 'social change' belief-system, a view that people cannot resolve their identity problems through individual action and mobility, but can only change their social situation by acting collectively in terms of their shared group membership. In social identity theory, then (but not self-categorization theory, in which ingroup identification and the relative salience of that identification in a specific social context are given causal prominence – see, e.g., Ellemers, Spears & Doosje, 1997), it was impermeable group boundaries and the social change belief-system that were seen as the key factors in shifting behaviour along the continuum towards the intergroup pole. They played a central role in determining collective reactions by groups members to insecure status in the social system.

The hypothesis of an interpersonal–intergroup continuum has several implications. It points to the idea of a qualitative psychological distinction between individual and group behaviour. It draws a clear distinction between 'identification' with a social group and the current 'salience' of that social identity in a specific social situation, similar to the distinction between the 'stored' and the 'working' self-concept (Markus & Wurf, 1987; Turner, 1982). It also directs one to look more carefully at the issue of how social identity processes come into play and, in particular, at how social identities become 'salient' (Oakes, 1987). Finally, the questions are raised of the interrelationship of interpersonal and intergroup behaviour and of the processes that determine their specific characteristics. These questions, amongst others, led to the development of self-categorization theory (see Turner & Oakes, 1989), which began with the insight that the distinction between interpersonal and intergroup behaviour could be explained by a parallel and underlying distinction between personal and social identity (Turner, 1978a, 1982).

Self-categorization theory

Self-categorization theory began (Turner, 1978a, 1982, 1984) with the distinction between social identity (self-definitions in terms of social category memberships) and personal identity (self-definitions in terms of personal or idiosyncratic attributes). It drew on evidence of situational variations in self-concept functioning (salience) to suggest that 'social identity is sometimes able to function to the relative exclusion of personal identity' (Turner, 1984, p. 527) and hypothesized that: 'The adaptive function of social identity . . . is to produce group behaviour and attitudes . . . it is the cognitive mechanism which makes group behaviour possible' (ibid.).

The basic process postulated is self-categorization, leading to self-stereotyping and the depersonalization of self-perception. It is argued that where people define themselves in terms of a shared social category membership, there is a perceptual accentuation of intragroup similarities and intergroup differences on relevant correlated dimensions. People stereotype themselves and others in terms of salient social categorizations, leading to an enhanced perceptual identity between self and ingroup members and an enhanced perceptual contrast between ingroup and outgroup members. Where social identity becomes relatively more salient than personal identity, people see themselves less as differing individual persons and more as the similar, prototypical representatives of their ingroup category. There is a depersonalization of the self – a 'cognitive redefinition of the self – from unique attributes and individual differences to shared social category memberships and associated stereotypes' (Turner, 1984, p. 528) – and it is this process that transforms individual into collective behaviour as people perceive and act in terms of a shared, collective conception of self: 'The identity perspective . . . reinstates the group as a psychological reality and not merely a convenient label for describing the outcome of interpersonal processes and relations' (Turner, 1984, p. 535).

Thus, social identity was reconceptualized as the process which transforms interpersonal into intergroup behaviour. Initially, following the hypothesis of the interpersonal–intergroup continuum, it was assumed that personal and social identity were also at the poles of a bipolar continuum. However, subsequently (Turner, 1985; Turner, Hogg, Oakes, Reicher & Wetherell, 1987; Turner & Oakes, 1989), this conception was substantially revised. The idea that salient personal and social identities would tend to have opposing effects on self-perception, producing, respectively, personalization and depersonalization, was retained, but the conceptualization of personal and social identity as forming a bipolar continuum was replaced by the notion that they represented different levels (of inclusiveness) of self-categorization. The self can be categorized at many different levels and the factors which make for the salience of any given level need not be inversely related. On the contrary, it can be assumed that in many situations there will be factors making for the salience of both the personal and the social categorical levels of self-definition. It is the relative salience of different levels of self-categorization in a specific situation which determines the degree to which self-perception is personalized or depersonalized, the degree to which behaviour expresses individual differences or collective similarities. Thus, although the forces determining the salience of different levels of self-categorization need not be inversely related, the perceptual effects of the different levels will still tend to work against each other as a function of their relative strength.

In its present form the theory provides an analysis of variation in self-categorization. It assumes that self-conception reflects self-categorization, the cognitive grouping of the self as identical to some class of stimuli in contrast to some other class of stimuli. As is the case with all systems of natural categories, self-categorizations can exist at different levels of abstraction related by class inclusion. That is, a given self-category (e.g., 'scientist') is seen as more abstract than another (e.g., 'biologist') to the extent that it can contain, but cannot be contained by, the other: all biologists are scientists, but not all scientists are biologists. Self-categories can be both more or less inclusive than personal and social identity, but these are the most important levels for understanding group behaviour.

Personal identity refers to self-categories which define the individual as a unique person in terms of their individual differences from other (ingroup) persons. Social identity refers to social categorizations of self and others, self-categories which define the individual in terms of his or her shared similarities with members of certain social categories in contrast to other social categories. Social identity is the social categorical self (e.g., 'us' versus 'them', ingroup versus outgroup, us women, men, whites, blacks, etc.). It is a more inclusive level of self-perception than personal identity in the sense that the category 'scientist' is more inclusive than 'biologist'.

The theory implies that when we perceive ourselves as 'we' and 'us' as opposed to 'I' and 'me', this is ordinary and normal self-experience in which the self is defined in terms of others who exist outside of the individual person doing the experiencing and therefore cannot be reduced to purely personal identity. At certain times the subjective self is defined and experienced as identical, equivalent, similar to or interchangeable with a social class of people in contrast to some other class. Psychologically, the social collectivity becomes self.

The central hypothesis for group behaviour is that, as shared social identity becomes salient, individual self-perception tends to become depersonalized. That is, individuals tend to define and see themselves less as differing individual persons and more as the interchangeable representatives of some shared social category membership. For example, when an individual woman tends to categorize herself as a woman in contrast to men, then she (subjectively 'we') tends to accentuate perceptually her similarities to other women (and reduce her idiosyncratic personal differences from other women) and enhance perceptually her stereotypical differences from men (Hogg & Turner, 1987a; Lorenzi-Cioldi, 1991; Onorato & Turner, 1996, 1997). Her self changes in level and content and her self-perception and behaviour become depersonalized. Depersonalization of the self is the subjective stereotyping of the self in terms of the relevant social categorization.

The theory explains variation in the salience of any given level of self-categorization as a function of an interaction between the relative accessibility of a particular self-category (or 'perceiver readiness', the readiness of a perceiver to use a particular categorization) and the fit between category specifications and the stimulus reality to be represented (the match between the category and reality). Relative accessibility reflects a person's past experience, present expectations and current motives, values, goals and needs. It reflects the active selectivity of the perceiver in being ready to use categories which are relevant, useful and likely to be confirmed by the evidence of reality. One important factor affecting a person's readiness to use a social category for self-definition in specific situations is the extent of their identification with the group, the degree to which it is central, valued and ego-involving (see, e.g., Doosje & Ellemers, 1997; Gurin & Markus, 1988).

Fit has two aspects: comparative fit and normative fit (Oakes, 1987). Comparative fit is defined by the principle of meta-contrast (Turner, 1985), which states that a collection of stimuli is more likely to be categorized as an entity (a higher-order unit) to the degree that the average differences perceived between them are less than the average differences perceived between them and the remaining stimuli which comprise the frame of reference. Stated in this form, the principle defines fit in terms of the emergence of a focal category against a contrasting background. It can also be used to define fit for the salience of a dichotomous classification. For example, any collection of people will tend to be categorized into distinct groups to the degree that the intragroup differences perceived within the relevant comparative context are smaller on average than the perceived intergroup differences.

Normative fit refers to the content aspect of the match between category specifications and the instances being represented. For example, to categorize a group of people as Catholics as opposed to Protestants, they must not only differ (in attitudes, actions, etc.) from Protestants more than from each other (comparative fit), but must also do so in the right direction on specific content dimensions of comparison. Their similarities and differences must be consistent with our normative beliefs about the substantive social meaning of the social category (Oakes, Turner & Haslam, 1991; Turner, Oakes, Haslam & McGarty, 1994).

Self-categorization is seen as a dynamic, context-dependent process, determined by comparative relations within a given context. The meta-contrast principle indicates that, to predict categorization, the entire range of stimuli under consideration, rather than isolated stimulus characteristics, must be considered. By proposing that categories form so as to ensure that the differences between them are larger than the differences within them, meta-contrast contextualizes categorization, tying it to an on-the-spot judgement of relative differences. For example, we might categorize an individual as 'Australian' to the extent that, in the current comparative context, the differences between individual Australians are less than the differences between Australians and Americans. Alternatively, the salient category might be 'English-speaking' in a context where the difference between various English-speaking groups (such as Americans and Australians) is less than the difference between English and non-English speakers (Haslam & Turner, 1992).

The emphasis on categorization as highly variable and context-dependent produces a concomitant emphasis on the context-dependence of perceived similarity and difference, the major outcome of categorization. People who are categorized and perceived as different in one context (e.g., 'biologists' and 'physicists' within a science faculty) can be recategorized and perceived as similar in another context (e.g., as 'scientists' rather than 'social scientists' within a university) without any actual change in their own positions. Whether people see themselves as similar or different, and the extent to which they do so, is not a fixed, absolute given, but varies with how, and the level at which, people categorize themselves and others. Arising from the comparisons specified in the meta-contrast principle, self-categorization subjectively transforms people's relations into similarities and differences, and from perceived similarities and differences flow, the theory hypothesizes, perceptions of attraction and dislike, agreement and disagreement, cooperation and conflict. Self-categorization is assumed to provide the fundamental basis of our social orientation towards others.

In sum, as an account of the psychological group, the theory's key ideas are that, first, the level and kind of identity used to represent self and others vary with one's motives, values and expectations, one's background knowledge and theories, and the social context within which comparison takes place; second, the salience of shared social identity leads to the depersonalization of self-perception; and, third, depersonalization produces group behaviour (i.e., collective action and, processes regulated by a shared social categorical self).

Implications and Criticisms of the Social Identity Perspective

The social identity perspective has generated and is generating a vast amount of empirical research. It has stimulated a plethora of specific analyses, hypotheses and approaches in a wide range of different areas. Apart from the particular findings and ideas generated in specific studies, perhaps its chief value has been to open up areas by providing new ways of thinking about major social psychological phenomena, in particular, the individual–group relationship and group processes, prejudice and intergroup relations, social stereotyping, and, most recently, the self-concept and personality. The perspective represents a major new approach to social psychology in that it embodies a general metatheory, which we have termed social psychological 'interactionism' (see Tajfel, 1972b, 1979; Turner, 1996a; Turner & Bourhis, 1996; Turner, Hogg, Oakes, Reicher & Wetherell, 1987; Turner & Oakes, 1986, 1997). In what follows we shall not try to review specific studies or areas (which is simply impossible in the space), but to indicate the radical thrust of its contributions and discuss briefly some of the relevant criticisms that have been aired.

A new way of thinking about groups

The fundamental principle that follows from self-categorization theory is that psychological group formation is an adaptive process that produces socially unitary, collective behaviour and makes possible group relations of mutual attraction, cooperation and influence between members. Factors which, in a given social setting, tend to create and make salient shared group membership, shared social identity, tend to produce a mutual orientation of attraction, cooperation and influence, as members define and react to each other in terms of their common social category membership rather than as differing individual persons. Group formation is a not merely an effect of interpersonal relationships; it actively determines and qualitatively changes people's attitudes and behaviours towards each other. This view has provided new analyses of group formation and cohesion, social cooperation, social influence (conformity, polarization, minority influence and leadership), crowd behaviour and 'de-individuation'.

The key idea is that group behaviour represents a shift from action in terms of differing personal identities to action more in terms of a shared social identity. The evidence that salient social identity depersonalizes the perception of self and others is now quite extensive (e.g., Oakes, Haslam & Turner, 1994; Spears, Doosje & Ellemers 1997; Turner, Oakes, Haslam & McGarty, 1994). Reasonably direct evidence comes from studies on self-stereotyping (e.g., Hogg & Turner, 1987a; Onorato & Turner, 1996, 1997; Simon, 1993; Simon & Hamilton, 1994; Simon, Pantaleo & Mummendey, 1995; Spears, Doosje & Ellemers, 1997), perceived ingroup and outgroup homogeneity (Ellemers & Van Knippenberg, 1997; Haslam, Oakes, Turner & McGarty, 1995, 1996) assimilation and contrast effects (Brewer & Weber, 1994; Haslam & Turner, 1992, 1995; Wilder & Thompson, 1988) and the effects of differences in ingroup identification (Branscombe & Wann, 1994; Doosje & Ellemers, 1997; Ellemers, Spears & Doosje, 1997).

Anastasio, Bachman, Gaertner and Dovidio (1997), Hogg (1992) and Turner (1984) report research on the role of self-categorization in producing social cohesion within groups and between (sub)groups. The main idea here is that psychological group formation is not based on interpersonal attraction (attraction between members as unique individual persons) but creates identity-based liking between members in terms of their mutually perceived group similarities (Hogg, 1992; Turner, 1982; Turner, Sachdev & Hogg, 1983; Turner, Hogg, Oakes, Reicher & Wetherell, 1987). There is also evidence of its role in social cooperation (Brewer & Kramer, 1986; Brewer & Schneider, 1990; Caporael, Dawes, Orbell & van de Kragt, 1989; Dawes, van de Kragt & Orbell, 1988; Kramer & Brewer, 1984; Morrison, 1995a, 1995b; 1998; Orbell, van de Kragt & Dawes, 1988; Turner & Bourhis, 1996; Tyler & Dawes, 1993). It is proposed that the perceived interdependence of people can function as both a cause and an effect of psychological group formation (Turner, 1981, 1982, 1985). Any variable such as common fate, shared threat, proximity, similarity, shared interests, cooperative interaction or positive interdependence, which can function cognitively as a criterion of social categorization to produce an awareness of shared social identity, can lead to group formation. We can define ourselves as a distinct we-group on the basis of our shared interests in contrast to others. Similarity of fate, shared goals, etc. can directly create a group through social identification prior to any experience of positive outcomes mediated by group membership. Conversely, group formation can produce perceived interdependence; it can transform people's perception of their goals. It is assumed that, in depersonalizing the self, salient social identity also depersonalizes self-interest, transforming differing personal self-interests into a collective we-group interest and creating a cooperative orientation within the group.

Probably most work applying self-categorization theory to group processes has looked at social influence (Turner, 1991). As with cooperation, the theory argues that shared social identity is the basis of mutual influence between people. It is assumed that depersonalization, the creation of mutually perceived similarity between ingroup members, not only leads to more consensual behaviour in terms of the norms and values that define one's group, but that it also produces shared expectations of agreement between ingroup members. Where the latter are disconfirmed (i.e., where there is disagreement within the group), subjective uncertainty about the validity (appropriateness, correctness, etc.) of one's judgements is produced, which has to be resolved. The uncertainty is created by individuals' implicit awareness that people who are similar and who are judging a similar (shared, publicly invariant) stimulus situation ought to agree (i.e., react in the same way). Furthermore, where they do so agree, the agreement provides evidence that ingroup members' responses reflect an external, objective reality, rather than personal biases or idiosyncrasies. If some response to the stimulus situation is depersonalized, shared with similar others, if it is consensual and normative for the group, then it can be attributed to external reality, it provides information about reality. In fact, the response is experienced as subjectively valid and appropriate precisely because it is perceived as in some sense 'objectively demanded' by reality. By the same token, disagreement within the group raises basic questions to do with the perceived cause of one's response, which amount to the experience of uncertainty: do we differ in some relevant way after all? are we confronting the same reality, approaching it from the same perspective? am I or are they wrong?

Thus the basic ideas are that (a) shared social identity is the precondition of mutual influence, (b) disagreement within the ingroup creates uncertainty, which must be resolved (through recategorizing self and others as different, differentiating the stimulus situation into one that is not shared, or engaging in mutual influence) and (c) one's own judgement or behaviour is subjectively validated (as correct, desirable, appropriate, informative of reality) to the degree that it participates in and exemplifies an ingroup norm. The traditional distinction between 'informational' and 'normative' influence (see Turner, 1991) is rejected in this formulation. It is assumed that ingroup norms induce private acceptance rather than merely public compliance because they provide information about appropriate behaviour. They define congruent responses as informationally valid for members, as shared within the ingroup and hence as reflecting reality rather than personal bias or the incompetence and/or prejudice of outgroups. Informational influence is influence as a function of the perceived validity of information, and here perceived validity is a function of the degree to which the message (judgement, response, etc.) is consensual (i.e., normative) within the ingroup. Thus for self-categorization theory, informational and (ingroup) normative influence represent the same process. Compliance, on the other hand, going along with social norms as a function of the social power of the source, rather than its capacity for persuasive influence, is seen as specifically a reaction to the norms and power of an outgroup.

Several hypotheses follow from this analysis (see Turner, Hogg, Oakes, Reicher & Wetherell, 1987; Turner & Oakes, 1989). One currently being applied to the issue of leadership (e.g., Fielding & Hogg, 1997; Haslam, 1998; Haslam, McGarty, Brown, Eggins, Morrison & Reynolds, 1998; Platow, 1998; Turner, 1998; Turner & Haslam, in press) is the idea that group members will differ in their relative persuasiveness as a function of the degree to which they embody the ingroup and its norm. The notion that people vary in the extent to which they represent the group as a whole is operationalized by means of the concept of relative prototypicality (in turn based on the meta-contrast principle). To the degree that, on average, an individual differs more from outgroup members and less from ingroup members on some dimension or attribute than other ingroup members, the more he or she can be defined as relatively prototypical of the ingroup (compared to other ingroup members), that is, the more he or she will be perceived as representative of the ingroup as a whole in this intergroup context, and the more influential will he or she be within the ingroup:

> In self-categorization theory, the expert/leader is the individual who best represents the group consensus . . . The theory uses the concept of 'prototypicality' derived from research on categorization (Rosch, 1978) to explain how there can be differences between category members in the degree to which they represent categorical identity. Thus there can be individual differences between members in the degree to which they exemplify the group as a whole . . . and a person can be perceived as different from one's individual self in better expressing one's shared social identity. The idea of levels of self-identity clarifies that [a leader] may be different from one's personal self at the same time as being (and indeed just because they are) more similar to our shared social categorical self. (Turner, 1991, pp. 164–5)

This notion that there is variation within groups in the degree to which particular individuals and subgroups represent the group as a whole, and the additional notion that the relative prototypicality of extremist and moderate members varies as a function of the social context within which the ingroup is defined, have been used to explain group polarization (Turner, 1991). The related idea that who is categorized as part of the ingroup at any given time varies with the social context of comparison has been used to explain minority influence and conversion (David & Turner, 1992, 1996, in press a and b). It is hypothesized that ingroup minorities (radical subgroups who are 'on our side' but more extreme than the moderate ingroup majority) will tend to be categorized as outgroup in the context of intragroup comparisons and as ingroup in the context of intergroup comparisons. In the context of disagreement within the sociological group, we shall tend to define who 'we' are as the majority in contrast to the deviant minority. 'We' will be defined as excluding the deviant minority, as 'us' the majority as opposed to 'them' the minority. However, in the context of a wider intergroup conflict with a more different 'them', some more fundamentally discrepant outgroup, the deviant minority will tend to be recategorized as 'us' in contrast to the even more opposed outgroup. 'We' will not now be restricted to the orthodox majority of the ingroup, but will be extended to include all ingroup members in comparison to the higher-order outgroup. In self-categorization terms the 'ingroup' changes from being a lower-level, majority 'us' to being a higher-level, combined majority and minority 'us'. Whether a minority is ingroup or outgroup, therefore, will vary with the specific social context and it is this variation in self-categorization which determines when minorities influence.

A new way of thinking about intergroup relations and prejudice

Rabbie and colleagues (Horwitz & Rabbie, 1989; Rabbie, 1991; Rabbie & Horwitz, 1988; Rabbie, Schot & Visser, 1989) have criticized the social identity analysis of the group and intergroup discrimination on a number of grounds. Their arguments have already been answered in some detail by Turner and Bourhis (1996) and Bourhis, Turner and Gagnon (1997), and this debate will not be reproduced here. There, we have answered the criticism that the effects of the minimal group paradigm can be explained by interdependence and individual self-interest, providing a conceptual critique and empirical evidence against this reductionist move. Social identity theory never denied the importance of the material basis of conflicts, or the role of self-interest, although by now it should be clear that the self does not have to be conceptualized at the level of the individual. Indeed, social identity theory not only provides a specific theory of intergroup relations, it also resurrects the intergroup approach to social conflict pioneered in social psychology by Sherif (e.g., 1967) and his colleagues. Although Sherif was a realistic group conflict theorist, pointing to the role of conflicts of interest between groups in social conflict, he stressed as fundamental the idea that intergroup relations rather than individual and interpersonal processes determined intergroup attitudes. Social identity theory is an intergroup theory in exactly the same sense. It argues that intergroup attitudes are always the product of an interaction between people's collective psychology as group members and the perceived social structure of intergroup relationships. The interaction between collective psychology and social reality is assumed to be mediated by group members' socially shared and socially mediated understanding of their intergroup relations (i.e., their collective beliefs, theories and ideologies about the nature of the social system and the nature of the status differences between groups).

In this respect, as I have argued elsewhere (Turner, 1996b, 1996c), the social identity perspective provides a way of going beyond the 'prejudice' model of social conflict which has dominated the field since the 1920s. The implicit orthodoxy in intergroup relations research is that social antagonism in its various forms is a product of prejudice, that is, of defect, irrationality and pathology at the level of individual psychology. Negative outgroup attitudes are assumed to be inherently pathological, irrational, invalid and unjustifiable. This notion is summarized by three main ideas that pervade much research: that specific dysfunctional individual-difference or personality factors more or less directly predispose people to more or less hostility against outgroups; that there are individual-level cognitive and/or motivational processes which directly produce negative outgroup attitudes which are socially irrational since they are purely psychologically caused; and that intergroup attitudes are inherently mindless, meaningless and devoid of rational content.

The social identity perspective rejects each of these ideas. It emphasizes that we need to understand social conflict as psychologically meaningful, as an expression of how people define themselves socially and of their understanding of the reality of their intergroup relationships. Social conflict can be a rational reaction to people's historically evolved understanding of themselves in interaction with their theories of the social world and the reality of social structure. We do not need to posit defective personality types, individual-level psychological processes which directly cause outgroup hostility as a result of some single variable, factor or state (social categorization, ingroup identification, frustration, low self-esteem, low social status, positive or negative mood, etc.), or inherent defects in human cognition, motivation or emotions (e.g., the supposed over-simplification and over-generalization of stereotyping) to explain social antagonism. It is a result of ordinary, adaptive and functional psychological processes in interplay with the realities of social life. This is an important and radically different approach to social conflict which has implications for research in any and every area of 'prejudice'.

It is somewhat paradoxical then that the social identity perspective is often reduced to a 'prejudice' theory and then criticized because the evidence fails to support the revised version of the theory. Some of the main examples of this reduction are assertions that social identity theory predicts that social categorization automatically and inevitably leads to ingroup bias, that intergroup relations should be characterized by universal ethnocentrism, that there should be positive correlations between individual differences in ingroup identification and ingroup bias, that low status groups should always be more biased than high status groups, that intergroup discrimination is driven by an individual need for self-esteem and should directly enhance individual self-esteem and so on. There is a notion in many reviews that social identity theory is simply the assertion of a universal, irrational drive for ethnocentrism, unconstrained by social realities or the social meaning of intergroup attitudes, that this drive serves some individual, almost quasi-biological need for self-esteem, and that some simple, single factor which triggers or relates to this drive should be positively correlated with intergroup discrimination, virtually independent of social context or the perceived nature of intergroup relations. Any serious reading of the theory (let alone the explicit statements of its originators) illustrates that this is a caricature.

There are two major lines of research which illustrate these kinds of claim. These concern the hypothesis of a causal link (expressed as a positive correlation) between ingroup identification and ingroup bias and the so-called 'self-esteem hypothesis'. Another line of research, on positive/negative asymmetries in intergroup discrimination, can be understood as compatible with basic ideas of the social identity analysis (Mummendey & Otten, in press; Reynolds, Turner & Haslam, 1998a), but is sometimes used to argue that social identity theory is not applicable to real social conflict. Critics (e.g., Brown, 1995) underplay the subtleties of the social identity analysis of ingroup bias both as an experimental phenomenon and in its highly mediated relationship to real social hostility. A mistaken assumption is made that the theory directly equates ingroup bias (reflecting the search for positive distinctiveness) with aggression between groups (but see Tajfel & Turner, 1979).

Ingroup identification and ingroup bias   Several researchers (e.g., Hinkle and Brown, 1990; Kelly, 1993) state that the basic proposition of social identity theory is that there should be a direct causal link between ingroup identification and ingroup bias. This is understood to mean that positive correlations should be obtained between individual differences in identification with some ingroup and individual differences in the degree to which that group is favoured over the outgroups in the setting. In fact, such correlations are not uniformly positive but often tend to be weak and quite variable (Brown, Hinkle, Ely, Fox-Cardamone, Maras & Taylor, 1992; Hinkle & Brown, 1990). Such data are then cited as evidence against the theory, justifying attempts at major revision (Brown, Hinkle, Ely, Fox-Cardamore, Maras & Taylor, 1992). The inference that these data call the theory into question is unjustified on a number of grounds, ranging from the problematic nature of the derivation to weaknesses in the relevant studies. We can briefly note the main problems.

Social identity theory never advanced the hypothesis of a direct causal connection between ingroup identification and ingroup bias. The summary above indicates that the causal relationship was always assumed to be mediated by a number of complicating factors. Ingroup bias (or social competition) is only one of several individual and group strategies which group members can pursue to achieve positive distinctiveness (others being individual mobility and social creativity). Factors relevant to determining whether ingroup bias is likely to occur include: (a) the degree of identification with a group (understood in self-categorization theory terms as a 'readiness' to categorize self in terms of some group membership under appropriate conditions); (b) the salience of the relevant social identity in relation to which a specific comparative judgement is being made (which is not the same as degree of identification); (c) the perceived social structure of intergroup relationships; (d) the relevance of the comparative dimension to the intergroup status relationship; and/or (e) the relevance of the outgroup to the particular comparative judgement being made. Social identity theory did not derive ingroup bias directly from the motivation for a positive social identity. It always assumed that whether or not ingroup bias was observed was a function of the specific intergroup comparison being made and the interaction between the relative status position of the ingroup, the perceived impermeability of group boundaries and the nature of the perceived status differences on the relevant dimension. Turner and Brown (1978), for example, showed early on just how complex the relationship between ingroup bias and different intergroup status differences could be, just as the theory expected. In this light the variable relationship between measures of ingroup identification and ingroup bias is only to be expected. Nothing in the summary of the theory above implies simple positive correlations.

Three early studies widely cited as failing to confirm the hypothesis (Brown, Condor, Mathews, Wade & Williams, 1986; Brown & Williams, 1984; Oaker & Brown, 1986) illustrate other difficulties. Ingroup identification is not experimentally manipulated but is a correlational, individual difference measure. This raises the problem of other correlated individual differences which may be confounded with ingroup identification. Why, after all, do the respondents differ in their degree of self-reported identification? This issue is almost never discussed. The instrument used to measure identification focuses more on personal identity than social identity. For example, the questionnaire items commonly begin with 'I am a person who', where the implicit comparison in the self-report is within the ingroup between one's personal self and other ingroup members. It is not between the ingroup and the relevant outgroup(s) in terms of a collective self, that is, 'I am a person who identifies more with x than do my fellow members', not 'we identify more with x than with group y'. There is also evidence that the measure is not unitary; it has multiple components which may be only weakly correlated with each other (Hinkle, Taylor, Fox Cardamone & Crook, 1989).

Furthermore, use of an individual difference methodology is inconsistent with the discontinuity hypothesis of the social identity perspective, the hypothesis that there is a psychological discontinuity between people acting as individuals and people acting as group members (Turner, 1996b, 1996c; Turner & Onorato, 1999). A related point is that in these studies identification tends to be confused with salience. If one obtains intergroup attitudes from subjects responding in terms of their personal differences from others, in terms of their personal identities, then the attitudes obtained are not likely to remain unchanged when the subjects' social identities become salient. Where one makes a strong intergroup comparison and one's shared social identity becomes salient, intergroup attitudes are likely to become depersonalized, consensual and normative. Why would one expect such responses to reflect a personalized level of self? Self-categorization theory predicts directly that depersonalizing subjects enhances intragroup homogeneity and thus will modify correlations between the intergroup responses and a prior individual difference score (Haslam & Wilson, in press; Reynolds, Turner & Haslam, 1998b, Verkuyten & Hagendoorn, 1988.).

An example of this problem is provided by Brown et al. (1986), where different groups of workers (all unionized) rated the management least favourably of all outgroups. Where groups of workers make judgements about management as 'workers' rather than as members of some departmental or functional subgroup, one might expect their social identity as workers versus management to become salient, their personal and subgroup identities to decrease in salience and their attitudes to become more consensual and negative as a function of their superordinate identity as workers. This hypothesis was not tested directly, but perceived conflict between the subgroup and management was the strongest predictor of ingroup bias (against management) in the whole sample. If this conflict had become the focus of intergroup comparison and workers had reacted as workers and union members with more consensual anti-management attitudes, then, paradoxically, the relationship between pre-conflict individual differences in identification with the subgroup and attitudes to management might well have decreased or become irrelevant. Such an outcome would show the power of identification (with the superordinate group) in interaction with salience and perceived intergroup relations in predicting intergroup attitudes, but it would not be reflected in the predictive power of any prior individual difference measure of subgroup identification.

The actual social categorizations in the studies are selected by the researchers with often only weak or no evidence that they correspond to the subjective division of the social world by the subjects in relation to the intergroup attitudes obtained. For example, in Brown et al. (1986) only about a third of the subjects spontaneously mentioned the groups which the researchers employed as the basis for their measures of identification and ingroup–outgroup bias. Thus the researchers' ingroup–outgroup categorizations may have no real meaning or relevance to the subjects in relation to the outcomes measured. The same point applies to the dimensions of intergroup comparison selected to measure ingroup bias (which seem frequently to be selected a priori for the convenience of the researcher rather than because there is any real evidence of their relevance to the intergroup relationship they are supposed to reflect, e.g., Oaker & Brown, 1986). Similarly, bias is measured against all the 'outgroups' in the setting as if they were equivalent, even though it is clear that they may be in different relationships to the ingroup and differ in the degree to which they are included in superordinate social identities.

There is often good evidence that the intergroup relationships are not insecure, but relatively positive and that there are powerful superordinate social identifications at work (e.g., as nurses, workers, trade unionists). The latter often imply superordinate values and norms which prescribe that discrimination is not appropriate between the subgroups. This also means that the evaluative direction of the comparison can be ambiguous. Is it positive for a subgroup of nurses to discriminate against another group who work together with them in a complementary, cooperative relationship as nurses? Would this reflect a positive value held by the subgroup? No effort is made to determine whether the subjects are using other relevant strategies to achieve positive and secure social identity as social identity theory would predict. The claimed support for other theories is often quite contentious. Correlations between perceived conflict with another group and ingroup bias, for example (which seems close to an operationalization of insecure intergroup comparison), are cited as evidence for realistic conflict theory, even though it is admitted in the same paper that there are positively interdependent goals between the groups as 'workers' and 'trade-unionists', of which the subjects are aware. Perceived conflict, therefore, is not persuasive as a measure of objective or perceived conflict of interests.

This is not the place to review Hinkle and Brown's (1990) own taxonomic approach to ingroup bias. Suffice to say, the problems with taxonomic approaches were detailed long ago by Kurt Lewin (1931; see Oakes, 1996). Further, the evidence for this approach is not compelling or consistent (e.g., Capozza, Voci, Volpato & Pozzeto, 1996). Self-reported identification is not a static attribute. We know from research by Ellemers (e.g., 1993b) and self-categorization theory (Haslam & Turner, 1992, 1995, 1998) that self-reports of ingroup identification are a variable outcome of self-categorization and social identity processes in the specific setting; it cannot be assumed that they are direct reflections of fixed psychological structures (see Turner & Onorato, 1999). The same is also probably true of the other variables used to construct a supposedly stable taxonomy (individualist/collectivist and autonomous/relational orientations). We need a process account of intergroup relations which derives specific intergroup responses from the application of general principles to the concrete situation as defined by the values of relevant parameters.

This does not mean that differences in identification are unimportant. From a self-categorization viewpoint, measures of identification may be a way of getting at the individual's readiness to self-categorize in terms of some identity, reflecting the psychological resources a person will tend to bring to the task of understanding self and constructing self-categories in some setting. They will reflect the centrality of some group membership in a person's understanding of their place in the social order and their relationships to others and also their commitment to that identity as a consequence of that understanding and their social values. The mistake is to think that identification expresses some kind of fixed and stable self-structure or personality trait which is chronically salient and directly expressed independently of the social meaning of the situation. If we think of identification as measured in some relevant context as providing information about the different readiness of people to use certain social categories, then it becomes evident that it will be an important variable with relevance for predicting a whole range of effects. There is now good evidence (much of it reported in following chapters) that high versus low identifiers will react in a variety of different ways to various challenges to the ingroup, with high identifiers tending to act more in terms of a 'social change' pattern and low identifiers more in terms of 'individual mobility' (e.g., Branscombe & Ellemers, 1998; Doosje & Ellemers, 1997; Ellemers, Spears & Doosje, 1997; Kelly, 1993; Kelly & Breinlinger, 1996; Spears, Doosje & Ellemers, 1997). These effects, however, are more general than simply showing ingroup bias. This area is one where real progress has been made, but it is only comprehensible if one moves away from a simplified version of social identity theory and recognizes that one needs to incorporate a self-categorization analysis into its contemporary elaboration.

Self-esteem and intergroup discrimination   The self-esteem hypothesis refers to two supposed corollaries of social identity theory advanced by Hogg and Abrams (1990): that (a) successful intergroup discrimination elevates self-esteem and (b) depressed or threatened self-esteem promotes intergroup discrimination because of a need for self-esteem. Walsh & Banaji (1997) provide a recent discussion. The predictions which tend to be made and which receive very mixed support are that ingroup bias should increase or be correlated with (individual) self-esteem and that low (individual) self-esteem or ingroup status should increase or be correlated with ingroup bias. Some of the problems with these corollaries and the research have already been noted by Farsides (1995), Long and Spears (1997) and Rubin and Hewstone (1998). Many of the difficulties are similar to those applying to the hypothesis relating ingroup identification to ingroup bias. Social identity theory does not actually contain these corollaries. In fact, in many respects it specifically rejects them. Although the theory assumes that there is a need for positive self-evaluation, it does not equate this need with an individual-level motive. On the contrary, the theory refers quite specifically to social identity, not individual-level self-esteem as such, and, once again, it is quite explicit that insecure (not low) social status in interaction with other factors motivates efforts to achieve, restore or protect (in the case of high status groups) positive distinctiveness and that positive distinctiveness can be achieved through a variety of strategies, not simply ingroup bias.

Why therefore should an individual-level need for self-esteem motivate intergroup behaviour? Why should only low group status motivate a search for positive distinctiveness? Why should the latter only be expressed in intergroup discrimination and why should positive social identity be reflected in a measure of personal self-esteem? Under conditions where social identity is salient, it is insecure identity in interaction with high or low status that prompts the need for positive distinctiveness, and positive distinctiveness can take a variety of forms. Social identity processes are only expected to come into play where social identity is salient, and under such conditions people act in terms of their shared social identity, not in terms of their individual-level self-esteem.

For example, a low status group whose inferiority is stable and legitimate on the status dimension is not likely to discriminate on that dimension; it may display individual mobility and/or social creativity. A high status group whose superiority is subjectively legitimate but unstable may be highly discriminatory. The individual self-esteem of group members predicts nothing here, and nor even does positive or negative social identity on the status dimension. What matters is status position in interaction with the perceived nature of status differences. Further, where discrimination takes place and successfully achieves positive distinctiveness, this might be reflected in a relevant status-related measure of collective self-esteem (but perhaps not for a high status group protecting what it has), but there is no reason why it should be reflected in a measure of personal self-esteem (which is governed by intragroup comparisons). If positive distinctiveness is achieved through some strategy other than social competition on the status dimension, then collective self-esteem could increase or be maintained without any basis in intergroup discrimination.

To determine whether ingroup bias or some other intergroup strategy enhances positive social identity, one has to measure the self-evaluative aspects of the specific social not personal identity, in relation to the specific situational dimension of comparison, what Rubin and Hewstone (1998) refer to as 'social', 'specific' and 'state' self-esteem, not 'personal', 'global' and 'trait' self-esteem. Why would a more positive social identity affect personal, global and trait self-esteem? Perhaps, where there is no other outlet, the subjects may sometimes employ whatever measure is available to express the situationally relevant intergroup comparison, but this is prediction-testing on the basis of a hope and a prayer. It may be, as Long and Spears (1997) hypothesize, that individual self-esteem interacts in complex ways with high or low social identity in particular conditions. For example, perhaps low ingroup status is more threatening to high personal, global, trait self-esteem persons. Data supporting or disconfirming this kind of hypothesis may be interesting for all kinds of reason, but whether they are directly relevant to the validity of social identity theory depends on how ultimately they are explained.

The social identity perspective makes a core assumption of a psychological discontinuity between individual and group behaviour, personal and social identity and, therefore, personal and social categorical self-esteem (e.g., Branscombe & Ellemers, 1998, Brewer & Weber, 1994; Crocker & Luhtanen, 1990; Turner, 1982; Turner, Hogg, Oakes, Reicher & Wetherell, 1987, pp. 57–65). As Rubin and Hewstone (1998) show, research on the self-esteem hypothesis has by and large proceeded in blithe disregard of this discontinuity, looking at 'global, personal, trait' self-esteem (but see Branscombe & Wann, 1994; Gagnon & Bourhis, 1996; Long & Spears, 1997; Platow, Harley, Hunter, Hanning, Shave & O'Connell, 1997). Abrams (e.g. 1996) and Hogg have acknowledged the need for a self-categorization analysis of self-esteem (see Turner, Hogg, Oakes, Reicher & Wetherell, 1987, pp. 57–65). The misunderstandings embodied in the self-esteem hypothesis seem to arise because instead of seeing the social identity analysis as being concerned with self-evaluative motives which arise from the interaction of social identity, social comparison and valued dimensions of comparison, there is an implicit model of self-esteem as a fixed psychological structure which drives and motivates behaviour independently of the social context. In general, the social identity perspective provides a different way of thinking about self-esteem from the traditional personality way. It distinguishes between personal and collective self-esteem and other levels as a function of different levels of self-categorization (e.g., Brewer & Weber, 1994). It relates self-esteem to judgements of self (at various levels) in relation to higher-level identity-based norms and values through relevant self–other comparisons on specific dimensions. It does not reify self-esteem as an abstract chronic drive independent of the social comparative nature of self. Self-esteem is an outcome of a social psychological process of self-categorization and social comparison in the context of group values and ideologies, not a fixed universal biological or learned structure.

A new way of thinking about stereotyping

For 60–70 years, with only a few highly distinguished exceptions, the great majority of social psychologists have taken for granted the invalidity of stereotyping,
that it is cognitive distortion, over-simplification and over-generalization, in the
service of cognitive economy and social prejudice. Self-categorization researchers
have finally broken with this view on the basis of a coherent and empirically novel
and testable theoretical analysis (Oakes & Turner, 1990; Oakes, Haslam & Turner,
1994). Self-categorization theory argues that stereotypes are social categorical
judgements, perceptions of people in terms of their group memberships. They
represent categorizations at the level of social identity, in which people are defined
in terms of the characteristics of the group as a whole in the context of intra- and
intergroup relations. They are fluid, variable and context-dependent. A stereotype
of the same people may vary in categorical level, kind, content and prototypical
meaning as a function of the relationship between self and others, the frame of
reference, the dimensions of comparison and the background knowledge, expectations, needs, values and goals of the perceiver (Haslam, Turner, Oakes, McGarty
& Hayes, 1992; Haslam & Turner, 1992, 1995, 1998; Oakes, Haslam & Turner,
1994; Oakes & Turner, 1990; Spears, Oakes, Ellemers & Haslam, 1997; Turner
& Oakes, 1997; Turner, Oakes, Haslam & McGarty, 1994).

Contrary to popular wisdom, it suggests that stereotypes are not rigid or fixed,
but vary with intergroup relations, the context of judgement and the perspective
of the perceiver. They are probably not stored in the head as enduring cognitive
structures, but are better seen as the product of a dynamic process of social judgement and meaningful inference. We do not impose fixed mental images, but construct stereotypes flexibly to explain, describe and justify intergroup relations.
The myth of rigidity arises from looking for stereotype change in the wrong place,
from the assumption that stereotypes should change with information about the
individual-level characteristics of group members. Nor can stereotypes be seen as
irrational, invalid cognitive prejudices. Social groups and collective relationships
exist as much as do individual personalities and individual differences. Social
categorizations become salient to fit group realities and provide veridical contextual representations of people's group relationships. Stereotypic accentuation reflects the rational selectivity of perception in which it is more appropriate to see
people in some contexts at the level of social category identity than at the level of
personal identity. It is no more a distortion to see people in terms of their social
identity than in terms of their personal identity. Both are products of the same
categorization processes. It is not true that individual differences are real but that
social similarities are fictions. It is unjustifiable to assume that one level of categorization is inherently more real than another.

Stereotypes reflect fit in interaction with perceiver readiness. They are selective,
constructive, evaluative and motivated. Like all perception, they vary with the
expectations, needs, values and purposes of the perceiver. Their psychological

validity is relative to the perspective of the perceiver. Psychological validity, however, is not the same as social validity. As social beings, human perceivers engage in social reality testing to validate or invalidate their judgements (Haslam, Turner, Oakes, McGarty & Reynolds, 1998; Turner, 1991). Social and political conflict over stereotypes is not evidence of underlying psychological deficit, but of the political dimension of stereotype validity (Oakes, Haslam & Turner, 1994; Oakes, Reynolds, Haslam & Turner, 1998). Disagreement, argument and conflict between individuals and groups over the correctness of specific stereotypes is part of the social, political, historical process through which society moves (or tries to move) towards stereotypes which are valid from the perspective of the whole community. Individual cognition and social influence are interdependent processes for producing valid stereotypes.

At any given time, a stereotype may be produced which is wrong in the sense that it will be rejected later. At any given time, we may, as a matter of fact, be in error. But self-categorization theory sees nothing in the functioning of stereotyping as a psychological process which in principle works to promulgate error (see Oakes & Turner, 1990, and Spears & Haslam, 1997, for a discussion of the supposed role of limited information-processing capacity). It may be plausible that there are social processes which systematically distort the images which some groups form of certain other groups (indeed, social psychologists are expert in creating experimental arrangements which lead people into error), and this issue is one which deserves further exploration.

There are several implications of this perspective on stereotyping. Perhaps the most important are, first, that the general cognitive model of stereotyping implicit in the field for so long is in need of revision. It may not be meaningful to think of stereotypes as fixed mental representations, stored in memory. This picture is consistent with rigidity but awkward if social categorizations are fluid, contextual judgements. Second, social categorical perception is a basic, normal and adaptive process of group life. It defines people in terms of their group relationships and underlies group formation and collective behaviour (Turner, Oakes, Haslam & McGarty, 1994). Group life is not based on a cognitive distortion of the self and prejudice: it is, in Asch's words, one of 'the two permanent poles of all social processes' (1952, p. 251) and is an authentic expression of self. Third, much of the plausibility of the 'cognitive miser' metaphor of social cognition has rested on the dominant view of categorizing and stereotyping as over-simplification. Self-categorization theory argues that this view is false. It is not necessary to assume that people have limited information-processing capacity to explain why people stereotype. Stereotyping does not impoverish, but enriches social perception, since it captures one of the two poles of human social behaviour; without it, we should be seeing only one half of human life and sociality. It reflects important aspects of social reality and is meaningful, explanatory, theory-laden, with content derived from people's complex higher-order beliefs about the nature of intergroup relations (Tajfel, 1969, 1981b). It is time to lay the cognitive miser metaphor to rest; it embodies an ideology of one-sided individualism which rejects the distinctive psy-

chological reality of group life a priori. Consistent with this message, we note that
the heyday of research on cognitive biases, errors and illusions seems already past.
Researchers are once again talking of social perception as flexible, adaptive, complex, meaningful and purposeful. Self-categorization theory has gone a step further in exploring how and in what sense stereotyping is veridical. This is not a
simple but a complex matter, which goes to the heart of one's theoretical approach
to social cognition (Haslam & Turner, 1998; Oakes, Haslam & Turner, 1994;
Turner & Oakes, 1997). Fourth, much of the difficulty researchers have had in
understanding the rationality of stereotyping arises from a failure to put the analysis of cognition into a social context. Categorization processes do not function in
a social vacuum, in the minds of isolated, asocial perceivers; human cognition is
not purely individual, private, asocial, unaffected by group memberships, social
norms and values. We believe that individual cognitive activity is always mediated
by the social context within which it takes place, and that research on stereotyping
shows the need for a fully social psychological perspective on cognition.

A new way of thinking about the self and personality

The nature of self and its relationship to cognition is at the theoretical core of
social psychology (Turner & Oakes, 1997). Explicit research on the self-concept
has never dominated social psychology in the way that research on group dynamics, attitude change or social cognition has. Yet, in fact, virtually all the phenomena and theories of social psychology touch on the self-process in one way or
another. This is not accidental. The idea that the mind is social psychological can
be rephrased as the idea that the human mind cannot be understood by theories
which leave out the self and its activities. It is the fact of self which makes human
cognition social cognition. It is the self-process which is the dynamic principle
which acts to internalize society as part of cognitive functioning. In the words of a
recent paper, the self is 'a mechanism for the social determination of cognition, for
translating variation in one's "social place" into relevant "cognitive choice"'
(Turner, Oakes, Haslam & McGarty, 1994, p. 462). What we mean by 'cognitive
choice' is the selective representation of phenomena from the vantage point of the
perceiver.

Recent work on the self, however, has tended to borrow theories and concepts
from individual cognitive psychology in order to devise models of self which reduce it to a cognitive structure which processes information just like other cognitive structures (e.g., Kihlstrom & Cantor, 1984). The self is seen as a relatively
fixed, separate mental structure which is activated according to the situation and
which defines one's personality (or personality core). The 'true' self is personal,
unique and private and stored as an organized system of interrelated self-concepts.
The public self is what one presents to and is perceived by others, though it is not
a self that one shares with others in the sense of social identity. In its cognitive

aspects, therefore, the self-structure is strangely asocial, a set of cognitive generalizations largely built up from one's past experience, from observations of one's past behaviour. It comprises core self-schemata reflecting past experience and providing stability of interpretation and resistance to change.

This idea of self as a fixed cognitive structure or system that processes information has a number of problems (Turner & Oakes, 1997; Turner & Onorato, 1999). For example, it must face the empirical fact that there is great variability in self-perception. The idea of an underlying mental structure sits awkwardly with this fact and complicates the task of explaining such variability. Understanding the fluidity of self-perception has thus become a matter of explaining when, why and how some specific subset of cognitive structures is activated. The idea of structure itself makes no direct contribution to the answer. It simply puts the question of variability at second remove: not why does self-perception vary, but why does some (completely hypothetical) mental structure (which is supposed to produce self-perception) get activated?

Our research suggests a different approach (Turner & Oakes, 1989, 1997; Turner, Oakes, Haslam & Turner, 1994; Turner & Onorato, 1999). It argues that self-categorizing varies lawfully and systematically (in level of inclusiveness, specific kind of self-category at each level, comparative attributes and relative prototypicality of instances) so as to express the varying social comparative properties of the perceiver. The self is a varying, reflexive representation of the perceiver which is inherently fluid and flexible because it is a comparative, relational judgement. It defines the individual in a social context or, if one prefers, it defines the individual in social relational terms. To define the self as male is to represent it in terms of similarities with other males and differences from females, reflecting the perceiver's goals, theories and knowledge and employing particular relevant dimensions of comparison in a given situation. This is the outcome of an active process of judgement in which the self-category of male is given a specific meaning and form as a function of the particular set of relations being represented. It is not the activation of some stored, invariant generic concept of 'maleness'.

The argument we have made is that self-categorizing provides a varying social definition of the perceiver, and that the varying, socially defined self actively shapes and determines cognition by directing its functioning from the specific vantage point of a given self. Changing one's self-definition can, in turn, change values, self-relevance, goals, knowledge, the boundaries of social influence, the perception of agreement and disagreement, and so on. Are we Australians very similar to each other, or very diverse? Does one share the values of radical feminists, does one agree or disagree with them? Is one's discussion partner creative and tolerant, or is she systematic and logical? Our research has shown that these judgements vary, as salient self-categorization is affected by the demands of different comparative contexts. The answers will vary depending on whether one is comparing Australians with other nationalities, whether there are anti-feminists around or not, and whether one is taking part in this discussion as a science student or as a woman (see David & Turner, in press a; Haslam, Oakes, Turner & McGarty, 1995; Oakes, Reynolds,

Haslam & Turner, 1998; Reynolds, 1996). All cognition, including basic processes such as categorization, takes place from a specific vantage point, a singular
perspective: that of the self currently salient. Perception and thought are not neutral or disinterested, but actively involved in representing and understanding the
world from the point of view of the participating perceiver. Hence, cognition
varies as the socially defined self varies, and there is socially mediated cognitive
variation within and between individuals.

These arguments cannot be fully elaborated here. In essence, we are suggesting
that the self is indissolubly social and that all cognition is social because of the
impact of self. It is the fact of self that transforms cognition into social psychology.
Cognitive principles can only provide an adequate account of human perception if
they involve the self, and in so doing they become social psychological. This is
what Tajfel (1972b) meant when he described cognitive dissonance theory as social psychological because it used concepts such as 'commitment' and 'justification', concepts which invoke the self. Far from being able to reduce the self to a
cognitive structure, it is the socially variable self that transforms cognition into
social psychology.

This general view has implications for the link between self and personality.
Much contemporary work in social psychology is guided by a 'personality' model
of the self-concept (Turner & Onorato, 1999). This model is apparent in four
major themes: that, first, the self-concept is a representation of one's personal
identity; second, the self-concept is a unique psychological property of the perceiver,
not shared with others; third, the social self is a 'looking-glass' self, a reflection
and internalization of others' reactions to one's public self as presented in social
interaction; and, fourth, the self-concept is a relatively enduring, stable cognitive
structure. These ideas indicate a strong affinity between traditional views of self
and personality. In a sense the self-concept is a person's implicit theory of their
own personality (Epstein, 1973; Kihlstrom & Cantor, 1984). It is 'an intimate
counterpart of personality, constituting its subjective representation as it were'
(Kruglanski, Miller & Geen, 1996, p. 1061). Likewise, it functions as a scientific
theory of personality for social psychologists, providing an explanation of individuality, stability across time and consistency across situations. It is the core
psychological structure which embodies personal history, relates the individual to
the social situation, shapes cognition and functions as the anchor for a range of
individual motives, goals and needs. The personality view of the self is the idea
that the self-concept is one's idiosyncratic and relatively stable knowledge structure about one's personal identity, reflecting personal experience and the internalized appraisals of others.

Research and thinking in the social identity tradition, however, qualifies each of
these major themes. Self-categorization theory argues that the self is not based
predominantly on personal identity, but varies in level and includes collective
identities, reflecting group memberships and collective similarities, that actively
depersonalize self-perception. Social identities are not idiosyncratic but under appropriate conditions, can be shared and highly normative (Haslam, Turner, Oakes,

McGarty & Reynolds, 1998) and produce relatively unitary, collective behaviour when salient. Further, social identity is not personal identity as reflected in the looking-glass of social interaction, but is a subjective collective identity which includes others defined as ingroup members. Finally, social identities and other self-categories arise from an active process of judgement and meaningful inference, in which they are constructed from an interaction between motives, expectations, knowledge and reality, rather than being passive activations of a fixed self-structure. All these points are at odds to some degree with the personality model. Do they also call into question traditional ideas of individuality, stability and consistency? What of stable individual differences, of personality structure? Is the self completely fluid and malleable, merely an epiphenomenon of the immediate social context? Individuality, stability and consistency under certain conditions are not incompatible with the self-categorization perspective, but the latter does reinterpret and limit the significance of these phenomena.

The social identity analysis posits that people are both individuals and group members and display both individuality and collective identity. Individuality, expressed in personal identities and individual differences, is one basic level at which the self is categorized and behaviour takes place. It may be an empirically prevalent level under many conditions, in that people's relationships and social interactions are almost by definition more commonly with ingroup than outgroup members. We live our lives ordinarily, but not always, in intragroup contexts, within which the individual differentiates him- or herself in terms of personal differences from ingroup members.

Just like groupness, however, individuality is seen as dynamic, variable and context-dependent. It is not seen as some fixed, basic substratum of the self. It, too, is a function of an interaction between motives, expectations, knowledge and reality. People are relatively personalized in some contexts just as they are depersonalized in others. Further, the dimensions and attributes of personal identity will vary with the ingroup contexts and the level of the social identity that provides the frame of reference. It is not universalistic. It appears so only to the degree that the higher-order group, society or culture is invisible, implicit, unquestioned. Individual differences are not theoretical primitives. They are products, not abstract causes. As Epstein and O'Brien (1985) note, they are there to be explained, not in themselves explanations.

Similarly, the analysis is not arguing against the stability of self-categories as an empirical fact or possibility. It is not saying that self-categories vary chaotically, whimsically. The same general processes that predict variation under some conditions also predict stability under others. Self-categorizing is an active, interpretative, judgemental process, reflecting a complex and creative interaction between motives, expectations, knowledge and reality, but the outcomes can still be similar and stable. If perceiver motives and expectations do not vary, if background knowledge does not vary and if the stimulus reality to be represented does not vary, then the interactive outcomes will be similar. Groups and cultures do not, after all, change their values on a daily basis, and these values become individual motives which constrain variation. Similarly, ideologies, theories, scientific knowledge and reality, the relevant social contexts, do not change overnight, but they can change and sometimes do, sometimes gradually and moderately, sometimes rapidly and dramatically. Stability of self-categories across time is assumed to reflect the stability of the perceiver factors and judgemental conditions which interact to produce them, and is restricted to conditions which are invariant in these respects. One does not need the concept of a fixed underlying self-structure to explain why and when self-categories may be stable.

Are there broad stable consistencies across situations in self-conception as, apparently, in personality? It can be assumed that self-categorizing is always determined by an interaction between characteristics of the 'person' and characteristics of the 'situation', just as in individual behaviour. Thus consistency at the level of specific self-categories across specific situations is not to be expected other than where situational differences are irrelevant to the factors determining the self-categorization process. Indeed, there seems to be wide agreement in social psychology, personality and self-concept research for variability at the level of the specific situation (Epstein & O'Brien, 1985; Markus & Wurf, 1987; Mischel & Shoda, 1995; Ross & Nisbett, 1991). As we move from specific to more global self-concepts, then consistency across situations may well become more likely. If we think of global as opposed to specific self-concepts as more abstract, summary judgements of the self in relation to some broad class of situations, then consistency across situations seems plausible, providing that the situations being compared are all contained within the broad class from which the global judgement is abstracted. However, it is assumed that even such global self-categories are the product of an active, interpretative process. Thus the same general principle applies: consistency in self-categorizing at either the specific or global level can only be expected where there is similarity or consistency of the perceiver motives, knowledge bases and situational realities or broad class of situational realities which determine self-categorizing.

The picture of the self that emerges from social identity work is one more suited to research on intergroup relations and group processes than is the personality model, but one that is also compatible with research on individual differences and interpersonal relations.

Conclusion

This chapter has outlined selected themes in current research on social identity and self-categorization theories as a prelude to the chapters to come and as general background for the book as a whole. In the space available it has been necessary to put ideas more boldly and generally than might otherwise be desirable, without the tentativeness which is ideal in science and without the details and qualifications they deserve in terms of dealing with other viewpoints and empirical research. Apart from space limitations, given the extent of the ground to be covered (and much has still been omitted), the only excuse is that many of the elaborations and empirical illustrations of the ideas are referenced in the text. The social identity perspective is not a dogma but a view that emerged from and is based on research. The ideas in this chapter should be read as hypotheses to be tested further both by those who find them congenial and those who wish to dispute them.

The themes emphasized in this book – context, commitment and content – emerge as central in varying ways to all the issues discussed in the chapter. Social identities, self-categories and stereotypes are social comparative and reality-based representations of self and others, and hence vary with the social context. The need for positive social identity emerges from an interaction between salient social identities, specific contexts of comparison and situationally relevant social values. Its effects depend on the interplay between collective psychology, shared beliefs and ideologies, and the character of the particular intergroup relationship.

Commitment to and/or identification with group membership are fundamental variables for conceptualizing the subjective aspects of group belongingness, for recognizing that the social identity perspective, just like the earlier Gestalt and Lewinian tradition, focuses on psychological or reference-group processes, not sociological categories as defined by an outsider. Commitment is also a way of tapping the centrality of a particular identity to a person's background knowledge and naive theories of their place in the social world, to their model of the social world (Reicher, 1996b). It is relevant to Tajfel's concept of a 'social change' orientation, solving group problems through group actions, in that it indicates the process of investing the self in the group, of binding them together so tightly that individual action ceases to be a subjective option. For some people in relation to some groups, to leave the group for another or as an individual is as meaningful as trying to become someone else. The situation can only be dealt with collectively because it's particular challenges only arise in relation to the collective self which defines it.

The theme of content is apparent in the idea that specific values, expectations, knowledge, theories and ideologies are used to construct self-categories, that self-categories reflect the social location of the perceiver and that judgements are socially relative even where determined by the same psychological processes. It is apparent in the role of relative status position and shared beliefs about the social system and the nature of intergroup status differences in predicting which specific strategy group members will adopt to solve identity problems and pursue other goals, and in the political dimension of stereotype content reflecting the group ideologies which describe, explain and justify intergroup relations. Content is important in a more general way. Individualism in social psychology leads to the reification of socially specific beliefs, actions and motives as universal processes or structures, to the creation of an abstract individual psychology which supposedly functions independently of rather than in interaction with a socially structured life (Reicher, 1987; Tajfel, 1979; Turner, 1996a). Process theories such as social identity and self-categorization require the incorporation of specific content into their analyses before they can make predictions either in the laboratory or the field, and are designed to require such an incorporation. They cannot be reduced to abstract, one-factor notions in which some purely psychological event leads to some purely psychological outcome. As Tajfel put it: 'The processes of social categorization, social identity and social comparison, as used in the theory, cannot be conceived to originate outside of their social contexts' (1979, p. 185). Acknowledging the causal role of social and psychological content is a way of facing the specific political, historical and ideological facts of society and moving to the interactionist social psychology which Tajfel advocated so powerfully.

2

The Context and Content of Social Identity Threat

Nyla R. Branscombe, Naomi Ellemers, Russell Spears and Bertjan Doosje

The concept of threat has occupied a central position in much psychological theorizing. It does, however, continue to be a controversial construct for both conceptual and methodological reasons. At the theoretical level, there has been considerable variation in how threat has been defined within various research traditions and the level of identity at which it is assumed to operate. Empirically, threat induction has resulted in diverse consequences. Furthermore, because of its potentially reactive nature, the operation of threat has often been inferred from its effects on a variety of factors rather than via direct assessment, resulting in interpretational difficulties. Our main focus in this chapter will be on distinguishing the different forms that identity threat can take, particularly those operating in intergroup contexts, but we will return to concerns of measurement in the concluding section.

Research, especially that stemming from a Freudian (1930) conception of development, has often considered threat in strictly personal identity terms. As part of the authoritarian personality syndrome (Adorno, Frenkel-Brunswick, Levinson & Sanford, 1950), it was expected that individuals would experience chronic feelings of threat to the extent that they were recipients of rigid and harsh treatment during their formative years. As a result of the growing feelings of hostility and inadequacy that were produced by such experiences, people might display defensive derogation of devalued social groups. In a similar vein, frustration–aggression theory (Dollard, Doob, Miller, Mowrer & Sears, 1939) explained the occurrence of prejudice and discrimination by suggesting that the frustration resulting from the failure to satisfy some personal need would be displaced onto specific scapegoats, such as minority-group members. Likewise, realistic group conflict theory (Sherif, 1966) proposed that conflicts between social groups arose because of individuals' instrumental concerns (see Spears, Oakes, Ellemers & Haslam, 1997).

Preparation of this chapter was facilitated by a Visiting Professor Award from NWO (Dutch Organization for Scientific Research) to the first author.

This approach suggested that threat results when people's personal interests are jeopardized because their group has to compete with other groups for scarce resources.

Similar predictions concerning who is most likely to be responsive to threat can be found in more recent social psychological research, where a number of studies have assessed whether people who differ in their levels of personal self-esteem also differ in their likelihood of engaging in outgroup derogation (Crocker, Thompson, McGraw & Ingerman, 1987; Hogg & Sunderland, 1991; Pelham, 1991; Tice, 1991). Although it has been demonstrated that even short-term or transient threats to personal self-esteem can elicit derogation of outgroup members (e.g., Meindl & Lerner, 1984), this literature is characterized by substantial inconsistencies in terms of the empirical findings. Indeed, recent reviews of this research have concluded that manipulation and measurement of self-esteem in a strictly personal sense are ill-suited to inform us about the likely responses of those whose group-based self-esteem is threatened (see Long & Spears, 1997; Rubin & Hewstone, 1998).

Thus, while there is a variety of forms of temporary and chronic threat to the individual's personal identity that have been investigated (Higgins, 1987, for a review), what has not been systematically examined are the different classes of threat that can be experienced at the social identity level. To the extent that previous theoretical and empirical work has considered social identity threat (see Breakwell, 1986), it has mainly addressed what we will call threats to the value of a group identity or its distinctiveness, as well as various strategies people may use to cope with these kinds of threat. In this chapter we delineate a taxonomy of four distinct classes of social identity threat, incorporating the different kinds of threat that can be implied in the relation between the individual and the social group. Although certain examples might touch on more than one class of threat, we believe this taxonomy has conceptual utility in clarifying the primary differences among them. These classes of identity threat can be distinguished as follows (see table 2.1 for a summary of the expected effects following each type of identity threat):

1 'Categorization threat' (being categorized against one's will).
2 'Distinctiveness threat' (group distinctiveness is prevented or undermined).
3 'Threats to the value of social identity' (the group's value is undermined).
4 'Acceptance threat' (one's position within the group is undermined).

With this classification scheme, we will be able to describe the most common social contexts in which each kind of threat is likely to be encountered or induced, and how the content of the resulting social identity determines the nature of this threat. In line with a central theme of the volume, we further argue that different classes of response are likely to be exhibited by people who vary in the degree to which they feel committed to a particular social group.

Table 2.1   Responses by low and high identifiers to different kinds of threat

Class of threat	Who is likely to respond?	Type of response
Categorization	Low identifiers	Stress ingroup heterogeneity
		Further disidentification
		Stress unique personal qualities
	High identifiers	None
Distinctiveness	Low identifiers	Perceive groups at superordinate level
	High identifiers	Display outgroup derogation
		Perceive ingroup homogeneity
		Increased self-stereotyping
Value		
(a) Competence	Low identifiers	Further disidentification
	High identifiers	Display outgroup derogation
		Perceive ingroup homogeneity
		Increased self-stereotyping
(b) Morality	Low identifiers	Undo morally objectionable behaviour
	High identifiers	Defensive reactions
		Perceive ingroup heterogeneity
Acceptance	Low identifiers	None
	High identifiers	Display outgroup derogation
		Sliming (to attain acceptance)

Categorization Threat

Because social categorization involves the assignment of stereotypical group characteristics to individual group members, it is possible that self-esteem may be affected,
and that the process of categorizing people into groups could constitute a social
identity threat (see Lemyre & Smith, 1985, for an early statement of this argument).
First, there is a whole host of social situations in which people expect to interact
primarily on an interpersonal basis and wish to be judged in terms of their personal
characteristics or merits (e.g., in an employment interview or when making new
friends). If, in such a situation, they are categorized in terms of their group membership and they are primarily treated in terms of their gender, their ethnic background
or their political orientation, for example, then people may resist it and consider the
situation to be unjust. Indeed, in this case, they are likely to feel that they are victims
of prejudice in the sense that they are being prejudged in terms of their category
membership rather than being seen as a unique individual.

Such resistance to being categorized is likely to be particularly strong when the membership category seems irrelevant or illegitimate given the situation at hand (e.g., gender, when applying for a business loan), even if it is a social category the person would otherwise identify strongly with. Recent empirical research, for instance, has revealed that women in leadership positions tend to emphasize that they are different from other women (Ellemers, 1993a) and indicate that a gender categorization is irrelevant in this context (Rojahn, 1996). In many social contexts, people might even choose not to reveal a stigmatized or group membership if such costs of being categorized could be avoided entirely. However, to the extent that some defining group features (such as gender or ethnicity) are evident from people's physical appearance, they cannot hide their group affiliation and hence cannot prevent others from categorizing them in terms of this group membership (see also Crocker & Major, 1989).

It is also the case that every individual could be potentially categorized in many different ways, and people might prefer to be considered in terms of certain social groups (e.g., their political orientation) rather than other group memberships (e.g., their ethnic background). Whether or not people are willing to be categorized in terms of a particular group membership is likely to depend on their level of identification with or commitment to that particular group relative to their involvement with another, competing categorization. Empirical work on cross-categorization (Vanbeselaere, 1991), subtyping (Weber & Crocker, 1983), superordinate categorization (Gaertner, Mann, Murrell & Dovidio, 1989) and multiple categorizations (Macrae, Bodenhausen & Milne, 1996; Stangor, Lynch, Duan & Glass, 1992) has demonstrated that people can and do use different social categories to classify the same target of social judgement. While such factors as cognitive accessibility and comparative or normative fit determine which of several different possible categorizations is likely to be used (see also Oakes, 1987), the bulk of the existing work on this issue has focused on how detached perceivers categorize social stimuli that are external to the self. It remains to be seen, however, the extent to which similar or different cognitive and motivational processes are operative when people's own self-categorization is at stake (see also Ellemers & Van Knippenberg, 1997; Smith & Zarate, 1992). Some preliminary work comparing different bases for categorization suggests that people are more likely to feel committed to groups that they self-select than to those that are externally imposed, and that they generally identify more with small face-to-face groups than with large encompassing social categories (Branscombe, Spears, Ellemers & Doosje, 1998; Ellemers, Kortekaas & Ouwerkerk, 1999). However, further research is necessary in order to assess systematically the conditions under which certain self-categorizations are more likely to be favoured than others.

In order to understand the implications of such categorization threats, looking at self-perceived group memberships alone is not enough. This is because the threat stems from the very fact that people's preferred self-categorizations do not correspond to the way they are perceived by others (see Long & Spears, 1997). In fact, Tajfel and Turner (1979) suggested that, when consensual category designations are applied by others, unless they are actively resisted, they may ultimately come to determine the way people perceive and define themselves (see also Tajfel, 1984). Although it is not self-evident whether and how the experience of such threats can be assessed directly, there is some suggestive evidence from recent empirical work that is relevant to this issue.

Other things being equal, we would expect low identifiers with a given social category to be the most resistant to such categorization, especially when it is explicitly imposed. Spears and Doosje (1996) showed that enhancing the salience of a categorization increases the tendency for low identifiers to distance themselves from the imposed categorization. Specifically, in research using the 'who said what' category-confusion paradigm (Taylor, Fiske, Etcoff & Ruderman, 1978), it was shown that participants who identified weakly with their group (i.e., psychology students) were less likely to categorize themselves as a group and were more likely to individuate group members, especially when they were forced to think in terms of the social categorization (see chapter 3 for further details).

Other research concerned with personal and collective self-esteem supports the idea that when internal and external categorizations are inconsistent or incompatible, defensive reactions can result. For example, research by Long and Spears (1997; see also Long & Spears, in press; Long, Spears & Manstead, 1994) proposed that people with the combination of low public collective self-esteem and high personal self-esteem might be particularly likely to be threatened by group categorization. This is because low public collective self-esteem represents an acknowledgement that one belongs to a group that is not valued by others, a situation that may be most threatening for people high in personal self-esteem. Because such people tend to define themselves in terms of their positive personal characteristics, they may therefore see themselves as being 'dragged down' by a negative group. Consistent with this increased threat hypothesis is the finding that a mismatch between personal and collective self-esteem levels can result in lowered identification with the group and this stems from reduced feelings of prototypicality and increased perceived distance from the group norm (Spears, Jetten & Van Harreveld, 1998).

Likewise, when high-performing individuals are included in a group that is low in status or that has received a negative evaluation, disidentification is likely to result (see Ellemers, Van Knippenberg & Wilke, 1990; Ellemers, Wilke & Van Knippenberg, 1993), and attempts to dissuade an audience of the applicability of that group membership for the self may occur. Those who lack an internal sense of commitment to the group, in particular if face-to-face interaction is lacking or unlikely so that ingroup repercussions can be avoided (see also chapter 6), may be tempted to distance themselves from the group or even 'put down' other ingroup members (see Ellemers, Van den Heuvel & De Gilder, 1996). Disidentification and discrediting the ingroup might be undertaken for the purpose of ingratiation with a higher status outgroup, especially in front of an outgroup audience (see also Ellemers, Van Dyck, Hinkle & Jacobs, 1998; Noel, Wann & Branscombe, 1995).

The intensity and type of emotion that is likely to be experienced when it is obvious that others have categorized the self according to a particular group membership will depend on a number of factors. Anger or other forms of distress such as depression may be exhibited primarily by those who are low in identification, especially if they are highly likely to be categorized in this way by others. Again, such affective responses following involuntary categorization might stem either from the belief that it is inappropriate to perceive individuals in terms of any category membership in that particular context (e.g., personal qualities should be the only basis of judgement), or because the persons so categorized do not think of themselves in terms of that particular group membership at all. To the extent that people feel they are treated unjustly as a result of such inappropriate categorization, they are not only likely to express anger, but they may also suffer from lowered self-esteem (see Koper, Van Knippenberg, Bouhuijs, Vermunt & Wilke, 1993; Lind & Tyler, 1988; Tyler & Lind, 1992).

Some suggestive evidence for the argument that categorization per se may have threatening affective consequences was obtained in a study by Van Rijswijk and Ellemers (1998). In this work, female students first completed a questionnaire to assess the extent to which they identified with their gender category. They were next presented with false information either indicating that women generally do worse than men at university, or that women generally do better, and they were asked to indicate the extent to which they experienced four positive (happiness, satisfaction) or negative (anger, disappointment) emotions as a result. While they received and responded to this information, participants' level of physiological arousal was assessed by measuring their skin conductance.

In this study, self-reported emotional responses, corresponding to the valence (evaluative direction) of the group-relevant feedback, were more pronounced among those participants who identified more strongly with their group (see also Branscombe & Wann, 1992). However, results with the physiological measure yielded a different pattern. From the skin conductance data, it turned out that, regardless of the valence of the information, participants were more aroused after having received the group-relevant feedback showing that they identified less with their gender group than do other women. Van Rijswijk and Ellemers explained this latter finding by arguing that the higher levels of arousal observed in low-identifying group members might stem from the threat they experienced from being addressed as members of a group they chose not to identify with, a response that was not assessed by the four emotion terms that were used. This post-hoc explanation should be tested more explicitly in further research, although the results converge with the general notion that people may feel threatened when they are categorized against their will.

Involuntary categorization might be especially threatening in a context where that group membership implies poor ability or performance. Accordingly, only those who feel strongly committed to their devalued social category should be willing to self-stereotype as members of that group (see Spears, Doosje & Ellemers, 1997). Further evidence that people resist being categorized under these circumstances was obtained in a study by Doosje, Spears and Koomen (1995). Members of experimental groups who were confronted with a better performing outgroup emphasized the heterogeneity of these two groups, presumably as an attempt to render the categorization less meaningful or diagnostic for themselves (see also Doosje, Spears, Ellemers & Koomen, 1999; chapter 6, this volume).

As Steele's (1997; Steele & Aronson, 1995) work has illustrated, categorization based on a poorly performing group may actually harm people's own perform-ances. Specifically, when Black American students think that they are likely to be categorized in terms of their racial group membership, their performance on di-mensions on which their group has historically fared poorly suffers. The extra burden of being seen as representative of one's group and the possible confirma-tion of the negative group stereotype appear to impede performance on verbal tests (a dimension on which there is stereotype vulnerability for this group; Steele, 1997; see also chapter 9, this volume). When Black Americans do not believe that they have been categorized according to their racial group membership, but as-sume instead that they are simply completing a reading test, their performance is equivalent to that of White Americans. Whether there might be psychological benefits to be gained by recategorizing the self in terms of an alternative group membership which is less subject to evaluation threat in such circumstances awaits future research.

Thus, as we have described, simply being categorized as a member of a group may be a threatening experience. For some, it is because they do not identify with that group in the first place, and for others it is because the group membership seems inappropriate for the context. In other instances categorization is threaten-ing in part because of the nature of the group categorization itself. It might be a group from which the individual derives little self-esteem, in contrast to the positivity of their personal self. Or, it might be a group membership for which self-esteem is at stake, but it is socially devalued to such an extent that the individual so catego-rized is vulnerable to confirming that group's performance expectancies.

Distinctiveness Threat

In the previous section we considered the problems of dealing with a contextually undesirable social categorization. In this section we wish to consider what is in many senses the opposite concern–namely, the threat associated with not having a distinct social identity, or one that is insufficiently distinctive from other compari-son groups. Starting with Tajfel's seminal work on categorization and perceptual accentuation effects (Tajfel & Wilkes, 1963), social identity theory has empha-sized the idea that people use social categories to structure their social environ-ment and to define their own place therein (see Tajfel, 1969, 1974; Tajfel & Turner, 1979). Social categories therefore help to provide us with meaningful identities, which allow us to make sense of our world (Tajfel, 1974, 1978a). More recently, self-categorization theory (Turner, 1987) has further developed the notion that people may actively use and enhance the meta-contrast (a measure of the distinctiveness of groups from each other) as a meaning-seeking device, in order to delineate more clearly our position in the social environment. Social identity theory also introduces an explicitly socio-motivational element driving a quest for group distinctiveness. Given that we derive part of our self-esteem from our social identities and positive social comparisons with other groups, it follows that social comparison with similar outgroups could threaten group distinctiveness and social identity.

According to this analysis, threats to identity associated with group distinctness can probably be broken down into two closely related aspects, which are complementary rather than competing. First, possessing a distinct and meaningful social identity may be functional in itself, for it provides a basis for action (see also Baumeister, 1986, for similar arguments in relation to personal identity). Second, once a distinct group identity is established, social comparison with similar groups can be potentially threatening to group distinctiveness. In short, the motivation to possess a 'distinct' social identity may be a prerequisite for, although it can be distinguished from, the quest for group 'distinctiveness', which is most likely to be at issue in the intergroup context. Below, we address each of these related aspects in turn.

Spears and Jetten (1998a) examined the ability of a categorization to furnish the meaning implied by a distinctive social identity in line with the earlier ideas of Tajfel (1969). The argument proposed was that if a social categorization already provides people with a distinct and meaningful identity, then differentiation and discrimination as typically experienced by minimal groups may not be necessary. This idea was tested in an experiment where people were categorized according to the minimal group paradigm (preference for Painter A versus Painter B in the 'minimal' condition). A further condition was added to the basic minimal one, however, stating that the preference for one painter over the other was said to be related to personality type, namely extroversion versus introversion (the 'maximal' or 'meaningful' condition). Whereas discrimination on the Tajfel matrices was significant in the minimal condition, it was reduced and non-significant in the meaningful. Moreover, these differences were unrelated to measures of uncertainty (e.g., Mullin & Hogg, 1998) and so cannot easily be explained as serving uncertainty reduction in any generic sense, which has been proposed as a basic purpose of differentiation and discrimination. Rather, these findings are consistent with the view that social categorization, especially when embellished with meaningful content, can provide a distinct identity for its members. Further attempts to achieve additional differentiation by discrimination may then become superfluous. Thus, only when the meaning or content of a group identity is not sufficiently clear or distinct (e.g., in minimal groups) will differentiation be used to enhance group distinctness.

It is interesting to note that Tajfel (1978a, p. 42) considered minimal groups to be 'maximal' in the sense that the minimal group context is stripped of all interpersonal contact and context: the group is the only identity made available to the participants in this situation and discrimination is perhaps the only means available to them for asserting group identity (see also Spears, 1995). The anonymity and 'depersonalization' associated with the minimal group paradigm may also, however, provide the most fertile conditions for increased group salience. In line with the social identity model of deindividuation effects, increased intergroup discrimination has been found in this paradigm (Reicher, Spears & Postmes, 1995; Spears, 1995a; Spears & Lea, 1994: see also chapters 6 and 8, this volume). Nevertheless, minimal groups do remain minimal in terms of the content of group identity, and, as the study by Spears and Jetten suggests, embellishing this content may abrogate the need for more active differentiation. Indeed, at times, the content of a group identity may even explicitly proscribe discrimination (see chapter 5), helping to explain why differentiation and discrimination in natural social groups are not universal, as the minimal group literature might suggest they should be.

Yet, there is also clear evidence based on more established groups that a distinct and meaningful group identity is important. Indeed, possession of a distinct identity may be even more important than having a positive identity. Evidence of this was provided by a study involving Dutch and Polish students, where it was demonstrated that the desire for ingroup distinctness could override the concern for a positive group image (Mlicki & Ellemers, 1996). Specifically, among Polish students, for whom establishing a distinct national identity was of paramount importance, the negative nature of characteristic national traits was emphasized as a means of enabling them to derive a distinct national identity rather than emphasizing similarity to other European countries with respect to positive national traits. In a laboratory study using students from the University of Amsterdam, Doff (1998) further showed that when their social identity was threatened by an unfavourable comparison with a rival outgroup (i.e., students from the Free University), high but not low identifiers were more likely to stereotype their group on negative but stereotypic dimensions (e.g., 'sloppy'). In short, the importance of having a meaningful and distinct social identity may well outweigh the fact of its negativity, especially for those who strongly identify with that group.

The importance of group distinctness leads directly to the issue of group distinctiveness in the intergroup context. Many theorists have pointed to the psychological consequences of group distinctiveness. However, distinctiveness has been conceptualized and operationalized in a number of different ways. Following social identity principles we have, thus far, emphasized the importance of the psychological boundedness of the group (group distinctness), which then logically implies its differentiation from other groups (intergroup distinctiveness). However, some previous research has conceived of group distinctiveness in more contextually specific ways. In particular, distinctiveness has been defined in terms of, first, the relative size or infrequency of the group (e.g., minority group status) and, second, the relative (dis)similarity of the two groups on some underlying content dimension. We consider below the social psychological implications of both these senses of distinctiveness in relation to the nature of the threat to identity that may be experienced.

Many theorists have analysed the cognitive effects of numerical distinctiveness (relative infrequency) in enhancing the salience of the group and endowing its members with a sense of uniqueness. The evidence supports the notion that people are more likely to perceive themselves spontaneously as members of numerically distinctive groups (McGuire, McGuire, Child & Fujioka, 1978; McGuire, McGuire & Winton, 1979; McGuire & Padawer-Singer, 1976) relative to majority groups. Similarly, Mullen (1991) has argued that numerical infrequency can form the basis of group salience. While, by their very nature, these kinds of cognitive factor can influence perceptions of distinctiveness, they cannot predict when distinctiveness will be undermined or why that would be threatening.

Other theoretical views have, however, included a more motivational component, which encompasses threats to group distinctiveness. Optimal distinctiveness theory (Brewer, 1991) argues for a basic motivational need where people seek a certain degree of group distinctiveness as well as inclusion (see also Snyder & Fromkin, 1980, for a similar argument). This approach, in keeping with the socio-motivational basis of group distinctiveness that is incorporated into social identity theory, regards group distinctiveness not just as a source of salient identity, but as something that will be actively protected when threatened.

Simon and his colleagues (Simon, 1992a; see Simon & Brown, 1987; Simon & Hamilton, 1994) have also argued that people will typically identify more strongly with distinctive groups (i.e., minorities) than with non-distinctive ones (i.e., majorities). The fairly strong identification that can be observed in minority group members has been explained by the observation that there is a relatively large overlap between social and personal identity for minority group members, which is lacking for dominant group members (Simon, Pantaleo & Mummendey, 1995).

At the same time, however, minority groups are often seen as inferior to majority groups (e.g., Blanz, Mummendey & Otten, 1995; Sachdev & Bourhis, 1984). Consequently, it is commonly assumed that minority group membership will be experienced as unattractive, and may therefore constitute an identity threat in its own right. In many contexts and societies, the majority group will often have the political and economic power to define itself as better and not just as numerically dominant. Some recent research has explicitly addressed this issue, by varying numerical distinctiveness (relative size) and relative status (differential value) as independent group characteristics that could influence the extent to which people are willing to identify with a particular group (Ellemers, Doosje, Van Knippenberg & Wilke, 1992; Ellemers, Kortekaas & Ouwerkerk, 1998; Ellemers & Van Rijswijk, 1997; Simon & Hamilton, 1994). These studies have consistently revealed that people are less willing to identify with majority than with minority groups, a finding that is in line with the notion that a lack of distinctiveness may constitute a threat to people's social identity. In addition, minority ingroup members have been shown to display greater ingroup bias than do majority group members, which may reflect the sense of threat that such lower status can bestow (e.g., Bettencourt, Miller & Hume, in press; Mullen, Brown & Smith, 1992).

There is now quite a considerable literature on the threats to distinctiveness arising from intergroup comparisons with groups that are similar to the ingroup (Brown, 1984a, 1984b; Brown & Abrams, 1986; Henderson-King, Henderson-King, Zhermer, Posokhova & Chiker, 1997, Jetten, Spears & Manstead, 1997a; 1998a, 1998b; Marcus-Newhall, Miller, Holtz & Brewer, 1993; Moghaddam & Stringer, 1988; Roccas & Schwartz, 1993; Turner, 1978b). Much of this work has supported the social identity theory prediction that groups will try to differentiate themselves from other groups that are too similar to the ingroup and which, accordingly, threaten group distinctiveness. This pattern is most notable for high identifiers for whom that group identity is important and central (Henderson-King, Henderson-King, Zhermer, Posokhova & Chiker, 1997; Jetten, Spears & Manstead, 1998b; Roccas & Schwartz, 1993). Because low identifiers, by definition, are less likely to be threatened by undermined group distinctiveness, they are more likely to consider the distinction between their own and a similar outgroup as less crucial. Indeed, low identifiers may prefer to self-categorize at the individual level or at a more superordinate level which includes both groups (see chapter 5).

Threats to intergroup distinctiveness can be manifested and responded to in ways other than direct intergroup differentiation. In fact, direct differentiation may sometimes be difficult, especially if it contradicts the social reality of the similarity between the groups (see chapter 6). Alternative strategies may be more likely to be employed by high identifiers, such as that of defining themselves in terms of the group ("self-stereotyping') when group distinctiveness is threatened by a similar outgroup comparison. Two studies have supported this prediction for both low self-perceived and low externally perceived ingroup distinctiveness (Spears, Doosje & Ellemers, 1997; see also chapter 3, this volume). Results from both studies were consistent with the notion that a lack of group distinctiveness may constitute an identity threat. Specifically, while there was no difference between high- and low-identifying group members when the ingroup seemed distinct from the relevant outgroup (the no threat case), these two classes of individuals showed differential strategic responses to the threat posed by low ingroup distinctiveness.

While many researchers have focused on the relative ease with which people can be induced to show outgroup derogation or discrimination when distinctiveness is threatened, the more general theoretical point is that people tend to differentiate their groups in order to achieve or restore distinctiveness (and, as we have seen, not necessarily always positively). As we have suggested, ingroup favouritism may occur in an experimental setting where people are forced to assess or evaluate both groups in terms of a single comparative criterion, because this is the only option for achieving intergroup distinctiveness (see also Mummendey & Schreiber, 1983). However, empirical evidence has now accumulated demonstrating that multidimensional intergroup comparisons are likely to yield different results (see also Van Knippenberg & Ellemers, 1990, for a review). In these studies, the usual pattern that is observed is for members of both groups to reach a consensual agreement that certain traits or abilities are more characteristic of one group, while the other group is deemed to be superior on other complementary comparative dimensions (Ellemers,

Van Rijswijk, Roefs & Simons, 1997; Mummendey & Schreiber, 1984b; Mummendey & Simon, 1989; Spears & Manstead, 1989; Van Knippenberg & Van Oers, 1984; Van Knippenberg & Wilke, 1979). Arguably, this is a desirable situation, as it enables members of both groups to maintain their own distinct identity (Van Knippenberg & Ellemers, 1990). In fact, it has been demonstrated that groups are likely actively to seek and propose additional comparative dimensions as a strategy for coping with a lack of positive group distinctiveness on the focal dimension (Lemaine, 1974; Van Knippenberg, 1978). Thus, the evidence suggests that increasing intergroup distinctiveness can actually reduce identity threat, with greater differentiation between groups diminishing ingroup bias (Deschamps & Brown, 1983), and improving intergroup relations (Brown & Wade, 1987).

Threats to Value

The notion that people will attempt to defend the value of an important group membership when it is directly attacked by an outgroup is derivable from the basic postulates of social identity theory (Tajfel & Turner, 1979, 1986). People can obtain or maintain positive feelings about their own group to the extent that a positive comparison with another group can be achieved. While different strategic responses are feasible (e.g., employment of social creativity strategies), exposure to a negative social comparison between the ingroup and a relevant outgroup may be perceived as sufficiently threatening to evoke ingroup favouritism and/or outgroup derogation as a means of defending that identity. In this section we further delineate the threat to a valued group membership by distinguishing between the source of the threat and the dimensions on which it can occur. The outgroup is often the 'object' of the identity threat, but it can also be the source in a more direct or active sense, such as when the threatening information or behaviour is intentionally directed at the ingroup by the outgroup. Sometimes the source is less explicit, however, with a third party generating the threat, or it may simply be activated based on a salient intergroup comparison (e.g., the group's poor performance, status or standing). Finally, and perhaps most unusual of all, the ingroup itself may be the source of the threat. That is, the domain of the evaluative difference between the groups may stem from the ingroup's prior actions or history. In particular, there may be an important distinction in terms of how threat will be experienced, depending on whether the difference between the groups is based on competence-related dimensions (e.g., performance, status) or those concerning morality (e.g., treatment of the outgroup). Reactions to such differing identity threats may depend on people's levels of identification with the group. We will begin by considering threats that stem directly from the outgroup, and then move on to cases where more neutral sources are operating, followed by instances where the ingroup itself plays a role.

A good demonstration of the hypothesis that threats to identity generated by an outgroup can provoke ingroup favouritism is provided by Bourhis, Giles, Leyens and Tajfel (1979). In that research, Belgian Flemish speakers were exposed to an outgroup member (a French-speaking Belgian) who was insulting about the ingroup's language group membership. Compared with a control condition, where this threat to social identity was absent, the Flemish respondents who were exposed to the language group insult were more likely to retaliate with obscenities directed towards the offending French-speaking experimental confederate. Thus, explicit attacks on a social identity can directly evoke outgroup derogation.

Group-level defensive strategies are equally apparent when the threatening behaviour of the outgroup is more chronic and ingrained. In a study of African Americans, responses to perceptions of discrimination by White Americans were examined (Branscombe, Schmitt & Harvey, in press). It was found that perceived discrimination across a variety of social situations predicted elevated minority group identification. Furthermore, the more Black Americans perceive themselves to be victims of racial discrimination, the more hostility towards Whites they exhibited. Thus, feeling discriminated against based on one's group membership encourages derogation of the rejecting outgroup member who does the discriminating (see also Crocker, Voelkl, Testa & Major, 1991), and psychological movement towards an accepting ingroup.

In a related vein, threats from an outgroup can also enhance self-affirmation (Steele, 1987) and self-stereotyping (see chapter 3). For example Dion (1986) reported that the more Jewish participants believed their Gentile evaluators were prejudiced against them, the more they described themselves as possessing positively evaluated stereotypic Jewish attributes. Such increased willingness to self-stereotype is suggestive of at least temporary increases in ingroup identification. More direct effects of this sort were obtained by Ellemers, Wilke, and Van Knippenberg (1993). They found that when people collectively suffered unjust treatment that resulted in low ingroup status (as opposed to the situation where they had been illegitimately categorized as a member of a lower status group), ingroup identification was strengthened, and increased intergroup competition occurred. When such outgroup-based threats to the ingroup's value in the form of discrimination and devaluation are severe enough, and the outgroup's penalties are not prohibitive, we would expect that most ingroup members would behave in this defensive fashion; closing ranks following explicit group-based exclusion allows devalued group members to protect their well-being (Branscombe, Schmitt & Harvey, in press).

When the source of negative evaluation is less explicitly derived from the outgroup per se, threats to identity can be no less evident. In a further refinement of the basic social identity theory predictions concerning identity management under conditions of threat, Branscombe and Wann (1994) exposed American participants who were either high or low in identification with their national group to one of two short video presentations of a boxing match. One version of the video was expected to create a threat to the value of being an American by portraying the American athlete as a loser when compared to his Russian counterpart. The other version was expected to support the value of being an American by portraying the American boxer as beating the Russian and winning the match. Notice that this manipulation did not involve a direct group membership insult, as the Bourhis, Giles, Leyens and Tajfel (1979) study did; it was a considerably more symbolic threat to identity. Yet, exposure to this implied inferiority of ingroup manipulation, among those who identified strongly with Americans, did significantly reduce their private feelings of collective self-esteem compared with when the identity-supporting video was viewed. Such reductions in self-esteem as a function of degree of identity threat were not observed among the participants who did not identify themselves strongly with the American. Furthermore, the degree to which exposure to the identity threat harmed the collective self-esteem of the highly identified predicted subsequent outgroup derogation. The amount of outgroup derogation that was expressed was, in turn, linked with subsequent positive self-esteem increases (see also Oakes & Turner, 1980).

This research illustrates how a threat to the value of a social identity is responded to differentially depending on how identified the individual is with a specific social group. Not all group members respond to such value threats by directly derogating the competing outgroup; only the highly identified respond with outgroup derogation. Furthermore, the potential consequences of outgroup derogation seems to be functional: for those who value the identity in question, derogation of the threatening outgroup can serve collective self-esteem restoration purposes.

In addition to direct outgroup derogation, when the ingroup is portrayed as 'less than' a competing outgroup on valued dimensions, other more subtle types of defensive responses can be exhibited. Social reality constraints may often limit the credibility of direct ingroup favouritism, at least on the status-defining dimensions (see chapter 6). In situations where the ingroup is portrayed as less successful than the outgroup because of its own failure (e.g., when one's own sports team loses, which can imply that the group as a whole is less valuable than previously thought) rather than because of an 'unfair' bias against the ingroup on the part of the outgroup, then only high identifiers are likely to display subtle collective responses as a means of reinforcing or displaying their commitment to the group. These include perceiving the ingroup as more cohesive or homogeneous (Doosje, Ellemers & Spears, 1995; Ellemers, Spears & Doosje, 1997), seeing the self as more representative of the ingroup (Spears, Doosje & Ellemers, 1997), and stereotyping the group on non-status defining stereotypic attributes, both positive and negative (e.g., Doff, 1998; Ellemers & Van Rijswijk 1997; see also Wann & Branscombe, 1990, 1993; and chapter 9 this volume). These processes may provide individuals with a clear and consensually agreed upon common group identity, which constitutes a first step towards ingroup favouritism, outgroup derogation, and other forms of collective resistance (see chapter 4). In this way, intergroup competition and defeat can elevate ingroup cohesion and make other group-level responses more likely (Rothgerber, 1997; Turner, Hogg, Oakes & Smith, 1984; see chapter 3, this volume).

Such increasing alignment with the ingroup among high identifiers can encourage attempts to rationalize and defend the ingroup's actual performance history. This type of defensive response can even occur in members of groups with superior social standing, when the group's moral value is called into question, as has been observed among various natural social groups. With such responses, the focus is shifted from the dimension of competence or status to questions of morality and the nature of the intergroup relationship itself. Consider the dilemma experienced by highly identified White American participants who are reminded of the unearned privileges that they have obtained because of their racial group membership (Branscombe, Schiffhauer & Valencia, 1998). In response to this threat to the image of the ingroup, where it is implied that the ingroup has been unfair to and exploitive of the other group, high White identifiers exhibit significant increases in their scores on McConahay's (1986) 'modern racism' measure compared with a control condition where their racial ingroup is not portrayed in this threatening manner. Because highly identified Whites cannot or will not accept this exploitive portrait of their group's past, the need to rationalize the contextually salient differences in outcomes received by the two groups can be accomplished by reducing the deservingness of the outgroup. In contrast, the low identified White participants, when they are reminded of the privileges they have received because of their racial group membership, do not show increases in anti-Black sentiments. Instead, they exhibit significant reductions in self-esteem, presumably because they accept the 'unearned advantages' claim about their group's history as true (see also Branscombe, 1998, for a similar demonstration in relation to gender).

The tendency to defend the group's history among high identifiers, and the induction of negative group-based emotions in low identifiers, was demonstrated more explicitly in a set of studies which examined how Dutch participants responded when they were reminded of their nation's colonial history in Indonesia (Doosje, Branscombe, Spears & Manstead, 1998; see also chapter 4 this volume). These results show that when people belong to a particular group they are likely to react differentially when the group's value is threatened, depending on their degree of identification with the group. In fact, we would argue that identification with a group allows people to feel emotions as a consequence of the fate of that group and the actions of its members, even if they personally cannot be held responsible for the outcomes delivered by their group to the other group (see chapter 4 for further discussion of this issue). Thus, an important conclusion we draw from this work is that emotions may be experienced by group members when their social identity is salient, and that those emotions may be very different from what would be expected if they were operating on the basis of their personal identity. In addition, such group-based emotions can be powerful determinants of intentions for future actions towards the outgroup (see also chapter 10).

A study by Ellemers and Haaker (1995) examined the self-esteem consequences of identity threat when either the outgroup or the ingroup was the source of the threat among high and low group identifiers. Natural group members were rated either positively or negatively on the basis of their group membership and subse-

quent self-esteem was assessed. After classifying the student participants according to their study major, a categorization that was made salient by asking them to
consider the similarities and differences between students with different majors,
participants rated an ingroup or an outgroup target on a number of personality
attributes. Before doing so, participants received a list with those same attributes
indicating how they themselves had been rated by another ingroup or outgroup
participant. The manipulated feedback was either favourable or unfavourable.
Not surprisingly, positive feedback was rated more positively, and was considered
more acceptable than negative feedback. Furthermore, regardless of its content,
feedback from an ingroup member was generally considered more credible and
important and was more easily accepted than feedback from an outgroup member
(see also Mackie, Worth & Asuncion, 1990). Thus, whereas threat from the
outgroup may be designed to incense or insult the ingroup, as revealed in the study
by Bourhis, Giles, Leyens and Tajfel (1979), rejection by the ingroup may carry
more impact, precisely because this group is more valued, is more a part of the
self, and because people expect its support (see also the next section on group
acceptance). The effects of the feedback on participants' self-esteem were actually
more consequential for low identifiers; their collective self-esteem suffered more
from negative feedback than did high identifiers' collective self-esteem, which was
independent of the evaluative direction of the feedback that they had received.
Therefore, these data are consistent with the notion that being evaluated on the
basis of one's group membership may threaten the self-esteem of those who prefer
not to identify as group members in this particular situation (see the section on
categorization threat). As with the case of the research on collective guilt, we see
that it is not always high identifiers who are the most sensitive to threats to identity. High identifiers may be generally more immune to threat, and are therefore
better able to rationalize any criticism precisely because of the strength of their
group identity.

Acceptance

Receiving negative feedback from the ingroup raises the question of acceptance by
one's own group and this constitutes our fourth class of identity threat. We now
consider threat pertaining to intragroup processes, albeit in an intergroup context.
Specifically, unwillingness on the part of the ingroup to accept the self as a group
member may be a source of threat to an ingroup member. One might be potentially threatened with a lack of ingroup acceptance for a variety of reasons. In this
section we will focus on the threat associated with the uncertainty of group acceptance that may occur when trying to gain entry into a new group, on the one
hand, and when being excluded from an existing group on the other.
   In a number of social contexts, groups to which people strongly desire admittance maintain strict requirements for prospective members. A certain set of skills

must be obtained or milestones passed (e.g., a high-level degree for academic promotion), a probationary period must be served (e.g., in trade unions; sororities and fraternities), or particular acts undertaken, which are often personally dangerous but can convey loyalty to the group (e.g., criminal acts in the Mafia or urban street gangs). It is commonly assumed that such initiation procedures, or 'rites of passage', serve as tests of the loyalty of prospective group members by the group's establishment, and they may enhance commitment to the group once individuals have actually gained group membership (see Aronson & Mills, 1959; Gerard & Mathewson, 1966), although these potentially beneficial effects of initiation severity have more recently been called into question (Lodewijkx & Syroit, 1997). We argue that while this class of threat may evoke similar responses to those resulting from a threat to the group as a whole (such as outgroup derogation), the motivation underlying such actions is fundamentally different.

A central component of self-categorization theory (Turner, 1987) is the notion that people can and do use expressive behaviour in order to indicate their preferred identity, and to act strategically in the service of their interests ('impression management'). Accordingly, research on attitude formation has demonstrated that people tend to adopt the position that is prototypical for the group they want to align themselves with. In fact, people may even express more extreme attitudes when this would serve as a means of differentiating the self from the position advocated by another group (Turner, 1991; Wetherell, 1987; see also chapters 6 and 8, this volume). As both Lewin (1948) and Tajfel (1978b) have argued, those who are marginal members of social groups are likely to experience an intrapsychic need to clarify what group he or she actually belongs to. An identity conflict situation of this sort might be most likely to arise in cases where the individual is a peripheral or non-prototypical member of two competing and incompatible group memberships. For example, Hispanic students, who are starting their first year at an Ivy League university, can either get involved in Hispanic activities on campus, or they may move away from their ethnic identity in order to integrate with the Anglo-Saxon students (see Ethier & Deaux, 1994). When one of the two social identity groups has greater social status than the other, attempts to 'pass' as a member of the higher status group may be a likely option. As a consequence, marginal group members are likely to devalue the lesser group as a means of convincing themselves, as well as other outgroup members, that they really are members of the more desirable ingroup.

Accordingly, we argue that those who feel uncertain about the extent to which others accept or recognize them as members of a particular group should display behaviour that is prototypical for members of the preferred group. Obviously, the specific content of this behaviour may vary, depending on the nature of the group, as well as the question of how it can be meaningfully differentiated from relevant comparison groups (see the section on distinctiveness threat and also chapter 5). Thus, people may display a variety of behaviours, ranging from physically hurting or even killing someone – for instance to get accepted as a member of a youth gang – to sponsoring the homeless as a means of getting accepted as a member of a

Rotary Club. However, the common denominator underlying these various behavioural displays is that, when facing uncertainty about acceptance into an ingroup
that is perceived to be desirable, people will try to present themselves to other
ingroup members as holding especially favourable and prototypical attitudes towards the ingroup (see Noel, Wann & Branscombe, 1995). Indeed, the applicant
may publicly report being honoured even to be considered for membership in the
group (see also Vonk, 1998).

As a result of the operation of such processes, a generic norm in many intergroup
situations will involve favouring the ingroup and/or to derogating the outgroup.
For instance, in social dilemma situations, people appear to be more competitive
in intergroup contexts as opposed to interpersonal contexts (see Insko, Schopler,
Hoyle, Dardis & Graetz, 1990). In a similar vein, in a series of experiments,
Platow, Hoar, Reid, Harley and Morrison (1997) demonstrated that group members are more likely to endorse a leader who accords them an unfair advantage in
intergroup situations, while fairness is clearly preferred in interpersonal decision
contexts. Furthermore, in line with our argument, the endorsement of ingroup-
favouring leadership behaviour appears to be more pronounced among those participants who strongly identify with their group.

Thus, given that it is normative in social groups to view one's own group more
positively than a relevant comparison outgroup, at least on group-defining dimensions, conforming to perceived ingroup expectations of this sort might seem to be
an effective means of securing greater acceptance on the part of more established
ingroup members. In fact, derogating the outgroup might even be a way of publicly proclaiming admiration for the sought-after ingroup and of attempting to
improve one's own status within the group (see also chapter 6). This strategy was
evident in a study by Breakwell (1979). She tested the prediction that more outgroup
derogation would be expressed by individuals who had obtained admittance to
the group via illegitimate means than by people who had gained acceptance into
the group legitimately. Those who were aware that their membership in the desirable group was not secure (because they cheated to gain admittance to it) did in
fact display more extreme outgroup derogation than those who felt their membership was secure. In this study, however, the extent to which this greater outgroup
derogation on the part of insecure group members served to clarify for themselves
which group they wanted to belong to, or was intended to convey their preferred
identity to others, remains ambiguous.

More conclusive evidence that outgroup derogation may be used for intragroup
ingratiation was obtained in a study where the individual's peripheral status was
explicitly related to the phase of seeking and achieving ingroup membership, and
participants were led to believe that other ingroup members either would or would
not learn about their responses (Noel, Wann & Branscombe, 1995, Study 2). In
this situation, outgroup derogation might be used as a means of providing convincing evidence to established ingroup members that the applicant will abide by
the ingroup's norms and should be accepted as a true ingroup member. The study
illustrated how fraternity and sorority group members' trait assignments for ingroup

members and non-members exhibited a consistent ingroup bias, regardless of the context in which those judgements were expressed. However, among the pledges from those who had not yet been fully accepted into the group, the assignment of traits to ingroup and outgroup members was affected by the social context in which their attitudes were expressed. When these not-fully-accepted group members' trait ratings could be publicly monitored by established group members who had power over them, then outgroup derogation occurred and ingroup members were evaluated most positively. If, however, the insecure applicants to the organization believed that their ratings would not be made known to the ingroup's powerful establishment, they failed to differentiate between the ingroup and outgroup in their ratings. Thus, this research illustrates that outgroup derogation can function as a means of strategically addressing intragroup self-presentational concerns by peripheral group members.

So far, we have considered the effects of insecure group membership for those who are trying to gain access to a particular group (newcomers). However, similar concerns may be evoked when people who currently belong to the group are faced with the risk of possible exclusion from the ingroup, with responses to such actual or implied rejection depending on how important that identity is to the individual. In some instances, the threat is not that one will be literally stripped of group membership, but, rather, it concerns the extent to which one will be accepted as a 'good' or 'typical' group member. That is, people may fear that they will not receive full recognition of their group membership because of their non-prototypicality. For those who are low in identification, a reasonable response to such a situation might be to disidentify in anticipation of being rejected by the ingroup (see also chapter 3). In fact, a positive emotional response to non-prototypicality could even be imagined for those who are not identified with the group, because this implies that their self-categorization is better matched with the way they are perceived by the group (see also Spears, Jetten & Van Harreveld, 1998).

Those who are high in identification, however, should show similar responses to people who are trying to gain access from the periphery of the group, as we have discussed above. Consequently, they are likely to continue admiring those who are more prototypical of the group. In fact, if the ingroup is of sufficient importance to the individuals who are threatened by being non-prototypical, they might even display a willingness to evaluate more positively someone who is prototypical of the group compared with someone who is personally similar to them (i.e., is also not prototypical of the group). A recent study of men who were either high or low in identification with their gender group provides empirical evidence that group-protecting evaluation ratings occur in the highly identified, but not among those whose identification with the group is weak (Schmitt & Branscombe, 1997). Such responses occur when high group identification is coupled with a perceived threat to group membership. That is, when highly identified men were told they were not prototypical of their group, they more strongly favoured an ingroup target who was portrayed as prototypical and at the same time they devalued an ingroup target who was non-prototypical. These results can be taken as quite compelling evidence of the high identifier's desire to protect the overall value of the group. Here they are willing to value someone who is apparently quite personally dissimilar to themselves but is a good representative of their valued group. This contrasts with the strong tendency, which has been observed in much social psychological research, to favour others who are similar to the self (Byrne, 1971; Griffin & Sparks, 1990). From a self-categorization perspective (Turner, 1987), however, the two forms of attraction exhibited by both the high and the low identifiers in this research are conceptually and empirically distinct. As Hogg and Hains (1997) have shown, social attraction of the sort observed among the highly identified males is indeed a function of level of identification with the group, while personal attraction would be a function of other strictly interpersonal variables.

In addition to not matching the ingroup prototype in terms of defining physical or psychological characteristics, people may be perceived as non-prototypical and be rejected because their commitment to the ingroup is not perceived to be firm enough by its highly identified elite members. One way in which a lack of commitment to the group, or even disloyalty towards the group, might be expressed is by attempts to distance the self from the group when it has failed or performed badly (see chapters 3 and 6). Such distancing from the group when its value is brought into question by a loss, if it is observed by highly identified group members is quite likely to be diagnosed for what it is: an attempt to salvage the personal self at the expense of the group. Thus, the low identified, who tend to behave in a more self-interested fashion, are likely to be subjected to such rejection or even expulsion from the group by those whose commitment to it is strong.

One step more extreme in terms of likelihood of evoking the ire of and total rejection by highly identified group members is an ingroup member who brings into question the entire group's value (see Marques, Yzerbyt & Leyens, 1988). Such a 'black sheep', who is disloyal to the ingroup, is particularly likely to be derogated by the highly identified when the ingroup's value is suffering, such as when it has endured a defeat (Branscombe, Wann, Noel & Coleman, 1993). Obviously, such patterns of disloyalty to the group and derogation by the ingroup can become cyclical and reinforce each other.

To investigate such intragroup processes systematically, we orthogonally manipulated the respect that fellow ingroup members accorded the individual as well as the prestige of the ingroup in the eyes of the outgroup (Branscombe, Spears, Ellemers & Doosje, 1998; see also chapter 4, this volume). In this research we defined prestige as the status of the ingroup based on the view of it as held by a relevant outgroup (closely related to the notion of public collective self-esteem: see Luhtanen & Crocker, 1992). Respect refers to the individual group member's perceived status within the group according to other ingroup members (see also Smith & Tyler, 1997). As predicted, people who belonged to a devalued group displayed fundamentally different responses, depending on the extent to which they felt respected or rejected by their fellow ingroup members. Specifically, highly respected members of a devalued group were more likely to discriminate against the outgroup when making intergroup allocations than were those accorded little respect by their fellow group members. Furthermore, they exhibited a greater willingness to work for and invest time in the group relative to their personal selves. Conversely, less respected members of a devalued group were significantly less inclined to invest in the group, and preferred to work for themselves. These differences were not evident in a group whose identity was not threatened by low prestige or standing, suggesting that the responses of respected group members were most consequential and necessary when the group suffered an external threat to its value (see the previous section on threats to value).

These results attest to the possibility that the group may antagonize its members by withholding respect from them, and the resulting disloyalty of the individuals in question provides further grounds for their rejection by the ingroup. In other words, when too little respect or too much rejection has been directed towards them, people may start to disidentify and feel little loyalty towards the ingroup. Consequently, they are the most likely to behave as a 'traitor' and switch camps when upward mobility is possible. When the rejecting ingroup is of a high status or if it cannot be easily replaced because it is basic in some important way for the individual's functioning, then adjustment following such rejection should be especially problematic (see Burris, Branscombe & Klar, 1997; Williams & Sommer, 1997). In fact, rejection by an important ingroup may be sufficiently difficult to adapt to psychologically that when individuals perceive themselves at risk for such treatment, they may display 'hyper-conformity' to perceived ingroup norms in an attempt to convince the ingroup that they are indeed loyal and want to retain their group membership.

Conclusions and Future Directions

In this chapter we have distinguished between four different types of social identity threat that can be experienced. We have summarized this taxonomy and the different effects that can be expected following induction of each sort in table 2.1. Furthermore, we have tried to illustrate how the nature of the threat depends on the social context in which it is encountered, and how the way in which people are likely to respond to each type of threat depends on the content of the social identity or the dimension of social comparison, and, above all, on the extent to which individuals feel committed to the group. For some types of social identity threat, those who are highly identified are most likely to show defensive responses (e.g., when the group's identity is not distinct, or when they face the possibility of rejection by the ingroup). However, the greatest responsiveness to other forms of social identity threat (such as the threat of being categorized against one's will) is likely to be observed among low-identified group members. With other forms of identity threat, such as threat to the group's value, reactions of high and low identifiers may be equally defensive but responses may take different and quite opposite forms, with low identifiers distancing themselves from the group or re-penting for its immoral behaviour, and high identifiers closing ranks and either symbolically or physically striking back at the group they perceive as representing the threat. Thus, social identity threat is not the sole province of those who are highly identified with a group. Rather, what is experienced as threatening and how it is responded to varies by level of group identification.

In addition to affecting their coping responses to identity threat, we argue that the content of the threat may vary depending on the way people define their social identity in a particular social context. For instance, a group that is generally deval-ued in the social structure at large may be perceived in a positive way by its members, perhaps because it accords them with a distinct identity, as is the case of alternative cultural identities such as can be found among body-piercers, for ex-ample. Alternatively, what is considered a valued identity may be culture-specific, as was illustrated in a study by Levy and Langer (1994). When they compared how Chinese and American research participants were affected by cultural stere-otypes about ageing, the responses of older people depended on the evaluation of their group in the larger society. Specifically, the memory performance of older people in China (where 'elderly' is a positive identity) was superior to that of American elderly (who are confronted with a negative group identity).

We have further illustrated that a similar response to threat, namely outgroup derogation, can occur for a variety of reasons (see table 2.1). Evidence in support of the most intuitively plausible possibility, where it is displayed in retaliation for a direct or indirect negative comparative evaluation between the ingroup and the outgroup, was discussed. However, outgroup derogation can occur for other rea-sons as well. It can be the result of a public self-presentational strategy designed to impress powerful ingroup members on the part of peripheral group members seeking admittance to the group or by ingroup members who fear expulsion. In this case it reflects a willingness to conform to perceived ingroup norms to gain approval, with outgroup derogation being the most obvious way of achieving this goal. It can also result from a lack of distinctness or distinctiveness for a group's identity, especially when no other means of meaningful differentiation are avail-able, as is typical in studies employing the 'minimal groups' paradigm.

In order to understand fully the possible implications of the different types of threat, the taxonomic scheme presented in this chapter and summarized in table 2.1 must be further developed and refined. First, there may be other distinct classes of threat not covered here that are relevant to the understanding of psychological reactions and behaviour in intergroup contexts. Second, further work is necessary to evaluate the importance of variations in context, content and commitment for these different classes of threat. Commitment, or degree of identification, is per-haps the theme that has attracted the most attention from researchers, forming a recurring motif in the research we reviewed. The context in which the threat occurs covers a range of factors, including the frame of reference (intragroup versus intergroup comparison) and the degree of salience of different identity levels that is likely to be evoked (personal versus group), amongst other factors.

This, too, has been the subject of much research, and the consequences of the combination of context and commitment have been an explicit theme in some of our own research in terms of both social perception (see chapter 3) and behaviour (see chapter 4). Perhaps the most fruitful direction for additional research is the issue of 'content' and how the content of social identity and group norms can be crucial to the sorts of response to identity threat that are likely to be exhibited (see, in particular, chapters 6, 8 and 10). In the present scheme we have only explicitly considered the content in relation to threats to group value (competence versus morality), but it is doubtless relevant to other classes of threat as well. In relation to group distinctiveness, we touched briefly on the importance of content in endowing us with a distinct identity and the possibility that differences in the content of group identity can sometimes provide the solution to group distinctiveness in the context of multidimensional comparisons, eliminating the need for more overt discrimination. Currently, we are engaged in research that examines the consequences of respect from fellow ingroup members in terms of the impact of differences in content (competence-based versus liking-based respect) for intergroup behaviour.

This scheme could also be conceptually extended by developing a taxonomy of groups and the ways in which these can vary, along with their implications for how reactions to identity threat might be moderated. Important factors that have not yet been sufficiently considered in systematic research include: (a) the controllability of inclusion (e.g., the visibility of group membership, see Frable, 1993); (b) whether the social identity itself is voluntary (self-selected) or is involuntary (assigned); (c) whether the group identity is long or short term and based on agreed-upon performance criteria, with the possibility that the position of the groups varies over time; (d) whether group members interact in face-to-face settings or are simply members of a social category; and (e) whether there is strong and widespread consensual devaluation of a group identity or whether its value is contextually dependent, with only some subgroups within the broader culture likely to evaluate the identity negatively. These factors are often correlated in real social groups, and there is considerable ambiguity about which are exerting the most crucial effects. In order to address these questions and assess their independent effects on intergroup behaviour they must be disentangled experimentally.

These kinds of conceptual issue are made all the more difficult by the methodological and measurement problems that plague the study of identity threat and its consequences. As we hinted at the beginning of this chapter, identity threat is a complex construct that can involve multiple meanings, making measurement a thorny problem. Indeed, the methodological issues associated with manipulation and measurement of threat may well require a chapter of their own. While we have not addressed these issues directly here, we see the problems involved in the study of threat as difficult to underestimate. Often it is difficult to obtain direct 'manipulation checks' of threat without revealing the real purpose of the manipulation itself and thereby undermining reactions to the critical dependent measures in the process. One well-known reaction to threat evident since the earliest psychodynamic treatises involves denying its presence or impact. This possibility makes it even more necessary, therefore, that we employ multiple methods, including those that are more 'direct' but less obtrusive or reactive (e.g., reaction-time data and physiological responses). Between-subjects treatments or even separate studies may be required to evaluate fully the impact of threat manipulations, if we are to convince critical consumers of the evidence concerning the operation of psychological processes as mediators of socially relevant outcomes (see Bettencourt, Miller & Hume, in press). Although the identity threat effects that we have presented here are interpretable and do make good sense in terms of the theoretical frameworks provided by social identity and self-categorization theories in particular, the richness of these grand theories may be seen by some as a weakness. Thus, attention to the measurement and methodological issues, in addition to theoretical developments, should be a priority in future empirical work.

In addition, an important direction for future research should be investigation of the consequences of exposure to longer-term threats to social identity than those examined thus far. Much of the existing literature concerns responses to immediate or temporary threats to identity, although some of the groups that have been studied (e.g African Americans, women) are subjected to long-term identity threat in society. With the exception of Breakwell's (1986) work on the consequences of loss of the ability to claim a valued identity (e.g., the movement from employed person to unemployed) and the addition or loss of major identities over the life-span (e.g., marriage, divorce, illness or criminal victimization), little is known about the options available to different types of people as they adjust to such social identity revisions and changes. Furthermore, when people might perceive a dimension in terms of a group membership or when they might perceive it as a feature of their personal selves requires additional theoretical and empirical work. As Simon (1997) has noted, any attribute or dimension can be used as the basis for group self-categorization or individual self-categorization. Under what circumstances people will move, in either direction, from conceptualizing themselves in group membership terms (e.g., as a member of one age group or another; as a member of the group 'healthy people' versus the group 'cancer patients') to personal identity terms, where those are simply individual attributes of the self, should be an important focus of further empirical investigation. It is unlikely to be the attribute itself that is critical; rather, some social contexts are likely to push towards one conceptualization of the self over another, and which level of identity is operating will have critical implications for how threats to identity are managed. The present chapter at least attempts to provide a heuristic framework in which the different faces of threat to social identity in intergroup contexts can be conceptualized and understood.

3

Commitment and the Context of Social Perception

Russell Spears, Bertjan Doosje and Naomi Ellemers

Is perception a product of the perceiver or the environment? We do not have to be psychologists to recognize this is a silly question, as both are clearly necessary for perception to occur. Nevertheless, in social psychology there is often a tendency in both theory and research either to emphasize or neglect one side of this equation. This chapter attempts to demonstrate the importance of both of these factors in the realm of self and social perception. The circumstances thrown up by the social context are clearly an important input into social perceptions, but how this context is interpreted and reacted to also depends on the nature of the perceiver's subjective identity and the degree of commitment to that identity. Although this appears obvious, some readings of social identity theory seem to assume that the mere presence of social categorization will result in group perception and behaviour, and neglect the say of the individual perceiver in this process. Theories that try to explain intergroup relations primarily in terms of individual differences are no less guilty of neglecting the import and impact of the social context. Social identity theory has always emphasized the interaction between the psychology and the context (Turner, 1996b; chapter 1, this volume), and in this chapter we try to show how the content of social perception is, quite literally, the product of an interaction between contextual factors and commitment to the particular social identities at stake.

Developing the central theme raised in the previous chapter, we start by examining how threats to identity can evoke divergent perceptions depending on degree of group identification. Group identification is a crucial moderating factor that forms the central leitmotif in all the studies discussed here. We propose that a degree of group identification is a critical factor that determines whether our cognitive reactions to identity threat are more individually oriented or more group-based. These social perceptions are not purely for cognitive consumption, but form a vital bridge to individual or collective behaviour. How these perceptions might facilitate overt group behaviour (e.g., social mobility, intergroup discrimination) is not the present focus, however, but is picked up and elaborated in chapter 4.

Our analysis is not confined to the effects of group identification on perceptual responses to identity threats. We extend it to examine the effects of group identification on less motivational and more 'cognitive' contextual factors, such as those facilitating category salience, and our ability to process information freely or under contextual restrictions ('cognitive load'). The argument in all of these domains is very similar, namely that group identification determines how we respond to these contextual conditions leading to divergent perceptual and judgemental outcomes in each case. The different dimensions of social perception that we examine are varied, including self-stereotyping, group stereotyping and intergroup differentiation, perceptions of group homogeneity, and indices of social categorization. However, all these measures share in common the fact that they reveal ways in which the social categories are more or less important and central for the social perceiver, and form important bricks in the bridge to social behaviour.

Social Identity Threat: The Moderating Role of Group Identification

One of our original interests in starting our programme of research was to consider the conditions necessary to elicit intergroup behaviour, and to examine the cognitive and perceptual processes that might accompany or even mediate such behaviour. However, as we will try to make clear, group behaviour such as discrimination might not be the best place to begin our search. Attempts to locate the bases of group behaviour in either contextual factors, person variables or their combination have proved elusive. A perusal of the literature on intergroup relations suggests that, despite evidence from the minimal group paradigm, mere categorization into ingroup and outgroup is not always sufficient to elicit intergroup differentiation or discrimination. In many naturally occurring groups ingroup bias is not observed (Mummendey & Schreiber 1984b; Spears & Manstead, 1989; Van Knippenberg, 1984). Indeed, even in the minimal group paradigm, ingroup bias does not always occur or, at least, not for all participants: fairness is also a prominent reward strategy for many people (see also chapter 5). Moreover, evidence of outgroup bias is often found in natural groups (Jost & Banaji, 1994; Spears & Manstead, 1989).

However, a closer reading of original statements of social identity theory (e.g. Tajfel, 1978a; Tajfel and Turner, 1979, 1986) clearly shows that an assumption of an automatic relation between social categorization and overt discrimination into groups is misguided. First, the theory suggests that objective categorization is not sufficient but must be accompanied by the subjective internalization of that social categorization by the ingroup members as important and relevant to them in the particular social context. People must identify sufficiently with a particular group for it to be a meaningful basis of self-definition before it can become a basis for social differentiation (see chapter 2). This idea is perhaps even clearer in self-categorization theory, where self-definition in terms of the category, as opposed to the external designation, is made even more explicit. Once again, group identification can be seen as an operational definition or indicator of the extent to which people are likely to see their categorization as relevant. It is perhaps, therefore, not surprising that some studies have shown a positive relation between identification and ingroup bias (e.g. Branscombe & Wann, 1994; Grant, 1993; Kelly, 1988, 1999). However, it would be equally misguided to see identification as sufficient to produce discrimination and even more problematic to expect there to be a general relation between the two, as some have proposed (e.g., Hinkle & Brown, 1990). The reasons for this are several and anticipate some of the arguments to be made later in this chapter and elsewhere in this book.

First, this prediction takes no account of the content of group identity and prescriptive norms. Assuming that identification will simply result in more ingroup bias neglects the ideological content of group norms and social identity. Although ingroup bias may be a very common and almost group-defining form of behaviour, it is by no means the only form of group behaviour. Group norms can prescribe fairness as well as discrimination, and in this case group identification might even lead to more fair behaviour (see chapter 5). Moreover, group norms might even more fundamentally be more individualistic and prescribe quite interpersonal reactions to others (see chapter 6).

The question of individualism raises a second point relating to the conceptualization of group identification itself. There is an inherent danger of defining group identification primarily as an individual difference variable, simply because it is measurable within individuals (Oakes, 1996; chapter 1, this volume). This would be to reduce the tendency to show ingroup bias or other relevant group responses to an individual process (i.e. 'individualism'), and tip the balance in favour of the perceiver at the expense of context from the very start. This is precisely what social identity theory has tried to escape from. For this reason we think it is important on principle not to see group identification as a static or stable individual difference variable. Rather, we view identification as the momentary and sometimes more long-standing crystallization of past contextual influences and ongoing allegiances, which will itself vary as a function of identity and context.

The notion that intergroup behaviour cannot be reduced to individual factors raises a third central point about social identity theory. This is that group responses such as ingroup bias should be seen as the product of psychological factors interacting with a (dynamic) social structure (Turner, 1996b). The individual is clearly embedded in a social field. Identification with the group, and the need to respond to this field, require that these social processes take into account this social reality, be it stable or shifting. Ingroup enhancement may be inhibited because of social reality constraints and power differentials which would render its expression problematic or lacking in credibility (see Reicher, Spears & Postmes, 1995; chapter 6, this volume).

These more social concerns remind us that perhaps the most basic reason for the absence of a general relation between identification and ingroup bias is that, for intergroup behaviour to occur, the situation has to be perceived to be intergroup in nature. Tajfel (1978a) defined an interpersonal–intergroup continuum, with group behaviour only occurring when the situation is an intergroup one. Even if people are likely to identify with their group, this does not necessarily mean that they will themselves routinely show ingroup bias. One of the points we shall make further below is that high identifiers are no less able to perceive a situation in interpersonal terms (and indeed may even be more able to do so). In short, group responses like ingroup bias are unlikely without features of the social context helping to define the situation as an intergroup one. One such feature that we have already seen in the preceding chapter is threat to social identity and this forms an important theme of this chapter.

Much research has been devoted to investigating the effects of threat to social identity as a precursor to group responses such as ingroup bias and discrimination. However, although much of this research has shown that identity threats can lead to bias or discrimination, this is not always the case. For example, the evidence that status-related threats to identity will automatically produce ingroup bias receives, at best, mixed support. For low status minimal groups, in particular, where threats to identity are presumably high, there seems a tendency to show less ingroup bias than for groups of high or equal status (Mullen, Brown & Smith, 1992). Once again, we can point to social structural and strategic factors, including reality constraints that help to explain such effects, and render the simplistic prediction problematic. However, the example of minimal groups again reminds us that, in order to display a basic ingroup bias, members have to identify with their group to some degree, and this may be less likely for minimal than for natural groups (chapter 5).

With these considerations in mind, we can locate the bases of group responses in the more subjective factor of group identification in combination with the more objective factor of identity threats caused by contextual factors (e.g. salient comparison with a higher status group). It seems that any general model of group-based responses needs, at a minimum, to take into account both features of social context and group identification (and objective and subjective factors more generally). However, for many of the reasons outlined above, a range of factors may intervene to impede or encourage the expression of ingroup bias which are extraneous to this basic interactive relation (see chapters 4 and 6). Intergroup discrimination is perhaps, therefore, not the best place to begin looking at the effects of these variables. Instead, we start with the more basic process of self and social perception, which might then help to explain the subsequent content of behaviour.

Self-categorization and self-stereotyping

Perhaps the most basic place to start when considering the effects of identity threat as a function of group identification concerns how one perceives oneself in relation to the group. Self-categorization theory (Turner, 1987) proposes that self-definition, as an individual or as a group member, is the basic categorization process from which many of the other perceptual and behavioural consequences follow: before we can judge others and decide how to behave ourselves, we have to decide who we are. Indeed, research by Lea, Spears and de Groot (1998) suggests that self-categorization and self-stereotyping actually precede and even mediate the stereotyping of others in the group.

We conducted a series of four studies to examine the effect of group identification in response to identity threat on self-stereotyping (Spears, Doosje & Ellemers, 1997). In these studies we define self-stereotyping quite generally in terms of similarity to the typical group member (self-perceived prototypicality). We did this in order to sidestep the fact that the content of identity and group stereotypes will vary with comparative context (e.g., Haslam, Turner, Oakes, McGarty & Hayes, 1992; Oakes, Haslam & Turner, 1994). The recurring prediction in these studies was that threats to identity would be responded to quite differently by people who only identify weakly with their group than by those who identify strongly. Specifically, we expected that threat would function to enhance self-stereotyping for those with high commitment to the group. Threats to identity not only make the social categorization more cognitively salient (see further below) but in more socio-motivational terms such threat suggests the group needs us, and that this is the time to stand up and be counted as group members. It follows that people who are committed to their group should see themselves more in terms of their group and self-stereotype themselves more in terms of the group identity under threat. Low identifiers, on the other hand, may try to distance themselves from the group when identity is being threatened, either by emphasizing their individual identity or by being driven to other social identities more relevant and dear to them. They may even fail to appreciate the threat to identity in the same way that high identifiers do – threat to social identity may be less cognitively salient and motivationally engaging for them (Ellemers & Haaker, 1995; see chapter 2, this volume). However, to the extent that low status (for example) is aversive, they may actively try to distance themselves from the group in various ways. This should result in reduced group self-perceived prototypicality.

Although a small number of earlier studies have simultaneously considered threat and group identification (e.g., Branscombe & Wann, 1994; Grant, 1993; Turner, Hogg, Oakes & Smith, 1984; Wann & Branscombe, 1990), none has looked directly at the basic process of self-stereotyping, and only three to our knowledge (Branscombe & Wann, 1994; Grant, 1993; Turner, Hogg, Oakes and Smith, 1984), provide evidence of an interactive relation between threat and group commitment (see further below where we discuss stereotyping of the ingroup generally). Some research by Dion and colleagues has examined the effects of threat to identity on self-stereotyping (Dion, 1975; Dion & Earn, 1975), but the moderating role of group identification was not assessed. Moreover, because self-stereotyping in this research was independent of the source of identity threat, it could be viewed as a positive response to that threat. In the studies we shall describe, because self-stereotyping is defined in terms of similarity to the typical group member, when information is given about unfavourable status of the ingroup, greater self-stereotyping implies taking on a negative identity. This, arguably, provides a strong test of the willingness to stereotype oneself in terms of the group.

In the first study, we manipulated identity threat by presenting the ingroup (psychology students at the University of Amsterdam) with a series of dimensions on which to compare themselves with an outgroup (either physics students or art school students). We varied the dimensions on which respondents rated themselves relative to the outgroup on bipolar scales (whether the trait was more characteristic of their group versus the outgroup). We also orthogonally varied the outgroup (physics/art students). We did this such that the comparative outcome was either stereotypically favourable ('high status') or unfavourable ('low status'). For half the sample the dimensions chosen were all concerned with intelligence (e.g. rational, analytic, etc.) so that where the outgroup was art students, a favourable social comparison resulted (psychology students are stereotypically seen as more academic and thus more intelligent than art students). However, the social comparison with physics students on this same dimension was unfavourable. The position was reversed when creativity-related dimensions were used as the comparative dimension: now comparisons with art students were unfavourable and those with physics students favourable. In this way we created favourable and unfavourable comparisons which were not specific to a particular group-stereotype or intergroup comparison (see Judd & Park, 1993). Manipulation checks confirmed that the favourability or status relation was perceived as we had intended for the various combinations. We collapsed across conditions to create high and low status comparisons for subsequent analyses.

Identification with the ingroup (psychology students) was measured on a scale at the beginning of the questionnaire, with high and low identifiers being distinguished by means of a median split. Our main measure of self-stereotyping was the perceived similarity/difference of self to typical group members. Principal components analyses assured us that the indicators of self-stereotyping were independent of the identification measure.

The predicted interaction between group status and group identification was significant and qualified a main effect showing that high identifiers self-stereotyped more in general. When group status was high (no identity threat) there was no reliable difference in degree of self-stereotyping. However, when status was low (identity threat), low identifiers showed significantly less self-stereotyping than high identifiers (and also compared with low identifiers in the high status condition). These results indicate that group identification does moderate the response to identity threat in terms of self-stereotyping. Low identifiers try to distance themselves from their group identity by self-stereotyping less under threat, and there was some evidence (albeit weaker) that high identifiers prefer to see themselves as more similar to their (negative) group under these same conditions.

In a second study we chose a slightly different way of manipulating identity threat in order to replicate this effect and evaluate its robustness. In this case we were interested not simply in whether participants themselves perceived a status difference on the relevant comparative dimension, but whether similar effects could obtain if respondents were informed that other people perceived such a difference. If the threat to social identity is genuinely social, the idea that other people perceived this difference should be enough to elicit feelings of threat, as this accords a wider legitimacy to the status difference (Tajfel, 1984). In the present study this was achieved by telling psychology students (our participant population) in a questionnaire that the general public in the Netherlands considered business students to be either superior (high threat) or inferior (low threat) to them on a range of dimensions. Once again identification was measured beforehand and a median split performed.

In this study we used our general group similarity measure and ratings on more specific dimensions relevant to the ingroup stereotype. Again, principal components analysis indicated identification and self-stereotyping measures were distinct, and also justified the averaging of the self-stereotyping items to form a single measure. As in the first study, high identifiers exhibited self-stereotyping, but this was qualified by an, albeit marginal, interaction between status and identification. Whereas there was no reliable difference between high and low identifiers in the high status condition (no identity threat), the critical difference for low status (identity threat) was clearly significant. This replicates the pattern for the first study and shows that public-perceived threat results in the same divergence for high and low identifiers, with low identifiers distancing themselves from the group stereotype, whereas high identifiers continue to embrace it and emphasize their similarity to the group.

In a third study we tried to extend the generality of this effect by considering a different threat to identity, namely the threat to group distinctiveness (see chapters 2 and 5). According to social identity theory, groups will try to gain or maintain a positive group distinctiveness from relevant other groups. Groups that are similar to the ingroup on relevant and meaningful dimensions are likely to threaten this sense of group distinctiveness, and we expect that this might be reflected in a greater tendency to self-stereotype and perceive oneself as prototypical of the ingroup. However, once again we do not expect this to be a universal tendency but to be particularly true of people for whom the group is important, namely high identifiers. Low identifiers are less likely, by definition, to be threatened by the similarity of a rival outgroup, and may even take this similarity to conclude that the distinction between the groups is not meaningful in the first place – preferring to see members of both groups as unique individuals or members of a more inclusive social category (Turner, 1987). In short, our predictions with regard to the effect of threats to group distinctiveness on self-stereotyping were very similar to the case of value- or status-based threats considered in the first two studies. We did not expect dissimilar outgroups to elicit much distinctiveness threat or to evoke any substantial difference in self-stereotyping between high and low identifiers.

In this study, the cover story to the questionnaire focused on the comparison between psychology students (the ingroup and participant population) and business students. We stated that the research was concerned with the similarities and differences between these groups, which had been the focus of some earlier research. In the distinctiveness threat condition we indicated that this research had shown that these two groups turned out to be very similar in terms of backgrounds and interests and that the purpose of the research was to assess further the basis of these similarities. In the non-threat condition we emphasized intergroup differences. As before, identification was measured at the beginning of the questionnaire and high and low identifiers were distinguished by means of a median split. Self-stereotyping was assessed with the same items as in the first study. Once again, our analyses revealed a strong main effect of identification, with high identifiers self-stereotyping more. Although the predicted two-way interaction was not reliable, simple effects analyses revealed the greatest difference in the outgroup similarity condition.

A fourth study produced more reliable support for the predicted pattern of means. In this study, as in the second, we manipulated the public-perceived distinctiveness threat, by suggesting that psychology and business students were generally seen as being similar or different. Otherwise, measures were similar to the previous study. Here the pattern of means was similar to the first two studies: there was no reliable difference between levels of self-stereotyping in the dissimilar outgroup condition (no threat), whereas self-stereotyping reliably diverged in the similar outgroup condition (distinctiveness threat). As expected, when the distinctiveness of the ingroup was threatened by comparison with a similar outgroup, high identifiers enhanced their similarity to the typical group member, whereas low identifiers did not (although in this case divergence from low identifiers in the non-threat condition was not significant as it was in our third study).

Taken together, the overall pattern of results was fairly consistent with predictions, and a subsequent meta-analysis confirmed that the predicted differences between adjacent cells of the basic 2 × 2 design were reliable across the studies as a whole (see Spears, Doosje & Ellemers, 1997). In short, diverging responses to identity threat in terms of self-stereotyping can result, depending on the initial level of group identification. Whereas low identifiers respond to this threat by trying to distance themselves from the group, high identifiers see themselves as more prototypical of their group. Self-stereotyping is perhaps one of the most basic antecedents of group perception and behaviour (Lea, Spears & de Groot, 1998; Turner, 1987). For this reason, establishing evidence of this predicted interaction is important, as, arguably, it forms the gateway into a range of other processes, including behaviour (see chapter 4). We now consider further social perceptions affected by identification and context.

Intergroup perceptions: evaluative and stereotypic differentiation

Having considered how threat and identification might combine to intensify or attenuate perceptions of ourselves in terms of our social self (self-stereotyping), the next logical step is to look at whether similar argument holds for our social perceptions and stereotyping of others. Specifically, does the presence of a threat to social identity lead high identifiers to stereotype the ingroup more than low identifiers, and to differentiate the two in either stereotypic or evaluative terms? In the first study to investigate this issue, Turner, Hogg, Oakes and Smith (1984) showed that social attraction to the group, which they labelled group cohesiveness, increased after failure feedback (identity threat), especially when initial commitment to the group was high. In a later study Branscombe and Wann (1994) manipulated threat by means of a video clip in which an American boxer lost to a Soviet boxer (taken from the film *Rocky IV*; the study was conducted before the Cold War had finished). Ingroup identification and outgroup derogation appeared to be more strongly related under identity threat.

In a series of studies using gender as the intergroup dimension, Grant (1992, 1993) showed greater positive differentiation on gender stereotypic dimensions when gender identity was threatened, especially for those identifying highest with their gender category. For example, Grant (1992) conducted a study in which participants were divided into all-male or all-female groups in order to make gender salient. These groups discussed gender-related topics. Pre-testing had established that stereotypically 'feminine' traits were characteristic of both male and female groups beforehand. Threat was manipulated by giving groups (false) feedback from the other opposite gender group present, stating that the their summary proposal on the issue they had discussed was not important (or was important: no threat). It was shown that group members with a 'strong group identity' with the *in vivo* group (in both all-male and all-female groups) described the ingroup in more feminine terms (i.e. stereotypic of the ingroup) and were more negative towards the outgroup when their identity was threatened. In the low threat conditions there was no relation between identity strength and positive differentiation.

In two studies described in more detail below we measured group ratings, and the perceived importance of these dimensions as a function of status and group identification (Doosje, Ellemers & Spears, 1995). In the first study, psychology students were led to believe that their group was either more or less intelligent than business students (the outgroup). Identification was measured beforehand and a median split performed. Participants then rated the ingroup and outgroup on a series of positive bipolar dimensions in which they had to say whether they associated the given characteristic more with psychology or with business students. They also rated the importance of these dimensions. More positive dimensions were associated with the ingroup overall. There was a main effect of identification such that high identifiers ascribed more positive rating to the ingroup, but this did not interact with the threat manipulation. However, dimensions stereotypically associated with psychology students were rated as relatively unimportant by low status low identifiers compared with other respondents, confirming once again that low identifiers under identity threat display the least group-favouring responses.

In a further laboratory study, groups were ostensibly categorized as 'inductive' and 'deductive' thinkers, although in fact all participants received feedback that they were inductive thinkers (Doosje, Ellemers & Spears, 1995, Study 2). They also received false feedback about their ability to solve 'personnel decision-making' problems. This was either positive (no threat) or negative (threat), compared with the outgroup. On this occasion, group identification was manipulated by means of a bogus pipeline procedure in which people were led to believe that they were high or low identifiers with their group. Participants subsequently rated the ingroup and outgroup on the status-defining dimension (proficiency in personnel decision-making) as well as four positive alternative dimensions (e.g., likeability, etc.). When group status was low, participants rated their own group as positively as the outgroup on the status-defining dimension, while participants rated their own group better when group status was high. On the alternative dimensions, however, participants in all conditions rated their own group as better than the other group. In short, the status manipulation seemed to exert a reality constraint on the expression of ingroup favouritism on the focal dimension on which they received feedback (see chapter 6). However, these ratings revealed no effects of group identification.

In a different study, the attempt was made to assess further the moderating role of group identification on threat in relation to group perceptions (Doff, 1998). Moreover in this study, the nature of the threat was varied in order to examine whether it was threat to social identity that is critical in producing group-level defensive responses or threat to identity more generally. This is important because many studies examining the evidence for group-level responses as a function of threat have done this by threatening individual identity (e.g., Hogg & Sunderland, 1991; Meindl & Lerner, 1984). From social identity and self-categorization theory, we would expect that responses such as ingroup favouritism and stereotypic differentiation should primarily result when the group identity is threatened. The response to a threat would be expected to occur at the same level as that of the identity being threatened. This was investigated in a design in which feedback was provided that was designed to imply a threat to personal identity (participants received feedback that they had scored substantially worse than other students on an intuitive intelligence task) or a threat to group identity (their group had scored substantially worse than the outgroup on this task). In this case participants were students at the University of Amsterdam and the outgroup consisted of students at the rival Free University of Amsterdam (see chapter 5). Identification was measured at the beginning of the experiment and a median split performed.

Checks confirmed that identity threat was successfully manipulated in both personal and group threat conditions. On a task involving the evaluation of group products (Jetten, Spears & Manstead, 1997a) there was evidence of an effect of the threat manipulation. Specifically, whereas people who received the group threat feedback showed ingroup bias in the evaluation of ingroup versus outgroup products, no such bias was evident when personal identity was threatened. This effect was not moderated by group identification, however. Furthermore, on a measure of positive but stereotypically neutral group ratings (pleasant, intelligent) the ingroup was rated higher than the outgroup, but this was not qualified by identification nor type of threat. However, the combination of the independent variables did have an effect on ratings of the ingroup on group stereotypic dimensions. In this study positive and negative dimensions were employed that stereotypically differentiated ingroup from outgroup. The ingroup was indeed rated higher than the outgroup on both the positive and the negative ingroup stereotypic dimensions ('independent' and 'sloppy', respectively). As one might expect, positive differentiation was significantly greater on the positive dimension. However, the theoretically more interesting effect was a significant triple interaction between type of threat, group identification and target university group on the negative dimension ('sloppy'). It turned out that the high identifiers characterized the ingroup relative to the outgroup significantly more in terms of this negative stereotype than did low identifiers, but only under conditions of social identity threat and not personal identity threat. This pattern of results is similar to that found for the self-stereotyping studies obtained earlier, where self-stereotyping was greater for high identifiers, even when this implied association with a negative group.

The effects for evaluative and stereotypic group ratings as a function of identity threat and group identification reviewed here are perhaps less clear-cut than for those relating to self-stereotyping reviewed earlier. As suggested, we propose that this is the case because self-stereotyping forms a more primary and thus a purer indicator of these effects, whereas additional factors contribute to or constrain the expression of ingroup bias. For instance, both high and low identifiers can benefit from positive group ratings so that self-serving biases may occur on positive dimensions regardless of identification level. Moreover, reality constraints may play a greater role where group evaluations are concerned, compared with general ratings of similarity to typical group members. However, the evidence of greater ingroup stereotyping on negative stereotypic dimensions, as demonstrated in the last study, is theoretically interesting, precisely because this seems to put the matter of the content of group identity above self (or group) serving bias (see also chapter 2). Although previous research has shown evidence of negative stereotyping of the ingroup (e.g. Mlicki & Ellemers, 1996), none to our knowledge has demonstrated the moderating effect of group identification. High identifiers, it seems, are most prepared to admit the negative as well as the positive aspects of the group stereotype, as well as internalizing group identity through self-stereotyping. The last study is also important in showing that it is critical to distinguish the level of threat to identity: social level threats are most likely to result in social level responses.

Intergroup perceptions: perceived group variability

Before we move on from considering the combined effects of identity threat and group identification, there is one important cognitive perception yet to consider.

Thus far we have examined self-stereotyping and stereotyping of the ingroup. Self-stereotyping is important, not only in itself, but in preparing one for collective behaviour (to go along with the group, or to opt out and take a more individualistic and instrumental path). Social stereotyping of both ingroup and outgroup provides the content of identity and group norms which can guide this collective behaviour: it is not enough to see ourselves as similar to the group, this must be translated into concrete content if it is to be transformed into collective behaviour or otherwise. However, a second important dimension of group perceptions, besides content (usually assessed in terms of judgements of central tendency of a given attribute for the group), is the perceived variability of the group. In terms of social identity theory, more homogeneous group perceptions provide the sense of solidarity that may subsequently encourage collective actions (Simon, 1992b). Put another way, whereas self-stereotyping may provide the key to individual motivation to act in and for the group, perceptions of homogeneity may provide the important social perception that group members are of like minds. Such perception may contribute to perceptions of collective efficacy (see chapter 9), which in turn feed into the coordination of collective behaviour (see chapter 4).

Once again, we expect high and low identifiers to react differently to identity threat. High identifiers should show the more group-oriented response of emphasizing group homogeneity and cohesion, whereas low identifiers are likely to perceive the group as more heterogeneous and fragmented. This may be partly to accommodate their own individuality in distancing themselves from the group ('If I am so different from the rest, there must be much difference within the group'). It could also reflect a more broadly strategic response whereby they try to undermine differences between the groups by emphasizing group heterogeneity, in order to play down unfavourable group differences (see Doosje, Spears & Koomen, 1995; chapter 6, this volume).

We have conducted a series of studies examining the moderating effect of group identification on the effects of identity threat in relation to group variability judgements. In the first study in this series, already outlined briefly above (Doosje, Ellemers & Spears, 1995, Study 1), recall that psychology students were compared favourably or unfavourably to business students with respect to the dimension of intelligence. In this study we also took a measure of intragroup similarity in order to assess group variability. On this measure we found the predicted interaction between identity threat and group identification: the ingroup was perceived as more homogeneous by high identifiers when group status was low (identity threat) and less homogenous by low identifiers under threat. This difference was absent when status was high (no threat). In short, the more group level and individual level responses of high and low identifiers respectively only become apparent when identity is threatened.

In the second study, also briefly describe above, which employed laboratory groups, group identification was manipulated by means of the bogus pipeline procedure (Doosje, Ellemers & Spears, 1995, Study 2). In this experiment we measured ratings of group variability by means of range scores (the difference between the perceived minimum and maximum scores on various status-relevant and also alternative dimensions; see above). The pattern of results was similar for all five dimensions and so a composite measure was formed. Once again the by-now familiar interaction between status/identity threat and group identification was obtained for the variability ratings for both ingroup and outgroup perceptions. Specifically, range estimates were similar for high and low identifiers in the high status (low threat) condition. In the low status (identity threat) condition, however, high identifiers perceived the ingroup range score to be much smaller (around 48 on a 100-point scale) than did the low identifiers (around 73 on the same scale). The patterns for ratings of outgroup variability were identical (we obtained no evidence here for the outgroup homogeneity effect). This study therefore provides further experimental proof that status threat produces divergent perceptions in group homogeneity amongst those weakly and strongly committed to their group. Moreover, by manipulating rather than measuring group identification, and replicating the familiar interaction, we were able to show that identification is a cause and not just a correlate of the dependent measure.

In a further study we also manipulated group identification among low status groups (identity threat). In addition, we manipulated the permeability of group boundaries (Ellemers, Spears & Doosje, 1997, Study 1). In this study we employed a similar procedure to generate laboratory groups as in the previous study (i.e. 'inductive' and 'deductive' thinkers) and used a simple rating of intragroup similarity. Permeability of group boundaries had no effect on the group variability measure and is not relevant to the present theme (see chapter 4). However, group identification did have an effect. In this study we found an asymmetry in the perceived homogeneity of the ingroup compared with the outgroup, with the ingroup being seen as generally more variable than the outgroup: the well-known outgroup homogeneity effect (see e.g., Park & Rothbart, 1982; Park, Judd & Ryan, 1991). However more theoretically interesting from the present perspective, this effect was moderated by group identification such that the asymmetry was displayed exclusively by participants manipulated to be low identifiers with their low status group (see also Castano & Yzerbyt, in press). For high identifiers, ingroup and outgroup were seen as equally similar or homogeneous. In sum, it is the high identifiers under threat who emphasize ingroup homogeneity, and this is sufficient to wipe out the classic outgroup homogeneity effect. This asymmetry was not evidenced at all in the previous study, a fact that may relate to the measures used (see Doosje, Spears, Ellemers & Koomen, 1999).

To summarize, we have now reviewed a series of studies that focus on the combined effects of identity threat and group identification on a range of self- and group-related perceptions. A fairly consistent pattern emerges from these studies. In some cases group identification has an independent effect, although this was most evident in the studies concerned with self-stereotyping. Threat to identity also occasionally had an independent effect, perhaps most clearly on intergroup differentiation measures. However, the more consistent finding was for an interaction between identity threat and group identification on the different perceptions studied. Differences between high and low identifiers became most apparent under conditions of identity threat. Under these conditions, low identifiers tend to self-stereotype themselves less (see themselves as less prototypical group members), to see group-defining characteristics as less important and to see their group as more variable and heterogeneous. There is little or no evidence that threat enhances intergroup differentiation for low identifiers. In contrast, under identity threat high identifiers tend to self-stereotype more, show greater ingroup bias and differentiate their group more from the outgroup on stereotypic dimensions, while they perceive both their own and the outgroup as more homogeneous. These differences between high and low identifiers are much diminished or even disappear when identity threat is absent.

These diverging responses make sense in terms of the different priorities implied by low versus high identification with one's group. Low identifiers have little psychological investment in their group, so they feel at liberty to dissociate themselves from the group or to deny the importance of intergroup distinctions as a way of coping with potential threats to social identity. This is confirmed by the fact that they are also less likely to see their identity as important under these conditions. High identifiers, on the other hand, should be reluctant to leave their group in the lurch, and conditions of threat are precisely those when the group needs its members. This helps to explain the effects of self-stereotyping, intergroup differentiation and homogeneity, respectively. These diverging perceptions are likely to form an important psychological springboard for equally divergent behaviours, from the more individualistic (low identifiers) to the more collectivist (high identifiers).

We now go on to consider other important factors that may bring out the diverging perspectives and psychologies of high and low identifiers. Threats to social identity are not the only conditions under which differences between high and low identifiers surface. In explaining the effects of threat on identity we have made reference to the fact that such threats may enhance group-based perceptions for high identifiers for both cognitive and motivational reasons. In motivational terms they reinforce the need to show solidarity for the group. However, in cognitive terms they may also increase the salience of group and intergroup distinctions. Put another way, they may move perception towards the intergroup pole of the interpersonal–intergroup continuum (Tajfel, 1978a; Tajfel & Turner, 1979). We have refrained from explicitly distinguishing these cognitive and motivational aspects hitherto, in part because they are so closely related (sometimes even confounded). A shift towards the intergroup pole of the continuum is arguably not only a shift in cognition but also a shift to a more socio-motivational level, where group members want and even need to see the context in intergroup terms. This is because social identification refers not simply to the cognitive process of social categorization, but also to the evaluative and emotional significance of this identity for the self (Ellemers, Kortekaas & Ouwerkerk, 1999; Tajfel, 1978a). This notwithstanding, it is theoretically important to see whether contexts which are perhaps less emotionally charged, but which vary the salience of the social categories involved, have similar effects in combination with identification, to those discussed above.

Social Category Salience: The Moderating Role of Group Identification

In this section we consider a smaller number of studies in which we examine the effect of various operationalizations of group salience, in combination with group identification on a range of social perceptions. This line of work is at an earlier stage than that concerned with identity threat and has not been conducted using the same broad range of dependent variables. However, we report three studies that illustrate similarities with the previous principles investigated, as well as highlighting some additional consequences.

In the first study (Ellemers, Spears & Doosje, 1997, Study 2), we carry on where we left off in the previous section and consider how the salience of social categorization on perceptions of group variability is affected by a degree of group identification. We used our familiar social categorization procedure to generate laboratory groups ('inductive' versus 'deductive' thinkers). We also used the same bogus pipeline procedure to manipulate group identification, as described earlier (Doosje, Ellemers & Spears, 1995). Category salience was manipulated by means of a simple procedure suggested by Leyens, Yzerbyt and Schadron (1994) to increase group salience (see also chapter 4). Specifically, in the high salience conditions participants were asked during an early phase of the experiment (i.e., after the social categorization and group identification induction) to complete a number of the Tajfel reward-allocation matrices (i.e. for ingroup versus outgroup recipients). In the low salience condition these matrices were omitted and only presented after all other dependent measures had been completed, and thus could not be influenced by them. The reasoning behind this manipulation is that the matrices force perceivers to think in terms of the ingroup and outgroup categories and to respond in terms of them (which is not to say that all participants necessarily show ingroup bias, of course). In this way the social categorization is rendered more salient.

In this study we employed 'range scores', such as those described earlier as a measure of perceived group homogeneity. As in the first such study reported above (see Doosje, Ellemers & Spears, 1995, study 2), the pattern of estimates was remarkably similar for ingroup and outgroup perceptions (i.e., there was little evidence of an outgroup homogeneity effect). In terms of the independent variables, there was a main effect of group identification such that high identifiers perceived both ingroup and outgroup to be more homogeneous than did low identifiers. However, most theoretically interesting, this effect was qualified by a significant interaction between the salience manipulation and group identification. The difference between high and low identifiers in these variability estimates was only reliable under conditions of high category salience, and not when category salience was low. This interaction is identical to that obtained when identity threat was manipulated by means of lower status in the earlier studies. In short the presence of category salience in itself appears sufficient to elicit the divergent perceptions of high and low identifiers, even when social identity is not directly threatened (although some have argued that social categorization can be perceived as threatening in itself: see Lemyre & Smith, 1985; chapter 2, this volume). At least from this measure it seems that high and low identifiers are differentially tuned in to the category salience, with high identifiers embracing the category when it is situationally relevant, and low identifiers continuing to resist the imposition of this categorization under these conditions.

In subsequent research we turned to a different paradigm and dependent measure and used a variant of the 'category confusion' paradigm (Taylor, Fiske, Etcoff & Ruderman, 1978), in which respondents are presented with statements made by members of two categories, and are required to remember 'who said what' when subsequently confronted with the same statements (i.e., unattributed to the group members). The sort of attribution errors made by perceivers provides an insight into the degree to which they use these categories as organizing principles in perception and recall. A very common finding in this paradigm is that people make more within-category errors than between-category errors, especially where 'chronically accessible' categories such as gender and 'race' are concerned (Hewstone, Hantzi & Johnston, 1991; Spears, Haslam & Jansen, in press; Taylor, Fiske, Etcoff & Ruderman, 1978). A high difference or ratio of within- to between-category errors implies that the category is being used more, providing an unobtrusive measure of the accessibility and importance of the categorization, and the degree to which perceivers see category members as interchangeable with each other (an indicator of 'depersonalization': Turner, 1987; see also Simon, Palanteo & Mummendey, 1995). This paradigm therefore provides a relatively subtle measure of the willingness of people to embrace or resist the imposed social categorization, permitting us to assess whether this varies as a function of group identification, as we predict.

Despite the popularity of this paradigm, it is perhaps surprising that it has rarely been used to examine the effects of the group membership of the perceiver in relation to the target group (i.e. ingroup versus outgroup), still less group identification. Where the relevant category membership of the perceivers has been coded, there has been no clear evidence that more within-category errors are made in the outgroup than the ingroup (e.g., Taylor, Fiske, Etcoff & Ruderman, 1978; Biernat & Vescio, 1993). Although this seems to go against the outgroup homogeneity effect, this is quite consistent with social identity and self-categorization theories (see Doosje, Spears, Ellemers & Koomen, 1999; Haslam & Oakes, 1995; Haslam, Oakes, Turner & McGarty, 1995; Simon, 1992). However, we might expect the degree of salience of the categories to result in different degrees of categorization generally.

A recent set of studies by Brewer, Weber and Carini (1995) has examined the effects of category membership in this paradigm as a function of group salience. For example, in their second study participants were categorized in one of two experimental groups (over-estimators versus under-estimators) and were exposed to a videotape comprising interviews with members from these two groups (group membership was designated by sweatshirts of different colours). The salience of intergroup context prior to viewing this tape was manipulated according to three conditions. In the categorization-only condition, participants were actually only put into groups after they had viewed the videotape (but before the 'who said what' assignments). In the 'salience' condition, group membership feedback was given prior to viewing the tape and the two groups were also given sweatshirts designating group membership and were placed in separate rooms where they worked individually on a problem-solving task. In the 'interdependence' condition groups worked collectively on the problem-solving task and it was emphasized that their performance as a group would be evaluated in comparison with the other group. In other words, there was cooperative interdependence within, and competitive interdependence between groups. Results showed that the degree of categorization as indicated by the within- versus between-category difference in name confusions was highest in the interdependence condition, as expected. More puzzling perhaps was evidence that categorization was lowest in the salience condition, where it was lower than in the categorization-only condition. We will return to this apparent anomaly below.

The study by Brewer, Weber & Carini (1995) is relevant to the present line of argument because it shows that a powerful manipulation of salience can indeed result in increased use of social categorization, although a more moderate manipulation seemed to have the opposite effect. In line with the current theme, however, we move a step further to consider how group identification might moderate such salience effects on categorization. In another study (Spears & Doosje, 1996) psychology students constituted the relevant ingroup, with economics students forming the outgroup. The study was conducted by means of a questionnaire in which statements attributed to members of these two groups were presented. The value connotations of the statements attributed to the ingroup were counterbalanced such that for half the participants the ingroup was represented by predominantly favourable statements and the outgroup by predominantly unfavourable statements, or vice versa. This ensured a degree of 'comparative fit' (Oakes, 1987), which was felt necessary to add some meaning and discriminability between the categories, especially as there were no visual cues to category membership in this study. Surprisingly perhaps there were no consistent effects of the manipulation of value connotations (which is, after all, akin to a manipulation of identity threat discussed earlier – but see the third study, reported below). Further analyses therefore collapsed over this factor.

Group identification with psychology students was measured at the beginning of the questionnaire. The salience of the social categorization was manipulated in a different way from previous research by the same authors and that of Brewer, Weber & Carini (1995). It was done by means of the instructional set introducing the presentation of the statements. In the high salience condition people were asked to try to form impressions of the two groups represented (impression set) thereby attracting attention to the categorization and the basis for group differences. In the low salience condition respondents were asked simply to try to remember as much information as possible, making no reference to the importance of the social categories (recall set) (see Hamilton, Katz & Leirer, 1980; Hirt, MacDonald & Erickson, 1995; McConnell, Sherman & Hamilton, 1994, for research using a similar distinction). After a filler task, respondents were then presented again with the (unattributed) statements and required to couple them with the correct names/affiliations listed on the same page.

As expected, there was strong evidence for the overall use of the categorization, as reflected by the greater proportion of within- to between-category errors. This was perhaps not surprising considering the high degree of comparative fit (see Spears & Haslam, 1997). There was also a significant interaction between salience and error type (within versus between), indicating that the categorization was used more in the high salience (impression set) condition. However, this effect was further qualified by the more theoretically interesting triple interaction between category salience, group identification and type of attribution error. Degree of categorization was highest for the high identifiers in the high salience condition; categorization was lowest for the high identifiers in the low salience (recall set) condition. In terms of the within- versus between-error difference, the salience manipulation made little difference to the low identifiers, who displayed a constant degree of social categorization. In short, it seems that the high identifiers are more prone to use the social categorization when the situation warrants it (i.e., under high salience), as one might expect. However, they also seem less likely than low identifiers to categorize when the context suggests that it is not relevant or appropriate.

Further insight into the processes involved was gained by looking at the breakdown of within-category errors into those that referred to the ingroup (psychology) and those that referred to the outgroup (economics). This resulted in a triple interaction between salience, identification and the source of the within-group errors (ingroup versus outgroup). For high identifiers, there was no difference in the proportion of within-category errors made up of confusions for ingroup or outgroup targets. However, for the low identifiers there was a clear tendency to make more within-category errors for outgroup targets under high category salience compared with low category salience. Low identifiers also correctly identified twice as many ingroup members compared with outgroup members in the high salience condition. These findings suggest that, under high salience, high identifiers tended to see both ingroup and outgroup in categorical terms, a finding consistent with our earlier findings for variability judgements (both for the effects of salience and group threat in combination with high group identification). However, for low identifiers under high salience there was clear evidence from the breakdown of within-category errors into ingroup and outgroup, and also from the correct identifications, that they were trying to individuate members of the ingroup when the social categorization was made salient. Under these conditions they confused ingroup members less, and recognized them more often correctly (correct identification has been used by some researchers as a measure of individuation in this paradigm: see Van Knippenberg, Van Twuyver & Pepels, 1994). Once again, this is similar to results for low identifiers on group variability measures that indicate evidence of an outgroup homogeneity effect (see also Doosje, Spears, Ellemers & Koomen, 1999; Castano & Yzerbyt in press). Low identifiers are keen to individuate their own group, but seem less concerned to do this for the outgroup. This is presumably because the outgroup is less relevant to their own identity and the goal of distinguishing themselves (and others) from the ingroup category.

This evidence of 'resistance' to the imposed categorization for low identifiers might help to explain the paradoxical result found by Brewer, Weber & Carini (1995) in their (moderate) category salience condition. Recall that participants in this condition actually used the categorization less than participants who had merely been categorized after viewing the videotape. Given that these were minimal groups, overall group identification may not have been high in this study. Moreover, working individually within the group, with no outgroup present to make the intergroup context salient, may have further enhanced individual identity and undermined the sense of category-belonging for these participants. If these respondents were similar to our low identifiers, the salience manipulation may have 'rebounded' and elicited resistance to the imposed categorization, evoking more individual than group-based perceptions. Presumably, the interdependence manipulation was strong enough to foster stronger bonds with the ingroup (and competition with the outgroup) and group-based categorization.

In sum, in another paradigm we have further evidence for the diverging responses of high and low identifiers to group salience, which is very reminiscent of the interaction found for identity threat (see also 'Identity Threat', in chapter 2). Indeed, low identifiers may have experienced heightened group salience as a form of identity threat (i.e., being forced to think of themselves and others in terms of a non-preferred social categorization). This would help to explain why, under these conditions, they prefer to see their own group in individual terms, rather than as members of the social category. For high identifiers, however, their social category is by definition a preferred form of self-definition, and thus it is logical for them to see themselves and others in terms of this categorization when the context warrants this (high salience). However, high identifiers are still capable of 'individuating' group members when this is contextually appropriate (low salience), and, indeed, the evidence suggests that they are even more likely to do this than low identifiers. Thus it seems that people for whom the category is important are more able to see people in both categorical and individual terms, depending on the context. Brewer, Weber & Carini (1995) have made a similar argument with respect to minority group members (see also Brewer, in press), and Van Twuyver and Van Knippenberg (in press) also report similar findings (see also Mlicki & Ellemers, 1996; Smith, Spears & Oyen, 1994; chapter 10, this volume). Although this would seem to contradict the principle of 'functional antagonism' between identity levels out-lined in self-categorization theory (Turner, 1987), it is important to note that functional antagonism, like our definition of group identification, is not proposed as a general dispositional tendency. It is therefore possible that evidence of both greater individuation and categorization could reflect rapid switches between lev-els.

In a third study (Spears & Doosje, in prep.) we also employed the category confusion paradigm to examine the effect of identification on different levels of group salience. The group membership (psychology versus economics students), identification measure and statements used in the questionnaire were very similar to those used in the previous study. However, here, group salience was manipu-lated by use of the Tajfel matrices, as described in the first study above; these were completed either before reading the statements or at the end of the questionnaire, where they could not have affected the 'who said what' assignment measure. As in the previous study, the value connotations of the statements were manipulated such that for half the sample the ingroup (psychology students) was represented by predominantly favourable statements and the outgroup (economics students) by unfavourable statements. Again, this manipulation was added to ensure some meaningful 'fit' distinguishing the two categories, but also represented a manipu-lation of identity threat akin to the identity threat manipulation of the studies described earlier.

Unlike the previous salience study, however, the valence manipulation did influ-ence the pattern of results on this occasion. In this case, the degree of categoriza-tion (as indicated by the proportion of within- to between-category errors) varied as a function of salience, identification and the favourability of ingroup versus outgroup. When category salience was low, degree of social categorization was moderate and fairly constant across high and low levels of identification. How-ever, when the social categorization was made more prominent by completing the Tajfel matrices beforehand, the pattern of categorization was different for high and low identifiers. Specifically, under high-category salience the degree of catego-rization was relatively high and constant for high identifiers, irrespective of whether their group was portrayed in favourable or unfavourable terms. However, under conditions of high-category salience, low identifiers were considerably more likely to use this categorization when their group was portrayed favourably, but much less likely to use it when their group was portrayed unfavourably. In short, iden-tity threat does not lead high identifiers to shirk from seeing the context in terms of their group (and the outgroup), and, indeed, category salience heightened this perception. However, low identifiers seem to be much more instrumental, viewing the stimuli in terms of the categorization when it suits them, and de-emphasizing the group when it is disadvantageous, but only when the category is made suffi-ciently salient. Under conditions of salience, they presumably cannot escape the implications of the categorization (see also Ellemers, Wilke & Van Knippenberg, 1993).

This pattern of findings brings together the two lines of research on identity threat and category salience and illustrates once again the contrasting response of high and low identifiers to these two variables. Whereas identity threat and category salience are precisely those conditions which render social categorization meaningful and relevant for the high identifier, the combination of the two is a reason to reject the validity of the social categorization, or escape its consequences for the low identifier. The 'die-hard' group members are prepared to embrace the social categorization even when it is disadvantageous to them, whereas the 'fair-weather' group members try to 'drop' the categorization when it does not suit them.

Cognitive Load: The Moderating Role of Group Identification

We have moved from the consideration of the role of group identification in relation to the (socio-) motivational processes implied by identity threat to consider the (at least potentially) more cognitive concepts of social category salience and social category use (although social categorization may well be threatening to low identifiers). We have shown that group identification affects not only our willingness to see ourselves and others in terms of the group when faced with adversity, but also our willingness to see people in terms of the group when the situation seems to suggest this is relevant. In the last study we move along the cognitive path one step further, and considered how group identification might affect our ability to categorize or stereotype as a function of contextual conditions that either help or hinder information-processing. Once again we propose that group identification is a critical factor in this process.

Perhaps one of the most central variables proposed to determine our tendency to see people in social categorical or stereotypic terms concerns the cognitive resources at our disposal. For example, the influential continuum model of Fiske and Neuberg (1990) proposes that we will tend to categorize and stereotype others if we are not sufficiently motivated to see them as unique individuals, and do not have the cognitive resources to individuate them. Our approach in which group identification plays a central role leads us to a slightly different conclusion. As we have seen in almost all of the research reviewed so far, although low identifiers may often prefer not to see themselves or others in terms of their category memberships, high identifiers seem quite happy to do so. According to this view, categorization is not a default process resulting from the lack of motivation or resources, or at least not for high identifiers. For high identifiers then, there should be little reason to see categorization and stereotyping increase as cognitive load increases. On the contrary, we argue that the availability of cognitive resources should make it easier for people who want to view others in categorical terms to do just that. We therefore predicted that, for high identifiers, low cognitive load experienced during the encoding of information should result in more evidence of category-use and stereotyping than high cognitive load. This is precisely the opposite of the predictions implied by the 'cognitive miser' analysis, which would suggest that cognitive load should increase our reliance on categorization (because it is resource-efficient), and reduce our ability individuate (because this is resource-consuming).

We tested this prediction in a laboratory study employing experimentally created groups (i.e., 'inductive' versus 'deductive' thinkers; Spears, Doosje, Yzerbyt, Rocher, te Brake & Haslam, in prep.). Identification was measured after group membership had been induced and reinforced, and a median split was subsequently performed. In a variant of the category-confusion paradigm participants then viewed statements made by members of the ingroup and the outgroup on the computer screen, coupled with a photo of each person (these were described as deriving from an earlier study using this categorical distinction). Although all the statements reflected favourably on the targets, for half the sample the ingroup made predominantly pro-social statements with the outgroup statements reflecting positively on their group's intelligence, and for half the sample this relation was reversed. In this way we one again introduced a meaningful comparative fit between the categories, in order to reinforce the minimal categorization and provide a basis for stereotypic differentiation, while keeping the favourability of the ingroup and outgroup statements constant. Load was manipulated during the performance of this task by requiring participants to attend to a modulating frequency by means of stereo headphones, and to tick on a sheet provided every time the sound channel switched from one ear to the other. In the high load condition the frequency of switching was five times as high as in the low load condition. The degree of social categorization was later measured by the category confusion index as well as by a clustering measure, and other measures of positive intergroup differentiation were also assessed.

In line with our predictions, evidence of social categorization on the basis of the within- to between-category index was highest in the low cognitive load condition for the high identifiers. In this study, the degree of social categorization did not vary as a function of load for people defined as low identifiers. On a free-recall measure we also examined evidence for the categorical representation of the social information by counting the number of names recalled that were clustered together within the same category. The idea here was that the more the names recalled were grouped together within categories, the more likely it was that perceivers had organized the social information according to category rather than as discrete individuals (see also Young, Van Knippenberg, Ellemers & de Vries, 1997). On this measure we found main effects of both load and identification. The mean number of names per cluster (controlling for the total number of names recalled) was highest in the high identification/low load cell, and lowest in the low identification/high load cell, which is broadly in line with our predictions. Finally, there was also evidence of greater positive differentiation of the ingroup from the outgroup for high identifiers on dimensions stereotypic for the groups (pro-social versus intellectual), although this appeared unrelated to load. Overall, group identification had a stronger effect on the dependent measures than did cognitive load, and it was most influential under low load. This supports the view that high identifiers were actually willing to categorize, rather than doing so because of a lack of resources, as implied by the cognitive miser analysis (see also Spears & Haslam, 1997; Spears, Haslam & Jansen, in press).

In sum, in this study we once again demonstrated the power of group identification to influence social perceptions and showed that for high identifiers this can lead to greater category use and stereotypic differentiation. Moreover, introducing cognitive load does not necessarily undermine this effect, as suggested by the cognitive miser metaphor. If anything, introducing load only served to undermine the ability of perceivers to make these categorical distinctions. Because the high identifiers actually want to categorize people in terms of their group membership, the cognitive resources available under low load were put to this end. In short, the characterization of social categorization as the default option for those who are unwilling or unable to individuate may be overstated. This could be true to some extent for low identifiers (see also the study in which salience was manipulated by means of an instructional set, when low identifiers seemed to individuate the ingroup less under low salience). However, high identifiers may be more likely to categorize and to stereotype, precisely because they are not only motivated but also able to do so (they have the cognitive resources available), and not because they are unable to individuate. This study therefore further emphasizes the importance of categorization and differentiation to high identifiers, not as a cognitive bias, but as a meaningful and relevant way of representing their social world (Spears & Haslam, 1997).

Conclusion

Overall, we have provided diverse evidence to show that various important contextual variables (social identity threat, social category salience, cognitive load) interact with group identification, to affect a range of important social perceptions (self-stereotyping, group stereotyping and intergroup differentiation, perceived group variability, and the degree of social categorization). The overall evidence is that the degree of group identification moderates the effects of these contextual factors on diverse social perceptions relating to group membership. The patterns of results are generally consistent with the view that conditions which impose the intergroup context on us (for either motivational or cognitive reasons) bring out the group in some of us (high identifiers) but not in others (low identifiers).

When the context motivates or enables perception in terms of the group, high identifiers rise to the bait, and begin to see the situation in intergroup terms. These social perceptions also arguably engage them in intergroup behaviour. Self-stereotyping focuses them on their own group membership, its centrality to themselves and on the appropriate content of behaviour for the intergroup context. Social perceptions of group stereotyping and intergroup differentiation, once expressed, become behaviour (discrimination, derogation, but also, in fairness, where normative for the group), providing a context for their perceptions. If self-stereotyping suggests that we are at one with the group, the group homogeneity judgements suggest that so also are our fellow group members. Such perceptions are essential to the perceived collective efficacy necessary to inspire collective action. More fundamentally still, heightened social categorization ensures that high identifiers see the context in intergroup and not in interpersonal terms. In short, all these social perceptions should contribute in different ways to translating social perception into social action.

However, we have also seen that the reactions of low identifiers to these contextual factors are fundamentally different. In many ways, these are the reactions one might expect and even consider rational from an individual point of view, especially where individuals are confronted with the aversive aspects of group identity. Little commitment to the group is reflected in reactions that emphasize the alternative and more individual identities available, especially when the social identity is unfavourable (identity threat) or imposed (e.g., category salience). These social perceptions help to explain behaviour in line with these individualistic priorities, such as social mobility (chapter 4).

In all of these studies the contextual variables were experimentally manipulated. However, in most of the studies, because of its very nature, group identification was measured, especially where it referred to natural groups. It can be argued that this aspect of measurement introduces a correlational element into this research, perhaps even an element of circularity (Wicklund, 1990). However, principal components analysis consistently showed the dependent measures employed to be conceptually distinct from group identification, and the interactive patterns obtained suggest that the relation between independent and dependent variables is far from trivial. Most important, in a number of studies we experimentally manipulated group identification by means of the bogus pipeline procedure. These studies show, generally, very similar effects to those using natural groups in which identification was measured. This procedure is important because it allows us to be more confident in the causal claims we are making for natural groups, as well as about the external validity of the more laboratory-based studies.

One central message of the present findings is that the meaning, content and fact of identity is sometimes more important and dear to us than having a positive (social) identity per se. Sometimes this point is forgotten in mechanical readings of social identity theory, in which having a positive social identity is seen as the primary goal or prize. Social identity is an important motivating principle (something to strive for), as well as an end in itself. If positive self-evaluation was the only goal, there would be little basis for solidarity and identification with low status and disadvantaged groups at all. Perhaps one of the most interesting aspects of our results, then, is that high identifiers, when threatened, can be prepared to see themselves more in terms of a negative group identity than a positive one, and enhance negative properties of their group if these are stereotypic. Such findings make little sense in purely self-serving terms, but suggest that the meaning of social identity is a valued end in itself for these people (Spears & Jetten, 1998a; Tajfel, 1978a). This would help to explain social cohesion and social loyalties: we may not be able to live with ourselves if we desert our group when it needs us – not least if our group is an important part of ourselves. The group is also the audience that matters most to high identifiers: positive evaluation formed outside the group may count for less than the respect of our fellow group members (chapters 2 and 4).

In conclusion, we hope to have made clear the importance of both context and commitment in social perception, and that the combination of the two help, on the one hand, to explain the content of social perception, while, on the other, they are steered by the content of group stereotypes. This content then determines the course of subsequent behaviour based on such perceptions, which need not necessarily be discriminatory in nature (see chapter 5). The interaction pattern found across our studies is a reminder that social identity theory always proposed group perception and behaviour to be the products of an interaction between psychological and socio-structural variables (Turner, 1996b; chapter 1, this volume). In the present chapter we have defined context as social structure (e.g., status relations) but also more generally to include 'micro-' elements of the situation (e.g., simply having the time and ability to process information meaningfully). In our studies we found quite literal evidence for this interaction, while the separate effects of context or group identification were less consistent. A primary focus on the context runs the risk of contextual or sociological determinism, and neglects the psychological make-up and history of the perceiver. Focusing primarily on perceiver characteristics neglects the input of the social contexts to which they react, and their social position in that context. Either exclusive focus is equally determinist and reductionist. In short, the interaction found in our studies provides concrete support for the metatheory of 'interactionism', in which both agent and social reality are integral parts of the dialectic underpinning perception and behaviour (chapter 1). Our research provides a reminder that readings of social identity theory that try to privilege either context or personal variables will be doomed to provide a partial account of the determinants of social perception.

4

Commitment and Intergroup Behaviour

BERTJAN DOOSJE, NAOMI ELLEMERS AND
RUSSELL SPEARS

Although the two teams did not play against each other that day, on Sunday, 23 March 1997, Dutch soccer hooligans of Ajax (Amsterdam) and Feyenoord (Rotterdam) agreed to meet each other. On a small field next to a highway near Beverwijk, the Ajax and Feyenoord supporters fought a battle that lasted about ten minutes. This fight resulted in the death of a 35-year-old Ajax supporter, Carlo Picornie, a husband and a father. This tragic incident elicited a wave of stunned reactions in the Dutch media. The main questions raised were (a) why do hooligans agree to meet each other outside the context of a football match?; and, more generally, (b) how is it possible that people engage in this kind of behaviour, which can even result in death? In answering these questions, we would argue that we need to take into account the role of commitment to one's group.

In this chapter, we focus on the consequences of group commitment for intergroup behaviour. In addition to mapping the cognitive responses and perceptual outcomes as influenced by ingroup identification (see chapter 3), it is important to examine the consequences of identification in terms of intergroup behaviour. In most general terms, we would argue that people for whom a particular group membership is important are more likely to behave in accordance with their group's norms and values than people who are less involved with their group (e.g., chapter 9, this volume; Tajfel & Turner, 1986; Terry & Hogg, 1996). Here, we illustrate this general principle by discussing research in which different kinds of group behaviour were examined. Furthermore, we demonstrate how different kinds of manipulation concerning the socio-structural context of a group in combination with group commitment may influence group-oriented behaviour. Finally, we will also illustrate how group-oriented behaviour depends on the content of the group's identity, again in combination with the degree of commitment.

This research was partially funded by grants from the Dutch Organization for Scientific Research (NWO) to B. Doosje and R. Spears.

Group Commitment

Group commitment (or ingroup identification) plays a crucial role in this chapter. For the present purposes we define it as the extent to which group members feel strong ties with their group. In other words, people may differ in the extent to which a particular group membership is important to them. If we introduce an often-reported distinction between 'die-hard' fans and 'fair-weather' fans (Wann & Branscombe, 1990; chapter 3, this volume) into our argument, we propose that 'die-hard' group members (i.e., those who feel committed to their group) are more predisposed to display group-oriented behaviour, and make sacrifices for it, than are 'fair-weather' members. The latter are more likely to be opportunistic and take an individualistic stance towards group membership (e.g., Doosje & Ellemers, 1997; Doosje, Ellemers & Spears, 1995; chapter 3, this volume). In other words, high identifiers are more likely to think and act in terms of their group membership than low identifiers. In addition, people who feel strong ties with their group are more likely to stick by it when it is facing hard times than people for whom this group membership is less important (e.g., Branscombe & Wann, 1994).

Some observations in natural group settings support this general argument, in the sense that high identifying group members appear more inclined to behave in terms of their group membership than less committed group members. For instance, De Weerd, Ellemers and Klandermans (1996) investigated a sample of Dutch and Spanish farmers in order to assess the factors that determine farmers' willingness to engage in political action on behalf of their professional group. The results showed that in addition to rational considerations, such as the expected chance of success resulting from coordinated action, social identity factors played an important role. Specifically, the more respondents identified with other farmers and the more anger they reported at the plight of their professional group, the greater their reported likelihood to participate in collective protest. Thus, empirical findings relating to real intergroup conflicts support an analysis in social identity terms (e.g., Simon, 1998).

Sometimes identification with one's group can lead to behaviour that is in accordance with the group without introducing an explicit intergroup context or conflict. For example, Ellemers, Spears and Doosje (1998) measured levels of identification with their study major among psychology students on a 6-item scale and divided the group into low and high identifiers. Subsequently, the participants were asked to indicate the time they usually spend on study-oriented activities (e.g., studying from a book and going to classes) and other behaviour (e.g., socializing with friends). It was shown that high identifiers displayed more study-oriented behaviour than low identifiers, who spent more time on other behaviour than high identifiers.

Much as these real-life examples speak to our imagination and attest to the profound implications that group identification may have, methodological weaknesses inherent in such correlational studies render it difficult, if not impossible, to draw conclusions about the causality of the observed patterns. This is all the more important as the theoretical perspective we have adopted explicitly allows for the possibility that shared experiences stemming from coordinated behaviour may further shape and reinforce a sense of common identity. Therefore, experimental research is necessary to exclude the possibility that differences in identification are merely a correlate or by-product of the action tendencies we observed, and to provide more unequivocal support for the notion that the initial level of identification determines whether or not people are inclined to behave in accordance with their group membership (see chapter 10).

Social identity theory (Tajfel, 1978a; Tajfel & Turner, 1986) and self-categorization theory (Turner, Hogg, Oakes, Reicher & Wetherell, 1987) are theoretical frameworks that are relevant in this context. According to social identity theory, individuals are motivated to perceive themselves favourably in relation to other people. In other words, people strive to maintain or enhance a positive self-esteem. In addition, the theory assumes that people partly derive their self-image from group memberships, and that they will therefore try to compare a group to which they belong (an ingroup) favourably with other relevant groups to which they do not belong (outgroups). This comparison will contribute to a positive social identity (that part of a person's self-image that is derived from group membership). Studies have shown that identification with a group can enhance self-esteem (Branscombe & Wann, 1991; Marmarosh & Corazzini, 1997). In addition, membership of self-perceived prestigious and satisfying groups leads to increased levels of self-esteem (Wright & Forsyth, 1997). A study in the domain of psychotherapy shows that people can benefit in terms of self-esteem (and collective self-esteem; Luhtanen & Crocker, 1992) from a treatment in which they are repeatedly reminded that they are members of a group and not just receiving individual treatment (Marmarosh & Corazzini, 1997).

An interesting earlier study also reveals that when a particular group membership is important and when the identity of this group is threatened, people may be willing to make personal sacrifices in order to establish a more positive view of their group. In this study, Lambert, Libman and Poser (1960, Study 1) first assessed the individual level of pain tolerance amongst their Jewish participants. Subsequently, they either told the participants that, typically Protestants have a higher level of pain tolerance (an experimental condition), or they told them nothing (a control condition). People in the experimental condition increased their level of pain tolerance on a second trial, whereas there was no difference in the control condition. These results suggest that group membership can be an important part of someone's self-image; a person may be prepared to maintain or establish a positive distinctiveness between their group and other relevant groups, even at the expense of individual costs such as pain.

Group Commitment and the Content of Group Norms

People are not only prepared to work on behalf of their group in order to change its image; they are also influenced by their group (see e.g., chapter 8, this volume;

Turner, 1991). When a particular group membership is salient, people are inclined to construct norms with respect to attitudes, feelings and behaviours (Terry & Hogg, 1996). These norms can become prescriptive, so that: 'Group membership causes people to think, feel, behave, and define themselves in terms of group norms rather than unique properties of the self' (Terry & Hogg, 1996, p. 780).

In our view, not all members of a group are likely to be equally influenced by the norms that exist in a group in a particular context. We would argue that the extent to which group members tend to act in terms of the group norms may depend on the context (and structural salience of group membership), as well as on differences in importance attached to a group membership. Specifically, people with low group commitment are less likely to act in accordance with the group's norms than do people for whom this particular group membership is more important.

Two studies by Terry and Hogg (1996) support these ideas. In their first study, they focused on the norm of engaging in regular physical exercise (an important general norm in the Australian context, in which this research was done). Terry and Hogg measured the perceived group norm (i.e., the extent to which participants believed that their friends and peers at the university would consider it a good thing to engage in regular exercise), subjective ingroup commitment (i.e., the extent to which participants identified with their friends and peers at the university), behavioural intention to engage in regular exercise during the next three weeks, as well as the actual behaviour after three weeks (i.e., the number of times participants actually engaged in exercise). Analyses showed that perceived group norms in combination with a subjective level of identification predicted behavioural intention. Specifically, for low identifiers perceived group norm did not contribute to a better prediction of behavioural intentions. In contrast, high identifiers intended to behave according to the perceived group norm. In addition, this behavioural intention did predict subsequent actual behaviour. However, there was no direct effect of group identification on actual behaviour. Thus, this research seems to indicate that group norms in combination with group identification have an influence on actual behaviour only via behavioural intentions.

In a second study, Terry and Hogg (1996, Study 2) tested the same ideas in a different behavioural domain: sun-protective behaviour (another relevant behaviour in Australia because it has the highest incidence of skin cancer in the world). Again, it was shown that the combination of perceived group norms and subjective commitment predicted behavioural intention, which itself predicted actual behaviour, and there was no direct effect of the interaction between perceived group norm and identification on actual behaviour. Taken together, these studies attest to the role of group commitment in combination with perceived group norms in predicting behavioural intentions, but not directly the behaviour itself. An obvious weakness in terms of methodology involves the correlational nature of the studies: in these two studies both group norms and level of identification were measured rather then manipulated, making it impossible to infer causal relationships.

Jetten, Spears and Manstead (1997b) tested the same theoretical argument as

Terry and Hogg (1996), but the study they report differed in two important respects: first, they manipulated both group norms and level of identification, and,
second, they focused on actual behaviour as a determinant of group norms and
identification. Like Terry and Hogg, Jetten et al. hypothesized that high identifiers
would be more likely to follow a specific group norm than low identifiers. In order
to test this prediction, they manipulated the group's norms (fairness or discrimination) by informing the participants that psychology students have always either
been fair towards an outgroup or discriminated against an outgroup. Level of
identification was manipulated by requesting participants to tick positive and
negative statements relating to their group membership. However, these statements differed in extremity depending on the experimental condition. In the low
identification condition, participants had the option to tick rather extreme positive statements (i.e., statements they most likely would not endorse) and moderately negative items (i.e., items they would most likely tick). In the high identification
condition, participants had to tick statements that were either extremely negative
or moderately positive, inducing them to agree with the positive rather than the
negative items. The main dependent variable was the allocation of pages of the
university magazine to the ingroup (psychology students) and the two outgroups
(physics and business students). Results show that high identifiers allocated more
pages to their group than low identifiers when the group norm was discrimination. In this condition, high identifiers allocated fewer pages to the business students than low identifiers (there was no difference between low and high identifiers
for the other outgroup). The introduction of a fairness norm did not result in
different allocation patterns for low and high identifiers. This study by Jetten et al.
shows that low and high identifiers are likely to respond differently to a group
norm: high identifiers were more likely to act in accordance with a group norm
than low identifiers, but only when this norm was discrimination. When the norm
was fairness, level of identification did not influence allocation behaviour, possibly because discrimination is a dominant response in intergroup contexts.

Whereas Terry and Hogg (1996) focused on norms that were specific for the
group (engaging in regular exercise and in sun-protective behaviour is relatively
typical for Australians), the study by Jetten, Spears and Manstead (1997b) focused on broader norms of discrimination and fairness that may not be specific for
the group (psychology students). This makes the connection between categorization and group norm arguably weaker, and may have resulted in a non-significant
effect of identification when fairness was the group norm. Ellemers, Spears and
Doosje (1998) further investigated this relation between manipulated group norms
and subjective level of identification, by examining behaviour and norms that are
specific to the group. In this study, Dutch psychology students were first requested
to indicate their level of identification on a 6-item scale, and were divided into low
and high identifiers on the basis of a median split. Subsequently, group norms
were manipulated by informing half of the participants that psychology students
are more work-oriented (during their study) than are business students, and the
other half were told that psychology students are more socially-oriented than

business students. The main dependent variables were self-described behaviour during the previous few weeks in terms of contact with other psychology students. High identifiers indicated having more contacts with fellow students when the norm reflected being socially-oriented rather than being work-oriented. For low identifiers, group norm did not influence self-described social behaviour. Thus, again, people for whom a particular group membership is important are more likely to follow a group-specific norm than people who attach less value to membership of a particular group.

Although the above discussed studies by Terry and Hogg (1996), Jetten, Spears and Manstead (1997b) and Ellemers, Spears and Doosje (1998) all investigated, theoretically, the same argument, the various researchers employed diverse methodologies to test these ideas. Some have focused on norms that are specific for a particular categorization, whereas others used broader norms. Some have used manipulations of group norms and/or level of identification, whereas others relied on measurements of these constructs. In all these cases, however, generally speaking, the hypothesized relation between group norms, group identification and subsequent behaviour received support. Low identifiers were less likely to be influenced by a group norm than were high identifiers. This supports the notion that people who value their group membership, in particular, are influenced by their group in terms of displaying normative behaviour, as suggested by self-categorization theory (Turner, 1991; Turner, Hogg, Oakes, Reicher & Wetherell, 1987; chapter 8, this volume).

Group Commitment and Intergroup Contextual Variables

Social identity theory and self-categorization theory not only posit that group members are likely to follow group-specific norms; they also assume that group members may follow more general norms. One such more general norm is that group members try to distinguish their own group favourably from other relevant outgroups (i.e., a general norm to display ingroup bias). Indeed, a meta-analysis by Mullen, Brown and Smith (1992) confirms the idea that people generally have an inclination to present the ingroup favourably in comparison to relevant outgroups: 'This effect, on average, is of moderate magnitude. In other words, this effect would be discernible to the naked eye' (p. 117).

An interesting situation occurs when people are confronted with a context in which it is difficult to achieve a positive view of their group in comparison to other groups (see chapter 2). Under some circumstances social reality puts constraints on the possibility favourably to distinguish an ingroup from outgroups (see chapter 6). Think of the example of a team that is ranked low in a competition. In this case, the inferred low standing of the group cannot be denied; membership of this group therefore cannot contribute to a positive social identity.

Tajfel and Turner (1986) clearly point to the role of group commitment when the status of a group, which is contextually determined, is relatively low. They state that 'negative social identity promotes subordinate-group competitiveness towards the dominant group *to the degree that . . . subjective identification with the subordinate group is maintained*' (p. 21, our italics). In other words, social identity theory argues that identification plays a crucial role as an input variable determining group members' responses to the status quo. Members of low status groups are considered to display group-oriented behaviour as long as their level of identification is maintained (chapter 9). Group members who do not feel strong ties with their group may express less interest in the improvement of their group's standing.

Ellemers, Spears and Doosje (1997, Study 1) explicitly tested this idea by investigating people's behavioural reactions to membership in a low status group. They examined the effect of level of commitment on willingness to stay in the group or to leave the group in order to become a member of a group with a higher status position (i.e., the desire for individual upward mobility). In addition, they focused on the role of permeability of group boundaries in this context. Previous research (e.g., Ellemers, Van Knippenberg & Wilke, 1990; Ellemers, Van Knippenberg, De Vries & Wilke, 1988; Lalonde & Silverman, 1994; Wright, Taylor & Moghaddam, 1990) has demonstrated that when group boundaries were flexible and open, people showed a low level of identification with their membership in a low status group, compared with a situation in which the group boundaries were fixed and not permeable. For members of high status groups, no such effects of permeability of group boundaries were observed. These results seem to indicate that people are willing to stay loyal to their group as long as it can provide them with a positive social identity. When this is not the case, and people are offered the possibility of changing group membership, they are tempted to do so.

However, subsequent studies have demonstrated that this may not be the complete picture. Specifically, most of the above-mentioned research has been conducted in a laboratory, in which the groups were formed on a random or trivial basis. When we look at the studies that have used a categorization that was somehow more meaningful (e.g., by letting group members believe they have a common trait), group members were less likely to opt for an individual upward mobility choice when this was presented as an option to cope with low status (e.g., Ellemers, Doosje, Van Knippenberg & Wilke, 1992; Ellemers, Wilke & Van Knippenberg, 1993). Thus, it seems that not all group members will choose to opt for membership of a higher status group when they have this possibility, and that the subjective importance of their group membership for their social identity is a crucial factor. Accordingly, Ellemers, Spears and Doosje (1997) argued that level of commitment is likely to influence the inclination to leave a group in order to become a member of another group independent of whether boundaries are permeable or not. They thus hypothesized that low status group members who feel less committed will indicate a greater overall willingness to become a member of a higher status group than members who value their group membership more.

Although, as we have indicated, from the outset social identity theory proposed level of identification as an important input variable, in most research level of identification or group commitment is measured. This variable is then used as a dependent variable in a correlational analysis (e.g., Simon, Kulla & Zobel, 1995), or at most used as a classification variable to split a group into two (e.g., Roccas & Schwartz, 1993). However, Doosje, Ellemers and Spears (1995) devised a method by which it is possible to manipulate level of identification experimentally. This makes it possible to infer causal effects of different levels of identification, while discounting the naturally occurring confounds of level of commitment in real-life groups with other factors such as perceived interdependence, familiarity and interpersonal loyalties. Ellemers, Spears and Doosje (1997) used the same experimental method to test the hypothesis that, in low status groups, high identifiers are less likely to show upward mobility than low identifiers (see also chapter 3).

Ellemers, Spears and Doosje (1997) led participants to believe that they belonged to a group named the inductive thinkers, and told them that there was another group that consisted of the deductive thinkers. Three electrodes were placed on a hand of each participant and they were told that the experimenters could infer their level of ingroup commitment from their bodily arousal, combined with their answers on a number of general questions about relations with other people. Subsequently, people were informed that their group involvement score was either lower (in the low identification condition) or higher (in the high identification condition) than the average score for these kinds of group, which was allegedly obtained from earlier studies. All participants were then informed that their group had performed worse than the other group. Subsequently, permeability of group boundaries were manipulated by informing participants that it was or was not possible to change group membership after the next group task. The main dependent measure assessed participants' pursuit of individual mobility by asking them to indicate the extent to which they preferred to perform another group task with their own group instead of the other group, and the extent to which they would rather collaborate with their own group than with the other group.

Manipulation of ingroup identification had an effect on the subjective degree of group commitment, such that members in the high identification condition showed stronger subjective commitment to the group than those who were told they had low involvement scores. Moreover, members in the high identification condition indicated a lesser preference for individual mobility than members in the low identification condition. Mediational analyses confirmed the notion that the manipulated level of ingroup identification resulted in differences in subjective level of group commitment experienced, and that this subjective level of commitment in turn determined people's inclination to change groups.

It is interesting to note that these effects were not contingent on the permeability of group boundaries. In other words, low and high identifiers differed in their readiness to pursue individual mobility, and this did not depend on the objective possibilities to do so. In fact, even when it was explicitly stated that the categorization would stay the same during the experiment, low identifiers still expressed a stronger preference to leave the group than did high identifiers. Conversely, even when membership in the alternative (higher status) group could be attained, high identifiers still preferred to stick to their low status group.

One reason this difference between low and high identifiers may have occurred is the fact that in their first study Ellemers et al. only investigated low status groups. Previous research has shown that it is typically under circumstances of threat to the image of the group that identification is most important (e.g., chapters 2 and 3, this volume; Branscombe & Wann, 1994; Doosje, Ellemers & Spears, 1995; Spears, Doosje & Ellemers, 1997). In order to rule out the possibility that the effect of group identification occurs only under conditions of group threat, Ellemers et al., in their second study, also examined groups where status was unknown. In addition, in this study category salience was manipulated by requiring half of the participants to perform an intergroup reward allocation task and the other half not (i.e., the 'Tajfel-matrices'; see Tajfel, Flament, Billig & Bundy, 1971). The idea here is that the intergroup allocation task serves to heighten the salience of the categorization (Leyens, Yzerbyt & Schadron, 1994; see also chapter 3, this volume). It was predicted that high identifiers would be less inclined to pursue individual mobility, especially when the categories were made salient. Results showed that, as predicted, low and high identifiers did not differ from each other in terms of inclination to leave the group when the category salience was low. However, when the category salience was high, low identifiers showed a stronger desire for mobility than did high identifiers. Subsequent mediational analysis again showed that it was the manipulated level of identification that led to subjective feelings of commitment, which in turn were predictive of the individual mobility scores.

This second study by Ellemers, Spears and Doosje (1997) demonstrates that, even in the absence of a threat to the identity of the group, low and high identifiers show different patterns of behavioural preference in terms of individual mobility, but only when the categories were made sufficiently salient. In line with the predictions, high identifiers are more likely to stick to their group than low identifiers when the categorization was made salient.

Taken together, these two studies by Ellemers et al. show that structural context variables such as group status and permeability of group boundaries may sometimes be less important than the subjective level of commitment to a group. When this commitment is sufficiently high, members do not seem to care whether it is possible to change group membership or not; they will still 'stand by their group'. At the same time, it seems that in their behavioural preferences low identifiers are also not much influenced by the objective possibility of leaving their group, and indicate their desire for individual upward mobility irrespective of the permeability of the group boundaries.

Group Commitment and Stability of Intergroup Status Hierarchy

In the previous section, we have shown how people's behavioural preference in terms of individual mobility is, to a large extent, dependent upon the subjective level of group commitment. In this section, we focus again on the nature of group identification, and, specifically, argue its importance both as determinant and a result of contextual changes. Tajfel (1978a; 1982c) stressed the importance of perceiving groups not as static entities, but in more dynamic terms. For example, he argues that 'Social groups are not "things"; they are processes' (1982c, p. 485). Tajfel also emphasized the context-dependency of the importance of group membership by stating that 'the psychological existence of a group for its members is a complex sequence of appearances and disappearances, of looming large and vanishing into thin air' (1982c, p. 485). In this section, we focus on the consequences of group commitment and another structural context variable that is highly dependent upon time (see Condor, 1996), namely stability of the intergroup status hierarchy. According to social identity theory (Tajfel, 1978a), social identity should be particularly salient when the status relations between groups are or become unstable. When these relations are unstable, the alternative status position (as a group) becomes a realistic possibility for members of both low and high status groups. The salience of this possibility is likely to elicit group action designed either to accomplish a change in the status structure or to defend the status quo (Turner & Brown, 1978). In line with social identity theory, we predict that group commitment underlies this coordinated group behaviour (see chapter 3). Group identification is arguably conceived of as an indicator of the behavioural intention to act collectively and may also be conceptualized as communicative behaviour (see chapter 6).

Earlier research has looked at the effect of stability of group status on group commitment primarily as a dependent variable. For instance, in a laboratory study by Ellemers, Van Knippenberg, and Wilke (1990), participants were assigned to either a low or a high status group, and were told that it was either possible or impossible that the status hierarchy would change during the experiment. For members of the low status group, an unstable status hierarchy resulted in higher group commitment than a stable status structure. This result was explained as an indication that members of low status groups try to achieve a better position for their group when the situation suggests that it is possible. In a further study by Ellemers, Wilke and Van Knippenberg (1993), it was shown that members of a group with illegitimately low status were more likely to display competitive behaviour towards the outgroup when the status structure was unstable than when it was stable. In addition, group members were less competitive towards their fellow ingroup members in an unstable status structure than in a stable one. Both studies lend support to the notion that, for members of low status groups, unstable status relations result more easily in group-level responses (such as higher identification and more intergroup competition) than a stable structure.

However, as we have indicated, in these studies discussed above identification with one's group is viewed as a dependent variable rather than an independent variable that can potentially moderate responses of members of low status groups, as originally suggested by Tajfel and Turner (1986). In Tajfel and Turner's view, members of low status groups will try to find a solution to the uncomfortable situation at the group level as long as there is a minimal level of identification with their group. In an attempt to test this notion, Doosje, Spears and Ellemers (1998) examined the temporal changes in levels of ingroup identification (i.e., both as an independent and a dependent variable) in response to both an anticipated change in the status structure (Phase 1) and an actual change in the status hierarchy (Phase 2). Furthermore, they extended the analysis of status stability by Ellemers, Wilke and Van Knippenberg (1993) by explicitly introducing the notion of necessity of an individual contribution to collective action. Doosje, Spears and Ellemers (1998) hypothesized that in low status groups low identifiers would only express a higher level of identification (as a behavioural intention for collective action) when a change in the status structure was likely and status improvement was expected to occur irrespective of the contribution of an individual group member. High identifiers were expected to be less instrumental and assert their level of identification especially when collective action seemed necessary to bring about a change in the intergroup status hierarchy.

In Doosje et al.'s experiment all participants received performance feedback which indicated that their group had a lower status than another relevant outgroup. Their initial level of identification was then assessed. Subsequently, they received information about the possibilities that the status structure would change during the experiment. In the no-change condition, it was explained that this structure would probably remain the same. In the potential change condition, it was stated that it was very difficult to predict the outcome of the groups' performances on subsequent tasks. In a likely change condition, participants were led to believe that their group was clearly expected to outperform the outgroup on the next task and that, thus, the status structure could be expected to change. Dependent variables, such as the subsequent level of commitment and perceptions of intragroup homogeneity, were related to group members' intention to engage in collective action.

Results showed that low identifiers were less likely to create a basis for collective action either when it was unlikely that the group's status would change or when change was contingent on a concerted group effort. This was evident from their relative low group commitment and perceptions of group heterogeneity in these circumstances. High identifiers, in contrast, were prepared to create a basis for social action when the status of the ingroup could potentially change, and were even willing to do this when it was unlikely that the group's status would change. Low and high identifiers did not differ in their responses when it was likely that the status structure would change in favour of their group.

The results of this part of the Doosje, Spears and Ellemers (1998) study indicate that low identifiers, especially, are attuned to the chances of gaining a more positive social identity. This instrumental depiction is supported by the fact that low identifiers are particularly likely to let their level of group commitment depend more on the present and future status of their group in the status hierarchy. High identifiers, on the other hand, are prepared to stick to their group, through 'thick and thin', and independent of the future of their group in the intergroup status hierarchy.

The second part of the Doosje, Spears and Ellemers (1998) experiment assessed group members' responses to actual changes in the status hierarchy. It was predicted that low identifiers would respond more strongly to actual status changes than high identifiers, because they were more likely to let their level of commitment depend on the status of a group than high identifiers. After another intergroup task, participants in the unlikely change condition received feedback that, as expected, their group was still inferior to the outgroup. In the likely change condition, participants were told that, as expected, their group was now superior to the other group. In the potential change condition, half the participants received the feedback that their group had performed better on the task, and the other half were told that their group had performed worse than the other group. Results showed that low identifiers in the potential change condition showed an increase in commitment when their group's status had changed from low to high. In all other conditions, the level of group commitment did not differ from the previous state of affairs.

These findings seem to indicate that low identifiers are particularly strategic in their behaviour towards their group. In the previous section, we have shown that low identifiers are more willing to leave their low status group in order to become a member of a high status group. In this section, we have tried to demonstrate that low identifiers are only prepared to increase their group identification when either a change in group status is likely, or an actual change in group status has been achieved. In contrast, high identifiers are more willing to stick to their group even when they have the possibility for individual mobility to a higher status group, as discussed in the previous section. Here, we have illustrated that high identifiers are also more likely to support their group irrespective of both its anticipated and actual status changes.

Given the fact that level of identification changes under different conditions, it is clear that group identification cannot simply be viewed as an individual difference variable (see Introduction and chapter 3). This is supported by the fact that people respond differently to various social structural configurations. For example, people are more likely to identify with a group that has a good chance of improving its status in the near future. However, in our view, identification is not just a dependent variable that will be influenced by structural relations, it is also an important input variable in intergroup situations (Reicher, 1996b; Tajfel & Turner, 1986). As Tajfel and Turner point out, for members of low status groups, a minimal level of identification is necessary in order to elicit responses to change the current status differences. Doosje, Spears and Ellemers (1998) point out that it is necessary to conceive of identification as both a dependent and an independent variable in order to capture the dynamic role of this variable in group life, and to reflect the fact that identification changes over time as a group develops in relation to its environment (Condor, 1996; Worchel, Coutant-Sassic & Grossman, 1992).

Intragroup Contextual Variables and Intergroup Behaviour

According to social identity theory (Tajfel & Turner, 1986) people try to derive to some extent a sense of esteem by attempting to compare their group favourably with relevant other groups. In other words, people try to establish a positive distinction between the in- and the outgroup. This search for positive distinctiveness is an intergroup phenomenon. However, it is also clear that intragroup variables play an important part in group life as well, especially in groups of relatively small size (e.g., Hogg, 1996).

One important intragroup variable discussed in the literature is the relative centrality of the various members in a group. Some have a central position and perhaps serve as the leader of the group, whereas others may fill a more peripheral or marginal role (e.g., Noel, Wann & Branscombe, 1995). Moreland and Levine (1982) also distinguish a number of different 'roles' people can play in a group (i.e., a new member, full member or marginal member). They argue that these roles are not fixed, but will change over time. The consequences of the centrality of the position within a group are not limited to intragroup processes, but can also have important effects for intergroup behaviour.

For example, Noel, Wann and Branscombe (1995) investigated the notion that group members who differ in the centrality of their position within the ingroup (peripheral of core group members) may express different levels of outgroup derogation. Specifically, it was argued that peripheral group members were more likely than core group members to display outgroup derogation as a means of showing their alliance to their fellow ingroup members. Noel et al. tested these ideas by investigating the expressed ratings of ingroup and outgroup products in two different situations: a private and a public condition. The idea was that peripheral group members only derogate an outgroup under public conditions, as a means of showing to their fellow ingroup members that they are worthy group members (see also chapter 2).

On the basis of answers on a mass-testing questionnaire, participants were categorized as Type P persons and were led to believe there were Type O persons as well. In the peripheral condition, participants were informed that they were just inside the Type P category, whereas core members were told that they were a very prototypical member of the Type P category. In the public condition, participants were informed that their responses to the main dependent variable (i.e., the endorsement of coercive strategy to persuade the outgroup) would be made public and that they had to explain their choice of strategy in front of other ingroup members. In the private condition, the confidentiality of the responses was emphasized.

Results showed, as predicted, that peripheral group members were more likely to derogate the outgroup (in terms of endorsing a coercive strategy to influence members of the outgroup) than central members were, but only in the public condition. In the private condition, there was no difference between core and peripheral group members in the extent to which they derogated the outgroup. Thus, it seems that for peripheral group members publicly derogating an outgroup can be instrumental in making a positive impression on their fellow ingroup members. By publicly demonstrating their association, peripheral group members possibly try to enhance their acceptance by core ingroup members.

In a second study, Noel, Wann and Branscombe (1995, Study 2) tested the same hypothesis in existing and socially meaningful groups: fraternities and sororities. Participants were active (core) members, or pledge (peripheral) members, and the presentation condition (private versus public) was manipulated, as in the previous study. Results were similar to the first study: again, peripheral members showed most outgroup derogation in public conditions, presumably because they wanted to demonstrate their group-oriented behaviour to the core members and gain acceptance.

Taken together, these studies by Noel et al. suggest that group members are attuned to what other ingroup members think about them. These concerns lead them to present themselves as trustworthy ingroup members. By doing so, they hope to gain respect from their fellow ingroup members. Indeed, receiving respect from fellow ingroup members is an important concept in both traditional and more recent theoretical notions, as well as empirical research (e.g., Jackson & Saltzstein 1958; Smith & Tyler, 1997). As Smith and Tyler argue, respect may be an important instigator of group-oriented behaviour.

In a study designed to examine the role of respect, Branscombe, Spears, Ellemers and Doosje (1998) not only make a distinction between members who do and do not receive respect from fellow ingroup members, they also investigate the effects of prestige or status of the ingroup as accorded by an outgroup. This factor is similar to the status of the group and can potentially pose a threat to the ingroup's value when the prestige of the group is low. Previous research has shown that collective responses such as group solidarity, group cohesion and outgroup derogation are most evident when the value of the group is threatened by low status (chapter 2, this volume; Branscombe & Wann, 1994; Doosje, Ellemers & Spears, 1995; Turner, Hogg, Oakes & Smith, 1984) or low group distinctiveness (Jetten, Spears & Manstead, 1996; Spears et al., 1997; chapter 5, this volume).

In addition, Long and Spears (1997; Long, Spears & Manstead, 1994; see also Platow, Harley, Hunter, Hanning, Shave & O'Connell, 1997) have suggested that, in low status groups, stronger ingroup bias can be expected from members with high personal self-esteem than from members with low personal self-esteem. In their study, Long, Spears and Manstead (1994) measured personal self-esteem (see Rosenberg, 1965) as well as collective self-esteem (see Luhtanen & Crocker, 1992) of Dutch psychology students. The main dependent variables were the judgements of products of both the ingroup and a relevant outgroup (Swiss psychology students). They observed most intergroup discrimination when collective self-esteem was low, but personal self-esteem was high.

Translating these personal self-esteem differences to differences in respect from fellow ingroup members, Branscombe, Spears, Ellemers and Doosje (1998) predicted that, especially when the image of the group is threatened by low prestige, highly respected group members will be more likely to display group-level behaviour than will less respected group members. People who are not respected by their group have no particular loyalty to it either (Tyler & Lind, 1992). As a consequence, they should not feel the need to contribute collectively unless group prestige is high (Jackson & Saltzstein, 1958).

In their study, Branscombe, Spears, Ellemers and Doosje (1998) categorized participants as 'inductive thinkers', who were led to believe that other people belonged to the outgroup, the 'deductive thinkers'. Participants had to report one positive and one negative social behaviour that they had displayed recently. These statements were ostensibly evaluated by all group members, and thus a rank order was established. Half of the participants received the feedback that they were liked by other group members, and the other half were told that they were not popular in their group. In addition, participants received feedback at the group level, stating that on the basis of the self-provided information, their group as a whole was either positively or negatively evaluated by the other group. Behavioural responses were assessed by a point-allocation task and measures to tap the willingness to spend more time on a task with fellow ingroup members. Two of these items focused on willingness to improve one's own position within the ingroup (on a scale and in number of minutes), and two other questions concentrated on their willingness to improve the position of the ingroup in comparison to the outgroup (on a scale and in number of minutes).

Results showed that for the point-allocation measure, those who feel well respected gave more points to the ingroup than those who received less respect. On the outgroup allocation measure, it was shown that, as predicted, only when the group's prestige was low did highly respected group members give fewer points to the outgroup than those who had received little respect from their fellow ingroup members.

Analysis of the willingness to spend time on an extra task to improve either the personal standing within the ingroup or the standing of the ingroup showed that people with low respect were more willing to improve their personal standing than those who had received high respect. Highly respected group members, however, were more willing to spend time on a group task to increase the status of the ingroup than were group members who were less well respected. Inspecting the willingness in terms of the number of minutes participants were willing to work on a group task, a slightly more complicated pattern occurs: highly respected group members wanted to contribute to the improvement of their group's status more than less-respected group members, but only when the prestige of the ingroup was low (this pattern was in line with the outgroup allocation measure). On the other hand, less-respected group members wanted to contribute to the task in order to improve their personal standing, but only when the prestige of their group was high.

Thus, it seems that different group members may want to contribute to the same group task, but may have different (hidden) agenda's for doing so. Highly respected members of a group with low prestige want to work on the task to improve their group's status, as this is the group that consists of members that respect them. Low respected members of a high prestigious group want to work on the task to increase their personal standing, probably as a way to demonstrate to other members their willingness to work for this highly prestigious group.

The research of Branscombe, Spears, Ellemers and Doosje (1998) again demonstrates that group-oriented behaviour is more likely to occur when the identity of the group is threatened. Previous research has focused on the effects of low group status and low group distinctiveness on group-level measures such as ingroup bias, perceived group variability and self-stereotyping (e.g., Branscombe & Wann, 1994; Doosje, Ellemers & Spears, 1995; Jetten, Spears & Manstead, 1996; Spears, Doosje & Ellemers, 1997; chapter 3, this volume; Turner, Hogg, Oakes & Smith, 1984). At the same time, the results by Branscombe et al. also go one step further in that they point to the importance of intragroup variables such as ingroup respect in this context. The conclusion by Branscombe et al. is in line with work by Long and Spears (1997; Long, Spears & Manstead, 1994; see also Platow, Harley, Hunter, Hanning, Shave & O'Connell, 1997). Recall that Long et al. showed that people with high personal self-esteem (comparable with highly respected group members) exhibited the strongest ingroup bias when their group's prestige was low. Branscombe et al. point out that respect may be similar to personal self-esteem, and demonstrated that group-oriented behaviour when the group's image was threatened, depended on the level of respect from fellow ingroup members. When the group's image was threatened, high-respected group members (a) gave fewer points to an outgroup than less-respected members, and (b) were also more willing to work for the group in order to improve its image than were less respected members.

Thus, it can be seen that intragroup variables such as ingroup respect and personal self-esteem also serve as important predictors of intergroup behaviour (chapter 2). Especially when the image of the ingroup is threatened, these intragroup variables seem to play an important role. Future research might fruitfully examine the various forms of these intragroup variables as well as functions they may serve for the individual or the group.

Commitment and More Content: The Moral Status of One's Group

Social identity theory (Tajfel & Turner, 1986) argues that people are motivated to belong to groups that are superior to other groups in terms of status. However, being a member of a group that has been superior at the expense of another group may give rise to unpleasant feelings about the group (see chapter 2). At this point, we would like to make clear that the content of a group's identity plays a crucial role here. Having a history of morally objectionable behaviour to the benefit of the ingroup and at the expense of an outgroup may lead to feelings of guilt towards the mistreated outgroup. These feelings of guilt may in turn lead to reparative behaviour in an attempt to make up for the harm inflicted upon the outgroup.

For example, groups that could be described as having a history of economic success built on the exploitation of other groups include former colonizing powers such as Belgium, Britain, France, the Netherlands, Portugal and Spain. Other cases of exploitation are the treatment of the native populations in Canada, the USA and Australia by European immigrants, and the enslavement of Africans in the USA and Europe. In this section, we will review studies that examine emotional and behavioural reactions to exploitative behaviour of one's own group towards another group. More specifically, we will focus on feelings of guilt and reparation of the disadvantaged group when a history of exploitation has been made salient. A central argument is that the historical content of the group's identity may include a morally objectionable treatment of another group by one's own group, resulting in feelings of guilt, accompanied by inclinations to repair the harm inflicted upon the other group.

Guilt at the individual level can be experienced when there is a discrepancy between one's own rules or standards and one's behaviour (see e.g., Lewis, 1993; Tangney & Fischer, 1995). In other words, guilt may arise when there is a difference between how one thinks one should have behaved and how one actually behaved. These feelings of guilt are mostly accompanied by a tendency to act in ways that are aimed at undoing the harmed individual (Barrett, 1995; Roseman, Wiest & Swartz, 1994; Tangney, 1995). In this conception, guilt is an intrapsychic phenomenon, resulting from cognitive processes occurring within individuals. However, in the examples mentioned above, although it was not possible for some people (e.g., young British people today) to have been personally responsible for the colonization of another country (e.g., India), still, they may feel guilty when they are reminded about their nation's past. We would argue that this is because people are not only individual entities, they are also members of groups, and this group membership (and the behaviour of other members of one's group) may give rise to feelings and emotions as well.

A number of authors have discussed the possibility of feelings of guilt as a consequence of the behaviour of one's group. For example, in an essay entitled 'White guilt', S. Steele (1990, p. 8) states that: 'White guilt, in its broad sense, springs from the knowledge of ill-gotten advantage.' In this case, Steele argues that White Americans may experience feelings of guilt towards African Americans because the former realize they have exploited the latter in the past. Doosje, Branscombe, Spears and Manstead (1998) integrated these notions into existing theories of intergroup behaviour and set out to test experimentally some of the assumptions underlying the experience of collective or group-based guilt.

Based on social identity theory, Doosje et al. argue that people may experience specific emotions as a result of actions of their group, even if they personally have not behaved in an objectionable way. They hypothesize that, whereas people may experience personal guilt when there is a discrepancy between humanitarian values and personal behaviour, they may also experience group-based guilt when there is a discrepancy between humanitarian values and the behaviour of other members of one's group (Branscombe, 1998; Branscombe, Schiffhauer & Valencia, 1998).

Doosje, Branscombe, Spears and Manstead (1998, Study 1) tested these ideas in a laboratory study in order to try to separate the guilt that resulted from personal behaviour from that which resulted from the group's behaviour. Participants were categorized as a member of a minimal group ('inductive thinkers') and were told that there was another group ('deductive thinkers'). After an intergroup judgement task, they received bogus feedback concerning their fellow ingroup members' past and present behaviour towards the outgroup, which stated either that their group had systematically undervalued outgroup products, or that their group had always been fair in terms of judgements of outgroup and ingroup products. Subsequently, they also received feedback about their own judgemental behaviour (biased or fair).

Results showed that, when people have not personally displayed a bias against the outgroup, they felt more collective guilt when their group had undervalued the other group than when their group had been fair. When they personally showed a bias against the outgroup, the behaviour of their own group did not influence feelings of collective guilt. In an analysis of covariance, it was demonstrated that these effects of personal and group discrimination were independent of the level of vulnerability to experience personal guilt. Further analysis also showed that the feelings of collective guilt gave rise to compensatory behaviour. Specifically, even group members who had not personally displayed a bias were more willing to compensate the outgroup when their group had supposedly undervalued it than when they thought it had not systematically displayed a bias in favour of the ingroup. Analysis of covariance confirmed the idea that feelings of collective guilt were directly linked with inclinations to compensate the outgroup.

In a second study (Doosje, Branscombe, Spears & Manstead, 1998, Study 2), a more natural setting was chosen to explore further the same processes. In particular, Dutch reactions to different aspects of their forebears' behaviour during the colonization of Indonesia were examined. Indonesia was colonized by the Dutch for a very long period (about 350 years) and became officially independent in 1948. Moreover, in this real-life context, identification was introduced as a theoretically important variable. Branscombe, Schiffhauer and Valencia (1998) show that only low identified White Americans suffer a loss in self-esteem when they have to think about the advantages they have as White Americans compared with African Americans. They argue that high identifiers may not experience a loss in self-esteem, as they are less likely to accept the idea that White Americans do have advantages over African Americans. Translating these notions to our study, it was predicted that high identifiers may be less willing to acknowledge the negative aspects of their group's history. As a result, high identifiers may experience less guilt when the presented information includes both positive and negative aspects (i.e., mixed information). In addition, it was predicted that people are attuned to the social reality and do not want to make unrealistic claims when the information provided is unequivocally negative (e.g., Doosje, Spears & Koomen, 1995; Ellemers, Van Rijswijk, Roefs & Simons, 1997; Kunda, 1990; Spears & Manstead, 1989;

Stangor & Ford, 1992). It was therefore argued that when only the negative aspects of their group's history were made salient, people would experience more guilt than when only positive aspects about the history of colonization were made salient. It was argued that both these unequivocal messages would leave no options for different interpretations by low and high identifiers. As a result, the effect of the evaluative nature of the message on feelings of guilt was expected to occur irrespective of level of identification.

Dutch participants first had to indicate their level of identification with their nation, and then received one of three versions of a summary of the history of the Indonesian colonization by the Dutch: a clearly negative one (e.g., the Dutch had killed many Indonesians), a clearly positive one (e.g., the Dutch had introduced a solid legal system), or a mixed message including both negative and positive aspects. Results showed that in the negative history condition both low and high identifiers felt more guilty than in the positive condition, and in these conditions there were no differences between low and high identifiers. When the information was mixed, however, low identifiers experienced more collective guilt than did high identifiers. These results indicate that, when presented with unequivocal information about their group, low and high identifiers respond in the same manner. Even high identifiers are forced to accept the negative implications of the unfavourable information. However, when presented with mixed information, high identifiers are more likely to focus on the positive aspects of their group than low identifiers, and this results in different patterns of guilt.

Interestingly, political orientation was also measured, and there was a low, but significant correlation between political orientation and level of identification, such that people with a right-wing orientation were more likely to identify more strongly with being Dutch (see also Hilton, Erb, McDermott & Molian, 1996). This suggests that there is overlap between identification and political orientation which might potentially be a threat to the internal validity of this study. However, an analysis of covariance demonstrated that the crucial interaction between presented history and level of identification remained significant when political orientation was entered as a covariate. This makes it difficult to attribute the effects of commitment (in interaction with group history) to differences in political orientation.

The effects and pattern of the reparation measures generally matched the collective guilt findings. Again, when participants had received mixed information, low identifiers were more willing than high identifiers to compensate the outgroup (in terms of both global intentions and specific measures such as a donation of money). Mediational analyses also confirmed that collective guilt was responsible for the patterns of reparation, as the interaction between presented history and identification was no longer significant when collective guilt was introduced as a covariate.

Taken together, these studies of Doosje et al. empirically demonstrate that people may feel guilty because of what their fellow ingroup members have done, and not because of personal behaviour. Interestingly, it was not the high identifiers whose experience of this guilt was the most extreme. Indeed, when the history was portrayed as having both positive and negative aspects, low identifiers experienced more collective guilt than high identifiers, possibly because high identifiers were less willing to acknowledge the negative aspects of their history. However, high identifiers also want to be perceived as realistic and do not want to make claims that are not warranted by the presented information (e.g., Doosje, Spears & Koomen, 1995; Stangor & Ford, 1992). This was reflected in the responses when the information was unequivocally either negative or positive. In these conditions, low and high identifiers responded in the same way and felt more group-based guilt when the information was negative.

It is also clear that these feelings of collective guilt led to compensatory behaviour, as is the case with feelings of individual guilt (e.g., Barrett, 1995; Roseman, Wiest & Swartz, 1994; Tangney, 1995). When people feel guilty for their group's actions, they want to make up for this. Tangney (1995) discusses three possible means of doing so: confessing, apologizing or repairing the bad behaviour. For example, according to S. Steele (1990) 'White guilt' was at least partly responsible for the implementation of programmes of affirmative action in order to improve the position of African Americans in the 1960s in the USA. Our findings that the experience of collective guilt was driving the desire for reparation converge with this notion.

An interesting theoretical and practical implication of the Doosje et al. study is concerned with the relation between group identification and group behaviour. Often, at least implicitly, people who are committed to their group are viewed as moral because they value the collective good above self-interest, whereas people who feel less involvement are depicted as egoistic and bad. The work on collective guilt demonstrates that this may be an over-simplification. This work shows that it is the low identifiers who feel guilty because of their group's past actions, and are also willing to compensate the other group. This then leads to an image of low committed members as people who are able to have social feelings towards other people and are willing to act on it.

Although not directly investigated by us, we believe that these acts of confession, apology or reparation can sometimes be of great symbolic importance to the harmed group. For example, it was met with great enthusiasm when the US President Bill Clinton apologized for his country's history of enslavement when he was in South Africa. An official apology from such an important person can be of great symbolic value to the harmed group, and is often a first step towards improving relations between nations that may have a history of illegitimate unequal status positions or exploitation. Therefore, guilt can be classified as a productive emotion, as it motivates people to undo the harm being inflicted upon a target (e.g., Barrett, 1995), be it an individual or a group.

Conclusions

The present chapter focuses on the effects of level of commitment, structural context variables, and factors that influence the content of identity on group-oriented behaviour by group members. Generally, group-oriented behaviour is stronger among members who feel highly committed to their group than among those who feel less committed. Highly committed group members are more likely to stick to their group and show little inclination to become a member of another group. It is even more surprising that such group members are still not willing to become a member of another group when (a) this other group has a higher status position, and (b) the option for individual mobility is clearly presented as realistic (Ellemers, Spears & Doosje, 1997). This seems to undermine a strict individual or egoistic approach to group membership and group behaviour. Specifically, whereas some members of a group may only show their loyalty as long as their group provides them with a positive social identity, other group members are more willing to stick to their group through thick and thin, even when this implies that they have to make individual sacrifices.

However, it would not be fair to depict less committed group members purely as egoistic and antisocial, as we have also presented evidence of contexts in which low identifiers were likely to experience emotions on behalf the group (i.e., collective guilt), and behave in a pro-social manner as a response to that emotion (i.e., intention to make amends for the harm inflicted upon a group). High identifiers in this case were less likely to accept the negative implications for their group and were subsequently less inclined to act pro-socially (i.e., undo the harm done to another group).

Structural context variables also play a important role in group life. Specifically, in this chapter we have focused on the intergroup status hierarchy and observed that this is likely to interact with level of commitment. When the status of a group is high, level of commitment does not affect group-oriented behaviour. Both low and high committed members tend to perceive others and themselves in terms of their group membership (albeit for possibly different reasons). However, when the status of a group is low, level of commitment is an important moderator of group members' behaviour. Whereas low identifiers are dissatisfied with their group membership and want to change it, high identifiers are more willing to stand by their group during difficult times (Ellemers, Spears & Doosje, 1997).

Another important structural context variable discussed in this chapter is the stability of the status structure, in terms of both anticipated and actual changes in the status hierarchy. Again, the effect of anticipated status changes is moderated by group commitment, such that, for highly committed members, their group-oriented cognitions and behaviour are less likely to depend on the future prospects of their group. Even when their group is facing a definitely gloomy future in terms of group status hierarchy, they still show their loyalty to it. Low identifiers, on the other hand, are more instrumental, in the sense that they are only willing to express their affiliation to their group when its status is likely to change for the better (Doosje, Spears & Ellemers, 1998; Ellemers, 1993b). If we take a close look at the reactions to actual changes in the intergroup status structure, we find, again, that low and high identifiers differ in their responses when the status of their group has remained low (i.e., the low status position is not changed). In that case, low identifiers disassociate themselves from their group. In contrast, even in this unfortunate context, high identifiers are likely to support their group and stay loyal (Doosje, Spears & Ellemers, 1998).

Moving from the intergroup to the intragroup level, the degree of respect that people receive from fellow ingroup members is an important moderator of their responses to favourable and unfavourable group conditions (Branscombe, Spears, Ellemers & Doosje, 1998). Specifically, under unfavourable group conditions, highly respected group members are relatively likely to withhold rewards from an outgroup. They are also relatively willing to contribute to a group task, and the motivation to display such a willingness is to improve the position of their group. In a favourable group condition, a group member who receives little respect is more likely to contribute to a group task. The underlying motive in this case is not to improve the status of the overall group, but to improve his or her individual standing in the group. In other words, the aim is to gain more respect from fellow ingroup members by demonstrating a willingness to contribute to a group task. The fact that group members display group-oriented behaviour that looks similar from the outside (i.e., contribution to a group task), but represents different underlying motives (for well-respected members to improve the group's position, but for low-respected members to improve their personal intragroup position) is under-investigated and in our view deserves more attention in the intergroup literature (see chapter 2).

Finally, in terms of content of identity, in this chapter we have stressed the importance of existing group norms. We have shown that people are likely to act in line with these group norms (Turner, 1991), especially when they feel highly committed to their group (see also chapter 8). In addition, we focused on the role of content in terms of members of groups that have a history of exploiting another group. It is theoretically interesting to investigate the conditions under which people feel guilty about the past behaviour of their fellow ingroup members, and how they react to these feelings in the present in terms of trying to compensate the harmed group (e.g., S. Steele, 1990). We have argued that as long as people are implicated as group members, they may feel guilty about the behaviour of their fellow group members when they are reminded about the history of exploitation. Importantly, this collective guilt does not depend on personal contribution in the exploitative history of the group. In this chapter, we argued that people who feel committed to their group are relatively inclined to perceive both positive and negative aspects of their group's past when presented with mixed information about this. Subsequently, they experience less collective guilt and are also less willing to compensate the harmed outgroup than low identifiers, who are more willing to acknowledge the negative aspects of their group.

Taken together, it seems that high identifiers are not only more likely to display behaviour favouring the ingroup; sometimes they may also refrain from behaving in a compensatory fashion towards the outgroup. Low identifiers, on the other hand, may not always be loyal to their group when it takes a low status position, while they appear to be more willing to behave in a compensatory fashion towards a harmed outgroup. Although in this chapter we have reviewed the relevant empirical work in this area, we think there is a lot more to be done. Future research could be aimed at examining the influence of level of commitment on behavioural reactions to socio-structural context variables and content of group identity.

To turn back to our example mentioned at the beginning of our chapter (the death of the Ajax supporter Carlo Picornie after a fight with Feyenoord supporters), as it turns out, partly on the basis of evidence from a video of the incident, a number of Feyenoord supporters were sentenced because of their violent behaviour. What, then, can we say about the processes that resulted in the death of Carlo Picornie on the basis of the research described in this chapter? We can only speculate about the motives of the actors involved, and it is impossible to oversee all the aspects of this incident. If we were to speculate, however, it may be possible to conceive of this battle as a pure intergroup competition (which group is the toughest?). In addition, we may surmise that these Feyenoord supporters were trying to receive more respect from their fellow ingroup members by fighting members of the outgroup and thus demonstrating their ingroup loyalty at great individual risks. Finally, it is also possible that many Feyenoord fans who did not participate in the fight (and perhaps not the die-hard fans) experienced collective guilt when they heard about the behaviour of their fellow fans, which led to the death of the Ajax supporter. At any rate, we think that notions outlined in this chapter (such as group commitment, respect from fellow ingroup members and ingroup prestige) may have played a central role in the behaviour of the soccer hooligans during that unfortunate day, and that the notion of collective guilt may be relevant for the fair-weather fans of Feyenoord.

5

Group Distinctiveness and Intergroup Discrimination

JOLANDA JETTEN, RUSSELL SPEARS
AND ANTONY S. R. MANSTEAD

The phenomenon that people tend to favour their own group over relevant comparison groups (ingroup bias or positive differentiation) is perhaps one of the most researched topics in social psychology, and for obvious theoretical and applied reasons this interest shows little sign of waning. However, although ingroup bias has been found to be very robust (Mullen, Brown & Smith, 1992), it would be a mistake to conclude that ingroup bias is an inevitable response to being categorized in a group, or that intergroup hostility is the default in an intergroup context (Tajfel, 1982b; see chapters 4 and 6, this volume). Both the preceding and the following chapters confirm that the path from social categorization to discrimination, is far from direct. In this chapter we consider an important factor that could help to explain when discrimination and differentiation between groups is more (and less) likely. Specifically, we are concerned with the moderating role of perceived group distinctiveness on positive differentiation (see also chapter 2, 'Distinctiveness Threat'). We argue that the degree to which groups are perceived to differ from each other has important implications for attempts to differentiate between them.

The effect of perceived group distinctiveness on positive differentiation is far from straightforward. On the one hand, it can be predicted that groups may appreciate having something in common with each other. There is, after all, much evidence that similarity fosters attraction and liking in interpersonal relations (e.g., Byrne, 1971), although some theorists have warned of the dangers of generalizing from the interpersonal to the intergroup domain (e.g., Roccas & Schwartz, 1993). If a relation between similarity and attraction at the intergroup level is disputable, the notion that difference can elicit disliking between groups would seem to be on firmer ground. Freud (1922) argued, for instance, that differences of considerable magnitude between groups can lead to increased intergroup hostility: 'We are no longer astonished that greater differences should lead to an almost insuperable repugnance. Such as the Gallic people feel for the German, the Aryan for the Semite, and the white races for the colored'. As we shall see, self-categorization theory has also focused on the importance of intergroup difference as a basis of differentiation.

While intergroup discrimination is readily understood where groups differ a great deal or where fundamental values diverge (Rokeach, 1960), it is perhaps more surprising to find evidence of discrimination when the differences between groups are few or slight. It seems that groups can often feel threatened by the similarity or psychological proximity of the outgroup. As noted by the sociologist Williams (1956), groups can come 'too close for comfort': ' "Family quarrels" among religious groups are often intense – the just noticeable differences seem under some conditions to evoke especially strong reactions' (p. 15). Similarly, Staub (1989) notes that: 'The communist hatred of "revisionist" social democrats was often greater than their hatred for capitalist enemies. Small differences in dogma often result in the prosecution of religious heretics. The intense anti-Semitism of the early church fathers probably served their need to create an independent identity for Christianity' (p. 60). In these instances, groups display increased intergroup hostility in an attempt to restore group distinctiveness and to protect the unique identity of the group. Freud (1922) introduces the concept of 'narcissism of small differences' to refer to this perceived threat to the separate group distinctiveness when groups become too similar. This is in line with the classical predictions derived from social identity theory (e.g. Tajfel, 1982b). In sum, these anecdotes and examples suggest that intergroup similarity can be both attractive and threatening to the ingroup identity (Brown & Abrams, 1986).

The present chapter is concerned with the question of what conditions lead to an increase or decrease in positive differentiation as a function of perceived group distinctiveness. A range of empirical studies will be presented to demonstrate the importance of different forms of group distinctiveness in producing discriminatory intergroup behaviour. In a first series of studies the importance of group norms (content) in prescribing ingroup behaviour, and in defining group distinctiveness, is elaborated. It will be shown that, depending on the nature of the group, distinctive norms can result in enhanced intergroup discrimination, but also that threats to group distinctiveness produced by similar norms can produce discrimination. In the second section it is shown how intergroup distance and intragroup variability (context) can combine to create low, intermediate and high levels of group distinctiveness, producing variations in positive differentiation. The role of group identification (commitment) in moderating the relation between group distinctiveness and positive differentiation will be demonstrated, both in relation to the first series of studies, and in relation to the contextual manipulation of distinctiveness. In addition to reviewing other moderating variables, research will be reported to show that group identification moderates the distinctiveness–differentiation relation by specifying when group distinctiveness leads to more positive differentiation. The two main theories addressed in this chapter will be social identity theory (Tajfel & Turner, 1986) and self-categorization theory (Turner, Hogg, Oakes, Reicher

& Wetherell, 1987).[1] We start with an outline of predictions derived from these theories concerning the effect of group distinctiveness on intergroup discrimination.

Distinctiveness from the Perspective of Social Identity and Self-Categorization Theories

Although social identity theory and self-categorization theory are generally comparable in their predictions, it is possible to say that they differ in their emphases (more motivational versus more cognitive and perceptual in focus, respectively). More specifically, different aspects and processes concerning the relation between group distinctiveness and positive differentiation are stressed by these two theories and this can lead to opposing predictions.

Central to social identity theory is the principle that group members will generally try to seek group distinctiveness by viewing the ingroup as different from and better than other groups (Tajfel & Turner, 1986). Such a proposition leads to the prediction that ingroup–outgroup similarity is perceived as threatening and will stimulate the ingroup to create distinctiveness by differentiating itself from these outgroups (Tajfel, 1978a, 1982b). The underlying process proposed to maintain group distinctiveness is (socio)motivational in character: positive differentiation of the ingroup from relevant outgroups can benefit group evaluation and self-esteem (Tajfel & Turner, 1986). From this, it follows that the more that group distinctiveness is undermined by intergroup similarity, the greater should be the positive differentiation displayed in order to protect or restore group distinctiveness (Brown, 1984a, 1984b; Brown & Abrams, 1986; Dovidio, Gaertner & Validzic, 1998; Henderson-King, Henderson-King, Zhermer, Posokhova & Chiker, 1997; Mlicki & Ellemers, 1996; Moghaddam & Stringer, 1988; Mummendey & Schreiber, 1984a; Tajfel, 1982b; Turner, 1978b; Van Knippenberg & Ellemers, 1990).

Self-categorization theory builds in important ways on social identity theory, but tends to stress more perceptual or cognitive principles such as meta-contrast and comparative fit (Turner, Oakes, Reicher & Wetherell, 1987). Based on the meta-contrast principle, it can be predicted that it is more likely that social

[1] Belief congruence theory (Rokeach, 1960) is also concerned with the relation between perceived similarity and differentiation. From belief congruence theory it is predicted that individuals are attracted to those who have similar attitudes or opinions (see also Byrne, 1971; Festinger, 1954; Insko, Nacoste & Moe, 1983; Struch & Schwartz, 1989). Although these predictions are mainly concerned with interpersonal relations, it is often assumed that this theory can be extended to the intergroup domain. However, several researchers have pointed out that this generalization of predictions from the interpersonal to the intergroup domain is problematic (Brown, 1984b; Brown & Turner, 1981; Tajfel, 1978a), and studies have demonstrated that the implication of similarity on differentiation is quite different in interpersonal compared to intergroup settings (see Diehl, 1988). Since the focus of this chapter is on intergroup similarity, belief congruence theory is less applicable.

categories will be perceived as separate entities and distinguished from other categories to the extent that the differences between groups exceed the differences within them (Turner, 1987). From this reasoning, it follows that a priori intergroup distinctiveness increases intergroup salience because it enables maximal differentiation between ingroup and outgroup. Previous research has associated intergroup salience with increased levels of positive differentiation (Oakes, 1987). Following from the emphasis on intergroup differences, it can be predicted that the similarity of the ingroup to the outgroup can undermine the intergroup distinction, making it is less likely that groups will be perceived as separate or as meaningfully different. It has been demonstrated that groups will be categorized at a higher level of inclusiveness (if a superordinate category is available), when the ingroup cannot be sufficiently distinguished from the outgroup (see Gaertner, Mann, Murrell & Dovidio, 1989; Vanbeselaere, 1996; Wilder & Thompson, 1988).

Predictions from the category differentiation model (Doise, 1978; Doise, Deschamps & Meyers, 1978) and accentuation principles (Tajfel & Wilkes, 1963) are quite similar to self-categorization predictions. It is argued that by accentuating the similarities within and the differences between categories, these categories become differentiated from each other. From these principles, one would also predict that differentiation increases with intergroup difference and decreases with intergroup similarity.

To summarize, although self-categorization theory and social identity theory are theoretically closely related and have similar points of departure, it seems at first glance that opposing and diverging predictions can be made with respect to the effect of group distinctiveness on positive differentiation. From social identity theory it can be inferred that too much similarity between ingroup and outgroup constitutes a threat to the distinctive identity of the ingroup, leading to an attempt to reassert positive differentiation by increased levels of positive differentiation. In contrast, self-categorization theory stresses that group members will act more in terms of their group membership (e.g., by displaying increased levels of ingroup bias), as the ingroup becomes more clearly distinctive from the outgroup.

A major aim of this chapter is to address and resolve the (apparent) contradictions between social identity and self-categorization predictions in this domain. We start by examining fairly simple intergroup contexts that vary in degree of similarity or distinctiveness at two basic levels (content-based distinctiveness) and consider the factors that might determine when principles from social identity theory and self-categorization theory are most applicable in this context (e.g., depending on type of group, level of identification). We move on to consider a more complex case where similarity or distinctiveness varies at more than two levels as a function of group distance and group variability (context-based distinctiveness). We then try to integrate these two strands within a common framework by considering the critical moderating variables, such as group identification, that help to explain when high levels of intergroup similarity will produce more differentiation rather than undermining group distinctiveness. The three guiding themes of this volume – content, context and commitment – will be recurring themes throughout the chapter.

Content as a Basis for Group Distinctiveness and Differentiation

Similarity or distinctiveness can take a number of forms, and groups can be similar or different on a range of different dimensions. Previous research has focused on similarity of attitudes (Brown, 1984b; Diehl, 1988; Henderson-King, Zhermer, Posokhova & Chiker, 1997; Jetten, Spears & Manstead, 1997a; Moghaddam & Stringer, 1988; Roccas & Schwartz, 1993), status (Brown, 1984b; Brown & Abrams, 1986; Dovidio, Gaertner & Validzic, 1998), group roles (Brown & Wade, 1987; Deschamps & Brown, 1983; Marcus-Newhall, Miller, Holtz & Brewer, 1993), and language (Giles, 1977). Whereas much previous research has defined distinctiveness simply in terms of the stated similarity between groups, or the distance between ingroup and outgroup (see the following section), in this section we consider the effect of group distinctiveness derived from the content of group norms. Specifically, we conducted a series of studies to investigate the effect of distinctiveness in the content of group norms on positive differentiation. A unique aspect of group norms, compared, for instance, with group attitudes, is that norms also prescribe suitable behaviour to group members more explicitly. Group members should be sensitive to the content of the group norm because acting in accordance with salient group norms expresses the salient identity (see Jetten, Spears & Manstead, 1997b). Manipulation of similarity of group norms should therefore also instigate group conformity processes (see also Terry & Hogg, 1996; see chapters 4 and 8, this volume).

Ingroup and outgroup norms were manipulated orthogonally in a minimal group (Study 1) and in a more natural group where the identification with the group was higher (Study 2) (Jetten, Spears & Manstead, 1996). The two norms manipulated were fairness and discrimination. In line with previous reasoning, manipulating ingroup and outgroup norms should vary not only the sort of behaviour they sanction or prescribe for the respective groups, but also the extent to which groups would seem similar or dissimilar according to these norms. From social identity theory it was predicted that the similarity of group norms with respect to discriminatory behaviour or fairness would lead to increased positive differentiation. However, a further consideration here was that where the ingroup and outgroup norms reflect fairness, discrimination against the outgroup would work against the content of the ingroup norm in prescribing behaviour. It was predicted that this would create a tension between conformity processes and processes directed at enhancing group distinctiveness by displaying positive differentiation. As a result, differentiation based on discrimination measures (e.g., the Tajfel matrices) was predicted to be strongest when the similarity of the ingroup and outgroup norms reflected discrimination rather than fairness.

On the basis of self-categorization theory principles of comparative fit and the meta-contrast principle (Turner, Hogg, Oakes, Reicher & Wetherell, 1987), one can predict that the 'fit' between the categorization and group norms will be higher when these norms are different for ingroup and outgroup. Different group norms for ingroup and outgroup should help to define and differentiate the group identity more clearly. This leads to the prediction that groups that are predefined as being distinctive in this way may display greater positive differentiation. However, positive differentiation may once again be reduced if the ingroup norm implies fairness. In sum, our analysis of the group distinctiveness–positive differentiation relation based on the content of group norms led to opposing predictions from the perspectives of social identity theory and self-categorization theory.

These opposing predictions were first tested in a modified minimal group setting (Study 1: Jetten, Spears & Manstead, 1996, Exp. 1). Participants were categorized on the basis of a task as detailed perceivers (versus global perceivers). The second phase of the study took the form of a distribution task. The purpose of this task was supposedly to investigate whether detailed and global perceivers used different strategies in dividing resources between two people (a detailed and a global perceiver). Participants were presented with an example of an allocation matrix and were instructed to use the matrices to allocate money between an anonymous detailed and a global perceiver. We informed participants that they could use four allocation strategies to distribute the money: (a) maximizing the joint profit of the detailed and global perceiver; (b) allocating the same amount of money to the detailed and global perceiver (i.e., fairness); (c) maximizing the profit for the detailed perceiver; and (d) maximizing the profit for the global perceiver. Hereafter, participants were provided with false feedback of information about the strategies used by fifteen detailed and fifteen global perceivers who had already participated in the experiment. Participants in the fairness condition (ingroup or outgroup) were told that ten out of fifteen detailed or global perceivers had allocated the money equally. In the discrimination condition (ingroup or outgroup), participants received feedback indicating that ten out of fifteen detailed or global perceivers had generally favoured their own group members. Ingroup bias and positive differentiation as measured by the Tajfel reward matrices (Tajfel, Flament, Billig & Bundy, 1971) were the primary dependent measure in this study.

The results revealed that the allocation behaviour was determined by conformity to the ingroup norm. That is, an ingroup norm of fairness led to more fairness and an ingroup norm of discrimination led to more discrimination towards the outgroup. Nevertheless, ingroup bias was significant in all conditions. The outgroup norm was less influential in determining the allocation behaviour. This is interesting because it suggests that processes relating to expressing one's social identity by conformity to ingroup norms were more influential than equity principles relating to outgroup norms. Another important finding was that the combination of ingroup and outgroup norms proved to be a key determinant of the level of positive differ-entiation. Dissimilarity of group norms (an ingroup norm of fairness and an outgroup norm of discrimination, or vice versa) led to more positive differentia-tion, as compared with similarity of intergroup norms (both group norms fairness or discrimination). This result was in accordance with the prediction derived from self-categorization theory that high comparative fit (reflected by dissimilar group norms) would produce a sense of group distinctiveness resulting in positive differ-entiation. No support was found for the social identity prediction that similarity of group norms would lead to more positive differentiation.

We reasoned that one explanation for the finding that groups differentiate the ingroup more strongly from the outgroup when norms are dissimilar may be related to the nature of the groups. The identity as a group member in a minimal group is not well developed, and so the lack of any basis for a group difference reinforced by intergroup similarity may undermine the very validity of the group distinction that is already quite ephemeral for the participants in any case (cf. Spears & Jetten, 1998b; chapter 2, this volume). It is possible that the positive differentiation pattern is quite different when groups are more well established and when the identification with the group is higher (see, e.g., Roccas & Schwartz, 1993). To test social identity predictions that similarity of group norms would lead to more differentiation, the first study was replicated using a natural group categorization where the identity was better established (Study 2: Jetten, Spears & Manstead, 1996, Exp. 2).

The only difference from the first study concerned the nature of the groups. In this study identity as a student of the University of Amsterdam was made salient (outgroup members were students of the rival Free University of Amsterdam). Ingroup and outgroup norms were manipulated in the same way as before, and Tajfel matrices were used to assess ingroup bias. Results of this study in a more natural group setting, where group members identified more strongly with the group, also showed that the ingroup norm was more influential than the outgroup norm in determining allocation behaviour. Moreover, in contrast to the previous study, here, the similarity of intergroup norms did lead to more ingroup bias and ingroup favouritism, in line with the social identity prediction. Ingroup bias and ingroup favouritism was reduced when ingroup and outgroup norms differed.

To summarize, different principles derived from social identity theory (Tajfel & Turner, 1986) and self-categorization theory (Turner, Hogg, Oakes, Reicher & Wetherell, 1987) seem to apply in different types of group when content distinc-tiveness was manipulated. In line with the self-categorization principle of com-parative fit, dissimilarity of the content of intergroup norms resulted in positive differentiation for the relatively unestablished minimal group. In contrast, the social identity prediction that similarity of the content of intergroup norms should lead to more positive differentiation did receive support when the group (and thus comparative fit) and group identification were already well established (Tajfel, 1982b; Turner, 1978b).

These opposite effects of similarity of ingroup and outgroup norms on ingroup

bias in minimal and natural groups were supported by group identification measures. Overall, degree of group identification was higher in the natural group study
than in the minimal group study. Furthermore, in the minimal group setting, perceived prototypicality as a group member was higher when the intergroup norms
were dissimilar than to when they were similar. In the more natural group study,
differences were found in the extent to which group members identified with the
outgroup. Outgroup identification, which can be seen as (negatively) complementary to the ingroup identification measure, was lower when both group norms
implied fairness or discrimination than when the group norms were different. In
sum, levels of group identification varied with expressed intergroup discrimination and, more importantly, opposite patterns of results were found between minimal and more natural groups, thereby suggesting the moderating power of this
variable.

A weakness of explaining the differences in the group distinctiveness–positive
differentiation relation between the minimal group study (Study 1) and natural
group study (Study 2) in terms of group identification is that this factor was
measured rather than manipulated. Moreover, minimal groups and natural groups
are likely to differ on a number of other dimensions. Further research was therefore conducted to examine the basis of such differences by experimentally manipulating the proposed moderating variable: level of identification (Jetten, Spears
& Manstead, 1998a).

In a minimal group setting (Study 3: Jetten, Spears & Manstead, 1998a, Exp.
2), identification was manipulated by means of a 'bogus pipeline' procedure (Doosje,
Ellemers & Spears, 1995; Ellemers, Spears & Doosje, 1997; see chapters 4 and 6,
this volume), leading participants to believe that they were strongly or weakly
involved with their group. Intergroup norms were manipulated as in Study 1 and
Study 2. However, the design of those studies was only partly replicated: the
ingroup norm was kept constant (i.e., discrimination) and the outgroup norm
differed across the two conditions (i.e., discrimination or fairness).

We predicted that dissimilarity of ingroup and outgroup norms would lead to
more positive differentiation for low identifiers, whereas similarity of group norms
would lead to more positive differentiation for high identifiers. The argument
underlying the prediction for high identifiers follows the classic social identity
prediction: an identity threat in terms of similar intergroup norms should motivate high identifiers, in particular, to differentiate their group positively by displaying increased intergroup discrimination (see also chapter 2, 'Distinctiveness
Threat'). It was predicted that low identifiers should be more concerned with clear
ingroup–outgroup distinctiveness, and that dissimilarity should therefore result in
most positive differentiation for low identifiers, in line with self-categorization
theory principles. Ingroup bias once again formed the primary dependent measure
of this study. We also measured evaluations of the ingroup and outgroup, ingroup
and outgroup identification, prototypicality and group cohesion. It was assumed
that these additional measures would reflect the degree of ingroup bias, and would
be similarly affected by possible effects of group norms and group distinctiveness.

Results showed that for high identifiers similarity of intergroup norms led to greater use of ingroup favouritism strategies, whereas for low identifiers dissimilarity of group norms led to more ingroup favouritism. This interpretation was reinforced by the fact that a similar pattern of results was found on a number of other dependent measures. When norms were similar, high identifiers evaluated the ingroup more positively, identified more with the ingroup (i.e., as a dependent measure) and saw their group as more cohesive. For low identifiers, any tendencies were in the reverse direction: the ingroup was evaluated relatively more positively when group norms were dissimilar. This study provides further insight into the underlying processes involved in determining when similarity or dissimilarity in the content of intergroup norms will lead to different effects on positive differentiation in minimal and more natural groups. Compared to the earlier studies, an additional strength of this study was that identification was manipulated rather than measured, providing a stronger test of the moderating power of group identification.

We shall return to the central moderating role of identification later in this chapter. First, we present another perhaps more parsimonious attempt to integrate the contrasting predictions of social identity and self-categorization principles, by considering their application to different levels of a similarity/distinctiveness continuum.

Context as a Basis for Group Distinctiveness and Group Differentiation

It can be argued that the contradiction between social identity theory and self-categorization theory with respect to the distinctiveness–positive differentiation relation is more apparent than real, and that it merely represents a difference in emphasis between the two theories. Whereas social identity theory focuses on the effects of perceived intergroup similarity leading to increased differentiation designed to restore threatened group distinctiveness, self-categorization theory concentrates on effects of intergroup difference as a basis for intergroup differentiation. Given these different foci, it is possible that a theoretical integration may be possible. One way to integrate the two theories is by specifying the level at which social identity and self-categorization predictions are more applicable. That is, it is possible that each theory can account for the group distinctiveness–positive differentiation relation in different domains.

Self-categorization theory proposes that a certain degree of distinctiveness may be necessary for groups to qualify as independent (Turner, 1987). Social identity theory stresses that groups have to be sufficiently similar on certain dimensions for them to be relevant or comparable, thereby evoking social comparison and potentially posing a threat to group distinctiveness (Tajfel & Turner, 1986). Although not encoded within the meta-contrast principle, self-categorization theory has also adopted the criterion of comparability from social identity theory. Combining these elements, it seems possible that an intermediate level of group distinctiveness will be associated with the highest levels of positive differentiation because this integrates both the difference and similarity specified by these two theories. That is, we propose that the relation between group distinctiveness and positive differentiation may well be curvilinear (inverted U-shaped). Low levels of positive differentiation are predicted when group distinctiveness is low and groups cannot be sufficiently distinguished (in line with the self-categorization principle), and when group distinctiveness is so high that groups are no longer comparatively relevant to each other. In short, the intermediate level of intergroup distinctiveness (and similarity) may combine the 'critical' level of intergroup difference (the self-categorization principle) and similarity (the social identity principle). Self-categorization and social identity theories differ from cognitive accentuation models (Doise, 1978; Doise, Deschamps & Meyers, 1978) with respect to the prediction for high intergroup distinctiveness. Accentuation models have not explicitly incorporated the comparability criterion and would predict that positive differentiation should increase as a function of group distinctiveness (a linear effect opposite to the one predicted by social identity theory).

The hypothesis that most positive differentiation would be displayed at intermediate levels of group distinctiveness was tested in two studies in which the group setting was varied from minimal groups (Study 4) to more natural settings (Study 5; Jetten, Spears & Manstead, 1998b). Intergroup similarity has usually been manipulated by varying the distance between the average ingroup and the average outgroup member on some attitude or status dimension (e.g., Diehl, 1988, Exp. 2). However, in recent research it has been emphasized that similarity between ingroup and outgroup entails not only information about central tendencies of ingroup and outgroup but also information about the variability or distribution of ingroup and outgroup scores (Jetten, Spears & Manstead, 1997a; Lambert, 1995; Park, Judd & Ryan, 1991). That is, even though the central tendencies of ingroup and outgroup may be quite different, if the distribution of ingroup and outgroup scores is heterogeneous, groups can still be perceived as being similar or 'overlapping' (see also Doosje, Spears & Koomen, 1995; Ford & Stangor, 1992; Oakes, Haslam & Turner, 1994). Although previous research on intergroup relations has been concerned with intergroup similarity and group variability (as an independent or dependent measure), little effort has been made to study their possible combined and interactive effects. This is particularly important because group distinctiveness may be impossible to assess where feedback about central tendency alone is provided (and where group variability information is unspecified), making it difficult to assess the effect of absolute level of distinctiveness on differentiation.

Group variability and intergroup distance (central tendency) were combined in our design to produce groups that are either clearly distinct, distinct but close, or overlapping and thus 'indistinct'. It was predicted that perceived intergroup distinctiveness would be greatest when groups are homogeneous and the intergroup distance between ingroup and outgroup is high. Distinctiveness should be moderate when groups are heterogeneous and the intergroup distance high, or when groups are homogeneous and the intergroup distance low. The perception of intergroup distinctiveness should be lowest when the intergroup distance between groups is low and groups are heterogeneous. In our studies the combination of high intergroup similarity and high group variability meant that groups overlapped on the underlying dimension, producing low intergroup distinctiveness.

In the first experiment (Study 4: Jetten, Spears & Manstead, 1998b, Exp. 1) participants were categorized in minimal groups (detailed versus global perceivers). They then received feedback about the distribution of scores of detailed and global perceivers. On a continuum ranging from detailed (0) to global perceiving (100), they saw a graphical presentation (i.e., a histogram) of the frequency distribution of their own group and the other group's scores. Distance to the outgroup was manipulated by varying the means of the ingroup and outgroup frequency distribution. Variability was manipulated by varying the range of scores of the two groups. As a consequence of the variability and distance to the outgroup manipulation, the heterogeneous/low intergroup distance condition resulted in an 'overlap' area between the two groups. Ingroup bias (evaluation of ingroup and outgroup products) and intergroup evaluations formed the primary dependent measures in these studies.

In line with our hypothesis concerning the integration of social identity and self-categorization principles, the results of the first study demonstrated that levels of positive differentiation (ingroup bias and intergroup evaluations) were highest at an intermediate level of group distinctiveness (heterogeneous/high intergroup distance and homogeneous/low intergroup distance). Only in these conditions were the ingroup evaluations significantly more positive than outgroup evaluations (significant ingroup bias). When relative distinctiveness was highest (homogeneous groups/high intergroup distance), thus making the intergroup comparison less relevant, positive differentiation reduced and was non-significant. When relative distinctiveness was undermined by an overlap between the two groups (heterogeneous/low intergroup distance), the basis for social categorization was undermined, and positive differentiation was also reduced and non-significant.

A second study was conducted to examine whether the predicted curvilinear relation between group distinctiveness and positive differentiation also holds for natural groups (Study 5: Jetten, Spears & Manstead, 1998b, Exp. 2). As we have seen in the previous section, group identification is generally stronger in natural groups and this can affect differentiation. Participants were all students at the University of Amsterdam and this identity was made salient. The outgroup consisted of students at the Free University of Amsterdam. The dimension of comparison was 'belief in supernatural phenomena'. The ingroup was situated near the 'no belief in supernatural phenomena' and the outgroup near the 'strong belief in supernatural phenomena' extreme of the continuum in all conditions. The manipulation of intergroup distance and group variability was similar to that used in the first study. The combined effect of group variability and intergroup distance did not lead to a substantially different pattern of results in natural groups (Study 5) from in minimal groups (Study 4). Similar to Study 4, positive differentiation was highest and significant at an intermediate level of group distinctiveness, when groups were clearly distinct but close enough to allow for a relevant intergroup comparison (homogeneous/low intergroup distance and heterogeneous/high intergroup distance). In this natural group setting, high group distinctiveness (homogeneous/high intergroup distance) and low group distinctiveness (heterogeneous/low intergroup distance) led to low and non-significant levels of positive differentiation.

In sum, these two studies support the theoretical integration of processes specified by self-categorization theory and social identity theory to explain the relationship between group distinctiveness and positive differentiation. Self-categorization theory is more cognitively and perceptually based (and more applicable to intergroup difference), whereas social identity theory is more motivationally based (and more applicable to intergroup similarity). These elements can be viewed as two interconnected steps or processes: a perceptual process ('social categorization') providing the conditions for a more motivational process ('social identification'). With these two components in mind, we propose that an intermediate level of intergroup distinctiveness combines the 'critical' levels of intergroup similarity and difference for promoting differentiation. This reasoning results in the prediction of a curvilinear relation between group distinctiveness and positive differentiation, which is what we observed in both minimal and natural groups. This finding is in line with some early research by Rokeach (1960), in which it was demonstrated that greater similarity between religious groups was associated with greater acceptance. However, there was a tendency for this linear effect to be reversed for groups that were perceived as being very similar (e.g., Catholics and Episcopalians). The two present studies also demonstrate the importance of taking into account group variability in addition to intergroup distance in order to define intergroup distinctiveness and understand its effects.

Moderating Variables: Commitment and Related Contenders

So far, we have proposed two somewhat contrasting solutions for resolving the tension between social identity principles, on the one hand, and self-categorization principles, on the other. In the first section we proposed that both sets of principle are valid, but probably have different domains of application, with social identity principles being more applicable for established groups where group identification is higher, and self-categorization predictions being more relevant to less well-established groups, where distinctiveness plays a more important role in establishing the groups in the first place. Thus, group identification appears to play a critical role, in that it is closely correlated with these two domains. In the research reported in the subsequent section we adopted a slightly different approach to resolving this tension, suggesting again that both sets of principle and prediction are valid, but that they apply to different regions of a similarity/distinctiveness continuum.

These two approaches to resolving this theoretical tension are useful in themselves, but on closer inspection they appear to generate their own theoretical tension. In short, are these two attempted theoretical resolutions themselves contradictory or complementary? In this section we consider both the critical levels of similarity and the moderating role of identification (in particular), in an attempt to provide a further theoretical resolution of the two proposed solutions to this problem set out above. Specifically, in this section we report evidence from empirical work examining the critical role of moderator variables at multiple, or at least critical, levels of similarity. In the last section we propose a final integrative model tying the two approaches (multiple levels and moderator variables) together in a single framework.

The final study reported in the first section (Study 3) makes it clear that one way of attempting to resolve the apparent contradiction between the contrasting predictions of social identity theory and self-categorization theory is by specifying moderating variables that predict when group distinctiveness leads to more and when it leads to less positive differentiation. There is empirical evidence for a range of variables that moderate the group distinctiveness–positive differentiation relation. In addition to the study described earlier, other research has also demonstrated the critical importance of group identification in this domain (Deschamps & Brown, 1983; Henderson-King, Henderson-King, Zhermer, Posokhova & Chiker, 1997; Jetten, Spears & Manstead, 1996; Moghaddam & Stringer, 1988; Roccas & Schwartz, 1993; Wilder, 1986). Group identification also forms the main focus of the present section, but it is worth mentioning other moderating factors that have been shown to moderate the distinctiveness–positive differentiation relation.

Other important moderators of this relation include the perceived threat in terms of similarity of a relevant outgroup (Brown, 1984b; Henderson-King, Henderson-King, Zhermer, Posokhova & Chiker, 1997; see also Roccas & Schwartz, 1993), and the threat to important versus more peripheral dimensions of comparison (Moghaddam & Stringer, 1988; Mummendey & Schreiber, 1984a; Roccas & Schwartz, 1993; Wilder, 1986). The imposition of a superordinate categorization on ingroup and outgroup (Dovidio, Gaertner & Validzic, 1998; Hornsey & Hogg, 1998), the degree of prototypicality of the ingroup member (Jetten, Spears & Manstead, 1997a), and the permeability of group boundaries (Spears & Jetten, 1998b) have also been shown to moderate the distinctiveness–positive differentiation link.

A recent study by Henderson-King et al. (1997) demonstrates that perceived similarity between ethnic groups only led to ingroup bias or positive differentiation when the outgroup was seen as a severe threat to ingroup identity. Other research has stressed the moderating power of the nature of the intergroup contact (Brown, 1984b; Brown & Abrams, 1986). The similarity of an outgroup is more likely to evoke differentiation and ingroup bias in a competitive as opposed to a co-operative setting. Intergroup competition presumably increased the concern for ingroup distinctiveness (Brown, 1984b).

In some of our own research the position of group members within their group proved to be an important factor (Study 6: Jetten, Spears & Manstead, 1997a). In a minimal group study it was demonstrated that a threat to the distinctiveness of group identity by similarity of the outgroup only led to increased positive differentiation among prototypical group members. It was argued that only group members who define themselves as prototypical for the group were motivated to defend their threatened identity by engaging in increased positive differentiation. This pattern of results was replicated in a more natural group setting (i.e., University of Amsterdam versus Free University students) where outgroup similarity was manipulated at three levels (low, medium, highly similar). Peripheral group members showed less or no positive differentiation in both studies, presumably because they were less motivated to defend their identity when threatened by outgroup similarity. Moreover, differentiation enhanced self-esteem for prototypical but not for peripheral group members.

The moderating factor that has attracted most attention in previous research is degree of identification with the group (Deschamps & Brown, 1983; Henderson-King, Henderson-King, Zhermer, Posokhova & Chiker, 1997; Jetten, Spears & Manstead, 1996; Moghaddam & Stringer, 1988; Roccas & Schwartz, 1993; Wilder, 1986). For example, Roccas and Schwartz (1993) studied the interaction between high levels of similarity and identification with the group in a school context. They found that for those who identified strongly with the school, high similarity was perceived as threatening and led to increased ingroup bias. For low identifiers, bias did not vary systematically as a function of the similarity manipulation. The reverse was found on a measure for readiness for social contact: similarity increased readiness for social contact for high but not for low identifiers. The results of a study that examined perceptions of similarity of Russians to Ukrainians, Moldavians and Georgians (Henderson-King, Henderson-King, Zhermer, Posokhova & Chiker, 1997) were less clear-cut. It was found that similarity to these groups was negatively correlated to ingroup favoritism but positively correlated to outgroup derogation. The importance of group identification in this context has also already been demonstrated in Study 3, described earlier in relation to content-based distinctiveness (Jetten, Spears & Manstead, 1996). Moreover, this study is the first to our knowledge actually to manipulate as opposed to measure group identification in assessing the impact of this variable. As we have seen, this study showed that high levels of similarity (i.e. where the ingroup and outgroup norm were identical) led to higher degrees of positive differentiation for high identifiers.

The first point to note from this brief review of the relevant group identification studies is that, hitherto, there have been no attempts to examine the role of group identification and distinctiveness according to the more context-based definition outlined in the preceding section. Second, the results of Study 3 would seem at first sight to contradict the findings of a curvilinear relation between distinctiveness and differentiation, at least for the high identifiers. Recall that according to the contextual manipulation studies, high levels of similarity led to reduced positive differentiation. In the content-based distinctiveness studies there was technically 100 per cent overlap between ingroup and outgroup (at least in terms of group norms) in the critical conditions. This suggests that intergroup distinctiveness was very low in these conditions (and similarity very high) and yet the high identifiers showed enhanced rather than reduced positive differentiation. This is at odds with the curvilinear prediction. It is of course difficult to compare the results of studies that use different manipulations of distinctiveness, but this suggests that for high identifiers, high levels of similarity according to a more context-based manipulation (distance and distribution feedback about the groups) might yet result in enhanced differentiation, in line with the classical social identity prediction.

Testing this idea was the objective of Study 7. We classified group members as high and low identifiers (Jetten, Spears & Manstead, 1998a, Exp. 1). As in Study 5, identity as a student of the University of Amsterdam was made salient, with Free University students forming the relevant rival outgroup. The dimension of comparison concerned 'level of extroversion', which was presumed to be more personally important than the dimension concerning 'belief in supernatural phenomena' used in Study 5. We followed a similar procedure to that used in Study 5, and participants were told that the study involved a comparison between students of the two universities on the dimension 'extroversion'. Scores of the ingroup and outgroup on the extroversion scale were displayed on a continuum ranging from 'very low in extroversion' (0) to 'very high in extroversion' (100). In accordance with existing stereotypes about typical students at these universities, the ingroup was situated near the 'high in extroversion', and the outgroup near the 'low in extroversion' extreme in all conditions. Intergroup distance was low in both group variability conditions, thus replicating the homogeneous/low intergroup distance and heterogeneous/low intergroup distance conditions from Study 4 and 5. The group identification factor was realized by selecting the top and bottom third (33 per cent) of participants on the basis of responses to the three items measuring social identification.

The results demonstrated that the social identity prediction that threatened group distinctiveness would lead to increased positive differentiation was supported for high identifiers. More specifically, high identifiers displayed more ingroup and outgroup stereotyping when group distinctiveness was low than when it was high. Furthermore, compared to low identifiers, low group distinctiveness led to increased ingroup and outgroup stereotyping for high identifiers. Although there was a tendency for low identifiers to display more outgroup stereotyping when groups were distinctive rather than similar (in line with the self-categorization prediction), this difference did not reach conventional acceptable levels of significance. The results further showed that when group distinctiveness was high and groups were clearly distinctive, identification did not influence the degree of ingroup or outgroup stereotyping.

In conclusion, in line with the results of Study 3 in which group identification was manipulated, the present study provides important additional information about the conditions under which processes specified by self-categorization theory and social identity theory operate. In particular, this study shows that high identi-fication with an established group can lead to increases in differentiation even for the highest levels of similarity on the continuum investigated in the previous sec-tion (at least for a comparison dimension of moderate personal importance). In other words, it seems quite possible that group identification does moderate the curvilinear relation between distinctiveness and differentiation proposed in the previous section. It is possible that the failure to find most discrimination under high levels of similarity in these studies may be due to relatively low levels of identification with the groups. Alternatively, it may be that the underlying dimen-sion of differentiation (belief in the supernatural) was not sufficiently central or important to the perceivers (see also Moghaddam & Stringer, 1988; Mummendey & Schreiber, 1984a; Roccas & Schwartz, 1993; Wilder, 1986).

Once again, we find that principles from both social identity theory and self-categorization theory are of heuristic value in helping us to provide a full account of the pattern of results. The effect of variations in group distinctiveness on posi-tive differentiation in groups in which members' identification is relatively low is best explained by self-categorization theory. Social identity concerns become more influential when members identify more strongly with their group. This implies that it is important to distinguish between cognitive and more motivational re-sponses to variations in group distinctiveness. Rather than regarding social iden-tity theory and self-categorization theory as contradictory, the present studies suggest that these two theories should be seen as complementary.

Summary and an Integrative Model

Two main classes of group distinctiveness have been distinguished and examined in this chapter: distinctiveness of content and distinctiveness of context. The first aspect of group distinctiveness (content) relates to the specific dimensions on which similarity or dissimilarity are perceived. Previous research has mostly focused on ingroup and outgroup similarity in the descriptive content of attitudes (Allen & Wilder, 1975; Diehl, 1988) or goals (Brown & Wade, 1987; Deschamps & Brown, 1983; Marcus-Newhall, Miller, Holtz & Brewer, 1993). Studies reported in the first part of this chapter manipulated content distinctiveness by varying the con-tent of ingroup and outgroup norms (Jetten, Spears & Manstead, 1996). In addi-tion to a descriptive component, group norms also comprise an influential prescriptive component. When a certain social identity is salient, group norms also become salient and regulate group members' behaviour (Jetten, Spears & Manstead, 1997b; see chapter 4, this volume).

Contextual distinctiveness refers to the relative clarity of a categorization as 'us' versus 'them', as determined by the absolute distance between ingroup and outgroup on some dimension of comparison, in combination with the variability within the groups. Importantly, it was demonstrated in two studies, which varied with respect to the nature of the intergroup setting (minimal versus natural groups), that contextual distinctiveness is not only determined by the mean difference between ingroup and outgroup, but also by the perceived variability of ingroup and outgroup (Jetten, Spears & Manstead, 1998b).

The central question in this chapter concerns the conditions under which positive differentiation decreases or increases as a function of perceived group distinctiveness. Diverging predictions were derived from social identity theory and self-categorization theory concerning the relation between group distinctiveness and positive differentiation. One way to resolve this apparent contradiction is to integrate these opposing predictions by assuming that most positive differentiation will be displayed when groups are at least sufficiently similar to evoke social comparison (social identity prediction) and at the same time sufficiently distinctive to qualify as clearly independent groups (self-categorization prediction). Two studies supported the prediction that an intermediate level of group distinctiveness provides the most fertile conditions for intergroup differentiation and that the relation between group distinctiveness and differentiation is curvilinear.

A second way to resolve this apparent contradiction between social identity and self-categorisation theory is to identify potential moderators of this relation (e.g., group identification, group prototypicality) in an attempt to specify domains of application of social identity theory and self-categorization theory. This approach has also proved to be quite successful. Studies in which participants were classified as low or high identifiers (Study 3, Study 7) demonstrate the moderating power of level of identification in accounting for the distinctiveness–differentiation relation. Moreover, as Study 7 shows, the group identification also seems able to qualify the curvilinear relation between contextual distinctiveness and positive differentiation: when the group and the underlying dimension of comparison are sufficiently important even high levels of intergroup similarity can be sufficiently threatening to evoke positive differentiation.

These two approaches to resolving the apparent contradiction between the social identity and self-categorization approaches to the distinctiveness–positive differentiation relation can be integrated within a single framework or model. Figure 5.1 shows the relation between levels of group distinctiveness and positive differentiation as moderated by group identification. In this model a central role is given to identification as a moderator of the relation between group distinctiveness and positive differentiation. For low identifiers, it is predicted that the relation between group distinctiveness and positive differentiation is basically curvilinear (inverted U-shaped), whereas it is predicted to be linear (increasing with increasing intergroup similarity) for high identifiers. The predictions for low and high identifiers are essentially identical when group distinctiveness is high or at an intermediate level. High group distinctiveness decreases the comparability of groups, leading to lower levels of positive differentiation independent of level of identifica-

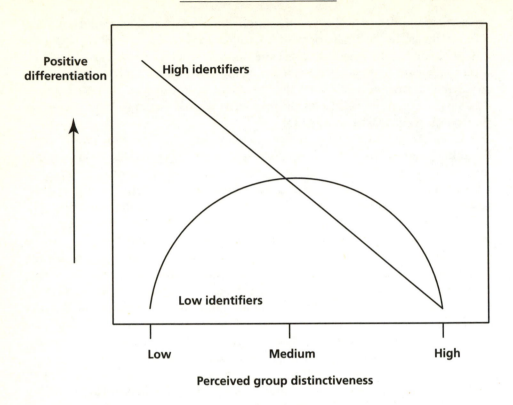

Figure 5.1 The relation between group distinctiveness and positive differentiation as a function of group identification

tion. This prediction from social identity theory and self-categorization theory can be contrasted with predictions derived from the category differentiation model (e.g. Doise, 1978). The latter model does not specify the criterion of comparability and would therefore predict that positive differentiation should increase as a function of group distinctiveness (a linear effect). At intermediate levels of group distinctiveness, groups are clearly distinctive and at the same time comparable enough to allow for a relevant intergroup comparison, and some threat to distinctiveness, leading to increased positive differentiation. The model predicts that the greatest differences between low and high identifiers will be observed when group distinctiveness is low. In line with the results of Study 3 and Study 7, high identifiers will display most positive differentiation when group distinctiveness is most threatened. Low identifiers, in contrast, are likely to focus on the fact that low intergroup distinctiveness undermines the basis for meaningful categorization, thereby undermining positive differentiation.

In other words, it is predicted in this model that processes relating to social identity theory will dominate for high identifiers, whereas self-categorization principles such as meta-contrast and comparative fit will be more important when identification with the group is low. When group distinctiveness is low, either no or low levels of positive differentiation are predicted from self-categorization theory, whereas high levels of positive differentiation are predicted by social identity theory (in order to restore threatened group distinctiveness). Predictions from self-categorization and social identity theory do not differ for low group distinctiveness and intermediate group distinctiveness.

As mentioned above, in this model we focus on the moderating role of group identification. Although the research reported in this chapter demonstrates that this is an important moderating variable, we also briefly summarized a range of other moderating variables of the group distinctiveness–positive differentiation relation (e.g., threat to ingroup identity, importance of the dimension of comparison, cooperative versus competitive intergroup setting, and perceived prototypicality of group members). It is also worth considering the role of these moderating factors within the general framework of this model. For example, the results of Study 6 concerning group prototypicality suggest that this variable may operate in a rather similar way to group identification.

This integrative model might be of help in explaining the inconsistent findings that have been found in research on the effect of similarity on differentiation. Some studies in this area have found a positive relation between similarity and positive differentiation (e.g., Diehl, 1988; Moghaddam & Stringer, 1988; Roccas & Schwartz, 1993; Turner, 1978b), whereas others found a negative relation (e.g., Hensley & Duval, 1976; Mummendey & Schreiber, 1984a; Rokeach, 1960), or no relation (Allen & Wilder, 1975). First, if differentiation is most likely under conditions of moderate distinctiveness or similarity, this would help to explain these inconsistent results. The pattern of differentiation would depend on how the continuum of intergroup distinctiveness is sampled in these studies. If the relationship is curvilinear, sampling the range of intergroup similarity on either side of this curve would lead to completely different and potentially misleading conclusions. Second, the model predicts that a threat to group distinctiveness (low group distinctiveness) will be perceived differently by low and high identifiers. It is possible that apparent inconsistencies in previous studies result from variations in the nature of the groups used in the intergroup setting (minimal versus more natural group settings), or as a result of differences in group members' identification with the group. In other words, in order to understand the process of intergroup discrimination it is necessary to focus not only on when a group displays more or less intergroup discrimination, but also on who within the group is more or less discriminatory.

Another more methodological reason for inconsistent results in previous research on the group distinctiveness–positive differentiation effect relates to the wide range of dependent variables that have been used to assess positive differentiation. It is unclear if variations in perceptions of group distinctiveness have similar effects on all of these measures. Among the dependent measures used to assess positive differentiation are: (a) evaluations of group traits (Brown, 1984b;

Deschamps & Brown, 1983; Dovidio, Gaertner & Validzic, 1998); (b) evaluations of group products and group performance (Brown & Williams, 1984; Jetten, Spears & Manstead, 1997a; Mummendey & Schreiber, 1984a); (c) resource allocations on matrices (Jetten, Spears & Manstead, 1996; Moghaddam & Stringer, 1988); and (d) intention to engage in positive or negative interactions with ingroup and outgroup members (Hornsey & Hogg, 1998; Roccas & Schwartz, 1993; Struch & Schwartz, 1989). Although patterns of results are sometimes remarkably consistent across different positive differentiation measures (see Jetten, Spears & Manstead, 1996, 1997a), this is not always the case, and different measures do not always reveal similar results (Brewer, 1979; Brown, 1984a; Brown & Abrams, 1986; Roccas & Schwartz, 1993; Struch & Schwartz, 1989). It is therefore worth examining whether differences in previous results vary systematically with the nature of the dependent measures.

The studies reported in this chapter make clear that the group distinctiveness–intergroup discrimination relation is a complex one. The research shows that small changes in the intergroup context in terms of perceived group distinctiveness in content and context can have quite substantial effects on intergroup relations. An example of one important implication concerns attempts to reduce intergroup conflict by stressing similarities between groups. According to our model, the effectiveness of this strategy will depend crucially on the level of identification of the group members: such an intervention is likely to be much more effective for low than for high identifiers. If it is not possible to tailor such an intervention to the different audiences with a group, it may be necessary to make the difficult choice between inciting further intergroup antagonism among the 'die-hard' members, or preventing antagonism developing among the others. At the very least, it is important to be sensitive to the factors that moderate positive differentiation in order to reach a better understanding of the underlying mechanism of intergroup hostility.

At the beginning of this chapter we cited Freud (1922) as presenting some of the first anecdotal evidence to a psychology audience that both difference and similarity could form the basis for intergroup hostility and discrimination. Less charitable readers might have taken this as evidence that the famous psychoanalyst was having it both ways. We hope that the evidence summarized here has persuaded the reader that Freud, far from being in two minds, was probably right on both counts. Whether he would have agreed with us that 'moderation' is the answer to this paradox remains a moot point.

6

Commitment and Strategic Responses to Social Context

Naomi Ellemers, Manuela Barreto and
Russell Spears

Introduction

A central tenet of social identity theory is that members of lower status groups should be motivated to establish a positive identity (Tajfel, 1978a; Tajfel & Turner, 1979). A host of studies has tried to assess the empirical validity of this prediction among members of natural as well as artificial groups (see Hinkle & Brown, 1990; Mullen, Brown & Smith, 1992 for overviews). In spite of the variety of groups that have been examined, the general methodology of these studies is more or less the same: participants are confronted with a specific intergroup comparison, from which their group emerges favourably or unfavourably. Subsequently, they are asked to allocate resources to members of the two groups, give their opinion of the two groups on specific rating scales, or both. The implicit assumption underlying this methodology is that such intergroup allocations or ratings tap people's evaluation of the two groups and, consequently, that these measures should reflect any attempts to establish positive ingroup distinctiveness.

Our point of departure for the present chapter is that this assumption is not necessarily valid. In fact, social identity theory never maintained that there should be a one-to-one relationship between relative group status and ingroup favouritism in outcome allocations or intergroup ratings. Instead, the motivation to establish a positive social identity may result in an array of overt behaviours, as people may use various identity management strategies to achieve the same goal. We further argue that it is possible to determine specific elements of the social context in which people operate, which restrict the ways in which group members are likely to express their identity needs. In this chapter we first look at how actual differences between social groups constrain the ways in which ingroup favouritism is expressed in group ratings. Then we turn to the communicative aspects of social judgements (and social behaviour) more explicitly. We assess how awareness of different audiences may affect the likelihood that ingroup ratings reflect privately held convictions about the group's worth, or are the result of strategic considerations that take into account the social reality in which people find themselves. Subsequently, we examine how statements of ingroup identification may be considered strategic responses to the social context and, finally, we look at how an audience affects group members' actual displays of ingroup normative behaviour.

Forms of Ingroup Favouritism

When we take a closer look at research on the relationship between relative group status and ingroup favouritism that has been done so far, it seems that empirical investigations have mainly tried to assess the extent to which group members compete for ingroup superiority on some central comparative dimension. However, from the outset (Tajfel, 1975, 1978a; Tajfel & Turner, 1979) social identity theory has emphasized that this is only one possible way to cope with a social identity threat, and has indicated that whether or not group members are likely to engage in social competition depends on the social circumstances. For instance, instead of engaging in attempts to improve the standing of one's group as a whole, people may prefer to use an individual-level identity management strategy. Indeed, a growing body of empirical evidence suggests that there is a difference in this respect between group members with different levels of commitment to the group (Branscombe & Ellemers, 1998), in the sense that those who identify strongly with their group are likely to favour the ingroup on evaluative and behavioural measures, while low identifiers aim to improve their identity by setting themselves apart from the rest of the group (see also chapters 3, 4 and 9).

Even when we limit our discussion to group-level responses to identity threat, the standard research paradigm that has been commonly used in this area seems too restricted to capture the essence of the phenomena that social identity theory aims to address. Indeed, previous attempts to summarize the work conducted within the minimal group paradigm, together with findings that were obtained in slightly more enriched situations, have resulted in contradictory conclusions rather than yielding converging evidence (see Hinkle & Brown, 1990; Mullen, Brown & Smith, 1992). In an attempt to examine actual group behaviour more directly, alongside the experiments with artificially created laboratory groups, there has been a growing body of research on the perceptions and behaviours among members of natural groups. There are two features of such natural intergroup comparisons that are likely to affect the expression of ingroup favouritism. First, people are aware that there are real differences between the groups under investigation and, second, they can compare the groups in many different ways, instead of only in terms of some criterion the experimenter presents as centrally important (see Mummendey & Schreiber, 1983; Spears & Manstead, 1989).

From this literature, there is by now converging evidence that in natural settings group members do not necessarily compete with each other for superiority on all available comparative dimensions (Mummendey & Schreiber, 1984b; Mummendey & Simon, 1989; Spears & Manstead, 1989; Van Knippenberg, 1978; Van Knippenberg & Van Oers, 1984; Van Knippenberg & Wilke, 1979). Instead, they are more likely to show some form of 'social co-operation' (Van Knippenberg & Ellemers, 1990), by mutually validating each other's superiority on different dimensions that characterize each group (see also Simon, 1992b). In the past, it has been suggested that this pattern of results may also arise from people's attempts to depict the ingroup positively, albeit in a rather subtle and creative way (see also Lemaine, 1974). Unfortunately, because this research was carried out with members of natural groups, the characteristics of the intergroup comparison could not be controlled by the experimenters, and hence it is difficult, if not impossible, to determine retrospectively whether the ratings that were given reflect actual differences between the groups, or are the result of ingroup favouring judgements.

Reality Constraints and Social Creativity

Some recent experiments have directly addressed this issue, by examining the use of social creativity as an identity management strategy under more controlled circumstances. In these studies group members' beliefs about existing intergroup differences were manipulated by the experimenters. The specific aim then was to investigate whether, while respecting these reality constraints, group members creatively use more ambiguous aspects of the intergroup situation to establish positive ingroup distinctiveness or defend against a negative social identity. Furthermore, in order to establish whether such ratings are part of an identity management strategy, it is important to assess whether responses are related to the importance that people attach to this particular group membership, that is, their level of ingroup identification.

The relative superiority or higher status of the outgroup on a particular dimension provides an obvious 'reality constraint' on the ability to define the ingroup as better, at least on the status-defining dimension. In such situations people may look for more subtle ways to side-step the unfavourable difference, or even to undermine it. In two studies, Doosje, Spears and Koomen (1995) investigated the operation of one such 'creativity strategy', namely by using variability judgements to cover up unfavourable intergroup differences (see also Doosje, Spears, Ellemers & Koomen, 1999; and chapter 4, this volume). In the first study participants were presented with evaluative sample information about behaviour of members of their own group and the other group. According to this information, their group was either superior or inferior in comparison with the other group in terms of pro-social behaviour. In addition, the reliability of this sample information (i.e., the severeness of the reality constraint) was manipulated by means of the variability of the sample. Half the conditions involved homogeneous ingroup and outgroup samples (high reality constraint), and the other half involved heterogeneous ingroup and outgroup samples (low reality constraint). In the conditions in which the ingroup was presented as superior to the outgroup, participants were willing to believe that this favourable difference was in fact typical of the groups generally, irrespective of group variability. When group members were informed that their group was inferior to the other group, however, participants only accepted that this was representative of the groups when the group feedback was homogeneous and thus reliable, implying a reality constraint. However, when the feedback about the groups was heterogeneous, and thus less reliable, participants indicated that these differences were not representative of the groups in general and also emphasized variation within each group, thereby undermining the importance of the unfavourable intergroup difference.

In a second study similar predictions were tested but this time the reliability of the sample information was manipulated by varying the size of the ingroup and outgroup sample (Doosje, Spears & Koomen, 1995, Exp. 2). It was assumed that evidence from a small sample is less compelling than information that is based on a large sample which puts a greater constraint on perception of social reality. Results were similar to the first study. When people were presented with favourable information about their own group and unfavourable information about the outgroup, they believed this favourable difference was generally typical for the groups, regardless of the size of the sample on which this information was based. However, when the ingroup was depicted less favourably than the outgroup, participants were only willing to accept that this difference in sample information was in fact typical for the groups in the large sample condition. In the small sample condition participants were less likely to accept that these differences were typical of the underlying population and once again they emphasized the heterogeneity of the groups on the status dimension.

The consistent pattern of results found across these two studies suggests that people seek a balance between the need for a positive identity and the need to stay in touch with reality, and do not make claims that seem unwarranted (e.g., Kunda, 1990; Stangor & Ford, 1992). By stressing the heterogeneity of both the ingroup and the outgroup people effectively undermine the significance of an unfavourable comparison ('our group may be bad, but we're not all bad'). Stressing the heterogeneity of both ingroup and outgroup in unfavourable intergroup comparison situations may serve the function of blurring the unfavourable intergroup distinction and also make it possible for group members to distinguish themselves as individuals from their fellow ingroup members ('I'm not like the rest of my group'). In other words, in this way variability information can be used strategically to protect both group and personal identity.

Further empirical evidence that group members take established intergroup differences into account when giving ingroup favouring judgements can be derived from studies that included several comparative dimensions on which the groups were rated, rather than relying on a single evaluative judgement. In an experiment by Doosje, Ellemers and Spears (1995; Study 2), members of artificially created groups (inductive versus deductive thinkers) were asked to complete a group task consisting of a series of personnel problems (see also chapter 4). Subsequently, they were led to believe that their group had either performed worse (low ingroup status) or better (high ingroup status) than the other group. When they were given the opportunity to rate the two groups on a number of comparative dimensions, it turned out that participants in the low ingroup status condition refrained from claiming ingroup superiority on the status-defining dimension (proficiency in personnel decision-making). At the same time, however, on four alternative dimensions (likeability, intelligence, friendliness, and judgement of character) they did favour the ingroup.

Similar results were obtained in a study by Blanz, Mummendey and Otten (1995). These authors randomly assigned participants to a minority or majority group, and manipulated the relative status position of these groups by providing false feedback on a 'concentration task'. Subsequent ratings of the groups revealed that those who received unfavourable ingroup information reflected their group's inferior standing (i.e., displayed outgroup favouritism) when rating the groups in terms of their ability. However, these low status group members favoured the ingroup when the comparative judgement was unrelated to the status manipulation, that is, when asked to indicate the relative worth of the two groups with respect to their morality (see also Poppe & Linssen, in press; Reichl, 1997; Spears & Manstead, 1989).

A more systematic attempt to investigate whether consensually defined aspects of social reality are reflected in group members' judgements, while claims of ingroup superiority only emerge with respect to more ambiguous aspects of the intergroup comparison, is reported by Ellemers, Van Rijswijk, Roefs and Simons (1997). In this study it was assessed how two student associations were rated by members of each of these natural groups, as well as by non-members. The authors argued that non-members would not have a vested interest in depicting one group more favourably than the other, and hence their ratings were most likely to reflect consensually defined ('real') differences between the two groups. By contrast, participants who were members of the groups under investigation were expected to hold more biased judgements favouring the ingroup.

As predicted, the consensual difference in the relative social standing of the two groups was reflected in the ratings given by non-members: the characteristic traits of the high status group were generally evaluated more positively than the traits that were typical for the low status group. In line with our previous argument, it turned out that the greater desirability of the traits that were typical for the higher status group was consensually acknowledged by members of both groups alike. At the same time, however, the lower status group members showed ingroup favouring biases when rating more ambiguous aspects of the intergroup comparison. While they would not deny that certain undesirable traits are typical for their group, they evaluated these traits more positively than did members of the other group or non-members. Furthermore, members of the lower status group claimed highly desirable but 'non-typical' traits as characteristic for the ingroup. Finally, in support of our previous argument that such biased ratings are part of a group-level identity management strategy, it turned out that the tendency to favour the ingroup was more pronounced, as respondents identified more strongly with their group.

However suggestive the evidence from this study may seem, it nevertheless relies on the assumption that non-members' ratings reflect the reality constraints which limit the ways in which group members can credibly claim ingroup superiority. In other words, in this study both the relative standing of the two groups and the nature and valence of typical group traits were given, and could, hence, only be independently assessed (but not controlled) by the experimenters.

In order to address this limitation of the investigation of Ellemers, Van Rijswijk, Roefs and Simons (1997), Ellemers and Van Rijswijk (1997) conducted an experimental study that would enable them directly to manipulate relative group status, and explicitly look at group members' ratings on status dimensions (which refer to this manipulated reality), as well as other dimensions (which offer some more interpretational ambiguity). In this experiment students were randomly assigned to one of two groups (under- or overestimators; see Brewer, Manzi & Shaw, 1993), that differed in size ostensibly on the basis of their performance on a dot estimation task (we will not go into the effects of relative ingroup size here, as these are not relevant for our present discussion). Participants then performed a so-called 'group-creativity task', in which they were asked to provide creative solutions for a number of problematic situations at work. The feedback about the alleged performance of the two groups on this test was used to manipulate relative group status.

When asked to rate the two groups on a number of different dimensions, participants showed the predicted effects. While low status group members acknowledged their group's inferiority on the status-defining dimension (creativity), they denied that there was a difference between the groups on a number of more ambiguous, status-related dimensions (competent, valuable, intelligent and motivated), and they claimed ingroup superiority on an alternative dimension (honesty). Again, these ingroup favouring responses were mainly shown by those who identified strongly with the ingroup, underlining our previous conclusion that such biased group ratings can be considered to be part of an identity management strategy.

In sum, both the study of Ellemers, Van Rijswijk, Roefs and Simons (1997) with natural groups, as well as the experimental study of Ellemers and Van Rijswijk (1997) show that while people are likely to acknowledge consensually defined or (apparently) evidence-based differences between the groups (even when this is to the ingroup's disadvantage), at the same time they display ingroup favouring judgements when rating aspects of the intergroup situation about which they have more interpretational freedom. While this empirical evidence supports our previous contention that members of lower status groups creatively operate within the constraints that are posed by the current inferior standing of their group, it nevertheless remains unclear why exactly this is the case. Do lower status group members refrain from claiming ingroup superiority on specific comparative dimensions out of a lack of confidence in the worth of their group in these respects, or do they acknowledge the higher standing of the outgroup out of compliance with consensual views on the current standing of their group? In other words, the specific question of whether members of lower status groups are likely to internalize their inferior standing, as Tajfel and Turner (1979) assume, or whether their group ratings result from strategic considerations concerning how most successfully to cope with the situation at hand (see Van Knippenberg, 1989) remains to be addressed.

Effects of the Communicative Context on Strategic Group Ratings

So far, we have mainly considered how actual differences between groups may restrict the ways in which group members are likely to express ingroup favouring judgements. We now turn to the question of what psychological process leads members of lower status groups to respond in such a way. One possible reason why they opt for indirect identity enhancement strategies is that these group members have internalized their group's inferior standing in the social structure, and therefore lack the self-confidence to challenge it. In fact, in the self-esteem literature a similar hypothesis has been advanced in order to explain how people with low self-esteem may come to prefer information that is consistent with their negative self-image to information that is self-enhancing (McFarlin & Blascovich, 1981; Shrauger, 1975; Swann, Griffin, Predmore & Gaines, 1987). Another possibility, however, is that responses of lower status group members are mainly guided by strategic considerations, that is, by their judgement of whether claims of superiority are likely to be deemed reasonable or will be accepted by others. This would imply that issues of self-presentation and impression management might play a role in the expression of ingroup favouring judgements (Goffman, 1959; Schlenker, 1980). Before we address this question, however, it is important to consider the role of strategic self-presentation as it has been considered in intergroup contexts.

Traditional models of self-presentation and impression management have been relatively individualistic in that they have tended to operate on the assumption that the individual is motivated to present a positive (or defend against a negative) personal face to an undifferentiated audience or other person (Baumeister, 1982; Deutsch & Gerard, 1955; Reicher, Spears & Postmes, 1995; Spears & Lea, 1994; Turner, 1991). Social identity and self-categorization theory provide a context-sensitive notion of the self, which takes into account social identities, and thus also implies a social differentiation of the audience to whom self-presentation is directed (e.g., ingroup and/or outgroup). The social identity model of deindividuation effects (SIDE; Reicher, Spears & Postmes, 1995; Spears & Lea,

1994; see chapter 8, this volume, for a more detailed account of this model) explicitly combines the social specification of identity (the 'cognitive dimension'), with an analysis of the instrumental self-presentation that takes into account the nature of the audience or audiences present in the situation (the 'strategic dimension'). Self-presentation cannot therefore be understood or fully predicted without an analysis of the self being presented (e.g., personal versus group). When one's group identity is at the forefront, the expression of behaviour in line with this identity is likely to be facilitated and constrained by the presence of ingroup and outgroup audiences respectively. In particular, if the outgroup occupies a powerful position over the ingroup, its presence is likely to restrict the ingroup to behaviour deemed acceptable to and thus not punishable by the outgroup.

A study by Reicher and Levine (1994a) illustrates this point by showing that students for whom their 'student' identity was made salient (as opposed to a 'scientist' identity) were only willing to admit to behaviour punishable by lecturing staff (e.g. essay plagiarism, cheating on experimental reports, etc.) when their responses to this powerful academic outgroup were not identifiable. Interestingly, however, students tended to accentuate the expression of non-punishable behaviour deemed normative for the ingroup (e.g. anti-animal experimentation attitudes) when identifiable to the outgroup. The presentation of self therefore takes into account the power of sanction of the outgroup, but also provides an audience to whom one can express, or even flaunt, a distinctive ingroup identity (see also Reicher & Levine, 1994b). Further research shows that the co-presence of the ingroup can provide the social support necessary to transcend the fear of sanction and encourage less restrained ingroup responses (Reicher, Levine & Gordijn, 1998). In sum, similar to the research discussed earlier concerned with reality constraints, research on the SIDE model illustrates that intergroup behaviour does not automatically reflect the contents of identity, but that the social agents judge the impact of their responses strategically. Strategic self-presentation reflects the nature of the social self and the social nature of its audience. In this way the SIDE model attempts to complement the social dimension of social identity theory with a strategic dimension, and to complement self-presentation theory with a social dimension.

This theoretical framework allows us to reconsider the question of whether responses of lower status group members reflect a lack of confidence in the worth of their group or are, rather, affected by strategic considerations. This was empirically examined by Ellemers, Van Dyck, Hinkle and Jacobs (1998). They argued that by comparing private and public judgements of the groups in question, it should be possible to determine to what extent group ratings reflect internalized group images (i.e. genuinely accepted inferiority), or are the result of some communicative process by which overt responses are strategically adapted to the audience that confronts them. In two studies Ellemers et al. presented group members with an explicit audience, in order to test whether public expressions of ingroup favouritism reflected group members' private convictions, or were adapted depending on the social context. Although these studies were carried out in the laboratory, participants were members of natural groups, in order to ensure that people would care sufficiently about their group membership and its comparative implications.

In the first experiment, members of different sports clubs were asked about the self-perceived standing of their group. Subsequently, participants performed a group task, and were asked to estimate how well their group had performed on this task relative to the outgroup, and to give their ratings of the difficulty of ingroup and outgroup assignments. The crucial manipulation was that they could either express their opinions privately, or were led to believe that they were to defend their opinions in public. Both dependent measures together showed that whereas people who perceived their group as having relatively low social status favoured the ingroup in their private judgements, they showed outgroup favouritism in public.

These results offer preliminary support for the contention that we are looking at a form of strategic behaviour on the part of lower status group members, rather than a lack of confidence in the ingroup's worth (Reicher & Levine, 1994a; Reicher, Spears & Postmes, 1995). In order to investigate further the possible implications of such strategic behaviour, Ellemers et al. conducted a second study, in which they distinguished an intra- from an intergroup public context. They argued that if people indeed use their group ratings in a strategic way, the content of their communications should vary, depending on the audience in question. Specifically, it would seem that an ingroup audience would be more likely to approve of claims of ingroup superiority, while the confrontation with an outgroup audience might lead members of a lower status group to admit to their inferior standing. However, on the basis of theoretical considerations, as well as previous empirical results, the authors pointed out that people may be differentially motivated to uphold the worth of the ingroup towards an ingroup or outgroup audience, depending on the extent to which they identify with the ingroup.

In Ellemers, Van Dyck, Hinckle and Jacobs's (1998) second experiment, the relevant comparison was between students of the two universities in Amsterdam, in terms of their performance on training placements. After this comparative context was introduced, participants were asked to indicate the extent to which they identified as students of the Free University. For this purpose, they were asked to complete Luthanen and Crocker's (1992) identity subscale, adapted to this particular group membership, and divided into two groups at the median. Furthermore, in this second study, the relative status position of the ingroup was externally assigned, instead of self-perceived (as was the case in the first study). The status manipulation consisted of false information indicating that it had been established that students of the Free University (the ingroup) generally performed better (high ingroup status) or worse (low ingroup status) in their practical trainee posts than students of the University of Amsterdam (the outgroup). The alleged purpose of the present investigation was to learn more about the background of these performance differences, and therefore participants were asked to work on a series of tasks that were supposedly related to their performance in practical situations.

The main dependent measure consisted of participants' judgements about the relative task performance of the two groups. They were either led to believe that their group ratings would remain strictly confidential (private social context), that they would have to acknowledge and discuss their ratings with other ingroup members only (intragroup context), or that they would have to account for their ratings among outgroup as well as ingroup members (intergroup context).

Again, in their private ratings, high as well as low identifiers favoured the ingroup, in the sense that those who had received favourable information about the ingroup reflected this in their private judgements, while the assignment of an inferior position to the ingroup was not acknowledged. Furthermore, when publicly accountable for their group ratings, these were strategically adapted to the social context. However, the way in which group members responded to an ingroup or outgroup audience (intra- or intergroup context) depended on their level of ingroup identification. Specifically, highly identifying members of low status groups acknowledged their group's inferior performance in an intragroup context, while they denied the assigned status difference in an intergroup context. Conversely, those who identified less with the ingroup, did not differentiate between the two groups in the intragroup context, while they indicated that their group was inferior in the intergroup context.

Ellemers et al. explained these findings by referring to differential motives that high and low identifying group members are likely to have. On the basis of existing theoretical statements (e.g., Tajfel & Turner, 1979) as well as previous empirical work (e.g., Doosje, Ellemers & Spears, 1995; Ellemers, Spears & Doosje, 1997; Ellemers, Van Rijswijk, Bruins & De Gilder, 1998; Spears, Doosje & Ellemers, 1997), they argued that high identifiers are generally more prepared to incur personal costs for the benefit of their group. Consequently, when confronted with unfavourable information about the ingroup, high identifiers should be inclined to exert themselves to improve their group's current standing. Hence, they are most likely to uphold the worth of the ingroup in front of an audience that may sanction such claims (i.e., in an intergroup context). However, in order to mobilize the collective effort that is necessary to effect an actual change in the social situation, it is important that group members acknowledge among themselves (i.e., in an intragroup context) that there are problems with the current position of the ingroup.

Ellemers, Van Dyck, Hinkle and Jacobs (1998) argued that low identifiers are less likely to engage in similar efforts on behalf of the group, but strategically adapt their public behaviour to what the audience in question is likely to appreciate. Hence, in an intragroup context, low identifiers emphasize the ingroup's worth, instead of focusing on the fact that the group's position might be improved. However, they are not prepared to maintain this in front of an outgroup audience, and hence acknowledge the ingroup's inferior standing in an intergroup context. Accordingly, given this variation in group members' responses, depending on the communicative context, Ellemers et al. concluded that lower status group members who refrain from displaying ingroup favouritism in their judgements do this out of strategic considerations, rather than because of a lack of trust in the ingroup's worth.

Social Identity and Communicative Context

In social psychological research, strategic responses to the social context are likely to be more pervasive than has so far been acknowledged in the literature. It has been suggested elsewhere that it may often be useful to regard participants' responses to survey questionnaires as a form of social behaviour situated in a specific communicative context (Barreto, Spears, Ellemers & Shahinper, 1998; see also Klein & Azzi, 1998). Specifically, it would seem that participants' ratings of degree of group identification may in themselves constitute strategic statements of the right to claim membership in social groups to a given audience. This view does not imply that when engaging in such responses participants are not expressing a 'true' feeling of identification with a group. By contrast, it stresses the fact that 'true' social identities are not immutable cognitive structures, but that they are contextualized statements about how one wants to be positioned in the social system and how one wishes to relate to others.

Previous research has shown that people adapt their responses to the social context and to the audiences to whom they communicate (Krauss & Fussell, 1996; Reicher, Spears & Postmes, 1995; Schwartz, 1995), even when such audiences are only implicit in the language of the questionnaire (Bond, 1983; Bond & Cheung, 1984; Bond & Yang, 1982; John, Young, Giles & Hofman, 1985; Kosmitzi, 1996; Marin, Triandis, Betancourt & Kashima. 1983; Ralston, Cunnif & Gustafson, 1995; Trafimow, Silverman, Fan & Law, 1997; Yang & Bond, 1980). We have argued that audiences affect people's responses because they carry with them certain norms, which the respondent may be motivated either to comply with, or actively reject (Barreto, Spears, Ellemers & Shahinper, 1998). Whether participants will be motivated to comply with or reject the audience's norms is likely to be a function of the nature of the audience, as well as of whether individual responses remain anonymous, or participants are made personally accountable for their responses (see also Barreto & Ellemers, 1998a). Specifically, anonymous conditions are likely to foster salience of social identity. If a salient social identity is valued, anonymity is likely to increase adherence to group norms, as well as rejection of behaviour that conflicts with central ingroup values (see also Postmes, 1997; Reicher, 1996c; Spears & Lea, 1994; Spears, Lea & Lee, 1990; chapter 8, this volume). Accountability, however, enhances concerns with personal self-presentation, which results in increased compliance with the audience's norms. This may result in more or less ingroup normative behaviour depending on the nature of the audience (e.g., whether it includes a powerful outgroup as in Reicher & Levine, 1994a, 1994b). That is, since audiences are likely to differ in the norms that characterize them, it follows that different audiences may elicit different responses from the same participants.

In our own research (Barreto, Spears, Ellemers & Shahinper, 1998), we investigated migrant group members' expressions of identification with native and host groups as a function of linguistic context. Despite being commonly treated on the basis of their ascribed minority identity, migrant group members have been shown to define themselves by reference to both native and host groups (e.g., Berry, 1990; Deaux & Ethier, 1998; Hutnik, 1991; Verkuyten, 1997). In two studies, we investigated whether the degree to which migrants express their identification with native and host groups is a function of the (linguistic) context in which they make their claims. Linguistic context was manipulated by varying the language in which the questionnaire was written (i.e., native or host language). Under these conditions, we suggested that participants' reports of degree of group identification may serve to undermine the significance of an externally imposed category system. This is likely to be especially so if responses are directed at the audience that holds that category system as normative. Specifically, we argued that minority group members are likely to stress their bicultural identity (i.e., identification with both native and host groups) when responses are directed at an audience that questions the bicultural nature of their social identity. While enhancing identification with two groups simultaneously may at first seem problematic (see Turner, 1987), this might in fact be less so if statements of identification are seen as stemming from strategic concerns, that is, if they are seen as reflecting the motivation to be considered as a member of a particular group, rather than the relative salience of group membership. According to this view, independently of which identity is rendered more salient by the audience, members of minority groups that are generally seen as separate from the host society should be especially motivated to stress their bicultural identity to a host audience, thereby expressing their disagreement with the category system this audience imposes.

In our first study, two groups with different patterns of relation with the host society were examined: Turkish and Iranian immigrants in the Netherlands (Barreto, Spears, Ellemers & Shahinper, 1998). Turks in the Netherlands are generally seen as a separate group. For instance, within Dutch society they have their own institutions, and they prefer to marry within their ethnic group (see Lucassen & Penninx, 1997). In fact, this is one of the sources of criticism by some of the native Dutch, who feel that immigrants should adapt more completely to Dutch society. By contrast, the Iranians tend to be more personally involved with the host society, and are more inclined to integrate with the Dutch. The Turks may thus feel threatened when asked about identification with the host community when a Dutch audience is present, whereas this is less likely to be the case for the Iranians. At the same time, because the Iranians are mostly political refugees, they are expected to have a more problematic relation with their native society. Thus, when we compare how the two groups are likely to respond when asked to report about their native identity, we expect the Iranians to feel threatened when an Iranian audience is involved, while this is less likely to be the case for the Turks. This argument was corroborated by the empirical findings. Specifically, the relevant data revealed that Turks stressed their bicultural identity (Turkish and Dutch) in particular to a Dutch audience, while Iranians expressed higher levels of identification with both groups (Iranians and Dutch) in front of an Iranian audience.

In a second study (Barreto, Spears, Ellemers & Shahinper, 1998) we investigated expressions of native and host identification as a function of linguistic context, among members of a minority group which tends to be accepted by both native and host communities: Portuguese immigrants in the Netherlands (see Lucassen & Penninx, 1997). We reasoned that since neither audience presents an obvious threat to the participants' identity, participants should not be especially motivated to stress their bicultural identity. Instead, they would be expected to respond in terms of the identity that was cued by the linguistic context. As a result, native identification should be enhanced when the questionnaire was in Portuguese, and Dutch identification should be enhanced when the questionnaire was in Dutch.

In addition, we investigated whether personal accountability would modify such identity expressions. We argued that making people personally accountable for their identity ratings would enhance their awareness that an audience was to judge their group membership claims. Thus, accountability should motivate people to protect their personal 'face' by complying with the audience's norms and criteria for group membership. Therefore, participants were expected to identify less strongly with the Portuguese when accountable to a Portuguese audience, in order to make sure they did not make claims the audience considered unwarranted (e.g., claim to be fully Portuguese, while residing in Holland). In a similar way, accountability to a Dutch audience was expected to elicit weaker identification with the Dutch, since criteria such as birthplace or language proficiency would be likely not to allow full membership in the eyes of the Dutch audience. The results were consistent with these expectations: under anonymous conditions native identification was stronger when the native language was used, and Dutch identification was stronger when the Dutch language was used.

A reverse pattern was found for accountable conditions: native identification was weaker when the language was Portuguese, and Dutch identification was weaker when the language was Dutch. In addition, participants were more aware of being seen by the Dutch as minority group members when accountable to a Dutch audience than in any other condition. This latter finding supports the idea that in this condition participants were more aware of the audience's membership criteria, and adapted their identity claims accordingly.

Taken together, the results of these two studies show that people adapt their group membership claims to the social context in which these are voiced. People's expression of their social identity will depend on the nature of the audience, on the identity needs that the audience makes salient and on whether they are personally accountable for their responses. Statements of group identification may thus be viewed as strategic responses to specific (personal and social) identity needs made relevant in a given social context. It follows that the social context and the content of social identities are intrinsically related and cannot be understood without reference to each other.

Effects of Accountability and Social Norms on Group Behaviour

It has already been shown in this chapter that, despite strategic attempts at showing the ingroup in a favourable light in public, low status group members tend to admit their group's inferiority under private conditions (see Ellemers, Van Dyck, Hinkle & Jacobs, 1998). By doing so in front of the ingroup, high identifiers seem to be especially eager to show their fellow ingroup members that the group needs to be improved. This can be taken as an indication that, compared with low identifiers, high identifiers are more prepared to close ranks with the group and struggle for improvement of the status of the group as a whole.

However logical the connection between these judgements and the choice of identity management strategy may appear to be, little has as yet been done to show how those judgements are actually reflected in group members' behavioural efforts at status improvement. In fact, to date, research into people's willingness to exert themselves on behalf of the group has mainly focused on judgements or intentions, little yet being known about actual efforts at improving group status (but see also chapter 9). The lack of evidence regarding the connection between group identification and actual behaviour is the more important since it is not self-evident that differences found regarding judgements and intentions will also result in differential behaviour (Ajzen & Fishbein, 1980; Barreto & Ellemers, 1998a).

In particular, as Barreto and Ellemers (1998a) argue, the social context may render actual displays of behaviour socially costly and therefore subjectively unfeasible (Baumeister, 1982; Deustch & Gerard, 1955). For instance, under conditions of accountability, in order to avoid disapproval by others, people are likely to engage in strategic self-presentation and adopt behaviours that meet the audience's perceived preferences (see also Barreto, Spears, Ellemers & Shahinper, 1998; Ellemers, Van Dyck, Hinkle & Jacobs, 1998; Martin, 1988; Raven & Kruglanski, 1970; Reicher, Spears & Postmes, 1995). In effect, self-presentational concerns are especially relevant in regard to behavioural displays, since these tend to be visible and are thus more vulnerable to social disapproval than privately held attitudes.

In fact, while we argue that anonymity may reduce the extent to which people comply with group norms, work in the SIDE model has shown that anonymity can also increase adoption of group normative behaviour. However, it is important to note that this latter research has not differentiated between low and high identifiers' responses to anonymity manipulations (see chapter 8). In fact, while for high identifiers anonymity may increase salience of group membership, and thereby adoption of pro-group behaviour, for low identifiers anonymous conditions provide the opportunity to disregard the group's norms. Specifically, lowly identified group members may privately wish to disregard the group and work towards their personal status improvement. However, to the extent that this is seen to conflict with the audience's preferences, they may refrain from showing this individualistic behaviour when publicly accountable for their actions. High identifiers, by contrast, are likely to work on behalf of the group in both private and accountable conditions. In fact, when identification with the group is strong, group interests are internalized and adopted as self-interests, through the process of referent informational influence (see Hogg & Turner, 1987b; Turner, 1982; Turner, Hogg, Oakes, Reicher & Wetherell, 1987), and pro-group behaviour is likely to occur independently of context of response.

These predictions were tested by Barreto and Ellemers (1998a). In order to investigate these processes, low and high identifiers' responses to low group status under conditions of anonymity and accountability to the ingroup were compared. In the setting studied, and in all conditions, boundaries between groups were permeable and relative status was unstable, so that both individual and group improvement referred to feasible improvement possibilities. After dividing participants into groups and providing bogus feedback concerning group status, participants were given the opportunity to improve either their own personal standing, or the group's status. A median split on the basis of an identification measure (Ellemers & Mlicki, 1991), made it possible to divide participants into low and high identifiers. Accountability was manipulated by leading participants to believe that responses would be recorded and shared with the remaining ingroup members in a discussion at the end of the experiment. Importantly, participants were told that only behavioural responses were to be recorded by the experimenter. This procedure made it possible to compare privately expressed attitudes with public behavioural choices.

The results showed that low and high identifiers differed in their privately expressed inclinations to work with the group, with high identifiers being generally more willing to exert themselves in favour of the group (as measured by intentions, concerns with self and group improvement, and psychological involvement with the group). However, actual behavioural choices to work on individual or group status improvement also depended on whether responses were anonymous or to be shared with the ingroup. Specifically, high identifiers worked on group status improvement more often than low identifiers when responses were anonymous, whereas when accountable to the ingroup, low and high identifiers' responses did not differ. That is, while high identifiers exert themselves on behalf of the group independently of whether their behaviour is public or not, low identifiers only do so when subject to surveillance by the ingroup. The finding that low identifiers' private inclinations do not correspond to their behaviour in public renders support to the view that self-presentational concerns underlie their public choice of behaviour. The authors were also able to show that perceptions of the group norm were not affected by anonymity manipulations, rendering support to the view that the effect of anonymity may not be linked to differences in the perception of the group norm, but has to be attributed to differences in motivation to follow that norm (see also Ajzen & Fishbein, 1980).

Barreto and Ellemers (1998b) replicated this effect, both with the same forced choice measure and with the separate measure of efforts towards self- and group improvement. In this second study, time taken to read and solve each problem during efforts at status improvement was also measured. It was reasoned that when internal convictions and self-presentational considerations suggested conflicting strategies of action (as when low identifiers are accountable), participants would experience cognitive conflict, which, by itself or through its influence on degree of involvement with the task, would be reflected in longer response latencies (Fazio, 1990). Consistent with predictions, low identifiers, when accountable to the ingroup, showed longer response latencies than participants in any of the remaining conditions. Whether or not this stems from the simultaneous operation of conflicting motivations for low identifiers, this result underlines the fact that low and high identifiers' behaviour, when accountable, corresponds to different underlying psychological processes.

The results of this second study also made it possible to rule out various alternative explanations. Specifically, manipulations of anonymity were found to have no effect on awareness of the group norm, on salience of personal identity or on perceived group efficacy. In sum, both studies showed that degree of identification functions as a predictor of efforts towards group improvement only when choices are anonymous, while perceived acceptability of one's privately held intentions affects the public expression of behaviour. In this way, the results of these two studies underline the importance of both psychological factors (degree of identification with the ingroup) and socio-contextual factors (anonymity versus accountability) as determinants of whether people will be inclined to improve their social status by striving for individual or group status improvement.

In the two studies reviewed above, additional measures revealed that it was clear to all group members that the group preferred them to work together rather than to work individually. In fact, working together with other members of the group is commonly considered a default form of pro-group behaviour. It is however possible that some groups, in some settings, see individual improvement as a good way to achieve high status for the group itself. In such a situation, working on the improvement of each individual separately can correspond to a collectivist strategy, as long as it is done with the aim of improving the group's standing, and to an individualistic strategy if it is done with no concern for the group.

This situation was investigated in a second study by Barreto and Ellemers (1998b), in which the group norm was manipulated. Low and high identifiers were told either that their group preferred its members to work with the group, or that it approved both types of strategy (to work individually or to work with the group). In all conditions, psychological attachment to the group and concerns with group improvement were assessed in private, while behavioural choices were either kept private or made public to the ingroup. Low and high identifiers were expected to differ on their privately expressed attitudes towards the group, independently of the manipulated group norm. As to actual behavioural attempts at status improvement, low identifiers were expected to work with the group only when accountable to an ingroup which preferred its members to work with the group. High identifiers, in turn, were expected to follow the group norm more closely, working with the group when this was seen as the norm, and dividing their efforts between self- and group improvement, when this was normative, irrespective of accountability manipulations.

The results were consistent with predictions. Under anonymous conditions, while low identifiers worked individually irrespective of group norm, high identifiers worked towards status improvement in the way prescribed by the group. When accountable, however, both low and high identifiers worked according to the group norm (for the group, or dividing their efforts between both strategies, depending on the group norm). That is, while high identifiers followed the group norm closely in all conditions, low identifiers only acted according to the norm when accountable to the ingroup. Participants' private responses showed that, independently of norm or context manipulations, high identifiers expressed concern with improvement of the group's position, while low identifiers stated little concern with the group. This supports the view that, independently of the behavioural strategy chosen, the behaviour of high identifiers was intended to improve the group's standing.

The results of this experiment show that although high identifiers are clearly more willing than low identifiers to strive for the improvement of the group's status, they may do so by focusing on their own self-improvement as long as that is seen as normative for the ingroup. In turn, low identifiers may act in accordance with the group norm, either when their behaviour is public, or when the group norm converges with their internal motivations, but they do not do so out of concern with the position of the group.

Conclusions

In this chapter we have reviewed a selection of studies on natural groups as well as laboratory experiments, in order to emphasize the strategic aspects of group members' behaviour in social situations. In conclusion, we will try to illuminate the main theoretical implications of the work we discussed, by considering how these empirical studies relate to the main themes of this volume, namely the context, commitment and the content associated with social identities.

We started by describing how the comparative context in which group members find themselves may confront them with objective and often unpalatable differences between the ingroup and relevant comparison groups. From the research we reviewed, it seems that group members creatively adapt their group ratings to the status quo. That is, they consistently acknowledge established features of the social situation, while strategically biased judgements emerge when rating aspects of the intergroup comparison that are more open to interpretation, and where there is greater room for construal. While empirical evidence has been accumulating with respect to the occurrence of such socially creative group ratings, our argument in the present chapter went one step further, by investigating the psychological process underlying these effects. Specifically, we examined the extent to which group members' responses reflect an internalization of established intergroup differences or should be seen as a form of strategic behaviour. In doing this, we considered possible effects of the expressive (in addition to the comparative) context on group members' responses to the relative standing of their group, by varying the identifiability of their judgements and behaviour.

Inspired by Deutsch and Gerard's (1955) concept of normative influence, we hypothesized that members of disadvantaged social groups may refrain from displaying ingroup favouring judgements not only because they lack confidence in the worth of their group, but also out of fear for social sanctions which their claims of ingroup superiority might elicit. Sensitivity to the outgroup and acknowledgement of the power it possesses forms an important theme within the social identity model of deindividuation effects (Reicher, Spears & Postmes, 1995; Spears & Lea, 1994), which governs the willingness to express behaviour (the 'strategic dimension') in line with a particular identity (the 'cognitive dimension'; see also chapter 8).

A similar argument has been articulated by Melcher (1996a). This author characterized the distinction between anonymous and identifiable group ratings by maintaining that publicly expressed judgements not only speak to the rated object, but also inform the audience about properties of the agent that gives these ratings. In his research, Melcher observed that only anonymous ratings reflected people's personal attitudes, while their public judgements were affected by self-presentational motives stemming from their identification as group members.

In our own research programme we obtained converging evidence that group members' privately held convictions about their group's relative worth are not necessarily expressed in public. We further illustrated how the expressive context may influence group members' responses to their social identity by reviewing research demonstrating that, as is the case in many other domains, there is no one-to-one relation between people's attitudes and their (overt) behaviour. Moreover, we have showed that even people's attitudes (i.e., towards their group) must be understood in relation to the social context in which they are expressed, together with the identity issues it raises. In short, social context, both in terms of the constraints imposed by the social reality of the situation, and in terms of the domain in which behaviour is expressed (privately or publicly and to which audience) is an important factor predicting the nature of such behaviour.

These findings show that the assumption that behaviour simply reflects the contents of our identity and its associated interest is too simplistic, if not idealist. As reflexive beings, we reflect on the consequence of our actions and are able to act strategically, repressing and deferring overt expressions where this avoids conflict or loss of credibility, but perhaps thereby facilitating achievement of our identity-related aims in the longer term.

A factor that is closely related to the longer-term attachment to the group's goals and interests is social identification or 'commitment' to the group. A second conclusion to draw on the basis of our empirical review refers to the crucial role played by group commitment as a moderator of group members' behavioural expression. While various self-presentational models have emphasized the fact that audiences may influence behavioural expression, these different approaches have so far seemed incompatible, in the sense that they either conceive of this as an individual-level process, or specifically address this as a group-level phenomenon. Classic impression management theory (see Baumeister, 1982) has emphasized that social behaviour may contain self-presentational aspects which are intended either to please the audience or to construct an 'ideal' public self, for instance by avoiding blame for negative actions and seeking credit for positive actions (see Tedeschi & Riess, 1981). In doing this, impression management theory has analysed self-presentational behaviour as stemming from lay theories on person perception, while in this literature groups are merely considered as a vehicle for (indirect) self-presentation (Cialdini & Richardson, 1980).

An explicit focus on the group-level aspects of impression management in social behaviour, is provided by the SIDE model (Reicher & Levine, 1994a, 1994b; Reicher, Levine & Gordijn, 1998; Reicher, Spears & Postmes, 1995; Spears & Lea, 1994) as detailed above. This model builds on social identity and self-categorization theories, and particularly the analysis of social influence stemming from the latter ('referent informational influence': Turner, 1982, 1991). However, unlike these theories of the social self, the SIDE model makes explicit the role of strategic presentation of the social self in predicting behaviour, as well as analysing features of the social context that can influence this (for example, anonymity, identifiability). According to this theoretical perspective, self-presentation is determined by the level of self which is salient in a given context, although in practice research in this tradition has tended to focus almost exclusively on social identity (but see Spears, Lea & Lee, 1990), particularly in relation to strategic effects. Moreover, although based on the social identity and self-categorization tradition, in which a strong emphasis is placed on the importance of group identification, the research in this framework has previously failed to distinguish between the effects for high and low identifiers.

The research presented in this chapter makes a substantial contribution in addressing this lacuna, and thus clearly integrates research on more individual and group level forms of self-presentation. It also shows that at the group level, degree of identification is an important factor that determines whether people genuinely act more in group terms, or are engaged in more instrumental and individualistic self-presentation strategies that appear to be group based (see also Noel, Wann & Branscombe, 1995; chapter 2, this volume). As such, these studies enrich both our understanding of level of identity and strategic and self-presentational behaviour, by further demonstrating how the latter is inextricably linked to the former.

Finally, in this chapter we have illustrated the effect of group norms (content of identity) on the behaviour that is displayed. The seemingly paradoxical conclusion that emerged from the empirical work addressing this issue, was that high identifiers may end up working as little with the group as low identifying group members, if that behaviour seems prototypical for this particular group. Thus, although high identifiers consistently behave more in group terms, it is important to note that the specific content of their behaviour depends on the nature of the group's norms (see also chapters 5, 8 and 10). These findings remind us that it is essential not to neglect the contents of the identities we study and the role they have in guiding the process which they 'inhabit'. Whereas some have argued that social identity research has often ignored content at the expense of process, this research again shows that these are closely linked, and that an appreciation of both content and process is necessary to understand the often complex outcomes that constitute social behaviour.

The work reviewed in the present chapter underlines that we cannot rely on attitudinal measures or on expressed intentions in order to predict how group members will behave. While both evaluative judgements and behavioural expressions may be used in a strategic way, we have argued that in natural situations these responses are likely to differ from each other in terms of public accountability, and may therefore elicit different strategic considerations. Specifically, the desire to depict the ingroup favourably may conflict with the desire to avoid sanctionable behaviour. How group members are likely to deal with these conflicting motives and whose sanctions they are most keen to avoid depend on their level of ingroup identification, as we have tried to demonstrate.

One further direction for research is to investigate how strategic behaviour might eventually feed back to inform the nature of identity (Spears, 1995b). Thus far we have used level of identity (personal, group) and level of identification (high, low) as starting points for our analysis to show how these will determine the expression of behaviour in combination with a range of contextual factors. An interesting and important next step would be to investigate how the expression of strategic behaviour might itself transform identity or degree of identification. For example, does having the collective ingroup support to enable one to express group identity, even in the face of identifiability to an outgroup, lead in turn to more collective forms of identification and action? Even low identifiers might ultimately get swept along with a collective force of events, such that their private sentiments towards the group come in time to reflect public behaviour. For this more dynamic appreciation of the relation between identity and behaviour we may need an analysis and a methodology that takes the historical dimension into account (see, e.g., Doosje, Spears & Ellemers, in prep.; chapter 4, this volume).

In the meantime, the present research shows that, despite overt expressions of behaviour that might suggest otherwise, groups do not necessarily accept their lot and internalize inferiority. Although perception may be grounded in social reality, this reality is not pre-given or fixed, but socially produced and reproduced. Groups are continually trying to change as well as reflect this reality, in the process of providing a better reality for them and their members. Future research should help to build up a more complete picture of this process.

7

Categorization, Content and the Context of Communicative Behaviour

Daniël Wigboldus, Russell Spears and Gün Semin

Introduction

Whenever two or more people are divided into groups, positive and negative stereotypical views seem to emerge. For instance, Germans are industrious, Italians are romantic and English are gentle, but also, Germans have bad taste, Italians are sexist and English are stiff. To some extent, the stereotypes we hold are based on our personal experiences with individual members of the groups we stereotype. However, we may also hold strong stereotypical views about groups we have never encountered ourselves. Presumably, stereotypes are not only developed on the basis of personal experience, they may be learned through others as well. This communicative process and especially the subtle but crucial role played by language are central to the present chapter. In keeping with the central themes of this volume, we try to show how the content of stereotyping communicated between people is largely dependent on the communicative context in which they find themselves. More fundamentally, their commitment to the ingroup also defines the perspective from which they view the intergroup context.

Like Allport (1954), who devoted a chapter of his book *The Nature of Prejudice* to the influence of linguistic factors on the process of stereotyping, many other researchers have also acknowledged the importance of linguistic factors to the transmission and maintenance of stereotypes (e.g., Brigham, 1971; Hogg & Abrams, 1990; Maass & Arcuri, 1996; Moscovici, 1981; Park & Hastie, 1987; Tajfel, 1981a). Some have even argued that 'there is no completely non-verbal social stereotyping' (Fishman, 1956, p. 48). Although not everyone shares this extreme view, most researchers agree that linguistic factors do play an important role in the transmission and maintenance of collective stereotypes (see Stangor & Schaller, 1996). After all, for the most part, it has to be language by means of which educators influence the stereotypical views of their pupils (Stephan & Stephan, 1984), parents influence the stereotypes of their children (Epstein &

Komorita, 1966; Fagot, Leinbach & O'Boyle, 1992) and the mass media influence their readers, listeners and viewers (Van Dijk, 1984; 1987).

Research by Anne Maass and her colleagues (e.g., Maass, Ceccarelli & Rudin, 1996; Maass, Milesi, Zabbini & Stahlberg, 1995; Maass, Salvi, Arcuri & Semin, 1989) on the so-called linguistic intergroup bias has led to interesting new insights into the interface between language and stereotyping. The background and basis for this approach is, of course, the robust phenomenon of ingroup bias itself: the finding that in many intergroup contexts people will show a tendency to favour the ingroup over the outgroup, in terms either of their reward allocations or evaluations (Tajfel & Turner, 1979; 1986; see also chapters 2, 4 and 5, this volume). This phenomenon makes explicit what should already be apparent from reading the various chapters in this book, namely that people routinely perceive the intergroup context through the lens of their own group membership. Maass and her colleagues addressed the question of how language, as the medium of communication, and perhaps to a large extent the medium of perception and cognition, might contribute to ingroup favouring processes. In their research they suggest a linguistic mechanism that both parallels the more explicit instances of ingroup bias and, at the same time, provides a subtle mechanism for how such outcomes may come about and be maintained. They argued that communicating stereotypical information leads to systematic biases in the language people use, which in turn may lead to systematic biases in the recipients of this linguistically biased stereotypical information. The use of biased language is thus considered a subtle factor in the transmission and maintenance of stereotypes.

In the research performed so far on this linguistic phenomenon, the communicative context in which participants uttered their linguistically biased messages has been kept constant. That is, participants were asked to describe a stereotypical situation in a communicative context in which the recipient or addressee of their communicative act remained unknown to them. With respect to the communication of stereotypical information, the recipient's characteristics and, especially, group membership ('commitment') are crucial features of the communicative context. That is, conversing with an ingroup member creates a communicative context that is completely different from conversing with an outgroup member. A conversation between an ingroup member and an outgroup member is highly likely to be influenced by the group membership of the communication partners because it defines a mutual difference. In communication between two ingroup members, group membership is unlikely to become salient without the presence of an outgroup (Turner, 1987; chapters 6 and 8, this volume). Thus, in line with self-categorization theory (e.g., Oakes, Haslam & Turner, 1994; Turner, 1985; Turner & Oakes, 1989; Turner, Hogg, Oakes, Reicher & Wetherell, 1987), stereotypes and ingroup favouring motives can be expected to be more salient in an intergroup communicative context, in which the communicator and the recipient come from different groups, than in an intragroup context, in which both communication partners are ingroup members. In line with self-categorization theory principles, stereotypes are not rigid, but flexible and dependent on the social context (e.g.,

Doosje, Haslam, Spears, Oakes & Koomen, 1998; Ellemers & Van Knippenberg, 1997; Oakes, Haslam & Turner, 1994; Spears & Manstead, 1989; Spears, Oakes, Ellemers & Haslam, 1997). In this case the communicative context evoked by the group membership of two communication partners is likely to affect the production of linguistically biased messages, depending on whether an intragroup or an intergroup context is evoked.

In this chapter the linguistic intergroup bias and the influence of recipient characteristics on the communication process are introduced more extensively and discussed in relation to each other. Subsequently, on the basis of self-categorization theory (e.g., Oakes, Haslam & Turner, 1994; Turner, 1985; Turner & Oakes, 1989; Turner, Hogg, Oakes, Reicher & Wetherell, 1987) specific predictions are made about the influence of recipients' group characteristics on the production of a linguistic bias. Moreover, two studies are described that put these predictions to test. Finally, conclusions are drawn.

The Linguistic Intergroup Bias

Despite the fact that most stereotypes are socially shared and passed on from one person to another (e.g., Epstein & Komorita, 1966; Fagot, Leinbach & O'Boyle, 1992; Haslam, 1997; Stephan & Stephan, 1984; Van Dijk, 1984, 1987), relatively little attention has been paid to the interpersonal aspects of stereotyping and the linguistic factors that mediate this process (e.g., Brigham, 1971; Hamilton, Gibbons, Stroessner & Sherman, 1992; Harasty, 1997; Haslam, 1997; Maass & Arcuri, 1996). Although language plays an important role in most stereotyping research, this role is mostly confined to the content of national, ethnic and racial stereotypes in the language of traits (e.g., Katz & Braly, 1933; Linville, Fischer & Salovey, 1989; McCauley & Stitt, 1978; Miller 1982; Park & Judd, 1990; Peabody, 1968) or the organizing function provided by traits in associative networks (e.g., Allport, 1954; Stangor & Lange, 1994). The interpersonal functions of language in the stereotyping process, however, have for the greater part been neglected (Hamilton, Gibbons, Stroesser & Sherman, 1992; Harasty, 1997; Maass & Arcuri, 1996). As a result, little was known about the mechanisms underlying the factors responsible for the linguistic transmission of stereotypes.

However, the development of the Linguistic Category Model (LCM; Semin & Fiedler, 1988) initiated a host of new research in which systematically biased language use is considered an influential interpersonal factor in the maintenance and transmission of stereotypes (for an overview, see Maass & Arcuri, 1992, 1996). To a large extent this research is based on the linguistic intergroup bias hypothesis developed by Maass and her colleagues (Maass, Salvi Arcuri & Semin, 1989), in which the linguistic and cognitive functions of the LCM are used to provide an interface between language and intergroup processes.

An important conceptual and empirical link between overt intergroup discrimination and the linguistic intergroup bias is provided by research demonstrating the tendency for people to attribute the causes of ingroup and outgroup behaviour differently. This refers to the phenomenon whereby group members attribute negative behaviours of outgroups to stable dispositional characteristics, but positive outgroup behaviours to the demands of the situation, with positive ingroup behaviours being seen as more dispositional and negative ingroup behaviour more situationally determined. Echoing research in the person-perception domain on the 'fundamental attribution error' (the tendency to attribute behaviour more to the person's dispositions than to the situation) Pettigrew (1979) dubbed this intergroup phenomenon the 'ultimate attribution error' (see also Hewstone, 1990). The ultimate attribution error forms an important refinement of research on ingroup bias because in many ways it is much more implicit and subtle than previous demonstrations of explicit ingroup favouritism or outgroup derogation. With this manifestation of ingroup bias, perceivers are not directly favouring the ingroup; indeed, it is conceivable that both ingroup and outgroup are judged equally positively. Rather, the bias resides in how these evaluations are interpreted, generalized, seen as intentional, diagnostic and so on. It is important to note that subtlety underscores the power of this bias, because the more subtle it is the less likely are both the targets and the perpetrators to realize that it is being deployed.

The linguistic intergroup bias takes the greater subtlety of the ultimate attribution error a step further, while also drawing on the attribution implications of language use elaborated in this bias. In its original form (Maass, Salvi, Arcuri & Semin, 1989) the linguistic intergroup bias, or LIB, refers to the hypothesis that an ingroup member engaging in desirable behaviour and an outgroup member engaging in undesirable behaviour are described at a relatively high level of linguistic abstraction (e.g., 'The ingroup member is helpful' and 'The outgroup member is aggressive'), whereas an ingroup member engaging in undesirable behaviour and an outgroup member engaging in desirable behaviour are described at a relatively low level of linguistic abstraction (e.g., 'The ingroup member pushes someone' and 'The outgroup member opens the door for someone'). Although all the examples mentioned above may give an appropriate description of a specific desirable or undesirable event, the implicit meaning of each description varies systematically as a function of the level of abstraction of this description. For instance, relative to concrete descriptions, abstract descriptions give more information about the qualities of the subject and less information about the qualities of the specific situation in which the subject finds itself (Maass, Salvi, Arcuri & Semin, 1989, Exp. 3; Semin & Fiedler, 1988, 1992). Thus, in the four examples given above it is implied that desirable behaviour is typical for an ingroup member, while undesirable behaviour is typical for an outgroup member. Specific linguistic devices thus may be used strategically in an intergroup context. That is, depending on their current motivational needs, people may use either a concrete or an abstract linguistic device to describe a particular situation.

Maass, Milesi, Zabbini & Stahlberg (1995) distinguished two distinctive and different strategies or mechanisms that may underlie this biased language use, one based on ingroup protective motivations, and one based on differential expectancies. Based on ingroup protective motives and social identity theory (Tajfel & Turner, 1979, 1986), it may be argued that the LIB serves to maintain a positive ingroup image and therefore a positive self-image, even in the light of opposing evidence (Maass, Ceccarelli & Rudin, 1996; Maass, Milesi, Zabbini & Stahlberg, 1995). That is, when a LIB is exhibited, the desirable behaviour of ingroup members and undesirable behaviour of outgroup members are portrayed as highly diagnostic for those groups. Negative ingroup and positive outgroup behaviours, on the other hand, are portrayed as exceptions to the rule. This way, a positive ingroup image, and therefore a positive self-image, may remain intact.

On the other hand, based on differential expectancies (Maass, Milesi, Zabbini & Stahlberg, 1995), it may also be argued that the LIB derives from the fact that more positive and less negative behaviours are expected from ingroup members than from outgroup members (Howard & Rothbart, 1980). That is, the LIB may rely on the more general mechanism that expectancy-consistent behaviour is described at a higher level of abstraction than expectancy-inconsistent behaviour. After all, expected information by definition is considered to be more stable, typical and diagnostic than unexpected information, and therefore may be more appropriately described in abstract terms. Thus, positive ingroup and negative outgroup behaviours are described in more abstract terms because they are expectancy-consistent, while negative ingroup and positive outgroup behaviours are described more concretely because they are expectancy-inconsistent.

In most intergroup contexts, both explanations will lead to the same predictions because people generally expect more positive behaviours from the ingroup and more negative behaviours from the outgroup (Howard & Rothbart, 1980). In two recent series of experiments (Maass, Ceccarelli & Rudin, 1996; Maass, Milesi, Zabbini & Stahlberg, 1995), however, these alternative explanations were disentangled by orthogonally manipulating both the desirability and the expectancy-consistency of the behaviours. That is, participants were presented with a series of cartoons in which either an ingroup or an outgroup member (northern or southern Italian) showed a specific behaviour. Half the cartoons displayed desirable behaviours and half undesirable behaviours. Moreover, half the cartoons portrayed expectancy-consistent and half expectancy-inconsistent behaviours (typically northern Italian or typically southern Italian). Four descriptions were given underneath each cartoon and participants were asked to select the response that best described the scene.

Results demonstrated that a southern Italian performing typically southern behaviour and a northern Italian performing typically northern behaviour were described at a higher level of abstraction than a southern Italian performing northern behaviour and a northern Italian performing southern behaviour, independently of the desirability of these behaviours (Maass, Ceccarelli & Rudin, 1996, Exp. 2; Maass, Milesi, Zabbini & Stahlberg, 1995, Exp. 1). Thus, in general, expectancy-consistent behaviours were described at a higher level of abstraction than expectancy-inconsistent behaviours. On the basis of these results, Maass, Milesi, Zabbini and Stahlberg (1995) concluded that differential expectancies are sufficient to produce a linguistic intergroup bias.

This does not mean, however, that ingroup protective motives did not come into play at all. In intergroup settings, where the ingroup identity was threatened, the original LIB pattern based on differences in desirability was found (Maass, Ceccarelli & Rudin, 1996, Exp. 2). That is, positive ingroup and negative outgroup behaviours were described at a higher level of abstraction than negative ingroup and positive outgroup behaviours. Thus, it seems that only when motivated did participants show the original LIB. Interestingly, participants in the 'ingroup identity threat condition' showed a linguistic bias based on differences in desirability as well as the general bias based on differential expectancies. Further analyses revealed that these two biases operated independently of each other and were not mutually exclusive (ibid.).

Apparently, there are two distinct processes at play. On the one hand, there is the original linguistic intergroup bias or LIB, based on differences in desirability, which seems to operate predominantly when ingroup identity is threatened. On the other hand, there is a phenomenon based on differential expectancies, which describes the finding that expectancy-consistent behaviours are described at a higher level of abstraction than expectancy-inconsistent behaviours. This differential expectancy mechanism seems to be a much more general phenomenon than the original LIB. In line with this notion, additional research has shown that this mechanism also operates outside a specific intergroup context when expectancies are manipulated at an individual level (Maass, Milesi, Zabbini & Stahlberg, 1995, Exp. 3). Because this latter process seems to be distinct from and independent of the original LIB, theoretically as well as empirically, we propose to refer to this phenomenon as the linguistic expectancy bias, or LEB.

Thus far, strong support for the occurrence of the LIB and the LEB has been found in experimental as well as non-experimental studies, in a broad range of different intergroup contexts (e.g., gender, nations, political parties, sports teams) and in different languages (e.g., English, German, Italian), using closed-ended (multiple choice), as well as open-ended (free response) measures of linguistic abstraction (e.g., Arcuri, Maass & Portelli, 1993; Fiedler, Semin & Finkenauer, 1993; Guerin, 1994; Karpinski & Von Hippel, 1996; Maass, Ceccarelli & Rudin, 1996; Maass, Corvino & Arcuri, 1994; Maass, Milesi, Zabbini & Stahlberg, 1995; Maass, Salvi, Arcuri & Semin, 1989; Rubini & Semin, 1994; Webster, Kruglanski & Pattison, 1997; for overviews, see Maass & Arcuri 1992, 1996). Moreover, the LIB as well as the LEB have been shown to be highly related to other implicit, unobtrusive measures of intergroup discrimination and stereotyping, but not to explicit measures of that kind (Franco & Maass, 1996; Von Hippel, Sekaquaptewa & Vargas, 1997). Findings such as these not only demonstrate the validity of the LIB and the LEB, but also support the notion that linguistic processes such as these operate in an unconscious fashion (Schmid & Fiedler, 1996; Semin & de Poot, 1997).

Communication and Categorization

In most of the experiments performed so far on the linguistic intergroup bias participants were asked to transmit information to an anonymous other partici-pant, who functioned as a recipient. Although there are some forms of communi-cation in which most relevant characteristics of a recipient are completely unknown to the communicator (e.g., when writing a message in a bottle for an unknown rescuer), this kind of communication is quite rare in everyday life. Even in such a remote and indirect form of communication as mass communication, transmitters often try to gain as much knowledge as possible about their audience. In everyday life it is very rare for a communicator to know nothing about a recipient. Even when communicating with a total stranger, information about a recipient's most relevant social category memberships, such as gender, age and origin, is mostly directly available from the recipient's tone of voice, looks or accent. More impor-tant, recipients' perceived characteristics have been shown to play an important role in the communication process, because communicators adjust their messages to their audiences (e.g., Higgins, 1981; Martijn, Van der Pligt & Spears, 1996; McCann & Higgins, 1992). In view of the importance of recipients' characteris-tics on a communicative act, it seems rather surprising that the influence of recipi-ents' characteristics – and in particular recipients' group characteristics – upon the LIB and the LEB effect has never been addressed. To date, the linguistic intergroup bias research has extensively investigated the production of specific strategies that people use in their descriptions of ingroup and outgroup behaviours; however, the addressee or recipient of such communication have remained undefined. The cur-rent chapter addresses precisely this issue.

Early evidence for the influence of recipients' social category membership on communicators' construction of a message came from a field experiment (Kingsbury, 1968) in which a confederate of the experimenter presented himself either as a local or an 'out-of-towner' when requesting directions. Results indicated that re-sponses to the request of the 'out-of-towner' were longer and more detailed than responses to the request of the local. Presumably, participants adjusted their mes-sages to the assumed level of knowledge about the surroundings of the requester. Interestingly, asking for directions in a non-local accent elicited the same results as explicitly identifying oneself as an 'out-of-towner'. Likewise, in an experiment in which middle-aged and elderly adults were asked to describe nonsense figures to someone from their own age group or to a member from the other age group, Kogan and Jordan (1989) found that communicators used more 'ingroup-com-patible' descriptions with members of their own age group than with members of the other group. A final example constitutes of a phenomenon known as 'baby talk' (Ferguson, 1964, 1977) or 'motherese' (e.g., Newport, 1976; Shute, 1987). This phenomenon describes the type of language adults utter when communicat-ing with a small child. 'Baby talk' has been shown to differ from normal language use in numerous ways (e.g., pitch, content, grammar) and, therefore, may be considered a rather extreme example of the influence of recipient's group membership on the way communicators construct a message.

In addition to recipients' social category memberships, recipients' attitudes towards issues relevant to the communicative act have also been shown to influence communicators' messages (e.g., Higgins & Rholes, 1978; Higgins, McCann & Fondacaro, 1982; Manis, Cornell & Moore, 1974; Newston & Czerlinsky, 1974; Sedikides, 1990). In general, it seems that communicators change their messages to be consistent with recipients' attitudes towards a particular subject (for an overview, see McCann & Higgins, 1992). For instance, Manis, Cornell and Moore (1974) asked participants to summarize the main points of a speech concerning the legalization of marijuana to a recipient who either favoured or opposed legalization. Results indicated that summaries addressed to pro-legalization recipients were more favourable to legalization than were summaries addressed to anti-legalization recipients (see also Martijn, Van der Pligt & Spears, 1996).

In summary, there is substantial evidence suggesting that communication is not merely a linear transmission of information, but is strongly influenced by the context of the communication (e.g., Cushman & Whiting, 1972; Grice, 1975; Higgins, 1981; McCann & Higgins, 1992; Rommetveit, 1974; Searle, 1970). In particular, recipients' attitudes and social category memberships have been shown to play an important role in the communication process (e.g., Higgins, 1981; Kingsbury, 1968; McCann & Higgins, 1992).

With respect to the interpersonal transmission of stereotypical views via both the LIB and the LEB phenomena, recipients' social category membership seems to be of especial relevance, and in particular the question of whether a recipient is an ingroup or an outgroup member. After all, the LIB is, by definition, based on differences between ingroup and outgroup members, and the LEB, when referring to expectancies based on stereotypes, also relates to an intergroup context in which group membership plays a crucial role. Here, it is argued that group membership of a recipient may alter the social comparative context in a way that significantly influences the production of both the LIB and the LEB effect. To a large extent, this argument is based on self-categorization theory (e.g., Oakes, Haslam & Turner, 1994; Turner, 1985; Turner & Oakes, 1989; Turner, Hogg, Oakes, Reicher & Wetherell, 1987). First, therefore, a brief summary of this theory is given.

According to self-categorization theory the way people categorize themselves and others is not fixed, but variable, and depends on the social comparative context. With respect to the categorization process, self-categorization theory focuses mainly on the distinction between personal and social identity. Personal identity refers to a process in which the individual is seen as a unique person, distinct from other ingroup members. Social identity, on the other hand, refers to a group self-categorization process in which the individual is defined in terms of his or her shared similarities with members of a certain group in contrast to other groups. For instance, I may consider myself as a unique individual with my own specific characteristics, but I may also consider myself as a psychologist, having things in common with other psychologists and being different from, say, economists.

Self-categorization theory states that whether people categorize themselves and others on the basis of their personal or social identity is to a large extent dependent on the comparative context. More specifically, the type of categorization that becomes salient in a certain context depends on the accessibility of the relevant categorizations, and the fit between these categorizations and the stimulus reality to be represented (Oakes, Haslam & Turner, 1994; Turner, 1985; Turner & Oakes, 1989; Turner, Hogg, Oakes, Reicher & Wetherell, 1987). In line with this reasoning, it has been found that an intragroup context, in which only ingroup members are present, results in more individuation and less group level comparisons and subsequent stereotyping than an intergroup context, in which a clear outgroup is present (e.g., Doise, Deschamps & Meyers, 1978; Doosje, 1995; Haslam, Oakes, Turner & McGarty, 1995; Hogg & Turner, 1987a; Young, 1997).

On the basis of self-categorization theory (Turner, 1985; Turner & Oakes, 1989; Turner, Hogg, Oakes, Reicher & Wetherell, 1987), specific predictions can be advanced regarding the effects of recipients' group membership on the production of the linguistic biases. First, both the LIB and the LEB effect can be expected to be especially strong in an intergroup communicative context, in which either the recipient, the actor being described or both the recipient and the actor are outgroup members. From the research into self-categorization theory (e.g., Doise, Deschamps & Meyers, 1978; Doosje, 1995; Haslam, Oakes, Turner & McGarty, 1995; Hogg & Turner, 1987a), we know that in such an intergroup context a social categorization process is activated in which people's social identities become especially salient. As a result, intergroup processes such as stereotypes and ingroup favouring biases become activated. The increased salience of ingroup favouring motives is likely to manifest itself in an increased LIB effect. After all, the LIB effect is based on ingroup favouring motives, and thus may be expected to be especially prominent in an intergroup communicative context. Likewise, the increased salience of stereotypes is likely to manifest itself in a strong LEB effect, given that the expectancies underlying this LEB effect are derived from these salient stereotypical views. Note that the intergroup context is unlikely to have an effect when an LEB effect is based on expectancies derived from individual characteristics instead of group characteristics. However, in the current context of the interpersonal transmission of expectancies based on group stereotypes, the LEB effect may also be expected to be especially prominent in an intergroup communicative context.

When both the recipient and the actor are ingroup members, an intragroup context results, in which participants are more likely to view themselves and the actor at an individual level instead of a group level. In this case, differences based on group membership and group stereotypes become less salient, and individual characteristics become more important than group characteristics. As a result, both the LIB and the LEB effect are likely to be less pronounced in such an intragroup communicative context (although the LEB can operate at the interpersonal level, here we assume that the expectancy refers to stereotypes at the group level). After all, both group-based mechanisms underlying these biases are less salient in this case.

In the next section, empirical evidence from two recent studies is provided that aimed to test the assumption that both the LEB and the LIB effect are stronger in an intergroup communicative context than in an intragroup communicative context. In the first study, gender groups were used as a basis for categorization to subject the LEB to experimental scrutiny in a communicative context. In the second study, participants' views on an extreme right-wing political topic were utilized to test the LIB in a similar vein.

Empirical Evidence

Study 1: The LEB in a communicative context

In the first study (for a more complete account, see Wigboldus, Spears, Semin & Ham, 1999), participants communicated stereotype-consistent stories and stereotype-inconsistent stories via the computer to either an ingroup or an outgroup recipient. First, participants were asked to think of either a good male or good female friend whom they knew well. They were then asked to communicate four true stories about their friend. In each story, one specific behavioural event had to be described that participants had witnessed their friend engage in. Participants were asked to generate and communicate two stories in which their friend demonstrated typically male behaviour (one desirable and one undesirable example), and two stories in which their friend engaged in typically female behaviour. This resulted in both stereotype-consistent stories (males behaving in a typically male way and females behaving in a typically female way) and stereotype-inconsistent stories (males behaving in a typically female way and females behaving in a typically male way). Before writing the stories, participants were told that later on in the experiment they would have to read their typed messages out loud to another participant. Importantly, it was made clear whether this recipient was to be a male or a female (i.e., an ingroup member or an outgroup member).

The main independent variables in this study were, thus, the group membership of the actor (ingroup versus outgroup), the group membership of the recipient (ingroup versus outgroup) and the stereotype-consistency of the transmitted messages (consistent versus inconsistent). The main dependent variable consisted of the abstraction level of the stories that participants generated. The information each participant transmitted was coded according to Semin and Fiedler's (1988, 1991) Linguistic Category Model and its scoring criteria. That is, every verb (interpersonal as well as non-interpersonal) and every adjective referring to the actor of the story was coded according to the LCM. On the basis of these scores, a mean level of abstraction was computed for each story separately, which could vary between 1 (very concrete) and 4 (very abstract).

Results supported our hypotheses. First, in line with the linguistic-expectancy bias hypothesis, overall, stereotype-consistent information was communicated at a higher level of linguistic abstraction than stereotype-inconsistent information. This result confirms the findings reported by Maass, Milesi, Zabbini and Stahlberg (1995). That is, stereotype-consistent events are described in a way that implies high temporal stability and high diagnosticy. Stereotype-inconsistent events, on the other hand, are described in a way that implies low temporal stability and low diagnosticy, almost like an exception to the general rule. By doing so, communicators increase the chances of keeping stereotypical views intact, even in the light of evidence that denies stereotyping.

Our main hypotheses concerned the moderating effect of the communicative context evoked by the group membership of the recipient on the production of an LEB by a source (see figure 7.1). On the basis of self-categorization theory (e.g., Turner, 1985; Turner & Oakes, 1989; Turner, Hogg, Oakes, Reichter & Wetherell, 1987), it was predicted that the LEB effect would be most prominent in an intergroup context, in which either the actor, the recipient or both are outgroup members. After all, in such an intergroup context a social categorization process is activated in which people's social identities become especially salient (e.g., Doise, Deschamps & Meyers, 1978; Doosje, 1995; Haslam, Oakes, Turner & McGarty, 1995; Hogg & Turner, 1987a). As a result, intergroup constructs such as stereotypes are likely to become prominent. Indeed, evidence for a strong LEB effect was found whenever either the actor, the recipient or both were outgroup members. Presumably, the increased salience of gender stereotypes within an intergroup context led to a strong LEB effect based on expectancies derived from these salient stereotypical views.

Conversely, it was predicted on the basis of self-categorization theory that in an intragroup context, in which both the actor and the recipient are ingroup mem-

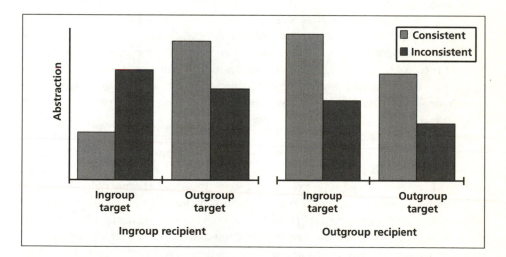

Figure 7.1   Mean level of abstraction as a function of actor group membership, behaviour consistency and recipient group membership

bers, a less pronounced LEB effect will be produced by communicators. After all, in such a context, people are more likely to view themselves and others at an individual level instead of a group level. As a result, group characteristics such as stereotypes become less salient, and individual characteristics become more prominent. Indeed, results indicated no evidence at all for an LEB effect based on gender stereotypes when both the actor and the recipient were ingroup members. Presumably, information based on gender stereotypes was not salient enough in this intragroup communicative context to elicit an LEB effect based on these stereotypes. Interestingly, in this intragroup context, participants even seem to demonstrate the reverse pattern to the LEB. The expectancy-inconsistent information gets communicated at a somewhat higher level of abstraction than the expectancy-consistent information. This reversal seems to run counter to the notion that the LEB is a general phenomenon that applies to groups as well as to individuals (Maass, Milesi, Zabbini & Stahlberg, 1995). However, it could be argued that when people self-categorize themselves and others without reference to groups or group membership, but as individuals, expectancy-inconsistent information is more informative, diagnostic and more salient than expectancy-consistent information (Fiske & Neuberg, 1990; Jones & Davis, 1965; Stangor & McMillan, 1992). Therefore, the expectancy-inconsistent information may be communicated at a higher level of abstraction when people describe others at an individual level, such as in an intragroup context.

No linguistic bias effects due to the desirability of the behaviour in the messages was found in this study. Thus, no support was found for a linguistic bias based on ingroup protective motives or LIB. The positive ingroup and negative outgroup behaviours were not communicated at a higher level of abstraction than the negative ingroup and the positive outgroup behaviours. These 'null-findings' are not surprising, considering the non-competitive context of the current experiment and the basis for categorization that was being used, namely gender. After all, while differential expectancies seem to be sufficient to produce an LEB effect, the LIB only seems to operate in an intergroup context where people are motivated to protect their ingroup identity (Maass, Ceccarelli & Rudin, 1996). Though gender is a very salient ingroup versus outgroup variable, the intergroup context that gender evokes by itself does not seem to be competitive, or ingroup-threatening enough to produce an LIB effect (Basow, 1992).

Because no LIB was found in the current study, the question remains open: to what extent is it possible to generalize from the moderating effect of the communicative context on the production of an LEB effect to the production of the original LIB effect based on ingroup protective motives? It seems likely that the presence of an intergroup context is as important for the production of an LIB effect as it is for the production of an LEB effect. That is, it seems highly likely that the self-categorization influence of the communicative context affects the salience of positive ingroup motivations in a way that is similar to the effect on the salience of stereotypes. However, since the LIB is different from the LEB and has been shown to operate independently of the LEB (Maass, Ceccarelli & Rudin, 1996;

Maass, Milesi, Zabbini & Stahlberg, 1995), we performed a second study to shed some light on the influence of recipients' group membership on the production of an LIB effect.

Study 2: The LIB in a communicative context

The results of the previous study indicated a more pronounced LEB effect in an intergroup communicative context than in an intragroup communicative context. On the basis of self-categorization theory (Turner, 1985) it may be expected that the communicative context elicited by recipients' group characteristics plays the same role with respect to the production of an LIB effect. After all, the increased salience of people's social identities in an intergroup communicative context (e.g., Doise, Deschamps & Meyers, 1978; Doosje, 1995; Haslam, Oakes, Turner & McGarty, 1995; Hogg & Turner, 1987a), should not only lead to increased stereotyping but also to an increased salience of other intergroup processes, such as ingroup favouring biases. Likewise, the increased salience of people's personal identities in an intragroup communicative context should not only lead to decreased stereotyping, but also to a decreased salience of other intergroup processes such as ingroup favouring biases.

Because of our specific interest in an LIB effect, an experiment was designed (for a more complete account, see Wigboldus, Spears, Semin & Ham, 1999) which was based to a large extent on recent American research demonstrating a strong LIB effect (Webster, Kruglanski & Pattison, 1997). In this research, participants' 'pro-choice' or 'pro-life' opinions on abortion rights were used to create a competitive intergroup context in which participants were motivated enough to demonstrate an LIB effect. Note that at the time this research was conducted (1993–4) abortion rights were such a hot issue in North America that people actually got into fights about it. Instead of participants' opinions on abortion rights, we used participants' opinions on the Dutch extreme right-wing slogan 'Full = Full' as a basis for categorization. This slogan implies that the population of Holland is already large enough and that political or economical refugees should not be allowed to seek asylum there. Like the abortion rights issue in North America, the rights of foreigners are a very hot issue in Holland. It was therefore expected that this issue would provide a similar basis for an LIB effect as the abortion rights issue in the USA.

The experiment was run on computers and was described as a study on 'impression formation and communication'. During the first part of the experiment participants filled out a questionnaire consisting of two parts. First, they were asked to give their opinion on a number of political issues. Embedded in this questionnaire was one critical item asking respondents to indicate their opinion on the Dutch extreme right-wing slogan 'Full = Full'. In the second part of the questionnaire, participants were asked to describe two events in which they had influenced the behaviour of someone else. That is, they were asked to generate two behavioural examples of a persuasive interaction with another person.

During the second part of the experiment, participants reviewed some of the information allegedly provided by a former participant. Before reading the two persuasive interaction examples of this actor, participants learned that the actor had either the same or the opposite opinion as they themselves had indicated on the critical 'Full = Full' issue. This randomly assigned difference served as the group membership manipulation. Then, participants read the two persuasive interaction examples allegedly written by the actor. In fact, all participants received the same two examples. In random order they read a desirable behavioural example in which the actor persuades a friend with a flat bicycle tyre to accept a ride home, and an undesirable behavioural example in which the actor persuades a friend to steal a room-mate's credit card.

In the final part of the experiment, participants were asked to communicate both persuasive interaction examples of their actor to a third participant, who joined the experiment at this stage. In addition to the experimental design employed by Webster, Kruglanski and Pattison (1997), participants received the opinion of the alleged recipient on the critical 'Full = Full' issue. Thus, participants learned that the recipients' views on this issue were either the same as or the opposite to their own. This randomly assigned difference served as the recipient group membership manipulation.

The main independent variables in this study were the group membership of the actor (ingroup versus outgroup), the group membership of the recipient (ingroup versus outgroup) and the desirability of the behaviour of the actor in the communicated stories (desirable versus undesirable). The main dependent variable again consisted of the mean level of abstraction of the stories that participants generated.

Results partly supported our hypothesis concerning the LIB. In line with the LIB effect, information about undesirable behaviour of an outgroup actor was communicated at a higher level of abstraction than information about desirable behaviour of an outgroup actor. Contrary to the LIB hypothesis, however, the undesirable behaviour of an ingroup actor was also communicated at a higher level of abstraction than desirable behaviour of an ingroup actor. Nonetheless, results did show an LIB-like effect, in that the difference between desirable and undesirable information was significantly greater when information about an outgroup actor was communicated than when information about an ingroup actor was communicated. In other words, although participants did not show an absolute LIB effect, relatively speaking they did show an LIB-like pattern.

With respect to the communicative context elicited by the group membership of the recipient, results again supported the predictions made on the basis of self-categorization theory (e.g., Oakes, Haslam & Turner, 1994; Turner, 1985; Turner & Oakes, 1989; Turner, Hogg, Oakes, Reicher & Wetherell, 1987). That is, the LIB-like effect described above was only produced in an intergroup communicative context in which the recipient was an outgroup member. In an intragroup communicative context in which the recipient was an ingroup member, no evidence for this LIB-like pattern was found.[1]

With this, evidence is again provided for the notion that the characteristics of a recipient may alter the communicative context in a way that influences the construction of a message. Similar to earlier research indicating that communicators take recipients' characteristics strongly into consideration when formulating a message (e.g., Higgins, 1981; Kingsbury, 1968; Kogan & Jordan, 1989; Krauss & Fussell, 1996; McCann & Higgins, 1992), the current research shows that communicators take recipients' group characteristics into account with respect to the production of an LIB effect. The way in which they do so seems to be very much in line with what could be predicted on the basis of self-categorization theory. The present study thus replicates the findings obtained in the previous study.

Conclusions

The main goal of the present chapter was to investigate the influence of a recipient's group membership on the production of both an LIB and an LEB effect. In general, recipients' attitudes and social category memberships have been shown to play an important role in the communication process because communicators take recipient characteristics such as these strongly into account when construing a message (e.g., Higgins, 1981; Kingsbury, 1968; McCann & Higgins, 1992). With regard to the production of an LIB or an LEB effect, recipients' group membership seems to be of special importance in this respect, because both effects are based on group characteristics and differences between groups.

Two experiments were discussed, which aimed to test the influence of the communicative context evoked by the group membership of the recipient on the production of both the LIB and the LEB effect. Importantly, the production of both linguistic biases was influenced by the intergroup context evoked by the group membership of the recipient in relation to the target and the subject of communication. Results indicated that when the recipient was an outgroup member, communicators produced the expected linguistically biased messages as a function of their stereotypical views or ingroup favouring feelings. However, when the recipient was an ingroup member, no evidence of an LIB effect was found and, with respect to the LEB, linguistically biased messages were produced solely when the

---

[1] Note that the meaning of the communicative context is not quite equivalent for the LIB and the LEB because it does not involve the group membership of the actor. This difference is due to the fact that the LEB effect is based on a main effect for stereotype-consistency, while the LIB effect is based on an interaction between group membership of the actor and desirability of the behaviour. Thus, while the LEB effect may be moderated by group membership of the actor as well as group membership of the recipient, the LIB effect can only be moderated by the group membership of the recipient, because group membership of the actor is involved in the effect itself.

behaviour of an outgroup target was being described. When the behaviour of ingroup targets was described to an ingroup recipient, no LEB effect was produced by communicators. Thus the content of stereotypic communication varied as a function of the communicative context (intragroup versus intergroup). Commitment to the ingroup formed a central feature of this context and the perspective from which it was viewed. Although degree of group commitment was not manipulated, we might expect the contextual effects (intra- versus intergroup) to become stronger the more people identify with their group.

These findings are very much in line with self-categorization theory (e.g., Oakes, Haslam & Turner, 1994; Turner, 1985; Turner & Oakes, 1989; Turner, Hogg, Oakes, Reicher & Wetherell, 1987). That is, the intergroup communicative context evoked by the outgroup membership of either the recipient, the target or both may have activated a social categorization process in which participants' social identities were especially salient (e.g., Doise, Deschamps & Meyers, 1978; Doosje, 1995; Haslam, Oakes, Turner & McGarty, 1995; Hogg & Turner, 1987). As a result, intergroup constructs such as stereotypes and ingroup favouring motives may have been especially prominent pieces of information when either the recipient, the target or both were outgroup members, which is reflected in the production of an LIB and an LEB effect. Conversely, the intragroup communicative context evoked by the ingroup membership of both the recipient and the target may have activated a self-categorization process in which participants were more likely to view themselves and others at an individual level instead of a group level. As a result, group characteristics such as stereotypes may have been less salient when both the recipient and the target were ingroup members, which was reflected in the absence of an LIB or LEB effect.

Although the findings presented in this chapter are supportive of self-categorization theory, it is important to note that in order to conclude that self-categorization processes underlie the current results, we need to demonstrate that category salience plays a mediating role in the processes outlined above. Because category salience was not measured in the current research, our claims about self-categorization processes remain somewhat speculative on the basis of the present results. The current findings should therefore be viewed with some caution. However, these findings do seem to provide further evidence for the important notion that recipients' characteristics and the communicative context evoked by them may play an important role in the communication process (e.g., Higgins, 1981; Kingsbury, 1968; McCann & Higgins, 1992). It is therefore important for future research to take into account the relevant recipient characteristics when studying the production of a linguistic bias.

On a more theoretical level, an intriguing implication of this work is the idea that the intergroup context evoked by the group membership of a recipient may influence the communication of stereotypes at an interpersonal level. As argued before by others (Doosje, Haslam, Spears, Oakes & Koomen, 1998; Ellemers & Van Knippenberg, 1997; Oakes, Haslam & Turner, 1994; Spears & Manstead, 1989; Spears, Oakes, Ellemers & Haslam, 1997), stereotypes and group perceptions should not be seen as fixed 'pictures in our heads' (Lippmann, 1922) but as dependent on relevant aspects of the social context and the perspective of the perceiver. In everyday life, the characteristics of the persons we are communicating with make up an important part of this social context. The research presented in this chapter demonstrates that contextual aspects such as these may even get reflected in the linguistic tools people use to communicate with others. Presumably, not only is the way people perceive social reality highly dependent on the relevant aspects of the social context, but also the way people describe social reality and thereby influence others' perceptions of social reality is dependent on contextual factors. In this way, stereotypes are not only maintained within individuals but also between individuals.

8

Social Identity, Normative Content and 'Deindividuation' in Computer-mediated Groups

TOM POSTMES, RUSSELL SPEARS AND
MARTIN LEA

This chapter reviews a programme of research that has developed around the social identity model of deindividuation effects (SIDE; Lea & Spears, 1991; Postmes & Spears, 1998; Postmes, Spears & Lea, 1998; Reicher, Spears & Postmes, 1995; Spears & Lea, 1992, 1994). In particular, we review intragroup processes in anonymous and identifiable settings in order to advance our understanding of normative influence in groups (see chapter 6 for a related analysis). In developing the theoretical background to this research, we first contrast the analysis of social influence by social identity and self-categorization theories with classical approaches to group influence (i.e. in small face-to-face groups). In addition to examining social influence in the group, we use the SIDE framework to consider related issues of stereotyping, ingroup favouritism and attachment to the group. Although we have studied these issues in the domain of computer-mediated communication (CMC), our approach also raises more basic theoretical questions of how the general features of this medium can moderate processes of social influence and group behaviour, sometimes in somewhat surprising and paradoxical ways. In the process, we add further empirical flesh to the themes of context, commitment and content that are central to this volume. Categorization in and commitment to groups provide the basic explanatory unit, in line with social identity principles. In line with self-categorization theory, content of group norms defines the direction of conformity and helps to explain the diversity of social behaviour that can follow. Finally the context of communication (face-to-face versus computer-mediated), forms the social setting

The authors are very grateful to Bertjan Doosje and Naomi Ellemers for their helpful comments on an earlier version of this chapter. This research has been made possible by a fellowship of the Royal Netherlands Academy of Arts and Sciences to Tom Postmes, and by a project grant from the British Council/NWO Anglo-Dutch Joint Scientific Research Programme to Martin Lea and Russell Spears.

which can accentuate or attenuate these processes. The SIDE model is, above all, an attempt to elaborate these contextual implications of social identity theory (Spears, 1995b), particularly those relating to anonymity and identifiability. CMC constitutes a ready-made externally valid context in which we can simultaneously examine and apply these theoretical ideas.

Social identity theory and self-categorization theory have hitherto had a fairly limited impact on studies of processes in small groups and of group dynamics. The small group literature has traditionally investigated processes within groups consisting of a few co-present individuals engaged in carrying out a shared task or fulfilling a common goal (e.g., Forsyth, 1990; Levine & Moreland, 1990; McGrath & Kravitz, 1982). By contrast, social identity theory has traditionally focused on intergroup relations and social categories characterized by less interpersonal contact than small groups (Tajfel, 1978a, 1982b). Self-categorization theory has addressed small group issues more directly, for example with research of group polarization and cohesiveness (e.g., Hogg, 1992; Turner, 1991; Turner, Hogg, Oakes, Reicher & Wetherell, 1987). Indeed, self-categorization theory has laid the theoretical foundation for an analysis of social influence exerted by factors (social identity, identification and group norms) which are present in small groups and social categories alike. Nevertheless, the empirical investigations of SCT and SIT have been geared more to processes at the level of social categories than to groups of a smaller size (Moreland, Hogg & Hains, 1994).

Possible reasons for the difficulty in wedding SIT/SCT with small group research may be that the levels of analysis for the two are difficult to reconcile, and that the different paradigms in which they have been studied, along with the theoretical assumptions underlying them, have not helped this rapprochement. The small group field has tended to define groups in terms of composition and structure, interpersonal bonds and roles (e.g., Levine & Moreland, 1990). Such a vision of the group has stimulated examination of social influence as exerted by (inter-) individual factors in interaction, such as personality characteristics, similarity and interpersonal attraction (Hogg, 1992). As a consequence, social influence is studied as a 'change in individuals induced by individuals' (Kiesler & Kiesler, 1969, p. 26). These individual and interpersonal factors are most apparent, and indeed studied, in co-present and face-to-face groups of a small size (typically two to seven members). Moreover, the emphasis on inter-individual sources of social influence suggests that larger social categories (or groups whose members are dispersed) exert either less social influence, or influence of a different nature.

In contrast, SIT assumes that 'The three aspects of group membership . . . – the cognitive, the evaluative and the emotional – can be made to apply equally well to small groups and to large social categories' (Tajfel, 1978a, p. 29). This assumption has been developed in SCT, which argues that social influence results from 'the transformation of individuals into a psychological group' (Turner, 1991, p. 160). What is proposed is that when a shared social identity becomes salient in a small group, members expect to act in unison and in line with shared ingroup norms derived from this common identity. Embedded in this analysis is the assumption that social influence is exerted by factors at the group level. Indeed, SCT argues that many characteristics of small groups at the individual level (such as attraction among group members) are caused by identification with the group as an entity, rather than vice versa, as small group researchers have argued (Hogg, 1992; Turner, 1991).

A central question then becomes under what conditions and in what research paradigms a social identity becomes salient within a small group of people. The self-categorization theory analysis of salience focuses on the 'accessibility' and (comparative and normative) 'fit' of the groups or social categories implicated to explain when a certain social identity will become salient (Oakes, 1987). This analysis is particularly tailored to suit intergroup comparisons, however, because an assessment of comparative fit requires that an implicit or explicit intergroup comparison must be made for a group identity to become salient. Yet, in intra-group contexts it is not always apparent what the relevant outgroup is, why a comparison would be relevant and functional for group members, or why a par-ticular ingroup identity might become more 'accessible'.

The present analysis focuses on an additional process, suggested by the SIDE model. Building on Reicher's (1982, 1984, 1987) analysis of collective behaviour, the model examines the consequences of being able to identify and individuate each member of the group (as is the case in most group dynamics research on small face-to-face groups). The reasoning in the SIDE model is that individuation of group members within a group may undermine the salience of possible social identities. This is because individuation entails making distinctions between group members deflecting from the common basis of the group, thereby undermining its unity (Spears, Lea & Lee, 1990). Individuation within a group may well contribute to interper-sonal influence of group members (e.g. social pressure due to accountability in a face-to-face encounter; see Barreto & Ellemers, 1998a). However, it can at the same time undermine influence deriving from the cognitive representation of the group (Postmes & Spears, 1998; Turner, 1982). This cognitive representation of the group has greater influence when people cannot individuate each group member ('deindividuation'[1] or, more accurately, 'depersonalization'), because the entitativity of the group is accentuated under such conditions. Moreover, 'deindividuation' within a small group should cause its members' actions to be seen as representative of the group, rather than typical of the specific individual, and thereby foster the development of a group norm through social interaction within the group. In sum, according to the SIDE model, the social influence exerted by factors at the social level in small groups is felt especially when people are 'deindividuated'.

In line with this analysis, the present chapter is primarily concerned with the power of anonymity to enhance the salience of a group identity. This is sometimes referred to as the cognitive aspect of the SIDE model because it has consequences for the level of identity or self-categorization activated or enhanced. However, the SIDE model also has a second 'strategic' component that refers to the conditions

---

[1] We use deindividuation here in the sense of the SIDE model, simply to refer to a lack of individuation, and not to imply anything about self or self-awareness, as in the traditional deindividuation literature.

facilitating the expression of behaviour once a given identity is rendered salient. This is particularly relevant in conditions where certain behaviour might be judged punishable by an outgroup or powerful authority figure and where responses may be accountable to this audience. However, this aspect of the SIDE model is less relevant to the present discussion (see Reicher, Spears & Postmes, 1995; Spears & Lea, 1994; chapter 6, this volume).

The cognitive effects of anonymity specified in the SIDE model are not elaborated in traditional statements of SCT, and, indeed, contrasting inferences from those of SIDE have been made on the basis of this theory. This contrast is particularly relevant within the context of the group polarization paradigm. Self-categorization theory explains polarization in terms of conformity to a prototypical but extremitized group norm (Turner, 1987, 1991; Wetherell, 1987). Some have claimed that the co-presence of group members (rather than isolation and anonymity) can serve to enhance group salience and group polarization (Abrams, Wetherell, Cochrane, Hogg & Turner, 1990). Along with the earlier explanations of group polarization effect, these claims suggest that there is powerful social influence at the group level in the co-present small groups typically deployed in the group polarization paradigm. Yet evidence for the SCT account of polarization has been most forthcoming in studies in which the intergroup context was made salient (Hogg, Turner & Davidson, 1990; Turner, Wetherell & Hogg, 1989; Van Knippenberg & Wilke, 1988; Van Knippenberg, de Vries & Van Knippenberg, 1990). Studies that have investigated polarization in the traditional (intragroup) contexts have not been able to demonstrate reliable polarization. It has been suggested by self-categorization theorists that 'members of such ad hoc groups are unlikely to feel much cohesiveness or sense of identity' (McGarty, Turner, Hogg, David & Wetherell, 1992, p. 16).

According to the SIDE model, the archetype of the small group of co-present individuals in a meeting may be precisely the paradigm to avoid if one wants to study the strength of social influence exerted by social identities and group norms. In such traditional small groups, individual idiosyncrasies are more likely to exert influence on the group processes. In contrast, paradigms in which group members do not meet face-to-face provide precisely those conditions predicted to maximize social influence exerted by social norms and social identities, according to the SIDE model. People are not always physically present in the groups and teams to which they belong, and group members do not spend all their time looking each other in the eye. Indeed, advances in communications technology mean that this is less and less the case. We are often confronted with an entirely different class of social group: groups bound together only by the use of CMC technology. And yet these non-present groups, or 'virtual communities', have a real and strong impact on participants, and sometimes perform important social functions for them (Baym, 1995; Van Dijk, 1997; Wellman, 1997).

Traditional theories of social influence in groups would suggest that the inherent anonymity in CMC make it an inappropriate medium for social influence, providing only a degraded version of the full richness of group life in the flesh. Although CMC is not absolutely anonymous, it has been argued that group members are much more individuated in person than as a 'name@somewhere' (Kiesler, Siegel & McGuire, 1984) so that in CMC there is a greater chance that people are not seen or paid attention to as individuals. However, in contrast to the SIDE model, this notion has been developed by influential theorists to imply a weakening of social influence in CMC. They have argued that the communicators' awareness of themselves as engaged in social interaction with an audience is hindered, so that in extreme cases of 'submergence' in CMC the communicator is deprived of awareness of the individual identity, in other words deindividuated (Jessup, Connolly & Tansik, 1990; Kiesler, Siegel & McGuire, 1984). Deindividuation in its traditional usage implies a reduced responsiveness to social norms (Diener, 1980; Festinger, Pepitone & Newcomb,1952; Prentice-Dunn & Rogers, 1989; Zimbardo, 1969). The implication is that CMC is a medium in which social influence is decreased.

The theory of 'normative influence' (Deutsch & Gerard, 1955) also argues that group influence depends on social pressure from others, and this pressure can best be exercised when groups members are identifiable and thus accountable to the group for their responses. Social impact theory (Latané, 1981) extends the theory of normative influence, and suggests that social influence will increase with the 'immediacy' of its members (their proximity in space or time). Short, Williams and Christie (1976) refer to a closely related concept of 'social presence'. Identifiability, as opposed to anonymity, would be expected to enhance immediacy and social presence and thus facilitate social influence. Similarly, theories of the group based on interpersonal attraction (Lott & Lott, 1965) or interdependence (Lewin, 1948/ 1997) of group members suggest that face-to-face interaction should strengthen the interpersonal bonds that serve to transmit social influence, whereas isolation and anonymity should weaken them.

In summary, in these theories anonymity in the group is argued, either explicitly or implicitly, to weaken social influence by and within the group. In contrast, the SIDE model would predict that the potential for deindividuation in such anonymous groups makes it precisely the context in which strong social influence is exerted by factors at a higher social level, in particular by social norms. In this sense, CMC provides the ideal paradigm in which to study meta-theories of the group and social influence. However, before moving on to CMC we must begin by re-examining classical deindividuation research. Although this theory has traditionally been used to explain large-scale collective behaviour, its invocation to explain (the lack of) social influence in CMC make it central to the present analysis of behaviour in small groups.

A Foundation for the SIDE Model: Deindividuation in Small Groups

Deindividuation is one of social psychology's most influential concepts. Although the concept has developed over time, successive generations of theorists have proposed that deindividuation is a psychological state of decreased self-evaluation, causing anti-normative and disinhibited behaviour (Diener, 1980; Prentice-Dunn & Rogers, 1989; Zimbardo, 1969). Deindividuation appears to be an empirically well-established phenomenon, and receives support in all major textbooks (e.g., Baron & Byrne, 1994; Deaux & Wrightsman, 1995; Feldman, 1995; Forsyth, 1990; Franzoi, 1996; Lippa, 1994; Lord, 1997; Sabini, 1995; Taylor, Peplau & Sears, 1994). Illustrative of the acceptance of the theory and the robustness of the effect, the concept has also been used to account for genocide (Staub, 1996; Staub & Rosenthal, 1994), and has been admitted as legal grounds for extenuation in murder trials (Colman, 1991).

The core of deindividuation theory is embedded in the ideas of some of the earliest scholars of social psychology, Gustave Le Bon (1895/1995) and Gabriel Tarde (1890/1921). These theorists wondered what causes the crowd to run amok, or what causes large assemblies to be persuaded by their leaders. Their answers revolve around a basic propensity for collective action based on suggestibility and imitation, which is caused by the submergence and anonymity in the crowd and a concomitant loss of awareness of individual identity. Reflection about the consequences of normally restrained actions diminishes when the individual is immersed in the crowd, and thereby rendered anonymous and unaccountable. These early theories of the crowd propose that anonymity can be associated with the breakdown of traditional values and norms. This simple idea has had a pervasive impact on social science and in society (Reicher, 1996a), and was reintroduced into mainstream social psychology in the form of deindividuation theory (Festinger, Pepitone & Newcomb, 1952). Like those early crowd theories, deindividuation theory proposes that anonymity causes the loss of a sense of self, termed deindividuation,[2] and thereby fosters anti-normative and disinhibited behaviour (Postmes & Spears, 1998; Reicher, Spears & Postmes, 1995).

Many experiments and studies have examined the deindividuation hypothesis over the past thirty years, reflecting the theory's popularity and status. A quantitative meta-analysis reviewed this body of research in order to evaluate deindividuation theory's most important claims (Postmes & Spears, 1998). Figure 8.1 graphically represents the results of the meta-analysis. In this graph, positive effect sizes indicate that a study supports deindividuation theory, while negative effects indicate the opposite. Such a graph is useful for visually inspecting the results of a meta-analysis, because the plotted effects are usually funnel-shaped around the average effect size. Figure 8.1, however, does not have this characteristic funnel shape: the average effect appears to be quite close to zero (it is actually $r = 0.09$) and effects are scattered across the whole graph (both statements are supported by the quantitative analysis; see Postmes & Spears, 1998, for details).

---

[2] Please note that this use of the phrase 'deindividuation' is different from the way used by SIDE. In SIDE, deindividuation refers to the diminished capacity to individuate one's environment, increasing attention to social dimensions of the self, whereas in classical deindividuation theory it refers to a loss of awareness of the self (Diener, 1980).

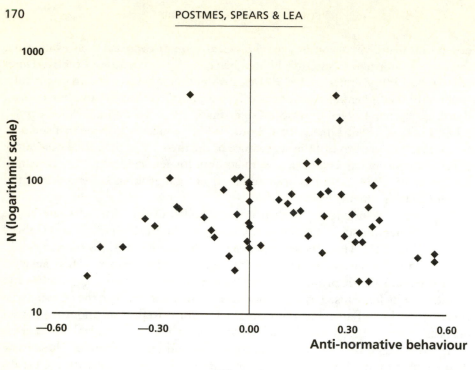

Figure 8.1   Funnel graph of effect sizes plotted by number of participants on a logarithmic scale

The weak support for deindividuation theory appears to be widespread. For example, studies in which self-awareness is lowered directly manipulate the theoretical construct that is supposed to underlie the deindividuated state, and therefore provide the best test of the theory (Diener, 1980). In these studies, however, support for deindividuation theory was absent ($r = 0.01$). Other manipulations of 'deindividuation' were equally unsuccessful. Differences in the operationalization of anti-normative behaviour also did not account for the lack of support. In sum, no support was found for deindividuation theory's two major claims: that deindividuation causes anti-normative and disinhibited behaviour, and that reduced self-awareness would underlie the deindividuated state.

Our meta-analysis revealed one predictor able to explain a large proportion of the variance in effects, and that was the situational norm. Unlike general social norms, such as laws or universal customs, a situational norm is specific to the participant groups in the study or to the experimental context. Contrary to the deindividuation theory prediction, however, the participants who are 'deindividuated' complied more with this situational norm. Thus, deindividuation increases the sensitivity to situational norms, and the responsiveness to cues indicating what is appropriate and desirable in a particular context. This increased responsiveness to situational norms was demonstrated in studies where group members were made anonymous to each other, as well as in studies that induced deindividuation via other means, such as direct reductions of self-awareness. The meta-analytic evidence is confirmed by experimental findings from several sources. For example in an experiment by Johnson and Downing (1979), participants were made anonymous by means of masks and overalls reminiscent of the Ku-Klux-Klan or by means of nurses' uniforms. Similar to the earlier studies of Zimbardo and others, participants were required to deliver electric shocks to a confederate, which was taken as a measure of aggression and anti-normative behaviour. Although compared to the control condition participants shocked somewhat more when dressed in the Ku-Klux-Klan uniforms, they actually shocked less when dressed as nurses. This finding is in line with a normative explanation, because participants appeared to be sensitive to normative cues associated with their clothing.

Deindividuation theory cannot readily account for the remarkable phenomenon that deindividuated individuals are apparently more responsive to the group's norms, and indeed most theories of social influence in small groups would have difficulty reconciling situations of decreased accountability with an increase in social influence. However, as elaborated above, the SIDE model predicts precisely this effect, provided that the group members share a common social identity.

This idea has some paradoxical implications for social influence in CMC. Although CMC is a radically different context from the crowd, people have suggested it is a cold and 'impersonal' medium partly because of its deindividuating potential. And yet if we believe the results of our meta-analysis are valid, the notion that deindividuation conditions foster negative or anti-normative behaviour are somewhat discredited. It follows that to the extent that people are deindividuated in CMC, they may actually become more responsive to the group and its norms. In this case this medium could be a vehicle for a cohesive and influential group life, assuming that communicators share a common identity or have (or develop) a clear group norm. Under such circumstances, the CMC medium may be far from cold and impersonal, but may be highly socially engaging and even intimate (Lea & Spears, 1995; Walther, 1996). Furthermore, if the medium is experienced as impersonal, this may reflect the operation of a local norm, rather than being a generic property of the medium. There are various examples such as electronic communities, cyberlove and other icons of virtual togetherness that would appear to support these counterclaims: 'virtual' groups do not seem to be any less cohesive or warm in general. A more systematic programme of research has been developed over recent years to investigate when and how interaction in CMC may actually epitomize social phenomena previously thought to be the province of 'real' face-to-face groups.

The propositions of the SIDE model have been tested mostly in studies of the effects of deindividuation and anonymity in computer-mediated groups (but see also Reicher, Spears & Postmes, 1995; and chapter 6, this volume). As elaborated above, the assumption is that visually anonymous CMC (and anonymity in general) renders individuals less susceptible to factors in the social sphere, such as the influence of norms, the influence of stereotypes and prejudice, ingroup favouritism, and attraction to those with whom one interacts. The research conducted on the SIDE model over the last decade has investigated each of these propositions. In keeping with the themes of this volume, these issues are united by a common focus on the content of identity and the ideal context for making identity salient and promoting group behaviour (Postmes & Spears, 1998; Reicher, Spears & Postmes, 1995; Spears & Lea, 1994; see chapter 6, this volume). We will examine the central findings for each area now in turn.

The Influence of Group Norms

As proposed above, the anonymity in deindividuation experiments enhances participants' susceptibility to group norms that are specific to the situation in which the study is conducted. Therefore, one may expect that the influence of group norms in computer-mediated interaction is strong when this medium is relatively anonymous or deindividuated. This prediction was confirmed in a series of studies. Spears, Lea and Lee (1990) conducted an experiment in which students discussed a range of politically relevant topics via a simple CMC system, which allowed them to interact synchronously by typing in their messages on a keyboard. The participants in this study were either separated from each other, or they were co-present in the same room and able to have visual contact. In addition, these participants were either made aware of their shared social identity as members of a superordinate group (psychology students) with strong norms (they received feedback about politically progressive student norms), or they were addressed as individuals throughout the experiment. In line with expectations, participants complied most strongly with the group norms when they were isolated and when their shared social identity was made salient, and less so when they were identifiable or when their individual identity was salient. These findings were also supported by content analysis of the actual messages exchanged (Lea & Spears, 1991).

Thus, anonymous CMC appears to foster a stronger influence of group norms. This finding was corroborated by a study in which the nature of group norms was experimentally induced. Using an experimental method by which group norms were 'primed' (see Bargh & Barndollar, 1996), Postmes and colleagues activated a norm for efficiency versus a pro-social norm in groups of three or four students (Postmes, Spears, Sakhel & De Groot, 1996). These students were then asked to solve a dilemma by communicating via a CMC system. During the interaction they were either personally anonymous to the extent that they were identified by a personal code only, or visually identifiable because their picture and that of other group members were displayed on the screen. As expected, the social norm that was induced had a strong impact on the style of interaction and the decisions made when group members were relatively anonymous. When they were identifiable by means of portrait pictures, in contrast, they did not comply with the experimentally induced norm.

A follow-up study replicated this finding (Postmes, Spears, Sakhel & De Groot 1996). Moreover, the follow-up showed that participants actually inferred the experimental norm from their interaction: they saw their group as more task-oriented when anonymous than when identifiable. It was also demonstrated that this process of establishing group norms occurs through interaction: only half the participants in a group were primed with the group norm in this study. The other half, who were originally neutrally primed, complied just as much with the norm by the end of the discussion as those who were primed with the task-oriented norm, confirming that interaction serves to bolster and communicate group norms. In other words, the transfer of the norm to the neutrally primed group members confirms that there is an active social influence process operating here, and not simply an individual behavioural priming effect. Moreover, this study provided direct evidence concerning the mediating process involved. It was reasoned that if anonymity enhances the salience of the group then people should report higher levels of identification with the group in the anonymous condition, and that this enhanced attachment to the group would account for the social influence effects. A mediational analysis supported this prediction.

A further study directly compared anonymous CMC, identifiable CMC and face-to-face communication in a group decision-making task (Postmes & Spears, 1997b). The group decision was to choose between applicants for a university lecturer position. Each participant was given a list of applicants' characteristics, which was composed such that one candidate (B) stood out as the best. This 'best' choice was misleading, however, because not all of the best applicant's (A) characteristics were given to each decision-maker. This is known as a 'hidden profile', where some of the characteristics of applicants are 'unshared', meaning that they are not given to each person in the group. Because of this uneven distribution, exchange of characteristics is vital to arrive at a good group decision, and the proportion of groups to reach a correct decision is a good measure of decision quality (Stasser & Titus, 1985).

Participants had to negotiate their choice, after being given these incomplete descriptions. Indeed, participants initially chose the wrong candidate (B), but after group negotiation things became better.[3] As in the earlier studies, the group norms were varied. It was predicted that a poor decision would be made in groups with a norm to reach consensus, because these groups would value unshared information less and shared information more. This line of reasoning corresponds to what would be predicted from a groupthink perspective (Janis, 1982), which identifies a strong drive for consensus as the main culprit for ignoring disconfirming evidence, with potentially disastrous consequences. In contrast, in groups with a norm for

[3] A special procedure was used to ensure that people exchanged the characteristics of each candidate, because previous research showed that groups are not particularly well equipped to do so.

critical enquiry, dissent would be tolerated and applauded. In such a critical group atmosphere the unshared information – necessary to reach a 'correct' group choice – should be valued highly and taken into account. In order to activate these group norms, prior group tasks were carried out that were pretested and known to foster a critical ambience (discussion of a controversial issue) or a more consensual and collaborative atmosphere (a creative joint task).

After the induction of a group norm, groups sat down to choose a candidate via a CMC system. During the interaction, participants were either isolated in separate cubicles and identified by a code number, rendering them relatively anonymous, or were co-present in the same room during the entire interaction, rendering them relatively identifiable.

Results showed that in isolated CMC groups the group norms had the predicted effect: critical norms improved the quality of group performance compared with consensual norms. Moreover, participants valued the unshared information more than the shared information in the critical norm condition, but not in the consensus norm condition. Thus, groups conform to group norms as expected in the isolated CMC condition and in the face-to-face condition. In contrast, participants in the co-present CMC conditions did not conform to the group norm, and showed a slight tendency to do the opposite. Their decisions were not improved when the group had a critical norm, and they valued unshared information no more than when they had a consensus norm. It appears that despite the co-presence of group members, and the relative abundance of visual and social cues, the co-present CMC groups experienced less norm-based influence than the isolated CMC members did.

What, then, may we conclude from all these findings with respect to the influence of group norms? The traditional accounts of behaviour in computer-communication is that sensitivity to social norms and standards is reduced by the lack of social cues and by increased 'deindividuation' in the classical negative sense. The anonymity in CMC also suggests a reduced accountability, freedom from social constraints and a reduced need to comply or conform. The findings, however, suggest quite the opposite: in line with the predictions of the SIDE model it seems that participants are more responsive to social norms and social cues in visually anonymous CMC.

The traditional view of social influence within small groups helps to explain this apparent paradox. Traditionally, 'normative influence' in the group has been equated with social pressure to conform, in order to gain the approval and avoid the sanctions of other group members (see Deutsch & Gerard, 1955; Turner, 1991). Here, normative refers not so much to the content of the group norm, but to the prescriptive or injunctive imperative to comply with a powerful group, which is contrasted with true 'informational' influence (Deutsch & Gerard, 1955). In these terms, the freedoms and reduced accountability associated with CMC would indeed be predicted to reduce group influence (see also chapter 6). However, we argue that this view of influence overestimates the degree to which norms are externally imposed, and underestimates the degree to which people desire to belong to a group and to behave appropriately within a specific group context. According to self-categorization theory, true group influence reflects this internal and willing process of conformity to one's group identity (as part of the self), and not compliance with the group defined as external to the self. The argument that visual anonymity, in enhancing group salience, promotes conformity to the group norms along these lines is sustained. Conversely, when people are able to differentiate each person individually in computer-based interaction, they appear motivated to set themselves apart and to differentiate their position from group norms (Spears, Lea & Lee, 1990; Postmes, Spears & Lea, 1998). Thus, it seems that individuation motivates people to assert individual identity, while anonymity is actually the setting that maximizes the self-imposed constraint of social norms.

In sum, anonymous CMC appears to enhance the influence of social factors within the group. With regard to the discrepancies between groups, CMC has been argued to dilute differences between high and low status social groups, and to render communicators truly 'colour-blind'. However, if visual anonymity heightens the impact of social norms within a group, it is quite likely that it may also accentuate the perceived differences between groups. Self-categorization theory argues, after all, that the salience of group identity is the product of at least an implicit comparison with a relevant outgroup (Turner, 1987). In the following section we consider the intergroup context more explicitly, and see whether anonymity in CMC might actually stimulate ethnocentrism and the stereotyping of other groups rather than deflecting from the differences between groups.

Stereotypes, Prejudice and Ingroup Favouritism

Many marginalized groups have embraced the Internet as a perfect forum for their activities to promote social change. The possibilities of CMC have raised hopes that traditional social relations and inequalities would be less influential in the emerging virtual communities (Balka, 1993; Haraway, 1990; Mantovani, 1994; Myers, 1987). The capacity to democratize and to empower the oppressed and powerless has been ascribed to new technology such as CMC (Herring, 1993). This 'equalization phenomenon' (Dubrovsky, Kiesler & Sethna, 1991) is said to occur as a result of the relative anonymity of CMC. For example, some influential theorists have argued that: 'Because it is harder to "read" status cues in electronic messages than it is in other forms of communication, high status people do not dominate the discussion in electronic groups as much as they do in face-to-face groups' (Kiesler & Sproull, 1992, p. 61). Thus there are high hopes that anonymity in CMC will reduce intergroup differences, because CMC renders all equal. Are these hopes warranted?

One striking aspect of the social psychological literature on ingroup bias is that the demonstration of ingroup favouritism has perhaps been most convincing precisely in minimal conditions that resemble this proposed Mecca of equality. Bias

has been argued to occur in the minimal group paradigm because the groups involved have little history and no obvious conflicts of interests (e.g., Diehl, 1990;
Mullen, Brown & Smith, 1992; Turner, 1981). One further property of this paradigm is that the allocations are made to anonymous members of the own and other
groups. Spears (1995a; see also Reicher, Spears & Postmes, 1995) demonstrated
that anonymity accentuates ingroup favouritism, and argued along the lines of the
SIDE model that the 'minimal' settings of this paradigm can be quite maximal, by
focusing attention on intergroup rather than interpersonal differences (see also chapter
2). Discrimination is perhaps the archetypal and, arguably, the only available 'group'
response in the minimal group situation. However, this effect was also sensitive to
the content of groups norms concerning discrimination, with ingroup favouritism
being eliminated under anonymity when a fairness norm was primed (see also
chapter 5). Unless such normative content is specified, ingroup bias may be the
most likely group-level response in the minimal situation. Indeed, in a series of
studies, Melcher (1996) also found effects of enhanced ingroup bias under anonymity, and demonstrated that when group members (of both in and outgroup)
are made identifiable, ingroup favouritism decreases.

Waldzus, Schubert and Frindte (1997) confirmed that this finding can be extended to electronic groups in a study conducted on the Internet. They allocated
people to imaginary groups as is customary in the minimal group paradigm. They
then gave these groups a shared group symbol to make their group identity salient,
or merely told them they were allocated to a certain group. Thus, in one condition
the shared identity was strengthened by a symbol, while in another condition no
symbol was available. Participants then had to judge products made by people
from the own group and people from another group. During these ratings, individuals were either consistently addressed as individual participants or as group
members. Although this latter manipulation was referred to as a deindividuation
manipulation, more precisely it could be seen as a further device for making individual versus group identity salient (cf. Spears, Lea & Lee, 1990). According to
the SIDE model, the anonymity associated with the Internet should operate to
deindividuate the participants and elicit the most group-level response in the condition where participants had a common symbol and were addressed as group
members. In line with predictions, they showed stronger ingroup favouritism here
than in any other condition.

These findings suggest that, despite the anonymity offered by CMC, people still
derogate other groups. In fact, as the results of the earlier studies would seem to
confirm, other things being equal, anonymity may actually exacerbate ingroup
favouritism. While this is suggestive of increased social inequity in CMC, further
evidence of this in natural groups was obtained in a research investigating gender
categories in this technology.

The small group literature has documented many differences between men and
women in face-to-face group discussions. Research has demonstrated gender differences in productivity (Wood, 1987), non-verbal behaviour (Hall, 1984) and
socio-emotional and task behaviour (Anderson & Blanchard, 1982; Carli, 1982;

Eagly, 1987). It appears from these reviews that males on average take on more powerful and dominant roles in small group discussions, while females perform more dependent and socio-emotional functions. Some theorists have suggested that these gender differences may disappear in anonymous CMC (e.g. Dubrovsky, Kiesler & Sethna, 1991; Siegel, Dubrovsky, Kiesler & McGuire, 1986). However, other research fails to show 'equalization' effects (Adrianson & Hjelmquist, 1991; Berdahl & Craig, 1996; Straus, 1996), or even show increased inequality in computer-mediated groups (Weisband, 1994; Weisband, Schneider & Connolly, 1995; see also Postmes, Spears & Lea, 1998; Spears & Lea, 1994). Qualitative studies of CMC also report substantial gender differences on the Internet (Balka, 1993; Herring, 1993; We, 1993), and indeed many female Internet users report that they suffer serious discrimination on such computer networks (Kramarae & Taylor, 1993). Thus, although some have argued that the anonymity of CMC allows gender to be obscured and its effects reduced, empirically there appears to be mixed evidence for equalization.

Postmes and Spears (1997a) investigated a SIDE model explanation for the variability of anonymity effects on gender differences in CMC. The SIDE model argues that the influence of contextual factors may be enhanced when people interact anonymously. Thereby, deindividuating settings may bolster the influence of social stereotypes and prejudice, rather than diminishing them. Therefore, participants in this study interacted with each other over a number of topics, and they did so while gender stereotypes were either activated during the interaction or not, by means of the scrambled sentence procedure described earlier (e.g., Bargh & Barndollar, 1996). In addition, people were either rendered relatively anonymous and deindividuated because they were identified by code numbers only, or they were individuated by giving them autobiographies of those with whom they interacted.[4]

An analysis of the content of discussion revealed that on the whole men made more dominant statements during the interaction than did women. This difference was especially marked when stereotypes were activated and when discussants were anonymous, and less accentuated when they were individuated by autobiographical information, or when stereotypes were not activated. Moreover, a postexperimental questionnaire revealed that people had a much more stereotyped perception of those they interacted with when they were anonymous and when stereotypes were activated.

These results show that, given the right circumstances, stereotyping and stereotypic behaviour can flourish under conditions of anonymity. It seems that the removal of social cues such as individual traits, appearance and even information about sex/gender does not guarantee 'gender-blind' perceptions and behaviour. Given our attempt to hide cues to gender categorization, the explanation of these

---

[4] These autobiographies were 'censored' so that they did not contain any cues as to the participants' gender: thus, people were personally identified by their age, interests and other personal details, but their gender remained unknown.

findings remains somewhat puzzling, however. It is striking that stereotyping and stereotypic behaviour occurs despite this complete anonymity, because this anonymity should obscure cues to gender (and recall that even when people were individuated, we tried to keep this information non-diagnostic with respect to gender). It seems that despite these efforts, evidence of gender 'leaked' through (this is comparable to the conditions on the Internet, where people might try to keep their gender secret). What could be the source of these gender effects? The source could be either the stereotypic treatment by group members who might have guessed or inferred other parties' gender despite the anonymity (cf. Herring, 1993). Alternatively these effects could derive from self-stereotyping: the greater application of stereotypes to oneself under conditions of anonymity. This latter explanation would be most likely from a SIDE-model perspective (see also Lea, Spears & de Groot, 1998).

Self-stereotyping occurs when the stereotypic attributes of one's social group are applied to oneself because this social identity is made salient (e.g. Oakes, Haslam & Turner, 1994; Spears, Doosje & Ellemers, 1997; chapter 3, this volume). For a man, this would mean that he might well become more 'macho' (assuming this is perceived as prototypically male) when placed in a context where his gender identity is activated. A follow-up study investigated this possibility (Brouwer, Kawakami, Rojahn & Postmes, 1997). Groups of four participants (two men and two women) interacted on a gender-sensitive issue for half an hour via CMC. Afterwards, we examined to what extent participants applied gender-stereotypes to themselves by means of a Dutch adaptation of the Bem Sex Role Inventory (Rojahn, 1996). Results indicated that those who interacted anonymously reported more gender-typical behaviour and traits, compared with people who were identifiable during the interaction. Thus, anonymous interaction appears to enhance the salience of gender stereotypes as applied to oneself. This enhanced salience may well be the source of the increased stereotyping and stereotyped behaviour found in other studies of anonymous CMC. A study by Lea, Spears and de Groot (1998), although not concerned with gender, provided further insight into the effects of anonymity and the processes involved. This study used structural equation-modelling techniques and confirmed that anonymity led to enhanced self-categorization in terms of the local group, which then enhanced the tendency to see other group members as prototypical.

It is clear, then, that visually anonymous electronic interaction cannot necessarily eradicate deep-rooted social divisions, such as those between men and women. Paradoxically, the social influence exerted by such (self-) stereotypes seem strongest when there is ostensibly least pressure to comply with the demands of one's gender role (i.e., when it is obscured). The strategic component of the SIDE model would suggest that we are more likely to defer to powerful outgroups when we are identifiable to them (Reicher, Spears & Postmes, 1995; Spears & Lea, 1994; chapter 6, this volume). However, the present effect suggests a more cognitive route to gender differentiation and deference.

Further research shows that such intergroup effects may not be limited to applications of stereotypes, but that inter-group hostility may also be triggered by anonymous CMC between groups. In one study, psychology students interacted via a CMC system with sociology or business students (Postmes, 1995; Postmes, Spears & Lea, 1996). Psychology students formed impressions of the outgroup that were much more negative after interaction that was relatively anonymous,[5] and much more positive after interaction during which pictures of outgroup members were displayed on the screen. This finding was especially surprising because, in fact, no actual interaction occurred: the computer simulated the exchange of a number of rounds of arguments, which were identical in all cases. Thus, the content of interaction was constant across conditions and could not have contributed to the negative impressions that were formed. Anonymity was the sole cause of increased intergroup animosity. The inability to see outgroup members as distinct individuals is also one of the features that social scientists have pointed to in trying to explain the hostility and even atrocities directed at such groups during extreme intergroup conflicts such as wars (e.g., Staub, 1996; Spears, 1995a; Wilder, 1978). Deindividuation of the enemy is an important step towards dehumanization.

In sum, there is converging evidence that anonymity in CMC does not eliminate intergroup distinctions, equalize participation or remove barriers between groups (even when these category cues are themselves not obviously available). On the contrary, there is mounting evidence that anonymous CMC increases the influence of social stereotypes on perceptions and on behaviour, the derogation of outgroups and ingroup favouritism. In contrast, when CMC allows us to individuate the people with whom we interact, derogation, prejudice and stereotyping are typically much reduced. On the whole, research suggests that identifiability during CMC ensures that people are treated more as individuals with idiosyncratic characteristics rather than as a member of a (devalued) social group, that possesses the properties we stereotypically associate with such groups. In the following section we try to look more closely at why the social dimension is sometimes more salient in these disembodied mediated settings by examining CMC's influence on the way people relate to each other.

Anonymity and Attachment to the Group

The central assumption of the SIDE model's argument is that the deindividuating properties of CMC shift people's attention away from individual idiosyncrasies, towards social identities that are shared in common, at least those that are salient. A group member may attempt to understand what goes on in the group by taking into account contextual factors such as the purpose of the interaction, the social

---

[5] In this study, participants were always identified by a group label plus a personal number (i.e. p4 for psychology student number four). In the individuated condition this number was augmented by a personal portrait picture of each discussant displayed on the screen.

identity of the group, group norms and the goal of the communication. Alternatively, a person may seek explanations by taking into account individual differences between actors, or by considering individual motives and rationales. We expect that the influence of situational and contextual explanatory variables will be relatively stronger when group members are deindividuated and anonymous to each other: when people are identifiable they are more likely to seek explanations and attributions on a personal level (at least in Western culture). In other words: when communicators are identifiable to each other, they will individuate each other, and thereby provide the basis for individual motives, impressions and explanations to influence their ideas of each other.

This line of reasoning received support in a study which examined to what extent people could recall who had said what during the interaction via CMC (Postmes, Spears & Lea, 1996, Study 2). This study examined how three people in one group interacted via a CMC system with three people from another group. Communicators were either personally identifiable during interaction because their portrait pictures were displayed on the screen, or they were identified by a group label and personal identification number only. When participants afterwards were asked to identify the source of statements made during the discussion, they were much better able to do so in the identifiable conditions: the portrait pictures helped to individuate the people they interacted with. Interestingly, though, despite the many errors made by anonymous participants, they performed just as well as identifiable participants in identifying the group from which messages came. Thus, despite a severely diminished attention for individual differences, the group membership received no less attention from anonymous participants. This finding confirms that, in a deindividuated setting, attention for individual differences diminishes but attention for social factors such as group membership does not.[6]

In addition to shifting attention to the group, deindividuation is hypothesized to enhance the salience of a social identity (as one of the relevant contextual factors). Although dependent measures of salience are inherently problematic (being very reactive), attraction within the group and identification may be used as substitutes, because both may be expected to co-vary with salience. A demonstration that attraction within the group may increase during anonymous CMC was provided by Walther (1997). In a longitudinal study of international CMC, Walther found that people whose shared social identity was made salient became more and more attracted to their fellow group members during the interaction via a relatively anonymous CMC medium, compared to people whose individual identity was made salient. This bolstering of attraction to people who had a shared social identity occurred on a number of dimensions, most notably on the dimension of physical attractiveness, of which none of these people could have had a clue, because they were separated by the Atlantic Ocean.

Finally, some studies have shown that anonymous interaction may enhance the

[6] As in the studies on normative influence, the anonymous participants responded more in line with the ingroup norms, and were less responsive to outgroup arguments.

closely related constructs of group self-categorization and identification, with the group, provided there is a basis for this identification such as a common social identity (Corneliusson, 1997; Lea, Spears & de Groot, 1998; Postmes, Spears & Lea, 1996; Postmes, Spears, Sakhel & de Groot, 1998, Study 2). In these studies, people who were relatively anonymous reported after the interaction that they identified more with their group compared to people who were individuated by means of portrait pictures. As described earlier in the study by Postmes, Spears and Lea, (1998), identification mediated the effects of anonymity on conformity to group norms in that study. In another study referred to earlier, Lea, Spears and de Groot (1998) looked at the processes responsible for mediating the finding that anonymity in CMC groups enhanced social attraction. Self-categorization as a group member was a critical factor here. This measure mediated the effect of anonymity on social attraction and also mediated an effect of anonymity on the perceived prototypicality of other group members, which in turn also enhanced social attraction.

These findings are generally in line with the predictions of the SIDE model: by focusing attention on the group as a whole the salience of self-categorization as a group member and identification with the group should be enhanced. Thus, deindividuated settings may foster a sense of belongingness to the overriding social entity (the group or the social category). However, it has not always proven easy to demonstrate this mediation empirically. Indeed, a demonstration of the mediation of identification or salience remains one of the major challenges of research on the SIDE model in the future (Postmes, 1997).

Conclusions

By now, we hope to have provided compelling reasons to believe that these 'virtual' CMC groups are no less real or open to social influence than are face-to-face groups. On the contrary, it seems that the virtual groups are actually more social and socially influenced, at least in the 'group' as opposed to the 'interpersonal' sense. The social groups with which we affiliate, the social categories to which we belong, and the social distinctions between ourselves and others do not necessarily disappear under the deindividuating properties of CMC. It is not denied that CMC has the potential to render us clueless as to the social characteristics of those with whom we communicate. Nor do we deny that visually anonymous communication on local networks or on the Internet gives people freedom to act out new identities and transcend the limitations that reality, custom or conventions can impose (Turkle, 1996). Yet the availability of this potential does not mean people will always use it to escape the pull of the group and its social influences and its interests. To assume this is to privilege individual identity and freedom above that of the group, and to forget both our embeddedness in the group and its embeddedness in us. Social norms and stereotypes are not only imposed on us from the outside, they also reside in the social self (Tajfel, 1978a; Turner, 1982;

Turner, Hogg, Oakes, Reicher & Wetherell, 1987). The group provides the content of identity as well as the context of interaction, and commitment (identification) is an important mediator of its effects. A critical feature of this context in CMC is visual anonymity, which may have the effect of reinforcing group influence, group identification, social attraction, stereotyping and ethnocentrism. This contrasts with the implications of traditional deindividuation theory (Postmes & Spears, 1998; Reicher, Spears & Postmes, 1995) and also classical group dynamics research on small groups.

Traditionally, small group research has emphasized that influence is exerted through factors such as social pressure, accountability, social presence, interpersonal attraction, interdependence and interpersonal bonds (Forsyth, 1990; Moreland & Levine, 1982). These forms of influence are implicitly or explicitly tied to models of the group that are based on co-presence: people who work closely together, who are proximate, meet regularly in the group and generally see a lot of each other (Hogg, 1992). Changing the research paradigm in which to investigate social influence in small groups from these traditional co-present groups to 'deindividuated' CMC groups has revealed that the strength of social influence exerted at a social level by group norms and social identity is particularly powerful when interpersonal cues are minimized. Our line of research supports social identity and self-categorization theories to the extent that they propose that social influence within small groups is guided by the same principles as influence at the level of social categories, but especially when group members are de-individuated (Tajfel, 1978a; Turner, 1991).

This raises the question of whether social influence exerted by social identity is present in the classic face-to-face small group. This is far from ruled out, particularly in intergroup settings where a social identity is likely to be made salient by the comparison between the two groups as distinct entities (Turner, 1987). In intragroup settings, however, we believe that people are open to several sources of influence at the interpersonal level, which may dilute or cross-cut the relative impact of social identity. This could potentially account for the lack of empirical success in confirming self-categorization theory's explanation for group polarization where it has used traditional small group settings to put the theory to the test. In this respect there may well be a fundamental difference between small groups based on 'common bonds' and those based on a 'common identity' (Prentice, Miller & Lightdale, 1994). Social identity and self-categorization theories apply particularly to the common identity group, but the more classical group dynamics approaches may provide a better explanation of social influence in groups tied together by interpersonal bonds. This is not necessarily problematic for social identity theory (or self-categorization theory) but applies more to behaviour at the interpersonal end of the interpersonal–intergroup continuum (Tajfel, 1978a). Recent research suggests that this distinction may well be useful in helping to explain the variety of social influence effects in groups, also in interaction with anonymity (Postmes & Spears, 1997b; Ter Haar, 1998).

Our increasing reliance on electronic interaction in various spheres of social life suggests that we rely on 'deindividuated' means of interaction and organization more and more. The members of such groups are dispersed, have irregular (asynchronous) interactions, and may never physically meet up. Although the research conducted shows that social influence is powerful in computer-mediated groups, it raises an issue that has been largely neglected in the experimental approach to studying CMC's effects. This line of research has consistently demonstrated social influence effects in existing social groups by using existing stereotypes, or by imposing the experimenters' norms and group boundaries on participants. This leads to an overly static view of what social influence is and how it is exerted. Now that we know that social influence can be strong in CMC, future research will need to take a closer look at the way in which social norms and social identities emerge in situ. Enhancing our knowledge of the processes by which identities and norms are socially constructed is central to our understanding of the way in which the individual and social mutually influence each other in a dynamic social environment.

9

Group Commitment and Individual Effort in Experimental and Organizational Contexts

JAAP W. OUWERKERK, NAOMI ELLEMERS AND
DICK DE GILDER

Introduction

One of the original aims of social identity theory (see Tajfel, 1975; 1978a; Tajfel & Turner, 1979) was to identify possible strategies that people may use to cope with an identity threat, and, drawing on real-life examples, Tajfel and Turner specified the conditions under which different strategies were likely to be used. As has been discussed in some detail elsewhere (see, for instance, chapter 6), empirical research in this area has largely focused on particular elements of social identity theory. Specifically, considerable research effort has been devoted to demonstrate the occurrence of ingroup favouritism in group ratings or outcome allocations (for overviews, see Brewer, 1979; Hinkle & Brown, 1990; Messick & Mackie, 1989; Mullen, Brown & Smith, 1992), while systematic attempts to examine different (perceptual or behavioural) strategies to cope with an identity threat have been relatively scarce (see chapter 6 for exceptions). By implication, in empirical research to date ingroup favouring judgements or allocations have been considered the prototypical form of social competition. Our point of departure for the present chapter, however, is that such measures may not offer an adequate or complete picture of the extent to which group members are likely to engage in behavioural efforts aimed at improving the current standing of their social group relative to other groups.

In order to gain further understanding of the situations in which a coordinated effort is mandatory to achieve a change in the position of one's group, previous researchers have commonly turned to the political arena, and have illustrated their reasoning by describing the circumstances under which members of socially deprived groups are likely to engage in collective action (e.g., Kelly & Kelly, 1994; Klandermans, 1997; Simon, Loewy, Stürmer, Weber, Freytag, Habig, Kaupmeier

& Spahlinger, 1998; Taylor & McKirnan, 1984). Thought-provoking as such analyses might be, we feel that participating in collective action as a behavioural response to social inequality is likely to be influenced by various factors that are difficult to control or even assess, such as historical momentum or political ideology. In this chapter, we therefore investigate group members' behavioural tendencies in less politically laden situations. For this purpose we will draw on observations in an organizational context to develop further our theoretical argument, after which we will systematically test the hypotheses that we derived by reviewing a series of experimental studies designed to study the antecedent conditions of individual effort aimed at improving the group's performance.

Behavioural Consequences of Intergroup Comparisons

As we briefly indicated above, the common procedure that has been used to investigate the effects of intergroup comparisons is to examine the occurrence of ingroup favouritism in evaluative judgements, or in the allocation of points or other resources. The use of such measures to assess attempts to achieve positive ingroup distinctiveness has been quite pervasive, in the sense that it has been used in research with artificially created laboratory groups as well as in investigations among members of natural groups (see Mullen, Brown & Smith, 1992, for an overview). The main conclusion that was reached on the basis of this research is that the results from different studies are inconsistent, indicating that, apparently, the confrontation with an unfavourable social identity (or enhancing the salience of the group's inferior social standing) is in itself insufficient to elicit ingroup favouritism (e.g., Brewer, 1979; Messick & Mackie, 1989). As has been argued in greater detail elsewhere (see chapter 6), one possible reason for this is that, depending on their level of ingroup identification, group members may engage in various direct or indirect identity management strategies, which may either focus on the improvement of one's personal standing or aim to enhance the position of the ingroup as a whole. Indeed, although previous research did not establish an unequivocal relation between ingroup identification and ingroup bias (see Hinkle & Brown, 1990), there is a growing body of empirical evidence suggesting that it is the combination of an identity threat and strong ingroup identification that elicits group-oriented coping responses (see also chapter 4).

Even if we address attempts at group-status improvement only, however, there are reasons to suspect that perceptual biases or strategic preferences do not necessarily predict the occurrence of actual behavioural efforts on behalf of the group. Arguably, both the general tendency to depict other ingroup members in a positive way and the inclination to allocate more resources to ingroup than outgroup members are unlikely to be costly to the individual. In this sense, it is relatively inconsequential to show these responses, so that the assessment of whether people do or do not engage in such forms of ingroup favouritism may not constitute a critical test of their preparedness to exert themselves on behalf of the group. Our current aim, therefore, is to uncover the conditions under which group members are willing actually to work for their group in order to improve its current standing. Viewed from this perspective, it is important to note that it is not self-evident that the measures of ingroup favouritism that have been used in research so far are suitable to predict actual behavioural effort on the part of group members (see also Fishbein & Ajzen, 1975).

Explicit consideration of the action-consequences of unfavourable intergroup comparisons can be found in relative deprivation research, investigating the conditions under which members of disadvantaged social groups are likely to engage in collective (political) action (e.g., Guimond & Dubé-Simard, 1983). In this research domain, a distinction is made between the consequences of personal or 'egoistic' deprivation and group or 'fraternal' deprivation (Runciman, 1966), with the latter being considered an important precursor for participation in collective action. Although relative deprivation theory has not systematically considered the circumstances under which either individual or group deprivation is likely to be experienced, it has been pointed out that the social identity of group members – that is, the extent to which they are inclined to identify as members of their social group – might play a crucial role in this (see Ellemers, 1993a). Specifically, the same disadvantage should result in feelings of group deprivation for those who identify strongly with their group, while eliciting feelings of personal deprivation in low identifiers (see Kawakami & Dion, 1995). A case in point is the situation of native entrepreneurs in Amsterdam, who feel threatened by the increasing presence of immigrant businesses in their city district (Ellemers & Bos 1998). Regardless of the results of their own business, questionnaire data revealed that native entrepreneurs felt more deprived as a group, and held more discriminatory attitudes towards immigrant entrepreneurs, the more they identified with other native shopkeepers.

Unfortunately, in the relative deprivation tradition, the moderating role of social identification has rarely been addressed in empirical work (but see chapter 10 for exceptions). Furthermore, the relative deprivation approach specifically focuses on people's responses to social injustice. In fact, several theorists have emphasized that the experience of a disadvantage per se (i.e., an unfavourable intergroup comparison) is not sufficient, and that people should feel unjustly treated for behavioural responses to occur (see Cook, Crosby & Hennigan, 1977; Folger, 1986). To some extent, this would seem to converge with Tajfel's (1978a) position. When laying out the foundations of social identity theory, he argued that people may find it difficult to conceive of possible alternatives to a social structure that is seen as legitimate. As a consequence, it is possible that they internalize their inferior social standing and/or cease to compare themselves with the superior group, both of which are likely to reduce their attempts at identity enhancement.

Our position, however, is that while members of lower status social groups may refrain from claiming ingroup superiority for a variety of reasons, recent empirical work has demonstrated that this does not necessarily reflect a lack of confidence in the abilities of the group (see chapter 6). Furthermore, there are other reasons to assume that the perceived illegitimacy of current status differences is not a necessary precondition for status improvement attempts to occur. In fact, we find ourselves on a day-to-day basis in situations in which it is quite likely that people try to improve their position vis-à-vis other individuals or groups, while their current inferior standing has been established in a perfectly legitimate way. In fact, when formulating social identity theory, Tajfel and Turner (1979) gave the example of two football teams that have emerged in first and second place in their league (i.e., in fair competition), and noted that, when the new season started, these teams would be just as competitive as they had been before.

Indeed, both in sports teams and in work groups, it is commonly acknowledged that the success of the group in competition largely depends on the extent to which its members are prepared to exert themselves in order to achieve common group goals. Therefore, we want to build on research into social perception (see chapter 3) and intergroup behaviour (see chapter 4), and use a social identity perspective to investigate the conditions under which people are motivated to improve the relative *performance* of their group (which may either be the result of fair or unfair competition), and actually exert effort on behalf of the group. Thus, rather than applying our theoretical reasoning to explain participation in collective action in a political domain (as has commonly been the case with research on behavioural consequences of collective disadvantage or injustice from a relative deprivation perspective), in the present contribution we aim to focus on an individual's willingness to improve collective performances, which is more relevant to the issue of behavioural motivation in an organizational context.

Social Identification and Organizational Commitment: Conceptual Issues

In the popular literature as well as in organizational practice, an often-expressed conviction is that a sense of common identity is essential for people in order to perform well at work (see Castells, 1997). In fact, the increasing flexibility of the relationship between organizations and their employees only seems to have intensified the concern with team building, or the creation of a corporate identity (see Reichheld, 1996). Despite this apparent consensus among practitioners about the beneficial effects of a common identity, results from scientific investigations so far have not offered unequivocal support for the relation between social identification and collective performance.

A case in point is the literature on the effects of group cohesion. The general assumption in these studies is that, as the group is more cohesive, group members will exert more effort towards achieving a common goal, which is likely to improve the group's performance. Unfortunately, the results of empirical investigations in this area are rather inconsistent. As has already become apparent from early reviews (see Lott & Lott, 1965; Stogdill, 1972), sometimes group cohesion results in higher productivity, sometimes it results in lower productivity, whereas in other cases there is no relation at all between cohesiveness and the productivity of a group (see also Hogg, 1992; Mullen & Copper, 1994). Furthermore, a recurring problem with the interpretation of the literature on group cohesion is that there is no single or unambiguous definition of the central concept, nor do researchers appear to agree about the best way to assess group cohesiveness (see Mudrack, 1989). Accordingly, in the organizational literature, there has been a recent increase in research that refers to social identity theory to analyse the behaviour of people in organizations, for instance to understand the behavioural implications of ethnic diversity at work (Nkomo & Cox, 1996). Unfortunately, rather than resolving the previously mentioned ambiguities, it seems that the application of social identity theory to the organizational domain has raised further conceptual questions, as there appears to be some confusion about the implications of the term 'social identification' in an organizational context.

Ashforth and Mael (1989), for instance, tried to develop hypotheses about individual behaviour in organizations, based on what was known from research on social identity. In order to distinguish between organizational *commitment* (see Mowday, Steers & Porter, 1979) and organizational *identification*, Mael and Ashforth (1992) then emphasized cognitive/perceptual aspects of identification, to indicate that organizational identification refers to the recognition that one's personal outcomes are tied to the fate of the organization. At the same time, they argued that organizational commitment refers more to affective aspects of the relation between the individual and the organization. When this distinction was made, it turned out that the affective construct ('organizational commitment') was a better predictor of work-related measures such as work satisfaction and job involvement than the cognitive/perceptual construct ('organizational identification'; Mael & Tetrick, 1992). This converges with other research, which reveals that *affective* organizational commitment (see Allen & Meyer, 1990; Meyer & Allen, 1991) is most strongly related to employees' behaviour, and hence appears to be the best predictor in an organizational context (Allen & Meyer, 1996; Burke & Reitzes, 1991; De Gilder, Van den Heuvel & Ellemers, 1997; Dunham, Grube & Castaneda, 1994; Meyer, Paunonen, Gellatly, Goffin & Jackson, 1989).

At first sight, this seems to undermine our previous assumption that social identity is a relevant concept that may help us predict the way people behave in organizations. In original theoretical formulations, however, social identification was defined as a *multifaceted* construct, which referred to cognitive, evaluative as well as affective components of the association between the individual and the group (see Tajfel, 1978a; Tajfel & Turner, 1979). In fact, in contrast to the approach of Mael and Ashforth (1992), the most widely used conceptualizations and measurement scales in the social identity tradition focus on identification as a sense of *affective commitment* to the group (Brown, Condor, Mathews, Wade & Williams, 1986; Ellemers, 1993b). Furthermore, research which explicitly addressed the separate effects of distinct aspects of social identity, revealed that the affective component (affective commitment), rather than the cognitive (self-categorization) or evaluative component (group self-esteem), is also the better predictor of group members' behaviour in an experimental group setting (Ellemers, Kortekaas & Ouwerkerk, 1999). Thus, laboratory research as well as data from organizations suggest that it is especially the strength of people's *affective* ties with a group (which we will refer to as affective identification or affective commitment) that determines the extent to which they are prepared to exert themselves on behalf of that group. We will now turn to the organizational literature more specifically, to examine further the evidence for a relation between affective commitment and individual effort at work.

Affective Commitment and Behaviour in Organizations

On the basis of social identity theory, specific predictions can be derived concerning the influence of people's affective commitment on their behaviour in an organizational setting. For instance, if we regard employee turnover as a form of individual mobility from one group to another, we may expect that weakly committed employees will be most inclined to leave an organization, whereas highly committed individuals are more likely to remain loyal to it. Furthermore, when we focus on behaviour that is beneficial to the organization, in contrast to employees with low affective commitment, those with strong commitment should show high attendance (low absenteeism). In addition, they may simply work harder at their jobs than weakly committed individuals, who might even show neglect (cf. Farrell & Rusbult, 1981). From a meta-analysis by Mathieu and Zajac (1990), it seems that each of these behaviours is indeed related to affective organizational commitment. That is, their analysis shows a strong negative relation between commitment and employee turnover, a positive correlation of commitment with attendance, and negative relations with tardiness and absenteeism. Furthermore, Mathieu and Zajac report a significant, although weak, positive correlation between commitment and in-role job performance. Likewise, Meyer and Allen (1997) summarize several studies investigating the relation between affective commitment and task-related performance in organizations, and report a number of positive correlations in more recent studies (e.g., Baugh & Roberts, 1994; Meyer, Allen & Smith, 1993; Saks, 1995). However, they also show that there is substantial variance in the correlations between commitment and performance measures, and note that a number of non-significant relations have been reported as well (e.g., Ganster & Dwyer, 1995). This suggests that the relation between commitment and performance is moderated by other variables. One likely candidate is the type of performance measure. For obvious reasons, for example, because the nature of the performance output differs across organizations, there is no single accepted measure of performance. A wide range of measures is reported in the literature, varying from self-reported measures of work effort (e.g., Randall, Fedor & Longenecker,

1990) and overall job performance (Darden, Hampton & Howell, 1989), to supervisor ratings of performance (Meyer, Paunonen, Gellatly, Goffin & Jackson,
1989), and more objective indicators such as control of costs (DeCotiis & Summers, 1987), and sales figures (Bashaw & Grant, 1994). This heterogeneity of
measures makes it difficult to draw general conclusions about the relation between affective commitment and 'performance' on the basis of previous studies.

Some researchers have argued that the relations between affective commitment
and the behavioural measures mentioned above are disappointingly low (e.g., Randall,
1990). However, it is not surprising that in most studies only modest correlations
are obtained. First, there are clear measurement problems associated with the behavioural measures mentioned earlier, turn-over being an exception (people either
leave or stay). For instance, tardiness and absenteeism are partly under volitional
control, but situational constraints (e.g., traffic jams, accidents, family illnesses) are
also likely to influence these behaviours. This is also true for simple output measures, as some machines dictate the working speed and may actually be designed to
prevent individual performance differences. Furthermore, both lack of insight and
insufficient motivation may undermine the validity of supervisor evaluations of
subordinates' job performances (cf. Meyer & Allen, 1997). Second, the degree to
which an employee's behaviour is determined by motivational factors such as affective commitment may be limited. The possibility that employees have to behave in a
way they would really like is constrained by daily reality. In an organizational
setting, people are subject to control mechanisms that limit their behavioural freedom. For example, even a weakly committed employee may be motivated to show a
satisfactory job performance and low absenteeism, because continuous below-stand-
ard performance and attendance will have serious repercussions in the end. The
organization is likely to refuse to give a rise in salary or may even try to terminate
the employee's contract in response to such behaviour. The turnover process is,
arguably, complex (cf. Mobley, Griffeth, Hand & Meglino, 1979), and is also largely
determined by motivational factors other than one's affective commitment, as people will have to consider various advantages and disadvantages of leaving an organization (e.g., a pay increase, an obligation to move, fringe benefits). Thus, the
extent to which people's affective commitment may influence the behavioural measures commonly used in organizational studies is often quite limited. Given these
problems, even modest correlations between organizational commitment and behaviour can be considered encouraging (cf. Johns, 1991).

If we look for a better indicator of an employee's willingness to exert effort on
behalf of their organization, we may focus on extra-role or so-called *organizational citizenship behaviour* (cf. Motowidlo & Van Scotter, 1994; Organ, 1988) –
that is, behaviour that is not formally required, but implies a voluntary effort to
support organizational goals (e.g., providing help to co-workers, volunteering for
special work activities, showing initiative). Organizational psychologists acknowledge the importance of these work-related pro-social behaviours as performance
criteria that may be unrelated to in-role job performance (George & Bettenhausen,
1990), although both types of performance are considered essential for organiza-

tional success (MacKenzie, Podsakoff & Fetter, 1991). Thus, displays of organizational citizenship behaviour may provide a less ambiguous indicator of individual willingness to exert oneself on behalf of common work goals. In line with our argument that such efforts should be related to the extent to which employees feel committed to the organization, a meta-analysis by Organ and Ryan (1995) revealed a strong positive correlation between affective commitment and organizational citizenship behaviour.

Our understanding of the influence that affective commitment has on individual effort on behalf of the group may be enhanced not only by investigating extra-role behaviour rather than more traditional performance measures, but also by examining the effects of more specific foci of commitment (cf. Becker, Billings, Eveleth & Gilbert, 1996). In an organizational setting, people may feel committed to different work-related entities at the same time (e.g., their career, work team, top management, the organization as a whole). Meyer & Allen (1997) argue, accordingly, that the relation between an employee's commitment to a specific entity and behaviour will be stronger when we examine behaviour that is relevant to that entity. This was illustrated in an investigation by Ellemers, De Gilder and Van den Heuvel (1998), who distinguished commitment to the work group (team-oriented commitment) from commitment to the organization as a whole, as well as commitment to individualistic work goals (career-oriented commitment). In a first study, which surveyed a representative sample of the Dutch working population, these different forms of work commitment turned out to be distinct, both at the measurement level and in terms of their interrelations with other relevant work aspects. Specifically, those who reported strong affective commitment to their team of co-workers indicated that they would work overtime to help a colleague complete his or her work, while no such relation could be established with organizational commitment or career-oriented commitment. The same sample of respondents was approached again one year later, in order to find out whether self-reported levels of commitment could also predict their subsequent behaviour. The results of this second measure confirmed that the extent to which people had previously indicated that they felt committed to their team (rather than to their career or the organization as a whole) predicted whether or not they had worked overtime during the past year.

To be able to investigate the relation between these different forms of commitment and individual performance at work more explicitly, Ellemers, De Gilder and Van den Heuvel (1998) carried out a second study among employees who all worked under similar conditions in the same organization. Furthermore, in addition to workers' self-reports, Ellemers et al. obtained supervisor ratings concerning their actual work performance. Again, a confirmatory factor analysis corroborated the distinction between the different foci of commitment, and these forms of commitment were differentially related to relevant work behaviours. Specifically, the performance ratings provided by the supervisors turned out to be unrelated to employees' levels of career-oriented or organizational commitment. By contrast, team-oriented commitment reliably predicted supervisor ratings of contextual performance (that is, extra-role behaviour directed at the work group), as well as the overall performance evaluation of the worker in question.

In a similar vein, an investigation by Becker and Billings (1993) revealed a positive relation between affective team commitment and pro-social behaviour directed at the work group. Furthermore, this research showed that affective team commitment contributes significantly beyond organizational commitment to the prediction of extra-role behaviour directed at the organization (Becker, 1992). Taken together, empirical results from different studies thus support our general hypothesis that people's willingness to exert effort on behalf of their group is related to the extent to which they feel affectively committed to it. At the same time, however, we are reminded that, to be able to observe these relations in an organizational context, we have to take care that the commitment measure focuses on the work environment that is relevant to the individual. Also, it should be noted that the consequences of strong work group commitment may not always be positive. By helping their colleagues, highly committed employees may obscure the fact that some team members do not function well (Kanter, 1996), which in the long run will result in poor group performances. Furthermore, strong affective team commitment may give rise to intergroup conflict and competition between different work units within the same organization. Although an investigation in a slipper factory suggests that intergroup competition can, under some conditions, lead to better group performances (Zander & Armstrong, 1972), competition between work teams is more likely to be harmful to the overall organization (cf. Leavitt, 1972), given that work units are often dependent on each other.

In discussing organizational psychological research on the relation between affective commitment and an employee's behaviour, we have used social identity theory as a theoretical background. Consistent with social identity theory, it seems that people with strong affective ties to their work group or organization are more willing to express behaviour that is beneficial for collective performances than weakly committed individuals (see also chapter 10). However, due to methodological and practical difficulties, research in organizational settings usually does not allow for explicit hypothesis testing. That is, the empirical support for our argument that can be obtained from research in an organizational context is based on correlational data, which do not provide conclusive evidence about the psychological processes involved. By contrast, the more artificial environment of a laboratory setting is more controlled (as is argued more extensively by Bruins, 1998), and therefore should enable us to make stronger causal inferences concerning the role of social identity processes in determining individual effort on behalf of the group.

Experimental Evidence on Commitment and Group Performance

Although the research in organizational settings that we cited previously provides some initial support for the notion that affective identification with (or affective commitment to) a group positively influences individual effort on behalf of that group, we have to turn to experimental investigations for more conclusive evidence. To date, experimental research within the domain of social identity theory has not addressed the issue of individual effort in group performance. However, some indirect evidence in support of our argument can be gained from a recent series of studies on cooperative behaviour in experimentally simulated organizations (Bruins, Ellemers & De Gilder, 1999; Ellemers, Van Rijswijk, Bruins & De Gilder, 1998). While these studies focused on the effects of autocratic leadership behaviour in dyads, the dependent measures assessed the extent to which subordinates felt committed to their superior and exerted themselves on behalf of the group. The results of three studies consistently showed that subordinates' sense of commitment to their supervisor differed, depending on manipulated aspects of leadership behaviour. More relevant to our present argument, mediational analyses indicated that commitment, in turn, led subordinates to decline an opportunity to leave the organization, and induced cooperative behaviour on a subsequent group task. Thus, although these experiments focused on dyads with asymmetrical power positions, the results of the organizational simulations corroborate the general hypothesis that in work situations affective identification or group commitment is an important determinant of individual effort, and thus may affect group performance.

Additional experimental evidence relevant to the effects of group commitment on behavioural motivation stems from research on 'social loafing' and 'social labouring'. Social loafing, defined as 'a reduction of individual effort when working on a collective task (in which one's outputs are pooled with those of other group members) compared to when working either alone or coactively' (Williams, Karau & Bourgeois, 1993, p. 131), has proved to be a robust phenomenon across a wide variety of tasks. At first sight, this may lead us to the pessimistic conclusion that, by definition, people are less motivated when working on collective tasks than when working as individuals. However, the groups used in research on social loafing are usually random aggregations of individuals, that is, these 'groups' are psychologically insignificant entities with neither a history nor a future, so that people have little reason to perceive themselves as group members, or feel committed to the group. Arguably, different processes should come into play when a common group membership is more meaningful, for instance when people expect their group's performance to be compared to that of other groups (e.g., Turner, 1985; Hogg & Turner, 1987a). Accordingly, intergroup comparisons have been found to increase the motivation of people to work on behalf of the ingroup (James & Cropanzano, 1994), and to reduce the social loafing effect (Karau & Williams, 1993). Furthermore, a series of experiments by Worchel and colleagues (Worchel, Rothgerber, Day, Hart & Butemeyer, 1998) showed that various conditions which are likely to enhance the level of commitment to a work group (e.g., having the perspective of future interaction, or wearing a common uniform in the presence of an outgroup) effectively eliminated group members' tendency to loaf.

In a similar vein, results from a meta-analysis by Karau and Williams (1993) suggest that people are less inclined to loaf when working with close friends or actual team-mates rather than strangers. Williams, Karau and Bourgeois (1993) have argued that this is the case because members of friendship groups identify more strongly with their group. Accordingly, they should also be more motivated to work on behalf of their group. Indeed, in a recent experiment directly comparing different kinds of group, Jehn and Shaw (1997) found that friendship groups outperformed mere acquaintance groups. Furthermore, and essential for our present discussion, this effect was mediated by affective commitment to the group. That is, the differences in group performance were explained by the fact that members of friendship groups were more strongly committed to their group than members of mere acquaintance groups.

In sum, the results of different studies suggest that when the group is sufficiently important to them, people may engage in social labouring rather than social loafing. Although this converges with our argument that the extent to which people feel committed to the group should predict their individual effort on behalf of the group, most of these investigations did not directly assess the effects of affective commitment as a cause of people's behaviour. More importantly, the social loafing research reviewed above essentially focuses on *intra*group processes, while, from a social identity point of view, *inter*group comparisons and the resulting desire to improve the standing of one's own group relative to other groups should constitute a crucial behavioural motivator. In the next sections of this chapter we will therefore review a series of experimental studies on intergroup performance comparisons, intended to investigate more explicitly the moderating effect of affective commitment on group members' performance motivation and individual effort.

Opportunities for Group Performance Improvement

A substantial amount of research within the domain of social identity theory has examined the effect of intergroup comparisons on ingroup identification. In this sense, social identification has predominantly been treated as a dependent variable (but see chapter 4 for exceptions). Findings show that, in general, people tend to dissociate themselves from their group when it compares unfavourably to other groups, whereas they identify more strongly with their group when confronted with a favourable intergroup comparison (e.g., Ellemers, Van Knippenberg, De Vries & Wilke, 1988; Snyder, Lassegard & Ford, 1986). However, in this research group members are rarely given an opportunity actually to improve their group's position on the comparison dimension in question. Thus, if they do not opt to protect their personal identity by dissociating themselves from an unsuccessful group, research participants can only hope to enhance or protect their group's image by denying the experimental feedback or by holding biased perceptions of established intergroup differences (e.g., Ellemers & Van Rijswijk, 1997; Ellemers, Van Rijswijk, Roefs & Simons, 1997). This limitation of much empirical research in the social identity tradition implies that it does not necessarily inform us about the occurrence of actual intergroup competition. In view of this, we propose that in order to study individual effort on behalf of the group, it is essential to offer group members future prospects that may enable them actually to improve the group's standing, as is usually the case in naturally occurring intergroup comparisons.

There is a limited number of studies that explicitly compared how group members respond when status relations are secure or insecure (see Tajfel, 1978a; Turner & Brown, 1978). This revealed that the relation between relative group status and strength of ingroup identification is much less pronounced when the group's relative position is unstable rather than stable (e.g., Doosje, Spears & Ellemers, 1998; Ellemers, Van Knippenberg & Wilke 1990). Arguably, when the status difference between groups has proved to be stable in the past, people have no reason to expect that change will occur in the future. In contrast, when the status difference between groups has been unstable in the past, people are likely to assume that further change is possible in the future. Thus, it would seem that both the current relative position of one's group and the perceived (in)stability of this position (based on intergroup comparisons over time) may determine how people respond to the present situation, and to what extent they are inclined to identify with their group.

However, as it appears from the research reviewed in this chapter, and consistent with social identity theory, ingroup identification also has consequences for an individual's motivation to improve the position of his or her group (see also chapter 4). In this sense, ingroup identification must not only be seen as a possible consequence of past and present status differences between groups, but also as a determinant of a group member's motivation to work at changing the status quo (see Doosje, Spears & Ellemers, 1998). Indeed, Tajfel & Turner (1979) note that a negative social identity (i.e., an unfavourable intergroup comparison) 'promotes subordinate-group competitiveness towards the dominant group to the degree that *subjective identification with the subordinate group is maintained*' (p. 45, our italics). On the basis of these theoretical statements it would seem that, for group members who maintain a sense of identification with a low status group, the awareness that another group has reached a superior performance can provide a source of motivation to improve the current standing of their own group.

In line with these arguments, Ouwerkerk, Ellemers, Smith and Van Knippenberg (1999) conducted two experiments in which they not only investigated how (temporal) intergroup comparisons affect ingroup identification, but also examined the subsequent consequences of ingroup identification for group members' motivation for group performance improvement. More specifically, they investigated how ingroup identification influenced people's *collective efficacy* beliefs for improvement. Collective efficacy is an extension of Bandura's (1977) concept of self-efficacy and refers to beliefs in the capabilities of one's group to organize and execute the courses of action required to produce given attainments (see Bandura, 1997). The social learning literature indicates that, at the individual level, exposure to a more successfully performing other increases people's confidence in their ability to achieve a higher performance level themselves, which, by inducing increased effort and persistence, in turn results in a better performance (Bandura, 1977, 1986). Analogously, Ouwerkerk, Ellemers, Smith and Van Knippenberg (1999) predicted that an unfavourable *intergroup* comparison should raise people's confidence in the ability of their group to improve itself, implying that they are more likely to invest more effort into the group's performance ('if they can do it, we can do it too'). However, as noted earlier, and in line with other research on intergroup perceptions (see chapter 3) as well as other forms of group-related behaviour (see chapter 4), people will only be motivated to improve the current position of a group to the extent that they have not dissociated themselves from that group as an immediate response to an unfavourable intergroup comparison (Ellemers, 1993b; Tajfel & Turner, 1979). In other words, knowledge of a better-performing outgroup will only elicit a motivation to improve the group's performance for those who have maintained a sense of identification with their group, despite its currently unfavourable relative position (i.e., the 'die-hard' members, see Branscombe & Wann, 1991).

In their first experiment Ouwerkerk, Ellemers, Smith and Van Knippenberg (1999) tested the prediction that collective efficacy beliefs are jointly determined by the outcome of previous intergroup comparisons, and the resulting level of ingroup identification. Additionally, in order to vary the likelihood that a performance improvement could be realized, the magnitude of the performance difference between two groups either seemed stable over time, or apparently decreased over time. At the beginning of the experiment participants were divided into two groups. Next, they completed three rounds of a group task. After each round, false feedback was provided concerning the scores obtained by the ingroup and the outgroup. The performance of one's own group always improved over time, and this was identical across experimental conditions. Although the performance of the outgroup also improved over time, it differed depending on the experimental condition. The performance of the outgroup was either better or worse than the score obtained by the ingroup. Furthermore, the difference in performance had either been stable over time or had steadily decreased over time (i.e., had been larger at previous rounds of the task). After they had received this feedback, participants were told that both groups would complete the task a fourth time. Before they started to work on the fourth round, affective identification with the ingroup was assessed. Subsequently, collective efficacy for improvement was measured by a cumulative scale modelled after Bandura's (1977) self-efficacy measure. That is, participants were asked to indicate how confident they were that their group could reach six successively higher performance levels.

As predicted, when the performance difference between the two groups had been stable over time, an unfavourable intergroup comparison resulted in less affective identification than a favourable intergroup comparison. However, no such effect was obtained when the performance difference between the two groups seemed to be decreasing over time. More relevant to our present discussion were the effects on collective efficacy beliefs for improvement. Knowledge of a better-performing outgroup led group members to have more confidence in an improvement of their group's performance than awareness of an inferior outgroup performance. Additionally, the more people identified with their group, the stronger their collective efficacy beliefs were. Importantly, both effects were qualified by an interaction between the group's relative performance and ingroup identification. As expected, a superior outgroup performance only resulted in stronger collective efficacy beliefs when ingroup members had maintained a sense of identification with their group. Furthermore, stronger identification only heightened collective efficacy for improvement when the current relative position of one's group was unfavourable. In other words, the positive effect of ingroup identification on people's motivation to improve the position of their group only occurred when their social identity was threatened.

In a second experiment, which was conducted to rule out an alternative explanation for the effects of stability on ingroup identification, these findings were replicated (Ouwerkerk, Ellemers, Smith & Van Knippenberg, 1999). That is, also with a modified version of the stability manipulation, a favourable intergroup comparison only resulted in stronger affective identification than an unfavourable intergroup comparison when the performance difference between the two groups had been stable over time. Additionally, the effects on collective efficacy beliefs for improvement replicated the findings of the first experiment. That is, a superior outgroup performance only resulted in higher collective efficacy for improvement than did an inferior outgroup performance for ingroup members, who still identified strongly with their group. Furthermore, stronger identification again only strengthened collective efficacy beliefs when the ingroup's current standing was unfavourable.

Taken together, the results of the two experiments described above remind us that ingroup identification should not just be regarded as a consequence of the present standing of one's group, nor can it be seen as a mere response to the perceived stability of intergroup differences. Instead, when we take into account opportunities for future performance improvement more explicitly, it turns out that the sense of ingroup identification resulting from past and present performance differences moderates group members' responses to the situation at hand. In this way, these data support the general hypothesis that group commitment constitutes an important determinant of people's motivation to improve the position of their social group.

However, in both these experiments relative group positions were established in fair and honest competition. Hence, these data mainly speak to situations in which performance differences between groups are legitimate. Even in performance domains, however, competition is often unfair. Some work departments may have better equipment at their disposal, or easier tasks to perform, than other departments. The referee in a sports contest may be biased against some teams, while showing favouritism towards others. Consequently, performance differences between groups are often illegitimate, and this may also influence how group members respond to the status quo. In general it seems that people are less likely to dissociate themselves from a low status group when its position is perceived as illegitimate, than when intergroup differences seem legitimate (Ellemers, 1993b; Tajfel & Turner, 1979). Furthermore, previous research has shown that group members are more inclined to improve their group's standing when low ingroup status stems from an unfair procedure, while they are more easily resigned to the present state of affairs when this is the result of a fair procedure (Commins & Lockwood, 1979a; 1979b; Taylor, Moghaddam, Gamble & Zellerer, 1987). Although these previous studies did not systematically differentiate between responses of low and high identifiers, in view of our general argument it may well be that people's level of commitment to the group also moderates these effects of group status legitimacy. That is, even though an unfair intergroup competition may elicit equally strong resentment in all members of the group that ends up having low status as a result, we predict that only those who feel strongly committed to the group are sufficiently motivated to invest the individual effort necessary to improve the group's current performance.

To test this prediction, in a further study Ouwerkerk and Ellemers (1999) investigated how an unfair intergroup competition would affect group members' identification, and assessed the subsequent consequences for their beliefs about group performance improvement. Similar to the experiments described above, participants were divided into two groups, both of which completed an anagram task containing twenty items, which either consisted of five, six, seven or eight letters (difficulty level 5, 6, 7 or 8). The difficulty level of the anagrams was allegedly randomly chosen by the computer. After completion of the task, false performance feedback was provided, informing participants that the performance of the outgroup had either been better or worse than that of the ingroup. In order to manipulate perceived fairness, participants received additional information concerning the difficulty level of the anagrams. Whereas the mean difficulty level for the ingroup was constant across experimental conditions, participants either learned that the ingroup had been disadvantaged (because the anagrams presented to the outgroup had had a lower difficulty level) or that the outgroup had been disadvantaged (because they had had a higher difficulty level). Next, participants were told that both groups would complete twenty additional anagrams. Before starting to work on this task, statements were presented to assess the level of affective identification with the ingroup. Subsequently, collective efficacy for improvement was measured by a cumulative scale similar to the one used in the two experiments described previously.

When the outgroup had been disadvantaged and participants were informed that their own group had nevertheless performed worse than the other group, they reported less ingroup identification than when their group had allegedly shown a superior performance. However, in line with previous findings, an inferior ingroup performance did not result in decreased ingroup identification when this could be attributed to ingroup disadvantage. In fact, under these conditions affective identification was enhanced, so that group members identified even more strongly with a low status group than a high status group.

Similar to the results of the previously described experiments, the degree of ingroup identification subsequently moderated the effect of intergroup comparison on collective efficacy beliefs for improvement. That is, when the outgroup had shown a superior performance, this only inspired higher collective efficacy (compared to when the outgroup's performance had been inferior) in participants who had maintained a sense of identification with their group. However, in this study, the moderating effect of ingroup identification was only observed after ingroup disadvantage. By contrast, no such motivational effects of the confrontation with a superior outgroup performance or of strong ingroup identification were observed when the outgroup had been disadvantaged. This suggests that people are relatively willing to be resigned to the status quo when they are outperformed by another group despite its disadvantage. Presumably, this makes people feel that their group deserves its inferior standing and/or think that it is unlikely that they will ever outperform the outgroup (see also chapter 6).

Group Commitment and Behavioural Attempts at Collective Improvement

Although the results of the three experiments described above consistently show that affective group commitment leads people to have more confidence in a collective performance improvement after being confronted with a better performing outgroup, the crucial question remains whether such motivational responses translate into actual behavioural differences aimed at improving the group's standing. A first result that may shed some light on this issue concerns an additional measure that was taken in the study of Ouwerkerk and Ellemers (1999). In order to explore further consequences of relative advantage or disadvantage in intergroup performance comparisons, they assessed the extent to which group members hindered the performance of the outgroup on a subsequent task. This was done by providing participants with an opportunity to determine the difficulty level of half the anagrams that would be presented to the outgroup in the second round. The higher the difficulty level that was selected, the harder it would be for the outgroup to show a good performance of this task, regardless of whether the ingroup would succeed in improving its own performance (see Rothgerber & Worchel, 1998, for a similar measure). Thus, the inclination to hinder the future performance of the outgroup might present an alternative means of achieving ingroup superiority.

However, from previous research on the positive–negative asymmetry in intergroup discrimination (e.g., Blanz, Mummendey & Otten, 1995, 1997; Mummendey, Simon, Dietze, Grünert, Haeger, Kessler, Lettgen & Schäferhoff, 1992) we know that group members are relatively ready to favour their ingroup by allocating more positive outcomes to it, while they are less willing to display such biases when this requires them to assign negative outcomes to another group. In fact, it seems that further 'aggravating' conditions (such as low group status or a minority position) are necessary for group members to show this latter kind of intergroup discrimination. In view of this, it might be that an unfair disadvantage constitutes such an aggravating condition, and may therefore lead group members to hinder the performance of the outgroup. This measure therefore taps into a slightly different process, which is not necessarily only driven by the motivation to improve the standing of the ingroup. Thus, it may well be that previous ingroup disadvantage in itself constitutes sufficient cause to hinder the outgroup, regardless of whether or not this resulted in an inferior ingroup performance.

In line with this argument, it turned out that relative group status and relative disadvantage had independent effects on this measure. Overall, group members were more inclined to hinder the performance of the outgroup when it had performed better than the ingroup, supporting the assumption that this behaviour is used to improve the relative position of the ingroup. Additionally, ingroup disadvantage elicited a similar response, but only for those who identified strongly with their group. This suggests that while either an inferior standing of the ingroup or a previous disadvantage may elicit group members' resentment against the current state of affairs, additional motivating factors seem necessary for outgroup hindering to occur. In the case of an unfavourable intergroup comparison, it may be that this was felt necessary to improve the relative position of the ingroup implied; in the case of previous disadvantage, people have to identify strongly with the group in order to show this response. Thus, these results again underline the importance of group commitment as a moderator of group members' behavioural tendencies, and indicate that the extent to which people identify with their group not only determines their motivation to improve the position of the ingroup, but also affects the extent to which they actually hinder the performance of an outgroup.

In a further attempt to assess behavioural consequences of differences in ingroup identification, Ouwerkerk, De Gilder, and De Vries (1999) designed a study to tap the extent to which group members actually exerted individual effort in order to improve their collective performance. At the beginning of their experiment, participants (first-year psychology students) were asked to complete a computerized reaction task consisting of sixty trials. At the start of each trial, four white squares were presented in a horizontal row on the computer screen. After one second the reaction stimulus appeared, consisting of one of these squares turning black. The participants' task was to indicate the position of the target by pressing one of four keys (labelled as 1, 2, 3 and 4, in left to right order) as fast as possible. When the second or third square turned black they had to make a compatible response (pressing 2 or 3, respectively). However, when the first or fourth square turned black they had to make an incompatible or 'cross-over' response (pressing 4 or 1, respectively). Their average reaction time served as a baseline for the effort they exerted on this task.

After completion of this task, participants were informed about the alleged purpose of the study, which was said to be part of a large ongoing study, the so-called 'Departmental Competition'. The alleged goal of this study was to determine whether students from nine different departments of their university (psychology, medical science, mathematics, physics, philosophy, economics, language studies, chemistry and law) differed in their performance on nine intelligence dimensions. Next, preliminary results of this study were presented. Supposedly based on their average performance on the nine intelligence dimensions, psychology students were either ranked second (high status) or eighth (low status). Subsequently, participants were asked to complete a questionnaire, which included statements concerning their affective identification with psychology students. Next, they were told that they were being randomly selected to be tested on one particular intelligence dimension, namely 'adaptability to inconsistent rules'. Their adaptability to inconsistent rules could supposedly be measured by the reaction task they had 'practised' at the beginning of the experiment. Participants were asked to complete this task again. Before starting, it was emphasized that although they would not receive any information concerning their personal score, their performance would influence the position held by the psychology students on the overall ranking. The extent to which participants worked harder on the reaction task (had a lower average reaction time) the second time compared to the first time served as a measure for individual effort on behalf of the ingroup (i.e., psychology students).

The pattern of results for male participants was highly consistent with the motivational effects found in the previously described experiments, and supports the argument that whether or not low group status elicits performance improvement depends on the extent to which individuals feel committed to their group. That is, an unfavourable intergroup comparison (low status) only resulted in more performance improvement than a favourable intergroup comparison (high status) for participants who identified strongly as psychology students. Again, it also turned out that identification was only related to performance improvement when the current standing of the ingroup was unfavourable.

Although these findings seem to offer encouraging support for the notion that the previously observed motivational responses should extend to differential amounts of effort exerted on the group task, a puzzling complication is that female participants tended to show an opposite pattern of results. That is, women who identified strongly with psychology students actually improved *less* in the low status condition than in the high status condition. In an attempt to find a post hoc explanation for this effect, Ouwerkerk, De Gilder and De Vries (1999) argue that the experimental procedure may have inadvertently evoked a so-called 'state of stereotype threat' (see Crocker, Major & Steele, 1997; Steele & Aronson, 1995) for female participants in the low status condition. In other words, the spatial choice reaction task may have been perceived as a typical male task, on which men are generally expected to perform better than women. Furthermore, the population of psychology students, in contrast to the population of students of most other faculties, is largely made up of female students (±75 per cent). Therefore, being informed of the poor performance of other psychology students, may have led female participants to take this as evidence of women's generally lower ability to perform the task (i.e., stereotype conformation), which in turned caused them to doubt their own ability and prevented behavioural attempts to improve their group's performance. Support for the plausibility of this explanation, as well as a possible solution to rule out these unintended effects, can be found in a study by Spencer and Quinn (1995). They demonstrated that stereotype threats concerning gender differences in abilities (and their negative effects on test performance) can be eliminated by simply describing a test as one on which there are no gender differences in performance.

In order to examine the validity of their post hoc explanation, and in an attempt to obtain more consistent support for the hypothesized effects of group status and ingroup identification on behavioural effort, Ouwerkerk, De Gilder and De Vries (1999) replicated their first experiment with some modifications. This time, they explicitly told participants that there were no gender differences in performance on the task. Additionally, participants were told that the preliminary ranking of the different departments (i.e., the status manipulation) was based on an equal proportion of male and female students for all study majors. These changes, which were intended to eliminate a gender-based stereotype threat, proved effective, in the sense that this time the predicted effects were obtained for *both* male and female participants. After being informed that the previous performance of psychology students compared unfavourably to that of other students, participants generally showed more performance improvement as they identified more strongly with psychology students. This replication and extension of the results obtained by Ouwerkerk et al. in their first study provides convincing experimental evidence that, when confronted with an inferior group performance, group members actually exert more individual effort on behalf of the group and consequently achieve a better collective performance as they feel more committed to the group.

Conclusion

Both the (largely correlational) data from organizational research and the experimental findings we discussed in this chapter provide support for our claim that the degree of affective identification with (or affective commitment to) a group influences an individual's behavioural motivation to enhance the performance of that group. At the same time, results from the experimental research suggest that the relation between one's affective ties with a group and the willingness to exert effort on behalf of the group is not as straightforward as one might expect. A consistent finding is that the positive motivational consequences of group commitment are only observed in situations where there is a potential threat to one's social identity, which may either be caused by an expectation of an intergroup comparison or a currently unfavourable relative position of one's group. This pattern converges with observations from research on the effects of group threat more generally, as reviewed for group perceptions by Spears et al. (chapter 3), and for other forms of intergroup behaviour by Doosje et al. (chapter 4). With respect to group performance improvement, the research reviewed in the present chapter accordingly indicates that *only* when the going gets tough, the 'tough' (i.e., high identifiers) get going. Research based on social identity theory has traditionally emphasized possible negative consequences of unfavourable intergroup comparisons, by pointing out that this is likely to result in an unsatisfactory social identity for group members, and specifying different strategies that can be used to cope with this identity threat. In this chapter we focus on the fact that when people maintain a sense of identification with their group, knowledge of a superior performance of an outgroup can have positive motivational consequences, which may lead them to invest more effort into the group in order to achieve a better group performance.

We think the research reviewed in this chapter attests to the important role of ingroup identification or group commitment in group performance. Nevertheless, in this contribution we have also tried to emphasize that, in order for people to become motivated to exert individual effort on behalf of the group, further conditions should imply that such increased effort might realistically result in a better group performance. While we have pointed out that the perceived instability of existing intergroup differences and future performance opportunities may provide such conditions, in principle, other (person or situation-related) characteristics may have similar effects. For instance, in a study of Pillegge and Holtz (1997), stronger group identification resulted in the setting of more ambitious goals, and a better performance, which is in line with the general pattern of results we have obtained in our own research. However, this effect was only observed for group members with high self-esteem, that is for those who felt confident about their ability to achieve a better performance, while no comparable effects of group identification could be established for group members lacking in self-esteem.

Another important issue that is often raised when examining possible consequences of group commitment is whether or not this should be conceived of as an individual difference variable, and if so, to what extent commitment can be distinguished from other similar constructs, such as collectivism (Triandis, 1995; Triandis, McCusker & Hui, 1990) or a pro-social value orientation (McClintock, 1978). Based on a social identity perspective, our position is that people can belong to many different (sometimes cross-cutting or overlapping) groups at the same time, but they are likely to feel more strongly committed to some groups than to others, and their sense of commitment to the same group may vary over time, depending on the salient social context. Obviously, there are also bound to be overall individual differences that limit the degree of cross-situational variation in commitment levels. However, a recent cross-cultural study revealed that in individualistic and collectivistic settings alike, people's level of identification with their work organization is predictive of their turnover intentions (see Abrams, Ando & Hinkle, 1998). Thus, as we argued when discussing people's commitment to different organizational constituencies, people's general 'groupyness' does not necessarily predict their behaviour in specific situations. Instead, as we have seen, a relation with people's individual performance could only be established when the commitment measure focused on the relevant work entity.

To develop our argument about the relationship between affective commitment and individual effort we have drawn upon research conducted in an organizational context. Despite the measurement and interpretative problems with these correlational data, the convergence of real-life observations with the results from more focused experimental studies seems encouraging. While the results of organizational investigations attest to the applied relevance and external validity of the phenomena under consideration, the experimental simulations enable us to draw firm conclusions about the causality of the observed relations, and illuminate the psychological processes underlying people's behavioural responses. Thus, in spite of the conceptual confusion this has caused in the past, we think that using social identity theory to understand people's behaviour in work organizations may lead to important new insights, even though much of the theoretical development in this area is based on experimental research. Conversely, as we have seen, observations in the organizational domain may give rise to additional theoretical questions, and in this way offer new and exciting research questions that can be further pursued in laboratory research. Thus, we think that social identity theory and the organizational context have much to offer each other, and we are convinced that the simultaneous pursuit of these research questions from both perspectives should prove highly fruitful.

While our argument here has mostly focused on commitment and its likely effects in a work context, the distinct contribution of this chapter also has to do with the content of the behaviour we studied. In contrast to research that focuses on biases in intergroup evaluations or outcome allocations, as well as work in the political domain on the pursuit of collective interests, the work we reviewed here focused on individual effort directed at improving group performance. As we spend much of our working life in collective settings, it is crucial to gain further understanding of the complex relation between social identification and people's willingness to exert themselves on behalf of their work group. Indeed, as a consequence of trends towards more group-based work, it seems that organizational success is more than ever dependent on voluntary individual effort (organizational citizenship behaviour) in work teams (e.g., Podsakoff, Ahearne & MacKenzie, 1997; Schaubroeck & Ganster, 1991). Unfortunately, to date, researchers within the domain of social identity theory have largely neglected this particular behavioural content, as well as the organizational context, when examining the causes and effects of group commitment. We hope that this chapter will inspire some to do otherwise, both in laboratory experiments and organizational studies.

10

Social Identity and the Context of Relative Deprivation

HEATHER J. SMITH, RUSSELL SPEARS AND
INTSE J. HAMSTRA

One of the recurring questions for social psychology concerns behaviour that appears to conflict with objective interests (Tyler & Smith, 1998). This is one factor that distinguishes social psychology from the economic theory of rational choice. This question is nowhere more apparent than in research on 'relative deprivation' (Runciman, 1966), the phenomenon that feelings of personal or group deprivation appear to be more dictated by comparison with others than by material circumstance. Why do people who suffer the most horrific conditions appear to accept their fate, whereas others who enjoy numerous advantages resent those who have still more? Why are some people willing to risk their personal security to champion a disadvantaged group, whereas others prefer to focus on their personal situation and ignore the larger context? In these examples, perceptions of one's lot do not seem to be based directly on material reality, but flow from social comparisons grounded in either individual or group identity. This comparative dimension opens the door to a social psychological analysis.

This chapter is concerned with how people react to their life conditions as individuals and group members, especially when these conditions reflect group disadvantage. In particular, we try to understand the material conditions and social psychological processes that predict diverse responses to collective deprivation, ranging from the individualistic and self-interested, to the collectivistic and group interested (see chapters 3, 4 and 9). We will demonstrate that it is all too easy not to identify with one's group and its plight. In common with the three guiding themes of this volume, the critical factors determining feelings of collective deprivation that we examine relate to context (identity salience), commitment (group identification) and content (the ideology of the group). This chapter is thus concerned with investigating the social psychological 'loop-holes' that allow the individual to escape collective commitments (see chapter 4), as well as the factors that foster a collective orientation despite the distractions of individual self-interest. More specifically, we consider in turn how the critical factors (context, commitment, content) influence the proposed mediating processes of social comparison

that help to explain feelings of deprivation and attributions for one's own outcomes, which in turn form the basis for individual versus more collectivistic behavioural intentions. Our first attempt to elicit feelings of deprivation, even for
group members who are personally advantaged, is by manipulating the contextual
salience of identity. We then go on to examine the effects of commitment and the
content of group ideology.

Theoretical Background: Relative Deprivation and Social Identity

A crucial insight in relative deprivation theory is the distinction between individual relative deprivation – feelings of resentment and perceptions of injustice
produced by a comparison between oneself and a similar other – and collective
relative deprivation – feelings of resentment and perceptions of injustice produced
by a comparison between one's membership group and another group (Pettigrew,
1967; Runciman, 1966; Tajfel, 1982b). Group deprivation is associated with two
important consequences that are typically not found with individual deprivation.
First, people appear more likely to acknowledge group injustice than they are to
acknowledge personal injustice. For example, in a Massachusetts survey underpaid working women described the situation for working women as dissatisfying
and unfair, but they reported little resentment or dissatisfaction with their own
personal working situation (Crosby, 1982). Second, people who believe their entire social group to be deprived are more likely to participate in social movements
and actively attempt to change the social system (Dubé & Guimond, 1986; Walker
& Mann, 1987). In contrast, people who feel deprived as individuals are more
likely to feel socially isolated, personally stressed and pursue individualistic strategies to achieve change (Abrams, 1990; Kawakami & Dion, 1992; Walker &
Mann, 1987). These individual reactions, characteristic of personal deprivation,
confirm that deprived individuals do not always relate their personal plight to
inequities in the intergroup situation (Postmes, Branscombe, Spears & Young,
1998; Taylor, Wright, Moghaddam & Lalonde, 1990).

For these reasons, it is particularly important to focus on feelings of collective
deprivation if we are going to understand and predict support and participation in
collective behaviour. Social identity theory and self-categorization theory (Tajfel
& Turner, 1986; Turner, Hogg, Oakes, Reicher & Wetherell, 1987) provide an
analysis of the self-concept that suggests when and how feelings of group deprivation will occur. According to these models, people can categorize themselves and
others at a number of different levels of abstraction. For example, people can
focus on unique idiosyncratic qualities that distinguish themselves from other
people (personal identity). Alternatively, they can focus on memberships in groups
and social categories that they share with some people but not with others (social
identity). According to this analysis, if personal identity is salient, people may be

more likely to make disadvantageous interpersonal comparisons between themselves and others, which can lead to feelings of individual relative deprivation. If group identity is salient, however, people should be more likely to make disadvantageous intergroup comparisons between their membership group and other groups, which can lead to feelings of group relative deprivation. Further, when a shared group membership is made salient, people should minimize differences within the group and emphasize differences between groups, suggesting that collective outcomes will become more important (Turner, 1987). In other words, the most important distinction between group deprivation and individual relative deprivation may not be whether the comparison target is a person or a group, but whether comparers consider themselves as group members or as isolated individuals (see also Kawakami & Dion, 1992; Postmes, Branscombe, Spears & Young, 1999; Taylor, Wright, Moghaddam & Lalonde, 1990; Tyler, Boeckmann, Smith & Huo, 1997; Walker & Pettigrew, 1984).

The consideration of both personal and group levels of identity means that we can distinguish between people who report both personal and group deprivation ('double deprivation', Vanneman & Pettigrew, 1972) and people who report group deprivation but no personal deprivation. We should perhaps not be surprised to find (as we and others generally do) that feelings of 'double deprivation' – the combination of personal and group disadvantage – is associated with a greater sense of injustice, more negative attitudes towards outgroups and more support for collective action (Foster & Matheson, 1995; Smith, Spears & Oyen, 1994; Vanneman & Pettigrew, 1972). However, the more theoretically interesting case concerns the situation where people view the group as a whole as deprived but themselves as not personally disadvantaged. Such people are especially interesting for practical, empirical and theoretical reasons.

In practical terms, a group that embarks on a 'social change' strategy of contesting the status quo needs as many group members 'on board' as possible. The success of collective action is likely to depend on perceived collective efficacy and real social support (e.g., Klandermans, 1997). Thus the proportion of group members who recognize the deprivation and who are willing to engage in collective action is likely to be critical. If the group relies just on those who feel personally most deprived, the momentum for collective change may be insufficient, especially given the disempowered nature of deprived groups. The success of a group action may be as strong as the weakest links in the chain. Furthermore, access to resources (e.g. in terms of education, status and respect, as well as material goods) may also make group members who enjoy personal advantages better placed to coordinate and lead a collective struggle.

The importance of such considerations is supported by empirical work showing that the taste for collective action on behalf of the group quickly dissipates among those who receive personal rewards, giving them potential mobility to higher status groups (Wright, 1997). This helps to explain why collective resistance is not more common than it is, and the potential for personal advantage to 'buy off' certain group members forms a central theme for our own work described below.

However, there is also substantial evidence from field research that it is not always those who are most personally deprived who experience collective deprivation or who form the vanguard of social movements and collective protests (Caplan & Paige, 1968; Flacks, 1970; Gurin & Epps, 1974).

Because of this empirical variation, the combination of personal privilege and collective deprivation also provides an important theoretical test case that demands the control provided by an experimental approach. For example, one difficulty with previous field and survey research in this regard is the lack of independent knowledge about people's objective situation. It is possible that the working women in previous research who evaluated their personal working situation as relatively satisfying and fair, but the situation for the group as a whole as unfair and dissatisfying, actually perceived the situation accurately. That is, they may actually have enjoyed personal advantages not shared by most or some other working women. An adequate test of this explanation requires knowledge of the objective working situation of the individual woman. Therefore, it is important to manipulate whether the participant was personally advantaged or disadvantaged within the context of collective deprivation. Pitting personal and group agendas against each other also forms a conservative test of the potential power of group identity to move us beyond the pull of personal self-interest. The power of group identity is most evident when it prevails despite being cross-cut with such interests. Conversely, an analysis of individual identity and interests (as exemplified by the research on tokenism, Wright, 1997) may help us to understand when and why group deprivation and collective action is relatively rare.

The Role of Context: Group Salience, Social Identity and Social Comparison

A social identity framework can help explain the numerous examples that have been documented in which felt personal deprivation has failed to mirror felt group deprivation. The inconsistent responses reported in this research may have occurred because respondents interpreted different questions as corresponding to different levels of abstraction or identity (Major, 1994; Postmes, Branscombe, Spears & Young, 1998; Taylor, Wright, Moghaddam & Lalonde, 1990). For example, when underpaid working women are asked to describe their personal work situation, their unique personal identity should be relevant. In this case, they may compare their situation to another employee (an interpersonal/intragroup comparison) and conclude they are doing rather well. However, when these same women are asked to describe the work situation for female workers in general, their social identity as a working woman should be more relevant. In this case, they may compare the situation of the average female worker to the average male worker (an intergroup comparison) and conclude that the situation for working women is unfair and dissatisfying.

If this analysis is correct, it should be possible to manipulate the salience of different identities and show that people focus on different aspects of the same situation, and that feelings of deprivation are greater when group identity is salient. In short, our model indicates that certain features of the social context will influence social comparison and subsequent feelings of deprivation and judgements of fairness. Clearly this context includes the actual disadvantage experienced by the individual and the group. However, our main interest is in how contextual variations in personal versus group salience influence perceptions of these two dimensions of (dis)advantage. Different levels of identity salience primed in the social context (personal versus group identity) are expected to evoke different levels of social comparison (interpersonal versus intergroup), which then help to explain feelings of deprivation and associated behavioural outcomes.

A first step was to see whether priming group identity actually makes people more concerned with individual or group outcomes, leaving aside for the moment the nature of these outcomes. In a pilot study (Smith, Spears & Oyen, 1994) designed to test the identity salience manipulation, participants who were primed to think of themselves as group members preferred to learn their group's and an outgroup's performance score, whereas participants primed to think of themselves as unique individuals preferred to learn their personal score and the score of a randomly selected other participant. It was hypothesized that the choice to learn about an outgroup's performance compared to the ingroup represented a preference for learning intergroup comparison information, whereas the choice to learn one's own score and the score of one other person represented a preference for learning interpersonal comparison information. As predicted, priming a group membership increased the desire to learn intergroup comparison information.

However, the situation is more complicated when the joint effects of personal and collective advantage and disadvantage are considered. The question arises of whether the comparison focus revealed by this contextual manipulation of identity salience is affected by personal outcomes. This is particularly interesting in the case of our theoretically critical combination of personal advantage and collective disadvantage. If a group identity focus manipulation is sufficiently powerful, we might expect people primed to think of their shared disadvantaged group membership to be more likely to notice and resent the collective disadvantage than those primed to think of themselves as unique individuals, even when they personally enjoy an advantage. Conversely, it is conceivable that when a disadvantaged group membership is primed for those who are personally advantaged, they may actually prefer to limit their comparisons to other ingroup members rather than to compare the ingroup with the outgroup. This intragroup perspective offers them the possibility of focusing on a favourable personal outcome and (personal) identity rather than an unfavourable group outcome and (group) identity. In contrast, collectively deprived group members who are also personally disadvantaged should have little to gain from such a personal comparison focus, and little to lose by focusing on the group disadvantage (i.e., the so called 'double deprivation' condition).

To test this idea, the salience of personal and social identity were manipulated independently of the participant's actual situation (Smith, Spears & Oyen, 1994, Study 1). In this study, both preferred comparison choices and feelings of fairness and satisfaction were measured. First-year Dutch psychology students arrived at the laboratory expecting both course credit and payment for their participation. However, during the experiment, they learned that the experimenter could not pay everyone. Participants assigned to the personally disadvantaged experimental condition learned that they would not be paid, and participants assigned to the personally advantaged experimental condition learned that they would be paid. For all four experimental conditions, the proportion of the participant's ingroup listed as receiving payment was substantially less than the proportion of the outgroup rewarded. (All participants eventually received the full compensation that they were promised after the debriefing.) Half the participants were primed to view themselves as psychology students (and not economics students) and half the participants were primed to view themselves as unique individuals.

With regard to the preferred social comparison, the results were quite complex and somewhat inconclusive. A slight majority of personally disadvantaged participants preferred to learn group averages regardless of the priming manipulation. Among personally advantaged participants, group-primed participants were more interested in learning the group averages and individual-primed participants were more interested in learning their personal score. The fact that individually primed people who are personally advantaged were more interested in their personal score than in group averages suggests a personal focus in line with their identity level and personal rewards. Among group-primed participants, there was no clear evidence that personally advantaged participants preferred intergroup comparisons any less than did personally disadvantaged participants, suggesting that comparison focus for group-primed participants was not moderated by personal (dis)advantage.

However, the perceptions of deprivation paint a slightly different picture. As expected, personally disadvantaged participants reported greater feelings of deprivation than did personally advantaged participants. Further, group-primed personally disadvantaged ('doubly deprived') participants reported the most deprivation. However, as shown in figure 10.1, group-primed personally advantaged participants reported the least deprivation (this resulted in a two-way interaction). This pattern of results is particularly intriguing in view of other results that showed that group-primed participants were more aware of the collective situation than were individual-primed participants. In other words, priming a shared disadvantaged group membership only increased feelings of deprivation when participants were personally disadvantaged, not when they enjoyed a personal advantage, even though checks confirmed that priming a group membership did make participants more aware of the collective disadvantage.

How can we explain the decreased deprivation reported by group-primed personally advantaged participants? Although group-primed participants were more likely than individual-primed participants to notice that another group received more money relative to their own group, it is still possible that group-primed

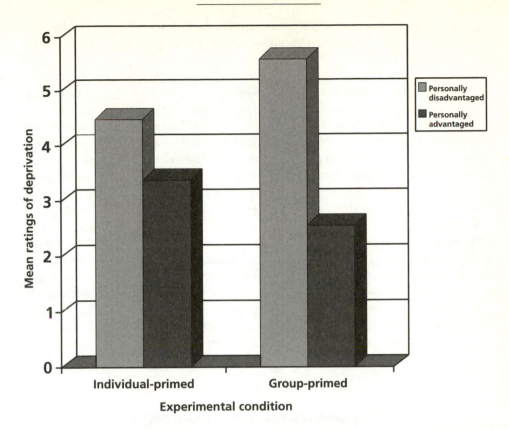

Note   Higher scores represent more deprivation (experiment rated as less fair and less satisfying). Scores could range from 1 (not at all deprived) to 7 (extremely deprived).

Figure 10.1   Participants' ratings of deprivation
Source: Smith, Spears & Oyen, 1994, Study 1

participants based their ratings of satisfaction and fairness on an advantageous intragroup comparison (as one of the few paid psychology subjects) and not on a disadvantageous intergroup comparison (as part of a significantly underpaid group). Given that the intergroup comparisons were unfavourable in this situation, downward interpersonal comparisons within one's own group may have been the most comforting for personally advantaged group-primed participants. In this case, rather than promote intergroup comparisons, increased group salience might have encouraged advantaged group-primed participants to redefine the frame of reference in terms of their position within the ingroup (Turner, 1987). Of course, this interpretation should be treated with some caution, given that the actual social comparison data reported above appear to give little direct support for this idea. However, in retrospect, this may reflect a fault in the measure of comparison preference used. In choosing the ingroup score (some) group members may have used this as a reference standard for evaluating their own score relative to the ingroup, and not because they were interested in differences between the two groups. We tried to resolve this ambiguity in later studies (see Smith & Spears, 1996, described below).

In conclusion, it seems that identity salience did not dictate feelings of deprivation in a straightforward way. Instead, people's evaluations of the situation may depend upon the benefits associated with making intragroup instead of intergroup comparisons in terms of maintaining a positive (social) identity. Positive intergroup comparisons can confirm the positive value of the ingroup and positive intragroup comparisons can confirm the positive value of the individual group member. Both processes may contribute to a positive identity. By looking 'inward' rather than 'outward', people for whom group membership is salient can protect their self-image by emphasizing their worth as a group member without minimizing the importance of their group membership (Smith & Tyler, 1997; see also chapter 2, this volume). For individuals who are doing relatively well compared with their group as a whole, making intergroup comparisons may be the less advantageous strategy. However, for people who experience both personal and group disadvantage ('double deprivation'), comparisons within the group offer no advantages over comparisons between groups. Therefore, they will be most likely to report general feelings of unfairness and relative deprivation. The use of group strategies to challenge the status quo when individual strategies fail to enhance self-esteem follows directly from social identity theory (Tajfel & Turner, 1986).

More Context: Forcing a Group Focus

These results confirm the difficulty of generating general feelings of group-level relative deprivation, and illustrate how easy it is to undermine them, despite drawing attention to one's collective situation. The results also echo experimental research on tokenism, which suggests that as long as there is a possibility for personal gain or individual mobility, people are less likely to be concerned with collective interests and action (Wright, Taylor & Moghaddam, 1990; Ruggiero & Taylor, 1995, 1997). Still, as we noted earlier, early relative deprivation research does show that leaders of student protests and civil rights activists were not the most absolutely deprived individuals, but often products of middle-class and even, upper-class backgrounds (Caplan & Paige, 1968; Gurin & Epps, 1974; Flacks, 1970). In those cases, personal rewards did not seem to prevent collective consciousness, involvement and action. Perhaps there were features of our experimental situation that may have enabled participants to focus on their personal advantage and to ignore the collective disadvantage.

One potential problem with the first experiment is the fact that participants were not asked explicitly about the group situation. We chose not to ask this question because we were afraid of priming group membership for participants assigned to the individual-primed experimental condition. However, the ambiguous nature of the questions meant that participants could interpret them as a request to de-scribe their personal situation rather than the collective situation. We assumed that people for whom group membership was made salient would perceive the situation in group terms. However, the results suggest that they may have used the group's disadvantage as a frame of reference for evaluating their personal fate. Therefore, in a second experiment (Smith, Spears & Oyen, 1994, Study 2), partici-pants were asked specifically about the collective situation of their ingroup. If they acknowledged dissatisfaction and unfairness when asked about the collective situ-ation, but not when they were asked about their personal situation, it suggests evidence that the pattern of results found in the first experiment was a conscious and strategic choice to focus on favourable personal circumstances.

A second feature that may have allowed group-primed participants to downplay the collective disadvantage was the relative salience of the advantaged outgroup. If an ingroup membership is salient but an outgroup comparison target is not, intragroup comparisons may be more likely than intergroup comparisons (Levine & Moreland, 1987).[1] For example, in the previous study, the relevant outgroup, economics students, was not especially obvious or salient. All the participants in the room were fellow psychology majors, the experiment took place in a psychol-ogy laboratory and economics students were never seen nor heard. Furthermore, psychology students as a group are not associated with a clearly 'reciprocal' outgroup (e.g., black and white, Pettigrew, 1985) nor are there clear political or collective attitudes and behaviours associated with being a psychology student that might encourage intergroup comparisons (as there might be for a feminist). This analysis suggests that if economics students, as a group, were made more salient, advantaged group-primed participants may have focused on disadvanta-geous intergroup comparisons and reported the greater deprivation we predicted.

In the second experiment, participants were asked about general and collective feelings of deprivation, gender rather than major was used as the shared group membership and whether or not advantaged outgroup members were present or absent from the room was manipulated. In this study, female psychology under-graduates in the United States were invited to participate in a pilot study designed to investigate decision-making styles. The majority of students who participated in this subject pool expected both short experiments and the requirements for participation to be the same for all participants. However, personally dis-advantaged participants were required to complete a second fifteen-minute decision-making problem, whereas personally advantaged participants were able to complete and leave the experiment significantly earlier. To manipulate collec-tive disadvantage, the distribution of task assignments indicated that the majority of female students and a minority of male students needed to complete a second problem. To manipulate the salience of the outgroup, for half the participants,

---

[1] We define interpersonal comparison choices as choices in which group membership is considered to be irrelevant, whereas group membership is important in determining an intragroup comparison choice.

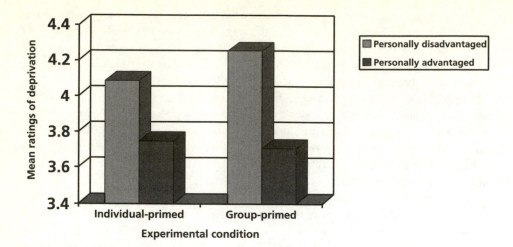

Note   Higher scores represent more deprivation (experiment rated as less fair and less satisfying). Scores could range from 1 (not at all deprived) to 7 (extremely deprived).

Figure 10.2a   Ratings of own deprivation
Source: Smith, Spears & Oyen, 1994, Study 2

two personally advantaged male participants completed the study early and left and for the other half, only female participants were present.

The key question is whether explicitly asking about the collective situation would make group-primed participants more likely to report dissatisfaction and unfairness regardless of their personal situation. As can be seen from figure 10.2a, when asked about deprivation in general, group-primed personally disadvantaged participants reported the most deprivation, whereas group-primed personally advantaged participants reported the least deprivation, just as in the first experiment. However, when asked specifically about the situation for the typical female participant, we see that both personally advantaged and personally disadvantaged group-primed participants acknowledge the collective disadvantage (see figure 10.2b). Most importantly, group-primed personally advantaged participants reported significantly more deprivation when they were specifically asked about the collective situation than about their personal situation. Interestingly, the presence of advantaged male participants in the room did make the advantage of the outgroup more salient, but it did not appear to make the corresponding disadvantage of the ingroup more potent.

This experiment suggests that if people are asked explicitly about the collective situation, and if they are reminded of their shared group membership, they will acknowledge the collective disadvantage. However, the question remains whether making a disadvantaged group membership salient can prompt people to notice

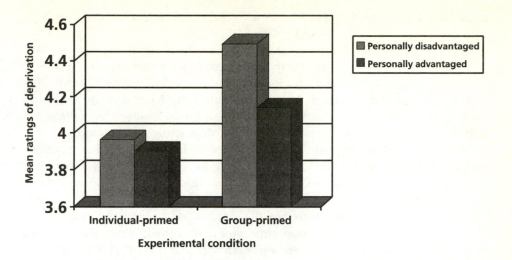

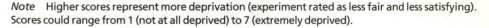

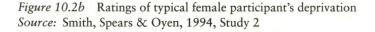

Note Higher scores represent more deprivation (experiment rated as less fair and less satisfying). Scores could range from 1 (not at all deprived) to 7 (extremely deprived).

Figure 10.2b   Ratings of typical female participant's deprivation
Source: Smith, Spears & Oyen, 1994, Study 2

and care about the collective situation without a specific request, and perhaps more importantly, whether identity salience can prompt behaviour. We pick up the thread of behaviour further below. First, however, we consider another route by which feelings of common fate and collective deprivation can be undermined by the salience of personal identity. Attributing personal outcomes to one's own inputs and ability can also deflect attention from the collective situation.

Additional Consequences of Context: Personal Identity Salience and Individual Attributions

The focus on ratings of deprivation ignores other ways in which people can respond to inequitable situations. When people do not get what they expect or think they deserve, they can react in a variety of ways (Mark & Folger, 1984). They can get angry, they can devalue the goal or outcome, or they can doubt their own abilities. 'Rationalizing' or reframing one's outcomes may be less risky and easier than confronting the inequity (Crosby, 1982; Ruggiero & Taylor, 1997). Of course, while there may be psychological costs to admitting personal inequity, there are also costs if they are not acknowledged. If members of disadvantaged groups justify arbitrary differences in rewards by downplaying effort or ability, it is not healthy in the long run, particularly in a society that emphasizes individual achievement and control. It can lead to self-fulfilling prophecies, and it does little to address systematic group-level injustices.

Researchers in other theoretical traditions have explored the variety of ways that people can react to disadvantageous situations, but this research has been limited to interpersonal contexts. However, the research presented already suggests that people may interpret the situation differently when they are primed to view themselves as group members. If making a group membership salient can influence people's feelings of satisfaction and fairness, it might also influence evaluations of personal ability and outcomes in inequitable situations. For example, imagine that you are a female employee working for a company and you have just received your year-end bonus. Then you discover that your male colleague down the hall has received twice the amount. You might focus on yourself as a unique individual, and decide that you are not all that good, do not really work that hard or that money is really not the most important part of the job. Alternatively, you might focus on the fact that you are a woman and he is a man. You might notice that not only did you not get as much as your male colleague, but that most female employees in the company earn less than their male colleagues. In this case, rather than doubt your own abilities, you might be motivated to challenge management to distribute the bonus money more equally.

With this example in mind, we can turn to several models which suggest that people, in general, will rationalize personal advantage or disadvantage. For example, according to equity theory, inequity produces anxiety (Adams, 1965; Walster, Walster & Berscheid, 1978). When faced with this anxiety, people can restore equity psychologically or in actuality. For example, if a person feels that they are unfairly underpaid, they can work less. Alternatively, they can view money as not important. The less likely it is that the real situation will change (or the more costly or risky real change might be), the more likely it is that people will try to adjust to the inequity psychologically. The Just World Hypothesis proposed by Lerner (1980) suggests a similar reaction to inequity. People have a need to believe in a just world in which everyone gets what they deserve and, therefore, deserves what they get. Most just world research focuses on reactions to suffering or deprivation of others, but there is also evidence that the disadvantaged use self-derogation to make sense of their personal situation. For example, strong believers in a just world were more likely to view their personal failure to win a desirable prize as fair than were weak believers in a just world (Hafer & Olson, 1993). Finally, people may assume personal responsibility for failure even in unfair situations because they have a need for control (Bulman & Wortman, 1977). For example, participants in a laboratory study who felt that they had a high level of control over whether or not they were exposed to discrimination were much less likely to mention discrimination as an explanation for personal negative feedback (Ruggiero & Taylor, 1997).

There are also more cognitive explanations for the tendency for the personally disadvantaged to deny their disadvantages. According to self-perception theory (Bem, 1967), people can use outcomes to infer their inputs or worth. For example, schoolchildren arbitrarily assigned to a disadvantageous position reported significantly less effort and comprehension of the experimental task than schoolchildren arbitrarily assigned to an advantageous position, even though their objective performances were the same (Gray-Little, 1980; Steil, 1983).

Our purpose here is not to determine what explanation best captures the phenomenon but to emphasize what these approaches have in common – they all focus on the individual level of abstraction. A shift to the social or group self might free the individual from some of the perceptions and motivations that underlie the tendency to rationalize one's personal situation. If social aspects of the self are made salient, they may influence evaluations of personal performance and outcomes in two ways. First, making a social self salient might 'release' people from individual-level concerns. In other words, protecting one's personal self-image, or having personal control may become less relevant or important when a social self is salient. An even stronger hypothesis is that making a social self salient replaces individual-level concerns with group-level concerns. In this case people might use evaluations of personal performance strategically to serve group interests. Imagine getting negative feedback about a task you just completed. An individual goal might be to look competent. You might argue that you did not really work that hard, so it is not surprising that you did not perform well. However, a collective goal might be to show collective injustice. In this case, you might 'emphasize' your personal failure to illustrate the unfairness of the situation: 'Look I worked really hard and I still didn't get rewarded.' You might even go so far as to deflate a personal triumph to demonstrate the unfairness of the system: 'Look I didn't work hard and I still got a good outcome' (see Van Knippenberg & Van Oers, 1984).

Evidence that people might evaluate their personal performance in different ways depending upon identity salience was found in the first experiment described above (Smith, Spears & Oyen, 1994, Study 1), in which Dutch university students expected to be paid for their participation in a study investigating creative problem-solving. As part of the experiment, participants completed two timed tasks in which they had three minutes to think of as many creative uses for an ordinary object as they could. Following the tasks, they rated how well they thought they and others may have performed on these types of task.

There was no difference across experimental conditions in how well participants performed. However, individual-primed participants who were personally advantaged reported working significantly harder and being significantly better at solving creative problems than did individual-primed personally disadvantaged participants. In contrast, group-primed personally advantaged and disadvantaged participants' ratings of their effort did not differ, just as their actual performance did not differ significantly. This pattern of results suggests that making a group membership salient undermines the importance of individual concerns. More interestingly, when asked how good they were at these types of problem, personally disadvantaged group-primed participants reported being very good (even though they were not rewarded), and personally advantaged group-primed participants reported being not very good (even though they were rewarded). This pattern of results suggests that making a group membership salient might replace individual concerns with collective concerns as argued above.

These results are suggestive, but there are several problems. First, it is unclear whether this pattern supports the strong version of our hypothesis (the ability evaluations) or the weak version (the effort evaluations). In other words, does making a group membership salient mean that people are released from individual level self-justification motives, or do they strategically use personal inputs to highlight collective disadvantage? One way to investigate this problem is to add a third factor to the design. If priming a group membership means that collective concerns replace individual concerns, then we should only see the strategic undermining of the rationalization of one's personal situation when the group as a whole is collectively disadvantaged. If the group is collectively advantaged, strategic evaluations are not needed. However, if making group membership salient means that personal impression management concerns are irrelevant, we should see evidence of the same pattern regardless of the group situation.

Another experiment also enables us to correct key difficulties with the original experimental design (Smith & Spears, 1996). For example, in the first experiment described earlier, all the participants learned their outcomes before they did the task. Although there were no significant differences in participants' performance, they could be behaving quite rationally. They believed that they adjusted their behaviour according to their expected outcomes. But if the same pattern occurred after people performed the task, it would support the argument that group membership salience actually undermines the personal justification bias. Therefore, a situation was designed in which personal outcomes were based on performance, but the performances required for the same outcome differed significantly. Personally disadvantaged participants were arbitrarily assigned to a much more difficult task, yet they were still required to meet the same performance standard as those arbitrarily assigned to a much easier task. This change in the design makes the situation more complicated, so participants were asked to evaluate effort, ability and the desirability of the prize. Objective effort and ability might vary, but the cash bonus was the same across conditions. As an outcome, evaluation of the cash bonus may be less susceptible to any impression management biases.

In this experiment, we manipulated personal advantage or disadvantage (whether the participant had to perform the more difficult task), collective advantage or disadvantage (whether the majority of one's group had to perform the more difficult task) and the salience of group membership (in this case, one's identity as Berkeley students versus one's unique personality).

The first question is whether we found any evidence that people 'rationalized' their personal situation. In other words, did the individually-primed participants report that they were worth what they were paid? As expected, individual-primed personally advantaged participants reported wanting the prize significantly more than did individual-primed personally disadvantaged participants. Personally ad-

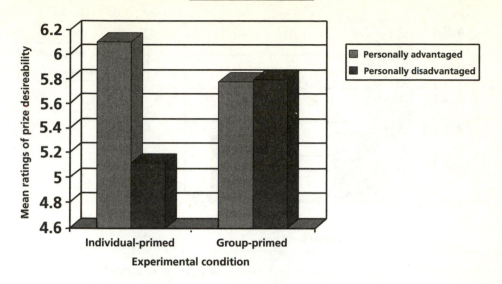

Figure 10.3   Participants' ratings of the cash bonus
Source: Smith & Spears, 1996

vantaged participants also reported being significantly better at signal detection tasks than did personally disadvantaged participants. Ratings of effort did not differ between the two experimental conditions. This means that we can only explore whether group salience undermines individual justification biases for ratings of ability and desirability.

The next question is whether making a group membership salient disrupted this pattern. As in the previous experiment, group-primed personally advantaged participants did not report wanting the prize any more than did the group-primed personally disadvantaged participants. Collective advantage or disadvantage did not influence participants' evaluations of the prize. Making a group membership salient did influence the tendency for participants to view the prize as more desirable if they won and less desirable if they did not (see figure 10.3).

For ratings of ability, the influence of group salience appears more strategic. Among group-primed collectively advantaged participants, personally advantaged participants reported significantly greater ability than did personally disadvantaged participants. However, for group-primed collectively disadvantaged participants, the ratings of ability did not significantly differ. This pattern suggests some evidence for the strategic explanation: only when the group was collectively disadvantaged, do the ratings of abilities converge (see figures 10.4a and b). If this was an automatic effect produced by group salience, convergence should also have been evident under conditions of collective advantage.

In this experiment, social comparison data was also collected. Given the am-

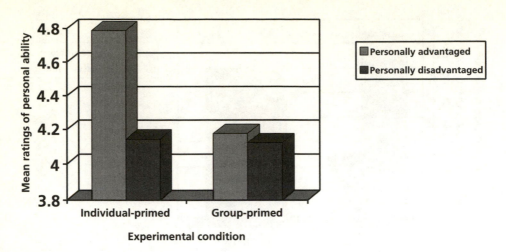

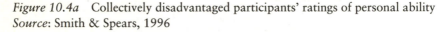

Figure 10.4a Collectively disadvantaged participants' ratings of personal ability
Source: Smith & Spears, 1996

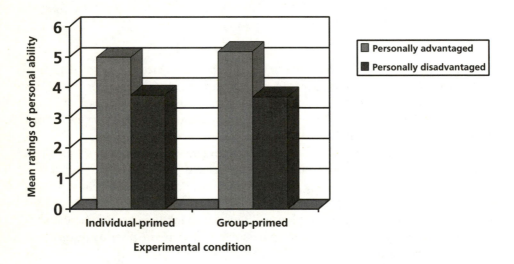

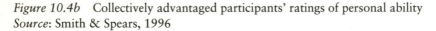

Figure 10.4b Collectively advantaged participants' ratings of personal ability
Source: Smith & Spears, 1996

Note Higher scores represent more ability. Scores could range from 1 (not at all good) to 7 (extremely good).

biguous results of the first study described above (Smith, Spears & Oyen, 1994, Study 1), a refined comparison choice measure was used. Recall that in the first study there was no clear evidence that personally advantaged group-primed participants preferred intergroup comparisons any less than did group-primed personally disadvantaged participants. However, this measure of comparison choice is potentially ambiguous and participants may have been interested in the ingroup score as a reference for evaluating their own score, not because they were interested in differences between the two groups. Therefore, in this experiment, we included four choices: (1) a comparison between their own score and the score of a randomly chosen participant; (2) their own score and the average score for their ingroup; (3) the average score for the ingroup and the average score for the outgroup; and (4) their own score and the average score for the outgroup. We hypothesized that the third and fourth choices represented a greater interest in intergroup comparison information (the fourth choice could include participants who view themselves as typical group members compared with the outgroup). We hypothesized that the second choice represented a greater interest in intragroup comparison information because the ingroup's performance could serve as a frame of reference for interpreting one's own score.

The majority of participants preferred to learn their personal score and the average ingroup member score. However, compared with individual-primed participants, group-primed participants were significantly more likely to choose to learn the score of the average outgroup member. Further, compared with personally advantaged group-primed participants, personally disadvantaged group-primed participants were the most interested in learning the score of the average outgroup member. In sum, in line with the effects of the personal advantage factor found in these studies, there is some evidence to suggest that personally advantaged group-primed participants were less interested in learning outgroup information. This supports the argument that they are more likely to turn their focus 'inward' and make more favourable intragroup social comparisons.

The results of the two studies discussed in this section show that the salience of group membership does appear to release people from individual-level judgement biases that can deflect attention from the collective situation. However, there was less evidence for the strategic explanation. Why? One possibility is that the situation was not perceived as illegitimate. When participants were asked to evaluate the general abilities of Berkeley students, collectively advantaged participants reported that Berkeley students were better at signal-detection tasks than did collectively disadvantaged participants. Further, this effect was only significant for participants who were primed to think of their shared group membership, suggesting that collectively disadvantaged participants may have viewed the group's collective disadvantage as reasonable. Therefore, there was, arguably, no collective injustice to be challenged. It is possible that by making the collective inequity appear more unfair, we would find more evidence of strategic judgemental bias. However, that goal might be especially difficult to accomplish (see Ruggiero & Taylor, 1997). Manipulation checks showed that group-primed and individual-primed collectively disadvantaged participants were equally likely to notice their collective disadvantage. Drawing attention to the unfair distribution of task assignments might undermine the group salience manipulation by creating feelings of common fate among individual-primed participants. It also remains possible that strategic biases related to group inequity are simply less robust than, for example, justification biases associated with personal identity.

To summarize the story so far, we have had mixed success in getting people who are personally advantaged to acknowledge group deprivation as a result of contextual manipulations of identity salience. Although priming a group identity does reinforce feelings of deprivation for those who are personally deprived, if anything, group identity salience seems to lead to reduced feelings of deprivation for those who are personally advantaged, especially when they are not forced to construe their feelings explicitly in terms of the group situation. However, we achieved greater success in cutting off the route to individual attributions associated with personal outcomes. Making group identity salient seemed to release people from the tendency to rationalize their personal outcomes in individual terms. Such individual perceptions are clearly one way in which people can be deflected from consciousness about the collective situation. In short, this contextual condition (salient group identity) is probably necessary but by no means sufficient to move people to think and behave in group terms rather than in line with their individual interests. In retrospect, this is perhaps not so surprising. As was argued by Spears et al. in chapter 4, there are good reasons to suppose that context alone will be insufficient to elicit collective perceptions and behaviour. Instead, the degree of group identification may be a critical moderator of reactions to context. We now consider how including the role of group identification might help to move us further along the road to increasing perceptions of collective deprivation. At the same time, we consider the importance of procedural factors in contributing to the perceived illegitimacy of outcomes and to the critical role of the content of group ideology.

Commitment and Content: Identification, Illegitimacy and Ideology

A fourth experiment (Hamstra, 1998) was designed to investigate whether group identification might promote greater attention to the collective fate and form a critical moderator of group-based perceptions of deprivation. In this study, we also tried to enhance the illegitimacy of discrimination more than in the previous experiments. We considered this important because legitimacy may provide a mechanism whereby group members accept their fate (Kappen & Branscombe, under review; Ruggiero & Taylor, 1995; 1997; Wright, 1997; see Jost & Major, 1999). As in most relative deprivation research, the focus in the previous two experiments has been on the large discrepancies in outcomes for the two different groups (Tyler, Boeckmann, Smith & Huo, 1997). However, outcome-focused models are incomplete in that they neglect people's perceptions of how outcomes are determined. People who feel they have been treated fairly in procedural terms (as compared to unfairly) are more likely to accept unfavourable decisions and outcomes (see Lind & Tyler, 1988; Tyler, Boeckmann, Smith & Huo, 1997; and Tyler & Smith, 1998 for reviews of the literature).

Closely associated with procedural fairness are perceptions of legitimacy (Tyler, 1997). As outlined in social identity theory, if a situation is perceived as legitimate without 'cognitive alternatives' to the status quo, a collective challenge is much less likely (Ellemers, 1993b; Tajfel, 1982b; Tajfel & Turner, 1979; 1986). Similarly, Folger (1987), in his referent cognitions model, argues that if an inequitable situation is justified, feelings of relative deprivation are unlikely. Perhaps if we made the situation appear more procedurally illegitimate, people aware of the collective disadvantage would be more willing to acknowledge the injustice and act regardless of their personal situation. Therefore, the experimental situation was designed to appear as illegitimate as possible (without losing participants because they decided to leave!).

The main purpose of this experiment was to determine whether group identification moderated reactions to collective disadvantage. Although the salience of a disadvantaged group membership may increase the focus on the group in the experiments described above, it does not necessarily enhance the degree of commitment to the group. Group identification is distinct from situational salience and also includes the emotional attachment to the group and (the degree of) positive and negative evaluations associated with the group as well as awareness of one's group membership (Tajfel, 1982b; see chapter 9, this volume). It is quite possible that group-primed participants may have been aware of their group membership but not have felt especially close to other group members. If so, intragroup comparisons and outcomes may have been more relevant and important than intergroup comparisons. It is possible that participants who felt particularly committed to their group would have reported greater deprivation than previously obtained. Guimond and Dubé-Simard (1983) offer a similar argument. They propose that the knowledge of unjust collective treatment represents the cognitive component of group deprivation, but that the level of identification influences the intensity of dissatisfaction with the deprived group's situation.

Recent experimental research shows that initial levels of group identification are critical to how people deal with disadvantaged group status (see chapters 3 and 4 for reviews of this work). In general, participants who identify strongly with the group tend to remain supportive of it, even or especially when the situation is unfavourable whereas those who identify weakly only show supportive responses when the group situation is favourable. For example, when group identity was threatened, those who identified closely with their group saw themselves as a more typical group member and the group as more homogeneous compared with low identifiers (Doosje, Ellemers & Spears, 1995; Spears, Doosje & Ellemers, 1997). People who do not identify with the group are less committed to it and want to change group membership even if it does not seem possible (Ellemers, Spears & Doosje, 1997). Most importantly, these differences between high and low identifiers are most evident when the intergroup context is made salient (see chapter 3). Together, this research suggests that making a disadvantaged group membership salient will only increase sensitivity to the collective situation for those participants who are closely identified with the disadvantaged group. For participants who are low identifiers, making the collective disadvantage salient might make them more inclined to distance themselves from the collective problem.

In the fourth study, we focused exclusively on the theoretically interesting combination of personal advantage and collective disadvantage (the case for the experience of double deprivation seems well enough supported by the data so far). To measure identification with the group, undergraduate engineering students completed an identification scale embedded in a short questionnaire given before the actual experiment. During the experiment, participants were primed to think of themselves as either engineering students (compared to business students) or as unique individuals. Participants were told that their performance would be measured on the same task (and those who did well would be able to participate in a $100 subject payment lottery). However, some students would be given the opportunity to practise (and receive the answers to) a similar task beforehand, clearly helping performance (the personally advantaged), and others would complete a totally unrelated task (the personally disadvantaged; only token data were gathered in this cell, which did not form part of the design). Across all experimental conditions, the task assignments showed that the majority of business students (outgroup) and a minority of engineering students (ingroup) would complete the practice task, creating a collective disadvantage. In order to make the illegitimacy of the situation especially clear, two confederates interrupted the introduction with the following comments: 'But doesn't this mean that whoever gets to practise has a far better chance of winning the $100 lottery?' and 'I heard that some of us get screwed!' (see Bylsma, Major & Cozzarelli, 1995 for a similar procedure).

The first question is whether those who identify closely with the group would be the most likely to prefer to make intergroup comparisons, particularly when their group membership is primed. In this experiment (personally advantaged) participants all knew their own score. Therefore, they simply chose what other score they would most like to learn (comparison choices were similar to Smith & Spears, 1996). In line with our predictions, we did find some indications that high identifiers are more interested in intergroup comparisons than low identifiers. Compared with high identifiers, most low identifiers preferred to know the average performance score of engineering students. High identifiers, on the other hand, were not only interested in the performance score of other engineering students but also in the average score for all students who participated in the study (e.g., the score for both engineering and business students). This pattern of results suggests that there is a tendency for low identifiers to adopt the ingroup as a frame of reference (hence the choice to learn the ingroup's average score). High identifiers not only showed an interest in their ingroup, but are also interested in the intergroup context (hence their interest in both the ingroup's average score and the overall score for both groups). Priming group membership did not appear to influence comparison choice.

Participants' behavioural intentions support their comparison choices. In this experiment, participants were asked if they would be willing to attend a psychology department discussion of research projects or to be contacted by a member of the committee on this matter. There were no differences in participants' willingness to attend a department meeting, but their willingness to be contacted for further information did vary across experimental conditions. For those who did not identify with engineering students as a group, being viewed as a group representative made them less likely to volunteer. However, for those who identified with engineering students as a group, being viewed as a group representative made them more likely to volunteer. Recall that high identifiers showed greater interest in the intergroup context (i.e., including the outgroup) whereas low identifiers seemed less interested in the intergroup context and more interested in the ingroup frame of reference. These data suggest that the behavioural commitment may well be more connected to the group's image relative to the outgroup for the high identifiers than is the case for low identifiers.

However, the most important question is whether priming group membership for highly identified participants, in particular, would lead to a greater acknowledgment of the collective disadvantage, even when they enjoyed a personal advantage. For low identified participants, priming group membership should not be as effective. In fact, high group identification might be sufficient to promote acknowledgment of the collective disadvantage even without the necessity of shared group membership being primed. Regardless of the identity salience manipulation, participants more accurately reported the collective disadvantage, rated the collective situation as significantly less fair than their personal situation and the task distribution as unfair and unequal. This pattern of results suggests that by making the situation more obviously unfair, we succeeded in making participants more sensitive to the inequity. Contrary to our expectations, identity salience did not influence participants' answers, with one exception: participants for whom their individual identity was salient reported being more satisfied with taking part in the lottery than those for whom their group identity was salient. Moreover, high identifiers downplayed their personal advantage to a greater extent than did low identifiers. For example, high identifiers reported being less personally advantaged than low identifiers; they reported that the possibility to practise was less helpful than low identifiers said it was; and high identifiers thought it was more fair that they could participate in the lottery than low identifiers thought it was. In other words, high identifiers, for whom disadvantaged group membership was primed, did not report more deprivation than low identifiers did, in contrast to what we had originally predicted. High identifiers constantly reported less deprivation than low identifiers, independent of identity salience. In short, advantaged participants who are members of a disadvantaged group recognize the inequity, but people who identify more closely with their group define the inequity as less of a problem than low identifiers.

There could be two reasons for this result. First, participants were confronted with inconsistent information (they are advantaged as a person while the ingroup is disadvantaged). This inconsistency could be especially distressing for participants who identify strongly with the ingroup. Following dissonance principles (Festinger, 1957), one way to reduce the inconsistency between their personal position and the position for the majority of the group would be to downplay the value of being able to practise the task. In contrast, for low identifiers, the inconsistency between their personal and group situation should be less anxiety-provoking, and they should be less motivated to downplay their personal advantage.

Alternatively, high identifiers may not be as collectively oriented as we assumed they would be. In retrospect, one could argue that key aspects of the engineering student identity are individual competence and success, especially for students at as competitive and prestigious a university as Berkeley. This emphasis on individual achievement and success could be interpreted as constituting a rather 'individualistic group norm' (see Barreto & Ellemers, 1998b; and chapter 6, this volume). If this 'individualistic group norm' is an important part of the engineering student identity, as we suspect, it is not surprising that differences between individual- and group-primed participants are not more dramatic. Identification with the group (and one's chosen career) might imply a fair degree of competition with one's peers to succeed on the important group-defining dimensions, perhaps even to be 'first among equals' (Codol, 1975). If the individual and group self-definitions are closely bound up with each other, it is explicable that ratings differ little between individual primed and group primed participants. It seems quite possible on the basis of group stereotypes that, compared with the other social groups used in our research (i.e. psychology students and women), engineering students may indeed be less collectively oriented. Furthermore, the groups chosen for the previous experiments – women, psychology students and university students – were paired with clear rival groups, which represented an equal or even higher status position. In other words, we may have primed a competitive intergroup context when we primed group membership. In contrast, engineering students may not have viewed business students as an equal or potentially higher status rivals (for jobs, for example). Together with the group ideology, this might explain why, for high identifiers, competition seems to have been directed inwards at the ingroup and they attempted to justify the situation in line with their personal disadvantage.

This albeit post hoc explanation suggests that one cannot focus on group identification and ignore group ideology. The results provide an important reminder that it is necessary to be aware of the content of group identity and norms before we can predict the actual products of context and commitment (see chapters 3, 4 and 6). This point is also clearly evident in social identity theory in which Tajfel (1978a) distinguishes between the 'social mobility' and 'social change' systems of beliefs that map onto the continuum of behaviour from interpersonal to intergroup respectively. For a disadvantaged group to act as a group, rather than as a set of individuals, it has to see itself as a group, and see the value in a collective rather than individual strategy for dealing with disadvantage. 'Cognitive alternatives' to the status quo are, arguably, important ingredients for predicting a collective strategy. However, their very cognitive nature means that such beliefs may be as much a product of group ideology itself as part of the situation.

In the present study the comparison and behavioural commitment data suggest that high identifiers do seem to be operating from a group perspective, even though this may be expressed in individualistic terms when their performance or achievement as prototypes of the group is at issue. More generally, the valence and the ideologies associated with a particular group membership may encourage the selection of particular comparison targets, influence the interpretation of disadvantaged comparisons and encourage or mitigate people's investment in the collective situation. For example, women who supported a feminist ideology indicated greater dissatisfaction with the pay difference between secretarial and sales manager jobs than did traditionally oriented women (Martin, 1986). Similarly, commerce students are more likely to attribute poverty and unemployment to internal characteristics, whereas social science students are more likely to attribute poverty and unemployment to institutional factors (Guimond & Palmer, 1990). We might expect feminists and social science students to be more likely to react to collective inequities.

Bringing the themes of context, commitment and content together, we find that priming a disadvantaged group membership can be a double-edged sword. For those who are personally disadvantaged, priming the collective disadvantage increases their feelings of general deprivation, as we would predict. However, for those who are personally advantaged, priming the collective disadvantage can actually decrease feelings of deprivation – particularly if people are not required to evaluate the collective situation, if the procedure is not especially illegitimate, if people do not identify closely with the disadvantaged group and if the ideology associated with the disadvantaged group membership does not support a collective focus. Yet priming a group membership does change how people frame the situation. Although they might not report greater deprivation, group-primed participants were more sensitive to the collective inequity and more willing to act as a group representative.

Commitment and Comparison Context: Further Evidence of Behavioural Consequences

We argue that if particular group memberships are made salient, and the ideological content of the group norms encourages collective behaviour, participants will be more likely to make the disadvantageous intergroup comparisons that lead to collective action. However, in the experiments described above, comparison information was measured rather than manipulated. Therefore, any causal conclusions are limited. In a questionnaire study, we returned to a clearly competitive intergroup context in which university membership was primed in comparison with another university viewed as having equal and possibly higher status (Smith, Ben-Moshe, Cummins, Irvin, Miller, Shull, Novasel, Warren & Werre, 1998). Participants in this study completed two separate questionnaires several weeks apart. The purpose of the first questionnaire was simply to measure how much students identified with being a Sonoma State University student. The purpose of the second questionnaire was to manipulate the type of comparison information participants read. Participants either read about a disadvantageous intergroup comparison between Sonoma State University and a rival university's students, or a disadvantageous interpersonal comparison between themselves and other Sonoma State students. Following the comparison information, students were asked a series of questions about their reactions to the information. For example, they rated their immediate reaction to the paragraph information on a series of adjectives. Interestingly, there was no difference in the emotional reactions of high and low identifiers to the disadvantageous intergroup comparison. However, low identifiers reacted significantly more negatively to the disadvantageous interpersonal comparison information compared to high identifiers.

The key question is whether greater identification with the group combined with disadvantageous intergroup comparison information would promote support for collective action. In the questionnaire, students rated whether they would sign a petition, attend a rally, write a letter to the Governor or picket a trustee meeting in order to protect Sonoma State University's unique atmosphere. The type of comparison did not influence low identifiers' ratings of these questions. However, high identifiers who read the intergroup comparison were significantly more likely to endorse these social change questions than high identifiers who read the interpersonal comparison. Furthermore, high identifiers who read the intergroup comparison were significantly more likely to report that Sonoma State students could improve the situation compared with high identifiers who read the interpersonal comparison. In contrast, low identifiers who read the intergroup comparison reported that Sonoma State students would be less likely to be able to improve the situation compared with low identifiers who read the interpersonal comparison (see chapters 3 and 4 for evidence of similar interaction patterns). In sum, in this study, both comparison information and strength of identification contributed to greater endorsement of collective action when a clearly competitive intergroup context was primed.

To summarize, whereas the first set of experimental studies suggest how group membership salience and strength of identification with a group can evoke different comparison preferences, the last questionnaire study shows how people who identify more or less closely with the group respond to different types of comparison information. For weakly identified group members, disadvantageous intergroup comparisons decrease their commitment to collective action and their belief in the group's influence. For highly identified group members, the reactions to disadvantageous intergroup comparison is to increase commitment to collective action and belief in the collective efficacy of such action (see also chapters 3 and 9).

Summary and Conclusions

Ironically, evidence from the laboratory suggests that group deprivation is more elusive than one might expect from the results of related field research. The salience of and identification with a disadvantaged group may not always promote collective strategies to overcome group disadvantage. In particular, personal advantage may be enough to undermine a general sense of injustice to one's group as a whole. However, both the experimental and survey results suggest that while group salience may not guarantee intergroup comparisons, it may guarantee greater sensitivity to the outcomes of intergroup comparisons. Regardless of their personal situation, group-primed participants reported the collective situation more accurately and, if asked directly, reported feeling collectively deprived. Further, making the group membership salient can disrupt the individual justification biases documented in other social justice research. Personally advantaged or disadvantaged participants primed to focus on their unique selves were likely to justify their plight, but were much less likely to justify the situation when primed to focus on their shared group membership. Our research also conceptualizes group identification as distinct from group salience and shows how strength of identification can encourage greater awareness of the intergroup context. Low identifiers were more likely to treat the group as a frame of reference for evaluating their personal outcomes. The questionnaire study in which comparison context was also directly manipulated confirms the importance of intergroup comparisons for promoting collective action, particularly for high identifiers.

Overall, this programme of research helps to explain the difficulties in generating collective consciousness and direct challenges to collective deprivation. The optimal conjunction of context, commitment and content seems to be necessary to ensure a collective reaction. The chances of people responding collectively to their group's fate will be maximized when their group identity is salient (context), when they identify strongly with their group (commitment) and when collective group behaviour is ideologically consistent with group norms (content). If these factors are in place, group members may be motivated to look beyond the comforts of their personal situation and consider the collective plight. Whether perceptions of deprivation are actually turned into collective action is likely to depend on yet further constraints, such as perceived collective efficacy and the perceived costs of expressing sometimes anti-normative and sanctionable behaviour in the face of powerful outgroups or authorities (Klandermans, 1997; Reicher, Spears & Postmes, 1995; Wright, 1997; chapters 6 and 8, this volume). In this respect the wider social structural context is also critical (Turner, 1996; see also chapter 1, this volume): unstable social relations and perceptions of illegitimacy will help to encourage collective action (Tajfel & Turner, 1986). With these conditions and constraints in mind, it becomes easier to understand why people routinely fail to recognize or act on the basis of collective deprivation. We do not need the blanket of false-consciousness to explain a lack of concern with the collective plight. Our findings suggest that reality-based experience grounded in identity and material interests are sufficient to explain the resilience of the status quo, while pointing to the necessary ingredients for social change.

References

Abrams, D. (1990). Political identity: relative deprivation, social identity and the case of Scottish Nationalism. *ESRC 16–19 Initiative – Occasional Papers*.

Abrams, D. (1996) Social identity, self as structure and self as process. In W. P. Robinson (ed.), *Social Groups and Identities: Developing the Legacy of Henri Tajfel*. Oxford: Butterworth Heinemann.

Abrams, D. & Hogg, M. A. (eds) (1999) *Social Identity and Social Cognition*. Oxford: Blackwell.

Abrams, D., Ando, K. & Hinkle, S. (1998). Psychological attachment to the group: Cross-cultural differences in organizational identification and subjective norms as predictors of workers' turnover intentions. *Personality and Social Psychology Bulletin*, 24, 1027–39.

Abrams, D., Wetherell, M., Cochrane, S., Hogg, M. A. & Turner, J. C. (1990). Knowing what to think by knowing who you are: Self-categorization and the nature of norm formation, conformity, and group polarization. *British Journal of Social Psychology*, 29, 97–119.

Adams, J. S. (1965). Inequity in social exchange. In L. Berkowitz (ed.), *Advances in Experimental Social Psychology* (vol. 2). New York: Academic Press.

Adorno, T. W., Frenkel-Brunswick, E., Levinson, D. J. & Sanford, R. N. (1950). *The Authoritarian Personality*. New York: Harper & Row.

Adrianson, L. & Hjelmquist, E. (1991). Group processes in face-to-face and computer mediated communication. *Behaviour and Information Technology*, 10(4), 281–96.

Ajzen, I. & Fishbein, M. (1980). *Theoretical Implications. Understanding Attitudes and Predicting Behaviour*. Englewood Cliffs, NJ: Prentice-Hall.

Allen, N. J. & Meyer, J. P. (1990). The measurement and antecedents of affective, continuance and normative commitment to the organisation. *Journal of Occupational Psychology*, 63, 1–18.

Allen, N. J. & Meyer, J. P. (1996). Affective, continuance, and normative commitment to the organisation: An examination of construct validity. *Journal of Vocational Behaviour*, 49, 252–76.

Allen, V. L. & Wilder, D. A. (1975). Categorization, belief similarity and intergroup discrimination. *Journal of Personality and Social Psychology*, 32, 971–7.

Allport, G. (1954). *The Nature of Prejudice*. Reading, MA: Addison-Wesley.

Anastasio, P., Bachman, B., Gaertner, S. & Dovidio, J. (1997) Categorization, recategorization and common group identity. In R. Spears, P. J. Oakes, N. Ellemers & S. A. Haslam (eds), *The Social Psychology of Stereotyping and Group Life*. Oxford, UK & Cambridge, MA: Blackwell.

Anderson, L. R. & Blanchard, P. N. (1982). Sex differences in task and socio-emotional behaviour. *Basic and Applied Social Psychology*, 3, 109–39.

Arcuri, L., Maass, A. & Portelli, G. (1993) Linguistic intergroup bias and implicit attributions. *British Journal of Social Psychology*, 32, 277–85.

Aronson, E. & Mills, J. (1959). The effects of severity of initiation on liking for a group. *Journal of Abnormal and Social Psychology*, 59, 177–81.

Asch, S. E. (1952) *Social Psychology*. Englewood Cliffs, NJ: Prentice-Hall.

Ashforth, B. E. & Mael, F. (1989). Social identity theory and the organisation. *Academy of Management Review*, 14, 20–39.

Balka, E. (1993). Women and media in Canada: A feminist sampler, *Electronic Journal of Communication/La Revue Electronique de Communication* (On-line), 3. Available: http://www.cios.org/www/ejc/v3n193.htm

Bandura, A. (1977). Self-efficacy: Towards a unifying theory of behaviour change. *Psychological Review*, 84, 191–215.

Bandura, A. (1986). *Social Foundations of Thought and Action: A Social Cognitive Theory*. Englewood Cliffs, NJ: Prentice-Hall.

Bandura, A. (1997). *Self-efficacy. The Exercise of Control*. New York: W. H. Freeman and Company.

Bargh, J. A. & Barndollar, K. (1996). Automaticity in action: The unconscious as a repository of chronic goals and motives. In P. M. Gollwitzer & J. A. Bargh (eds), *The Psychology of Action*. New York: Guilford.

Baron, R. A. & Byrne, D. (1994). *Social Psychology*. (7th edn). Boston, MA: Allyn & Baron.

Barreto, M. & Ellemers, N. (1998a). Psychological and contextual determinants of effort on behalf of a low status group. Paper presented at the first Jena workshop on intergroup processes, Jena, February 1998.

Barreto, M. & Ellemers, N. (1998b). You can't always do what you want: Social identity and self-presentational determinants of the choice to work for a low status group. Manuscript under review.

Barreto, M., Spears, R., Ellemers, N. & Shahinper, K. (1998). The influence of linguistic context on the expression of social identity. Manuscript under preparation.

Barrett, K. C. (1995). A functionalist approach to shame and guilt. In J. P. Tangney & K. W. Fischer (eds), *Self-conscious Emotions: The Psychology of Shame, Guilt, Embarrassment, and Pride*. New York: Guilford Press.

Bashaw, E. R. & Grant, S. E. (1994). Exploring the distinctive nature of work commitments: Their relationships with personal characteristics, job performance, and propensity to leave. *Journal of Personal Selling and Sales Management*, 14, 41–56.

Basow, S. A. (1992). *Gender Stereotypes and Roles* (3rd edn). Belmont, CA: Brooks/Cole.

Baugh, S. G. & Roberts, R. M. (1994). Professional and organizational commitment among engineers: Conflicting or complementing? *IEEE Transactions on Engineering Management*, 41, 108–14.

Baumeister, R. F. (1982). A self-presentational view of social phenomena. *Psychological Bulletin*, 91(1), 3–26.

Baumeister, R. F. (1986). *Identity: Cultural Change and the Struggle for Self*. Oxford: Oxford University Press.

Baym, N. (1995). The emergence of community in computer-mediated communication. In S. Jones (ed.), *Cybersociety: Computer-mediated Community and Communication*. Thousand Oaks, CA: Sage.

Becker, T. E. (1992). Foci and bases of commitment: Are they distinctions worth making. *Academy of Management Journal*, 35, 232–44.

Becker, T. E. & Billings, R. S. (1993). Profiles of commitment: An empirical test. *Journal of Organizational Behaviour*, 14, 177–90.

Becker, T. E., Billings, R. S., Eveleth, D. M. & Gilbert, N. L. (1996). Foci and bases of employee commitment: Implications for job performance. *Academy of Management Journal*, 39, 464–82.

Bem, D. J. (1967). Self-perception: An alternative interpretation of cognitive dissonance. *Psychological Review*, 74, 183–200.

Berdahl, J. L. & Craig, K. M. (1996). Equality of participation and influence in groups: The effects of communication medium and sex composition. *Computer-Supported Cooperative Work*, 4, 179–201.

Berry, J. W. (1990). Psychology of acculturation: Understanding individuals moving between cultures. In R. W. Brislin (ed.), *Applied Cross-cultural Psychology* (vol. 14). Newbury Park, CA: Sage.

Bettencourt, B. A., Miller, N. & Hume, D. L. (in press). Effects of numerical representation within co-operative settings: Examining the role of salience in ingroup favouritism. *British Journal of Social Psychology*.

Biernat, M. & Vescio, T. K. (1993). Categorization and stereotyping: Effects of group context on memory and social judgement. *Journal of Experimental Social Psychology*, 29, 166–202.

Blanz, M., Mummendey, A. & Otten, S. (1995). Positive-negative asymmetry in social discrimination: The impact of stimulus valence and size and status differentials on intergroup evaluations. *British Journal of Social Psychology*, 34, 409–20.

Blanz, M., Mummendey, A. & Otten, S. (1997). Normative evaluations and frequency expectations regarding positive versus negative outcome allocations between groups. *European Journal of Social Psychology*, 27, 165–76.

Bond, M. H. (1983). How language variation affects inter-cultural differentiation of values by Hong-Kong bilinguals. *Journal of Language and Social Psychology*, 2, 57–66.

Bond, M. H. & Cheung, M.-K. (1984). Experimenter language choice and ethnic affirmation by Chinese trilinguals in Hong-Kong. *International Journal of Intercultural Relations*, 8, 347–56.

Bourhis, R. Y., Giles, H., Leyens, J-P. & Tajfel, H. (1979). Psycholinguistic distinctiveness: Language divergence in Belgium. In H. Giles & R. St. Clair (eds), *Language and Social Psychology*. Oxford: Blackwell.

Bourhis, R. Y., Turner, J. C. & Gagnon, A. (1997) Interdependence, social identity and discrimination: Some empirical considerations. In R. Spears, P. J. Oakes, N. Ellemers and S. A. Haslam (eds) *The Social Psychology of Stereotyping and Group Life*. Oxford, UK & Cambridge, MA: Blackwell.

Branscombe, N. R. (1998). Thinking about one's gender group's privileges or disadvantages: Consequences for well-being in women and men. *British Journal of Social Psychology*, 37, 167–84.

Branscombe, N. R. & Ellemers, N. (1998). Coping with group-based discrimination: Individualistic versus group-level strategies. In J. K. Swim & C. Stangor (eds), *Prejudice: The Target's Perspective*. New York: Academic Press.

Branscombe, N. R. & Wann, D. L. (1991). The positive social and self concept consequences of sports team identification. *Journal of Sport and Social Issues*, 15, 115–27.

Branscombe, N. R. & Wann, D. L. (1992). Physiological arousal and reactions to outgroup
members during competitions that implicate an important social identity. *Aggressive
Behavior*, 18, 85–93.

Branscombe, N. R. & Wann, D. L. (1994). Collective self-esteem consequences of outgroup
derogation when a valued social identity is on trial. *European Journal of Social Psychology*, 24, 641–57.

Branscombe, N. R., Schiffhauer, K. & Valencia, L. (in press). Perceiving pervasive discrimination among African Americans: Implications for group identification and well being.

Branscombe, N. R., Schmitt, M. T. & Harvey, R. (in press). Coping with perceived prejudice among African-Americans: Attributions, group identification, and well-being. Manuscript under review.

Branscombe, N. R., Spears, R., Ellemers, N. & Doosje, B. (1998). Ask not what your group
can do for you (ask what it thinks of you!): Prestige and respect as determinants of group
affiliation and behaviour. Manuscript under review.

Branscombe, N. R., Wann, D. L., Noel, J. G. & Coleman, J. (1993). In-group or out-group
extremity: Importance of the threatened social identity. *Personality and Social Psychology Bulletin*, 17, 381–8.

Breakwell, G. M. (1979). Illegitimate group membership and intergroup differentiation.
British Journal of Social and Clinical Psychology, 18, 141–9.

Breakwell, G. M. (1986). *Coping with Threatened Identities*. New York: Methuen.

Brewer, M. B. (1979). In-group bias in the minimal intergroup situation: A cognitive-motivational analysis. *Psychological Bulletin*, 86, 307–24.

Brewer, M. B. (1991). The social self: On being the same and different at the same time.
Personality and Social Psychology Bulletin, 17, 475–82.

Brewer, M. B. (in press). Category-based versus person-based perception. *European Review of Social Psychology*, 9.

Brewer, M. B. & Kramer, R. M. (1986) Choice behaviour in social dilemmas: Effects of
social identity, group size and decision framing. *Journal of Personality and Social Psychology*, 50, 543–9.

Brewer, M. B. & Miller, N. (1996) *Intergroup Relations*. Buckingham, UK: Open University Press.

Brewer, M. B. & Schneider, S. K. (1990) Social identity and social dilemmas: A double-
edged sword. In D. Abrams & M. A. Hogg (eds), *Social Identity Theory: Constructive
and Critical Advances*. London: Harvester-Wheatsheaf.

Brewer, M. B. & Weber, J. G. (1994) Self-evaluation effects of interpersonal versus intergroup
social comparison. *Journal of Personality and Social Psychology*, 66, 268–75.

Brewer, M. B., Manzi, J. M. & Shaw J. S. (1993). Ingroup identification as a function of
depersonalization, distinctiveness, and status. *Psychological Science*, 4, 88–92.

Brewer, M. B., Weber, J. G. & Carini, B. (1995). Person memory in intergroup contexts:
Categorization versus individuation. *Journal of Personality and Social Psychology*, 69,
29–40.

Brigham, J. C. (1971). Ethnic stereotypes. *Psychological Bulletin*, 76, 15–33.

Brouwer, J., Kawakami, J., Rojahn, K. & Postmes, T. (1997). De effecten van de
(on)zichtbaarheid van sekse op zelf-stereotypering [The effects of gender (in)visibility on
self-stereotyping]. In C. K. W. De Dreu, N. K. De Vries, D. Van Knippenberg & C. Rutte
(eds), *Fundamentele Sociale Psychologie* (vol. 11). Tilburg: Tilburg University Press.

Brown, R. J. (1984a). The role of similarity in intergroup relations. In H. Tajfel (ed.), *The Social Dimension: European Developments in Social Psychology*. Cambridge: Cambridge University Press.

Brown, R. J. (1984b). The effects of intergroup similarity and co-operative versus competitive orientation on intergroup discrimination. *British Journal of Social Psychology*, 23, 21–33.

Brown, R. J. (1995) *Prejudice: Its Social Psychology*. Oxford: Blackwell.

Brown, R. & Abrams, D. (1986). The effects of intergroup similarity and goal interdependence on intergroup attitudes and task performance. *Journal of Experimental Social Psychology*, 22, 78–92.

Brown, R. & Turner, J. C. (1981). Interpersonal and intergroup behaviour. In J. C. Turner and H. Giles (eds), *Intergroup Behaviour*. Oxford: Blackwell.

Brown, R. & Wade, G. (1987). Superordinate goals and intergroup behaviour: The effect of role ambiguity and status on intergroup attitudes and task performance. *European Journal of Social Psychology*, 17, 131–42.

Brown, R. J. & Williams, J. A. (1984) Group identification: The same thing to all people? *Human Relations*, 37, 547–64.

Brown, R. J., Condor, F., Mathews, A., Wade, G. & Williams, J. A. (1986) Explaining intergroup differentiation in an industrial organization. *Journal of Occupational Psychology*, 59, 273–86.

Brown, R. J., Hinkle, S., Ely, P. G., Fox-Cardamone, L., Maras, P. & Taylor, L. A. (1992) Recognizing group diversity: Individualist-collectivist and autonomous-relational social orientations and their implications for intergroup processes. *British Journal of Social Psychology*, 31, 327–42.

Bruins, J. J. (1998). Experimental methods. In K. Whitfield & G. Strauss (eds). *Researching the World of Work: Strategies and Methods in Studying Industrial Relations*. Ithaka, NY: Cornell University Press.

Bruins, J., Ellemers, N. & De Gilder, D. (1999). Power use and differential competence as determinants of subordinates' evaluative and behavioural responses in simulated organizations. *European Journal of Social Psychology* 29.

Bulman, R. J. & Wortman, C. B. (1977). Attributions of blame and coping in the 'real world': Severe accident victims react to their lot. *Journal of Personality and Social Psychology*, 51, 277–83.

Burke, P. J. & Reitzes, D. C. (1991). An identity theory approach to commitment. *Social Psychology Quarterly*, 54, 239–51.

Burris, C. T., Branscombe, N. R. & Klar, Y. (1997). Maladjustment implications of self and group gender-role discrepancies: An ordered-discrepancy model. *European Journal of Social Psychology*, 27, 75–95.

Bylsma, W., Major, B. & Cozzarelli, C. (1995). The influence of legitimacy appraisals on the determinants of entitlement beliefs. *Basic and Applied Social Psychology*, 17, 223–37.

Byrne, D. (1971). *The attraction paradigm*. New York: Academic Press.

Caplan, N. & Paige, J. M. (1968). A study of ghetto rioters. *Scientific American*, 219, 15–21.

Caporael, L. R., Dawes, R. M., Orbell, J. M. & Van de Kragt, A. J. C. (1989) Selfishness examined: Cooperation in the absence of egoistic incentives. *Behavioral and Brain Sciences*, 12, 683–99.

Capozza, D., Voci, A., Volpato, C. & Pozzeto, S. (1996). Collectivism/individualism as a moderator of the relationship between identification and ingroup bias. Paper presented to the Small Group Meeting of the EAESP on 'Intergroup Relations: Current work and future perspectives', Catania, Sicily, 26–9 September.

Carli, L. L. (1982). Are women more social and men more task oriented? A meta-analytic review of sex differences in group interaction, reward allocation, coalition formation, and cooperation in a Prisoner's Dilemma Game. Unpublished manuscript, University of Massachusetts, Amherst.

Castano, E. & Yzerbyt, V. Y. (in press). The highs and lows of group homogeneity. *Behavioural processes.*

Castells, (1997). *The Power of Identity.* Oxford: Blackwell.

Cialdini, R. B. & Richardson, K. D. (1980). Two indirect tactics of image management: Basking and blasting. *Journal of Personality and Social Pyschology*, 39, 406–15.

Codol, J. P. (1975). On the so-called 'superior conformity to the self' behaviour: Twenty experimental investigations. *European Journal of Social Psychology*, 5, 457–501.

Colman, A. M. (1991). Expert psychological testimony in two murder trials in South Africa. *Issues in Criminological and Legal Psychology*, 1, 43–9.

Commins, B. & Lockwood, J. (1979a). Social comparison and social inequality: An experimental investigation of intergroup behaviour. *British Journal of Social and Clinical Psychology*, 18, 285–9.

Commins, B. & Lockwood, J. (1979b). The effects of status differences, favoured treatment and equity on intergroup comparisons. *European Journal of Social Psychology*, 9, 281–9.

Condor, S. (1996). Social identity and time. In W. P. Robinson (ed.), *Social Groups and Identities: Developing the Legacy of Henri Tajfel*. Oxford: Butterworth Heinemann.

Cook, T. D., Crosby, F. & Hennigan, K. M. (1977). The construct validity of relative deprivation. In J. M. Suls & R. L. Miller (eds), *Social Comparison Processes*. Washington DC: Hemisphere.

Corneliusson, R. (1997). Social identity in computer-mediated communication. Unpublished Master's thesis, University of Manchester.

Crocker, J. & Luthanen, R. (1990). Collective self-esteem and ingroup bias. *Journal of Personality and Social Psychology*, 58, 60–7.

Crocker, J. & Major, B. (1989). Social stigma and self-esteem: The self-protective properties of stigma. *Psychological Review*, 96, 608–630.

Crocker, J., Major, B. & Steele, C. (1997). Social stigma. In D. Gilbert, S. T. Fiske & G. Lindzey (eds), *Handbook of Social Psychology* (4th edn). Boston: McGraw Hill.

Crocker, J., Thompson, L. L., McGraw, K. M. & Ingerman, C. (1987). Downward comparison, prejudice, and evaluation of others: Effects of self-esteem and threat. *Journal of Personality and Social Psychology*, 52, 907–16.

Crocker, J., Voelkl, K., Testa, M. & Major, B. (1991). Social stigma: The affective consequences of attributional ambiguity. *Journal of Personality and Social Psychology*, 60, 218–28.

Crosby, F. (1982). *Relative Deprivation and Working Women*. New York: Oxford University Press.

Cushman, D. & Whiting, G. C. (1972). An approach to communication theory: Towards consensus on rules. *Journal of Communication*, 22, 217–38.

Darden, W. R., Hampton, R. & Howell, R. D. (1989). Career versus organizational commitment: Antecedents and consequences of retail salespeople's commitment. *Journal of Retailing*, 65, 80–106.

David, B. & Turner, J. C. (1992). Studies in self-categorization and minority conversion. Paper presented at the joint EAESP/SESP Meeting, Leuven/Louvain-la-Neuve, Belgium, 15–18 July.

David, B. & Turner, J. C. (1996). Studies in self-categorization and minority conversion: Is being a member of the outgroup an advantage? *British Journal of Social Psychology*, 35, 179–99.

David, B. & Turner, J. C. (in press a) Studies in self-categorization and minority conversion 2: The ingroup minority in intragroup and intergroup contexts. *British Journal of Social Psychology*.

David, B. & Turner, J. C. (in press b) Majority and minority influence: A single-process self-categorization analysis. In C. De Dreu & N. De Vries (eds), *Group Consensus and Innovation: Fundamental and Applied Perspectives*. Oxford: Blackwell.

Dawes, R. M., Van de Kragt , A. J. C. & Orbell, J. M. (1988) Not me or thee but we: The importance of group identity in eliciting cooperation in dilemma situations: Experimental manipulations. *Acta Psychologica*, 68, 83–97.

Deaux, K. & Ethier, K. A. (1998). Negotiating social identity. In J. K. Swim & C. Stangor (eds). *Prejudice: The Target's Perspective*. San Diego, CA: Academic Press.

Deaux, K. & Wrightsman, L. S. (1995). *Social Psychology* (5th ed.). Pacific Grove, CA: Brooks/Cole.

DeCottis, T. A. & Summers, T. P. (1987). A path analysis of a model of the antecedents and consequences of organizational commitment. *Human Relations,* 40, 445–70.

De Gilder, D., Van den Heuvel, H. & Ellemers, N. (1997). Het drie-componentenmodel van commitment [The three-component model of organizational commitment]. *Gedrag en Organisatie,* 10, 95–106.

Deschamps, J. C. & Brown, R. (1983). Superordinate goals and intergroup conflict. *British Journal of Social Psychology*, 22, 189–95.

Deutsch, M. & Gerard, H. (1955). A study of normative and informational social influences upon individual judgement. *Journal of Abnormal and Social Psychology*, 51, 629–36.

De Weerd, M., Ellemers, N. & Klandermans, B. (1996). Rationele en emotionele determinanten van de intentie tot participatie in collectieve actie onder Nederlandse en Spaanse boeren [Rational and emotional determinants of the intention to participate in collective action, among Dutch and Spanish farmers]. In E. C. M. Van Schie, D. Daamen, A. Pruyn & W. Otten (eds), *Sociale psychologie en haar toepassingen*, (deel 10). Delft: Eburon.

Diehl, M. (1988). Social identity and minimal groups: The effects of interpersonal and intergroup attitudinal similarity on intergroup discrimination. *British Journal of Social Psychology*, 27, 289–300.

Diehl, M. (1990). The minimal group paradigm: Theoretical explanations and empirical findings. *European Review of Social Psychology*, 1, 263–92.

Diener, E. (1980). Deindividuation: The absence of self-awareness and self-regulation in group members. In P. B. Paulus (ed.), *The psychology of group influence*. Hillsdale, NJ: Lawrence Erlbaum.

Dion, K. L. (1975). Women's reactions to discrimination from members of the same or opposite sex. *Journal of Research in Personality*, 9, 294–306.

Dion, K. L. (1986). Responses to perceived discrimination and relative deprivation. In J. M. Olson, C. P. Herman & M. P. Zanna (eds), *Relative Deprivation and Social Comparison: The Ontario Symposium* (Vol. 4,). Hillsdale, NJ: Lawrence Erlbaum.

Dion, K. L. & Earn, B. M. (1975). The phenomenology of being a target of prejudice. *Journal of Personality and Social Psychology*, 32, 944–50.

Doff, T. (1998). Is verdediging de beste aanval? Unpublished Master's thesis, University of Amsterdam.

Doise, W. (1978). *Groups and Individuals: Explanations in Social Psychology.* Cambridge: Cambridge University Press.

Doise, W., Deschamps, J. C. & Meyers, G. (1978). The accentuation of intracategory similarities. In H. Tajfel (ed.), *Differentiation Between Social Groups.* London: Academic Press.

Dollard, J., Doob, L. W., Miller, N. E., Mowrer, O. H. & Sears, R. R. (1939). *Frustration and Aggression,* New Haven: Yale University Press.

Doosje, B. (1995). Stereotyping in intergroup contexts. Unpublished PhD dissertation, University of Amsterdam, The Netherlands.

Doosje, B. & Ellemers, N. (1997). Stereotyping under threat: The role of group identification. In R. Spears, P. J. Oakes, N. Ellemers & S. A. Haslam (eds), *The social psychology of stereotyping and group life.* Oxford: Blackwell.

Doosje, B., Branscombe, N. R., Spears, R., Manstead, A. S. R. (1998). Guilty by association: When one's group has a negative history. *Journal of Personality and Social Psychology, 75,* 872–86.

Doosje, B., Ellemers, N. & Spears, R. (1995). Perceived intragroup variability as a function of group status and identification. *Journal of Experimental Social Psychology, 31,* 410–36.

Doosje, B., Haslam, S. A., Spears, R., Oakes, P. J. & Koomen, W., (1998). The effect of comparative context on central tendency and variability judgements and the evaluation of group characteristics. *European Journal of Social Psychology, 28,* 173–84.

Doosje, B., Spears, R. & Ellemers, N. (1998). The dynamic and determining nature of group identification: Responses to anticipated and actual changes in the intergroup status hierarchy. Manuscript under review.

Doosje, B., Spears, R., Ellemers, N. & Koomen, W. (1999). Perceived group variability in intergroup relations: The distinctive role of social identity. *European Review of Social Psychology, 10.*

Doosje, B., Spears, R. & Koomen, W. (1995). When bad isn't all bad: The strategic use of sample information in generalization and stereotyping. *Journal of Personality and Social Psychology, 69,* 642–55.

Dovidio, J. F., Gaertner, S. L. & Validzic, A. (1998). Intergroup bias: Status, differentiation, and a common ingroup identity. *Journal of Personality and Social Psychology, 75,* 109–20.

Dubé, L. & Guimond, S. (1986). Relative deprivation and social protest: The personal-group issue. In J. M. Olson, C. P. Herman and M. P. Zanna, (eds), *Relative Deprivation and Social Comparison: The Ontario Symposium.* Hillsdale, NJ: Lawrence Erlbaum.

Dubrovsky, V. J., Kiesler, S. & Sethna, B. N. (1991). The equalization phenomenon: Status effects in computer-mediated and face-to-face decision-making groups. *Human Computer Interaction, 6*(2), 119–46.

Dunham, R. B., Grube, J. A. & Castaneda, M. B. (1994). Organizational commitment: The utility of an integrative definition. *Journal of Applied Psychology, 79,* 370–80.

Eagly, A. H. (1987). *Sex Differences in Social Behaviour: a Social-role Interpretation.* Hillsdale, NJ: Lawrence Erlbaum.

Ellemers, N. (1993a). Sociale identiteit en sekse: Het dilemma van succesvolle vrouwen [Social identity and gender: The dilemma of successful women]. *Tijdschrift voor Vrouwenstudies, 14,* 322–36.

Ellemers, N. (1993b). The influence of socio-structural variables on identity enhancement strategies. *European Review of Social Psychology* , 4, 27–57.

Ellemers, N. & Bos, A. (1998). Individual and group level responses to threat experienced by Dutch shopkeepers in East-Amsterdam. *Journal of Applied Social Psychology* 28, 1987–2005.

Ellemers, N. & Haaker, M. (1995). Feedback and self-esteem: Individual and group level manipulations and responses. Unpublished manuscript.

Ellemers, N. & Mlicki, P. (1991). Refining the social identity concept: Some theoretical and empirical complexities. Unpublished manuscript.

Ellemers, N. & Van Knippenberg, A. (1997). Stereotyping in social context. In R. Spears, P. J. Oakes, N. Ellemers & S. A. Haslam (eds), *The Social Psychology of Stereotyping and Group Life*. Oxford: Blackwell.

Ellemers, N. & Van Rijswijk, W. (1997). Identity needs versus social opportunities: The use of group-level and individual-level identity management strategies. *Social Psychology Quarterly*, 60(1), 52–65.

Ellemers, N., De Gilder, D. & Van den Heuvel, H. (1998). Career-oriented versus team-oriented commitment and behavior at work. *Journal of Applied Psychology* 83, 717–30.

Ellemers, N., Doosje, B. J., Van Knippenberg, A. & Wilke, H. (1992). Status protection in high status minorities. *European Journal of Social Psychology*, 22, 123–40.

Ellemers, N., Kortekaas, P. & Ouwerkerk, J. (1999). Self-categorization, commitment to the group and social self-esteem as related but distinct aspects of social identity. *European Journal of Social Psychology*, 29, 371–89.

Ellemers, N., Spears, R & Doosje, B. (1997). Sticking together or falling apart: Ingroup identification as a psychological determinant of group commitment versus individual mobility. *Journal of Personality and Social Psychology*, 72, 617–26.

Ellemers, N., Spears, R & Doosje, B. (1998). Group identification, group norms and group behaviour. Unpublished manuscript.

Ellemers, N., Van den Heuvel, H. & De Gilder, D. (1996). Doorstroomproblemen van vrouwen in organisaties: Een gebrek aan motivatie, of een gevolg van sekse-stereotiepe denkbeelden? [Mobility problems of women in organizations: Lack of motivation, or a consequence of gender stereotyping?] *Nederlands Tijdschrift voor de Psychologie*, 51, 235–44.

Ellemers, N., Van Dyck, C., Hinkle, S. & Jacobs, A. (1998). Intergroup differentiation in social context: Identity needs versus audience constraints. Manuscript under review.

Ellemers, N., Van Knippenberg, A. & Wilke, H. (1990). The influence of permeability of group boundaries and stability of group status on strategies of individual mobility and social change. *British Journal of Social Psychology*, 29, 233–46.

Ellemers, N., Van Knippenberg, A., De Vries, N. & Wilke, H. (1988). Social identification and permeability of group boundaries. *European Journal of Social Psychology*, 18, 497–513.

Ellemers, N., Van Rijswijk, W., Bruins, J. & De Gilder, D. (1998). Group commitment as a moderator of attributional and behavioural responses to power use. *European Journal of Social Psychology,* 28, 555–73.

Ellemers, N., Van Rijswijk, W., Roefs, M. & Simons, C. (1997). Bias in intergroup perceptions: Balancing group identity with social reality. *Personality and Social Psychology Bulletin*, 23, 186–98.

Ellemers, N., Wilke, H. & Van Knippenberg, A. (1993). Effects of the legitimacy of low group or individual status on individual and collective identity enhancement strategies.

Journal of Personality and Social Psychology, 64, 766–78.

Epstein, S. (1973). The self-concept revisited or a theory of a theory. *American Psychologist*, 28, 404–16.

Epstein, R. & Komorita, S. S. (1966). Prejudice among Negro children as related to parental ethnocentrism. *Journal of Personality and Social Psychology*, 4, 643–7.

Epstein, S. & O'Brien, E. J. (1985). The person-situation debate in historical and current perspective. *Psychological Bulletin*, 98, 513–37.

Ethier, K. A. & Deaux, K. (1994). Negotiating social identity when contexts change: Maintaining identification and responding to threat. *Journal of Personality and Social Psychology*, 67, 243–51.

Fagot, B. I., Leinbach, M. D. & O'Boyle, C. (1992). Gender labeling, gender stereotyping, and parenting behaviors. *Developmental Psychology*, 28, 225–30.

Farrell, D. & Rusbult, C. E. (1981). Exchange variables as predictors of job satisfaction, job commitment, and turnover: The impact of rewards, costs, alternatives, and investments. *Organizational Behavior and Human Performance*, 27, 78–95.

Farsides, T. (1995) Why social identity theory's self-esteem hypothesis has never been tested – and how to test it. Paper presented to BPS Social Psychology Section Conference, York, UK, September.

Fazio, R. H. (1990). A practical guide to the use of response latency in social psychological research. In C. Hendrick & M. S. Clark (eds), *Research Methods in Personality and Social Psychology* (vol. 2). London: Sage.

Feldman, R. S. (1995). *Social Psychology*. Englewood Cliffs, NJ: Prentice-Hall.

Ferguson, C. (1964). Baby-talk in six languages. *American Anthropologist*, 66, 103–14.

Ferguson, C. (1977). Baby-talk as a simplified register. In C. Snow & C. Ferguson (eds), *Talking to Children: Language Input and Acquisition*. Cambridge: Cambridge University Press.

Festinger, L. (1954). A theory of social comparison processes. *Human Relations*, 7, 117–40.

Festinger, L. (1957). *A theory of Cognitive Dissonance*. Stanford, CA: Stanford University Press.

Festinger, L., Pepitone, A. & Newcomb, T. (1952). Some consequences of de-individuation in a group. *Journal of Abnormal and Social Psychology*, 47, 382–9.

Fiedler, K., Semin, G. R. & Finkenauer, C. (1993). The battle of words between gender groups: A language-based approach to intergroup processes. *Human Communication Research*, 19, 409–41.

Fielding, K. & Hogg, M. A. (1997) Social identity, self-categorization and leadership: A field study of small interactive groups. *Group Dynamics: Theory, Research and Practice*, 1, 39–51.

Fishbein, M. & Ajzen, I. (1975). *Belief, Attitude, Intention and Behavior: An Introduction to Theory and Research*. Reading MA: Addison-Wesley.

Fishman, J. A. (1956). An examination of the process and function of social stereotyping. *Journal of Social Psychology*, 43, 27–64.

Fiske, S. T. & Neuberg, S. L. (1990). A continuum of impression formation, from category-based to individuating processes: Influences of information and motivation on attention and interpretation. In M. P. Zanna (ed.), *Advances in Experimental Social Psychology* (Vol. 23). San Diego, CA: Academic Press.

Flacks, R. (1970). Who protests? The social bases of the student movement. In J. Foster and D. Long, (eds), *Protest: Student Activism in America*. New York: William Morrow.

Folger, R. (1986). A referent cognitions theory of relative deprivation. In J. Olson, C. P. Herman & M. Zanna (eds), *Relative deprivation and social comparison: The Ontario symposium*. Hillsdale, NJ: Lawrence Erlbaum.

Folger, R. (1987). Reformulating the Preconditions of Resentments: A Referent Cognitions Model. In J. Masters & W. Smith (eds), *Social Comparison, Social Justice and Relative Deprivation*. Hillsdale, NJ: Lawrence Erlbaum.

Ford, T. E. & Stangor, C. (1992). The role of diagnosticity in stereotype formation: Perceiving group means and variances. *Journal of Personality and Social Psychology, 63,* 356–67.

Forsyth, D. R. (1990). *Group Dynamics* (2nd edn). Pacific Grove, CA: Brooks/Cole.

Foster, M. D. & Matheson, K. (1995). Double relative deprivation: Combining the personal and political. *Personality and Social Psychology Bulletin, 21,* 1167–77.

Frable, D. E. S. (1993). Being and feeling unique: Statistical deviance and psychological marginality. *Journal of Personality, 61,* 85–110.

Franco, F. M. & Maass, A. (1996). Implicit versus explicit strategies of outgroup discrimination: The role of intentional control in biased language use and reward allocation. *Journal of Language and Social Psychology, 15,* 335–59.

Franzoi, S. L. (1996) *Social psychology*. Madison, WI: Brown & Benchmark.

Freud, S. (1922). Group psychology and the analysis of the ego. New York: W. W. Norton & Co.

Gaertner, S. L., Mann, J., Murrell, A. & Dovidio, J. F. (1989) Reducing ingroup bias: The benefits of recategorization. *Journal of Personality and Social Psychology, 57,* 239–49.

Gagnon A. & Bourhis, R. Y. (1996) Discrimination in the minimal group paradigm: Social identity or self-interest? *Personality and Social Psychology Bulletin, 22,* 1289–301.

Ganster, D. C. & Dwyer, D. J. (1995). The effects of understaffing on individual and group performance in professional and trade occupations. *Journal of Management, 21,* 175–90.

George, J. M. & Bettenhausen, K. (1990). Understanding prosocial behaviour, sales performance, and turnover: A group level analysis in a service context. *Journal of Applied Psychology, 75,* 698–709.

Gerard, H. B. & Mathewson, G. C. (1966). The effects of severity of initiation on liking for a group: A replication. *Journal of Experimental Social Psychology, 2,* 278–87.

Giles, H. (1977). *Language, Ethnicity and Intergroup Relations*. London: Academic Press.

Goffman, E. (1959). *The Presentation of Self in Everyday Life*. New York: Doubleday.

Grant P. R. (1992). Ethnocentrism between groups of unequal power in response to perceived threat to valued resources and to social identity. *Canadian Journal of Behavioural Science, 24,* 348–70.

Grant P. R. (1993). Reactions to intergroup similarity: Examination of the similarity-differentiation and similarity-attraction hypothesis. *Canadian Journal of Behavioural Science, 25,* 28–44.

Gray-Little, B. (1980). Race and inequity. *Journal of Applied Social Psychology, 10,* 468–81.

Grice, H. P. (1975). Logic and conversation. In P. Cole & J. Morgan (eds), *Syntax and Semantics*. New York: Academic Press.

Griffin, E. & Sparks, G. G. (1990). Friends forever: A longitudinal exploration of intimacy in same-sex friends and platonic pairs. *Journal of Social and Personal Relationships, 7,* 29–46.

Guerin, B. (1994). Gender bias in the abstractness of verbs and adjectives. *Journal of Social Psychology, 134,* 421–28.

Guimond, S. & Dubé-Simard, L. (1983). Relative deprivation theory and the Quebec nationalist movement: The cognition-emotion distinction and the personal-group deprivation issue. *Journal of Personality and Social Psychology,* 44, 527–35.

Guimond, S. & Palmer, D. (1990). Type of academic training and causal attributions for social problems. *European Journal of Social Psychology,* 20, 61–75.

Gurin, P. & Epps, E. (1974). *Black Consciousness, Identity and Achievement.* New York: John Wiley and Sons, Inc.

Gurin, P. & Markus, H (1988). Group identity: The psychological mechanisms of durable salience. *Revue Internationale de Psychologie Sociale,* 1, 257–74.

Hafer, C. L. & Olson, J. M. (1993). Beliefs in a just world, discontent and assertive actions by working women. *Personality and Social Psychology Bulletin,* 19, 30–8.

Hall, J. A. (1984). *Nonverbal Sex Differences: Communication Accuracy and Expressive Style.* Baltimore, MD: John Hopkins University Press.

Hamilton, D. L. Gibbons, P. A., Stroessner, S. J. & Sherman, J. W. (1992). Language, intergroup relations and stereotypes. In G. R. Semin & K. Fiedler (eds), *Language, interaction and social cognition* . London: Sage.

Hamilton, D. L., Katz, L. B. & Leirer , V. O. (1980). Cognitive representation of personality impressions: Organizational processes in first impression formation. *Journal of Personality and Social Psychology,* 39, 1050–63.

Hamstra, I. J. (1998). Personal advantage and relative deprivation: The role of social identification. Unpublished manuscript, University of Amsterdam.

Harasty, A. S. (1997). The interpersonal nature of social stereotypes: Differential discussion patterns about ingroups and outgroups. *Personality and Social Psychology Bulletin,* 23, 270–84.

Haraway, D. (1990). A manifesto for cyborgs: Science, technology, and socialist feminism in the 1980s. In L. J. Nicholson (ed.), *Feminism / Postmodernism.* London: Routledge.

Haslam, S. A. (1997). Stereotyping and social influence: Foundations of stereotype consensus. In R. Spears, P. J. Oakes, N. Ellemers & S. A. Haslam (eds), *The Social Psychology of Stereotyping and Group Life.* Oxford: Blackwell.

Haslam, S. A. (1998). Your wish is my command: The role of social identity and self-categorization processes in translating a leader's words into followers' actions. Paper presented to Conference on the Social Psychology of Leadership, Melbourne, La Trobe University, Australia, 3–4 October.

Haslam, S. A. & Oakes, P. J. (1995). How context dependent is the outgroup homogeneity effect? A response to Bartsch and Judd. *European Journal of Social Psychology,* 25, 469–75.

Haslam, S. A. & Turner, J. C. (1992). Context-dependent variation in social stereotyping 2: The relationship between frame of reference, self-categorization and accentuation. *European Journal of Social Psychology,* 22, 251–77.

Haslam, S. A. & Turner, J. C. (1995) Context-dependent variation in social stereotyping 3: Extremism as a self-categorical basis for polarized judgement. *European Journal of Social Psychology,* 25, 341–71.

Haslam, S. A. & Turner, J. C. (1998). Extremism and deviance: Beyond taxonomy and bias. *Social Research,* 65, 435–48.

Haslam, S. A. & Wilson, A. (in press) In what sense are prejudicial beliefs personal? The importance of an ingroup's shared stereotypes. *British Journal of Social Psychology.*

Haslam, S. A., McGarty, C., Brown, P. M., Eggins, R. A, Morrison, B. E. & Reynolds, K. J. (1998) Inspecting the emperor's clothes: Evidence that randomly-selected leaders can enhance group performance. *Group Dynamics: Theory, Research and Practice,* 2.

Haslam, S. A., Oakes, P. J., Turner, J. C. & McGarty, C. (1995) Social categorization and group homogeneity: Changes in the perceived applicability of stereotype content as a function of comparative context and trait favourableness. *British Journal of Social Psychology*, 34, 139–60.

Haslam, S. A., Oakes, P. J., Turner, J. C. & McGarty, C. A. (1996) Social identity, self-categorization, and the perceived homogeneity of ingroups and outgroups. In R. M. Sorrentino & E. T. Higgins (eds), *Handbook of Motivation and Cognition*. Vol. 3: *The Interpersonal Context*. New York: The Guilford Press.

Haslam, S. A., Turner, J. C., Oakes, P. J., McGarty, C. & Hayes, B. K. (1992). Context-dependent variation in social stereotyping 1: The effects of intergroup relations as mediated by social change and frame of reference. *European Journal of Social Psychology*, 22, 3–20.

Haslam, S. A., Turner, J. C., Oakes, P. J., McGarty, C. & Reynolds, K. J. (1998) The group as a basis for emergent stereotype consensus. *European Review of Social Psychology*, 9, 203–39.

Henderson-King, E., Henderson-King, D., Zhermer, N., Posokhova, S. & Chiker, V. (1997). Ingroup favoritism and perceived similarity: A look at Russian's perceptions in the post-Soviet era. *Personality and Social Psychology Bulletin*, 23, 1013–21.

Hensley, V. & Duval, S. (1976). Some perceptual determinants of perceived similarity, liking and correctness. *Journal of Personality and Social Psychology*, 34, 159–68.

Herring, S. C. (1993). Gender and democracy in computer-mediated communication, *Electronic Journal of Communication / Revue Electronique de Communication* (On-line), 3. Available: http://www.cios.org/www/ejc/v3n293.htm

Hewstone, M. (1990). The 'ultimate attribution error'? A review of the literature on intergroup causal attribution. *European Journal of Social Psychology*, 20, 311–35.

Hewstone, M., Hantzi, A. & Johnston, L. (1991). Social categorization and person memory: The pervasiveness of race as an organizing principle. *European Journal of Social Psychology*, 21, 517–28.

Higgins, E. T. (1981). The 'communication game': Implications for social cognition and persuasion. In E. Higgins, M. Zanna & C. Herman (eds), *Social Cognition: The Ontario Symposium* (vol. 1). Hillsdale, NJ: Lawrence Erlbaum.

Higgins, E. T. (1987). Self-discrepancy: A theory relating self and affect. *Psychological Review*, 94, 319–40.

Higgins, E. T. & Rholes, W. S. (1978). 'Saying is believing': Effects of message modification on memory and liking for the person described. *Journal of Experimental Social Psychology*, 14, 363–78.

Higgins, E. T., McCann, C. D. & Fondacaro, R. A. (1982). The 'communication game': Goal-directed encoding and cognitive consequences. *Social Cognition*, 1, 21–37.

Hilton, D., Erb, H.-P., McDermott, M. R., Molian, D. J. (1996). Social representations of history and attitudes to European unification in Britain, France and Germany. In G. M. Breakwell & E. Lyons Speri (eds), *Changing European Identities: Social Psychological Analyses of Social Change*. Oxford: Butterworth-Heinemann.

Hinkle, S. & Brown, R. (1990). Intergroup comparisons and social identity: Some links and lacunae. In D. Abrams & M. A. Hogg (eds), *Social Identity Theory: Constructive and Critical Advances*. London: Harvester-Wheatsheaf.

Hinkle, S., Taylor, L. A., Fox-Cardamone, D. L. & Crook, K. F. (1989) Intragroup identification and intergroup differentiation: A multi-component approach. *British Journal of Social Psychology*, 28, 305–317.

Hirt, E. R., MacDonald, H. E. & Erickson, G. A. (1995). How do I remember thee? The role of encoding set and delay in reconstructive memory processes. *Journal of Experimental Social Psychology*, 31, 379–409.

Hogg, M. A. (1992). *The Social Psychology of Group Cohesiveness: From Attraction to Social Identity*. Hemel Hempstead: Harvester-Wheatsheaf.

Hogg, M. A. (1996). Intra-group processes, group structure and social identity. In W. P. Robinson (ed.), *Social Groups and Identities: Developing the Legacy of Henri Tajfel*. Oxford: Butterworth Heinemann.

Hogg, M. A. & Abrams, D. (1990). Social motivation, self-esteem and social identity. In D. Abrams & M. A. Hogg (eds), *Social Identity Theory: Constructive and Critical Advances*. London: Harvester-Wheatsheaf.

Hogg, M. A. & Abrams, D. (1993). Towardss a single-process uncertainty-reduction model of social motivation in groups. In M. A. Hogg & D. Abrams (eds), *Group Motivation: Social Psychological Perspectives*. New York: Harvester-Wheatsheaf.

Hogg, M. A. & Hains, S. C. (1997). Intergroup relations and group solidarity: Effects of group identification and social beliefs on depersonalized attraction. *Journal of Personality and Social Psychology*, 70, 295–309.

Hogg, M. A. & Sunderland, J. (1991). Self-esteem and intergroup discrimination in the minimal group paradigm. *British Journal of Social Psychology*, 30, 51–62.

Hogg, M. A. & Turner, J. C. (1987a). Intergroup behaviour, self-stereotyping and the salience of social categories. *British Journal of Social Psychology*, 26, 325–40.

Hogg, M. A. & Turner, J. C. (1987b). Social identity and conformity: a theory of referent informational influence. In W. Doise & S. Moscovici (eds) *Current Issues in European Social Psychology* (vol. 2). Cambridge: Cambridge University Press.

Hogg, M. A., Turner, J. C. & Davidson, B. (1990). Polarized norms and social frames of reference: A test of the self-categorization theory of group polarization. *Basic and Applied Social Psychology*, 11(1), 77–100.

Hornsey, M. J. & Hogg, M. A. (1998). Intergroup similarity and subgroup relations: The role of threat. Unpublished manuscript, University of Queensland.

Horwitz, M. & Rabbie, J. M. (1989) Stereotypes of groups, group members, and individuals in categories: A differential analysis. In D. Bar-Tal, C. F. Grauman, A. W. Kruglanski & W. Stroebe (eds), *Stereotyping and Prejudice: Changing Conceptions*. New York: Springer Verlag.

Howard, J. & Rothbart, M. (1980). Social categorization and memory for ingroup and outgroup behavior. *Journal of Personality and Social Psychology*, 38, 301–10.

Hutnik, N. (1991). *Ethnic Minority Identity: A Social Psychological Perspective*. Oxford: Clarendon Press.

Insko, C. A., Nacoste, R. W. & Moe, J. L. (1983). Belief congruence and racial discrimination: Review of the evidence and critical evaluation. *European Journal of Social Psychology*, 13, 153–74.

Insko, C.A., Schopler, J., Hoyle, R. H., Dardis, G. J. & Graetz, K. A. (1990). Individual-group discontinuity as a function of fear and greed. *Journal of Personality and Social Psychology*, 58, 68–79.

Jackson, J. M. & Saltzstein, H. D. (1958). The effect of person-group relationship on conformity processes. *Journal of Abnormal and Social Psychology*, 57, 17–24.

James, K. & Cropanzano, R. (1994). Dispositional group loyalty and individual action for the benefit of an ingroup: Experimental and correlational evidence. *Organizational Behavior and Human Decision Processes*, 60, 179–205.

Janis, I. L. (1982). *Groupthink: Psychological Studies of Policy Decisions and Fiascoes* (2nd edn). Boston: Houghton Mifflin.

Jehn, K. A. & Shaw, P. P. (1997). Interpersonal relationships and task performance: An examination of mediating processes in friendship and acquaintance groups. *Journal of Personality and Social Psychology*, 72, 775–90.

Jessup, L. M., Connolly, T. & Tansik, D. A. (1990). Towards a theory of automated group work: The deindividuating effects of anonymity. *Small Group Research*, 21(3), 333–48.

Jetten, J., Spears, R. & Manstead, A. S. R. (1996). Intergroup norms and intergroup discrimination: Distinctive self-categorization and social identity effects. *Journal of Personality and Social Psychology*, 71, 1222–33.

Jetten, J., Spears, R. & Manstead, A. S. R. (1997a). Distinctiveness threat and prototypicality: Combined effects on intergroup discrimination and collective self-esteem. *European Journal of Social Psychology*, 27, 635–57.

Jetten, J., Spears, R. & Manstead, A. S. R. (1997b). Strength of identification and intergroup differentiation: The influence of group norms. *European Journal of Social Psychology*, 27, 603–9.

Jetten, J., Spears, R. & Manstead, A. S. R. (1998a). Intergroup similarity as a source of differentiation: The role of group identification. Manuscript under review.

Jetten, J., Spears, R. & Manstead, A. S. R. (1998b). Intergroup similarity and group variability: The effects of group distinctiveness on the expression of ingroup bias. *Journal of Personality and Social Psychology*, 74, 1481–92.

John, C., Young, L., Giles, H. & Hofman, J. E. (1985). Language, values and intercultural differentiation in Israel. *Journal of Social Psychology*, 125, 527–9.

Johns, G. (1991). Substantive and methodological constraints on behavior and attitudes in organizational research. *Organizational Behavior and Human Performance*, 2, 309–28.

Johnson, R. D. & Downing, L. L. (1979). Deindividuation and valence of cues: Effects on prosocial and antisocial behavior. *Journal of Personality and Social Psychology*, 37(9), 1532–8.

Jones, E. E. & Davis, K. E. (1965). From acts to dispositions: The attribution process in person perception. In L. Berkowitz (ed.), *Advances in Experimental Social Psychology* (vol. 2). New York: Academic Press.

Jost, J. T. & Banaji, M. R. (1994). The role of stereotyping in system-justification and the production of false consciousness. *British Journal of Social Psychology*, 33, 1–27.

Jost, J. T. & Major, B. (eds) (1999). The psychology of legitimacy: Emerging perspectives on ideology, justice and intergroup relations. Volume in preparation.

Judd, C. M. & Park, B. (1993) Definition and assessment of accuracy in social stereotypes. *Psychological Review*, 100, 109–28.

Kanter, R. M. (1996). Dilemmas of teamwork. In C. Mabey and P. Iles (eds), *Managing Learning*. London: Thomson Business Press.

Kappen, D. & Branscombe, N.R. (1998). Reasons for exclusion: Impaact on attributions and emotions. Manuscript under review.

Karau, S. J. & Williams, K. D. (1993). Social loafing: A meta-analytical review and theoretical integration. *Journal of Personality and Social Psychology*, 65, 681–706.

Karpinski, A. & Von Hippel, W. (1996). The role of the linguistic intergroup bias in expectancy maintenance. *Social Cognition*, 14, 141–63.

Katz, D. & Braly, K. (1933). Racial stereotypes in one hundred college students. *Journal of Abnormal and Social Psychology*, 28, 280–90.

Kawakami, K. & Dion, K. (1992). The impact of salient self-identities on relative deprivation and action intentions. *European Journal of Social Psychology*, 23, 525–40.

Kawakami, K. & Dion, K. L. (1995). Social identity and affect as determinants of collective action. *Theory and Psychology, 5*, 551–77.

Kelly, C. (1988). Intergroup differentiation in a political context. *British Journal of Social Psychology*, 27, 321–7.

Kelly, C. (1993) Group identification, intergroup perceptions and collective action. *European Review of Social Psychology*, 4, 59–83.

Kelly, C. & Breinlinger, S. (1996) *The Social Psychology of Collective Action: Identity, Injustice and Gender*. London: Taylor & Francis.

Kelly, C. & Kelly, J. (1994). Who gets involved in collective action? Social psychological determinants of individual participation in trade unions. *Human Relations, 47*, 63–88.

Kiesler, C. A. & Kiesler, S. B. (1969). *Conformity*. Reading, MA: Addison-Wesley.

Kiesler, S. & Sproull, L. (1992). Group decision-making and communication technology. Special Issue: Group decision-making. *Organizational Behavior and Human Decision Processes, 52*(1), 96–123.

Kiesler, S., Siegel, J. & McGuire, T. W. (1984). Social psychological aspects of computer-mediated communication. *American Psychologist, 39*, 1123–34.

Kihlstrom, J. F. & Cantor, N. (1984) Mental representations of the self. In L. Berkowitz (ed.), *Advances in Experimental Social Psychology* (vol. 17). New York: Academic Press.

Kingsbury, D. (1968). Manipulating the amount of information obtained from a person giving directions. Unpublished honours thesis, Harvard University, Department of Social Relations, Cambridge, MA.

Klandermans, P. G. (1997). *The Social Psychology of Protest*. Oxford: Blackwell.

Klein, O. & Azzi, A. (1998). The effect of the group membership of an audience on the communication of self-stereotypes. Unpublished manuscript: Université Libre de Bruxelles.

Kogan, N. & Jordan, T. (1989). Social communication within and between elderly and middle-aged cohorts. In M. A. Luszez & T. Nettelbeck (eds), *Psychological Development: Perspectives across the Life-span*. Amsterdam: Elsevier Science Publishers.

Koper, G., Van Knippenberg, D., Bouhuijs, F, Vermunt, R. & Wilke, H. (1993). Procedural fairness and self-esteem. *European Journal of Social Psychology, 23*, 313–25.

Kosmitzi, C. (1996). The reaffirmation of cultural identity in cross-cultural encounters. *Personality and Social Psychology Bulletin, 22*(3), 238–48.

Kramarae, C. & Taylor, H. J. (1993). Women and men on electronic networks: A conversation or a monologue. In H. J. Taylor, C. Kramarae & M. Ebben (eds), *Women, Information Technology, and Scholarship*. Urbana, IL: The Center for Advanced Study, University of Illinois.

Kramer, R. M. & Brewer, M. B. (1984). Effects of group identity on resource use in a simulated commons dilemma. *Journal of Personality and Social Psychology, 46*, 1044–57.

Krauss, R. M. & Fussell, S. R. (1996). Social psychological models of interpersonal communication. In E. T. Higgins & A. W. Kruglanski (eds), *Social Psychology: Handbook of Basic Principles*. New York: Guilford.

Kruglanski, A. W., Miller, N. & Geen, R. G. (1996). Introduction to the special issue on the self and social identity. *Journal of Personality and Social Psychology, 71*, 1061.

Kunda, Z. (1990). The case for motivated reasoning. *Psychological Bulletin, 108*, 480–98.

Lalonde, R. N. & Silverman, R. A. (1994). Behavioral preferences in response to social injustice: The effects of group permeability and social identity salience. *Journal of Personality and Social Psychology, 66*, 78–85.

Lambert, A. J. (1995). Stereotypes and social judgment: The consequences of group variability. *Journal of Personality and Social Psychology*, 68, 388–403.

Lambert, W. E., Libman, E. & Poser, G. (1960). The effect of increased salience of a membership group on pain tolerance. *Journal of Personality*, 28, 350–7.

Latané, B. (1981). The psychology of social impact. *American Psychologist*, 36, 343–56.

Lea, M. & Spears, R. (1991). Computer-mediated communication, de-individuation and group decision-making. Special Issue: Computer-supported cooperative work and groupware. *International Journal of Man Machine Studies*, 34(2), 283–301.

Lea, M. & Spears, R. (1995). Love at first byte? Building personal relationships over computer networks. In J. T. Wood & S. Duck (eds), *Understudied Relationships: Off the Beaten Track*. Beverly Hills: Sage.

Lea, M., Spears, R. & de Groot, D. (1998). Knowing me, knowing you: Effects of visual anonymity on self-categorization, stereotyping and attraction in computer-mediated groups. Manuscript under review.

Leavitt, H. J. (1972). *Managerial Psychology* (3rd edn). Chicago: The University of Chicago Press.

Le Bon, G. (1995). *The Crowd: A Study of the Popular Mind*. London: Transaction Publishers. (Original work published in 1895.)

Lemaine, G. (1974). Social differentiation and social originality. *European Journal of Social Psychology*, 4, 17–52.

Lemyre, L. & Smith, P. M. (1985). Intergroup discrimination and self-esteem in the minimal group paradigm. *Journal of Personality and Social Psychology*, 49, 660–70.

Lerner, M. J. (1980). *The Belief in a Just World*. New York: Plenum.

Levine, J. M. & Moreland, R. L. (1990). Progress in small group research. *Annual Review of Psychology*, 41, 585–634.

Levy & Langer, E. (1994). Ageing free from negative stereotypes: Successful memory in China and among the American deaf. *Journal of Personality and Social Psychology*, 66, 989–97.

Lewin, K. (1931) The conflict between Aristotelian and Galileian modes of thought in contemporary psychology. *Journal of Genetic Psychology*, 5, 141–77.

Lewin, K. (1948). *Resolving Social Conflicts*. New York: Harper.

Lewin, K. (1997). *Resolving Social Conflicts: Selected Papers on Group Dynamics*. Washington, DC: APA (Original work published in 1948.)

Lewis, M. (1993). Self-conscious emotions: Embarrassment, pride, shame, and guilt. In M. Lewis & J. M. Haviland, *Handbook of Emotions*. New York: Guilford Press.

Leyens, J-P., Yzerbyt, V. & Schadron, G. (1994) *Stereotypes and Social Cognition*. London: Sage.

Lind, E. A. & Tyler, T. R. (1988). *The Social Psychology of Procedural Justice*. New York: Plenum.

Linville, P. W., Fischer, G. W. & Salovey, P. (1989). Perceived distributions of characteristics of ingroup and outgroup members: Empirical evidence and a computer simulation. *Journal of Personality and Social Psychology*, 57, 165–88.

Lippa, R. A. (1994). *Introduction to Social Psychology* (2nd edn). Pacific Grove, CA: Brooks/Cole.

Lippmann, W. (1922). *Public Opinion*. New York: Harcourt Brace.

Lodewijkx, H. F. M. & Syroit, J. E. M. M. (1997). Severity of initiation revisited: Does severity of initiation increase attractiveness in real groups? *European Journal of Social Psychology*, 27, 375–400.

Long, K. & Spears, R. (1997). The self-esteem hypothesis revisited: Differentiation and the disaffected. In R. Spears, P. J. Oakes, N. Ellemers & S. A. Haslam (eds), *The social psychology of stereotyping and group life*. Oxford: Blackwell.

Long, K., Spears, R. & Manstead, A. S. R. (1994). The influence of personal and collective self-esteem on strategies of social differentiation. *British Journal of Social Psychology*, 33, 313–29.

Lord, C. G. (1997). *Social Psychology*. Fort Worth: Harcourt Brace.

Lorenzi-Cioldi, F. (1991). Self-stereotyping and self-enhancement in gender groups. *European Journal of Social Psychology*, 21, 403–17.

Lott, A. J. & Lott, B. E. (1965). Group cohesiveness as interpersonal attraction. *Psychological Bulletin*, 64, 259–309.

Lucassen, J. & Penninx, R. (1997). *Newcomers: Immigrants and their Descendants in The Netherlands 1550–1995*. Amsterdam: Het Spinhuis Publishers.

Luhtanen, R. & Crocker, J. (1992). A collective self-esteem scale: Self-evaluation of one's social identity. *Personality and Social Psychology Bulletin*, 18, 302–18.

Maass, A. & Arcuri, L. (1992). The role of language in the persistence of stereotypes. In G. Semin & K. Fiedler (eds), *Language, Interaction and Social Cognition*. Newbury Park, CA: Sage.

Maass, A. & Arcuri, L. (1996). Language and stereotyping. In N. Macrae, C. Stangor & M. Hewstone (eds), *Stereotypes and Stereotyping*. New York: Guilford.

Maass, A., Ceccarelli, R. & Rudin, S. (1996). Linguistic intergroup bias: Evidence for ingroup-protective motivation. *Journal of Personality and Social Psychology*, 71, 512–26.

Maass, A., Corvino, P. & Arcuri, L. (1994). Linguistic intergroup bias and the mass media. *Revue de Psychologie Sociale*, 1, 31–43.

Maass, A., Milesi, A., Zabbini, S. & Stahlberg, D. (1995). Linguistic intergroup bias: Differential expectancies or ingroup protection? *Journal of Personality and Social Psychology*, 68, 116–26.

Maass, A., Salvi, D., Arcuri, L. & Semin, G. (1989). Language use in intergroup contexts: The linguistic intergroup bias. *Journal of Personality and Social Psychology*, 57, 981–93.

MacKenzie, S. B., Podsakoff, P. M. & Fetter, R. (1991). Organizational citizenship behaviour and objective productivity as determinants of managerial evaluations of salespersons' performance. *Organizational Behavior and Human Decision Processes*, 50, 123–50.

Mackie, D. M., Worth, L. T. & Asuncion, A. G. (1990). Processing of persuasive ingroup messages. *Journal of Personality and Social Psychology*, 57, 812–22.

Macrae, C. N., Bodenhausen, G. V. & Milne, A. B. (1996). The dissection of selection in person perception: Inhibitory processes in social stereotyping. *Journal of Personality and Social Psychology*, 69, 397–407.

Mael, F. & Ashforth, B. E. (1992). Alumni and their alma mater: A partial test of the reformulated model of organizational identification. *Journal of Organizational Behavior*, 13, 103–23.

Mael, F. & Tetrick, L. E. (1992). Identifying organizational identification. *Educational and Psychological Measurement*, 52, 813–24.

Major, B. (1994). From social inequality to personal entitlement: The role of social comparisons, legitimacy appraisals, and group membership. *Advances in Experimental Social Psychology*, 26, 293–355.

Manis, M., Cornell, S. D. & Moore, J. C. (1974). Transmission of attitude relevant information through a communication chain. *Journal of Personality and Social Psychology*, 30, 81–94.

Mantovani, G. (1994). Is computer-mediated communication intrinsically apt to enhance democracy in organizations? *Human Relations,* 47(1), 45–62.

Marcus-Newhall, A., Miller, N., Holtz, R. & Brewer, M. B. (1993). Cross-cutting category membership with role assignment: A means of reducing intergroup bias. *British Journal of Social Psychology,* 32, 125–46.

Marin, G., Triandis, H. C., Betancourt, H. & Kashima, Y. (1983). Ethnic affirmation versus social desirability: Explaining discrepancies in bilinguals' responses to a questionnaire. *Journal of Cross-Cultural Psychology,* 14(2), 173–86.

Mark, M. & Folger, R. (1984). Responses to relative deprivation: A conceptual framework. *Review of Personality and Social Psychology: Emotion, Relationship and Health,* 5, Beverly Hills: Sage Publications.

Markus, H. R. & Wurf, E. (1987). The dynamic self-concept: A social psychological perspective. *Annual Review of Psychology,* 38, 299–337.

Marmarosh, C. L. & Corazzini, J. G. (1997). Putting the group in your pocket: Using collective identity to enhance personal and collective self-esteem. *Group Dynamics: Theory, Research, and Practice,* 1, 65–74.

Marques, J. M., Yzerbyt, V. Y. & Leyens, J-P. (1988). The 'black sheep effect': Extremity of judgements towards ingroup members as a function of identification. *European Journal of Social Psychology,* 18, 1–16.

Martijn, C., Van der Pligt, J. & Spears, R. (1996). Judging attitudes: Description, evaluation and type of implication of judgemental language. *Social Cognition,* 14, 77–91.

Martin, J. (1986). The tolerance of injustice. In J. Olson, C. P. Herman and M. Zanna, (eds), *Relative Deprivation and Social Comparison: The Ontario Symposium.* Hillsdale, NJ: Lawrence Erlbaum.

Martin, R. (1988). Ingroup and outgroup minorities: Differential impact upon public and private responses. *European Journal of Social Psychology,* 18, 39–52.

Mathieu, J. E. & Zajac, D. (1990). A review and meta-analysis of the antecedents, correlates, and consequences of organizational commitment. *Psychological Bulletin,* 108, 171–94.

McCann, C. D. & Higgins, E. T. (1992). Personal and contextual factors in communication: A review of the 'communication game'. In G. Semin & K. Fiedler (eds), *Language, Interaction and Social Cognition .* Newbury Park, CA: Sage.

McCauley, C. & Stitt, C. L. (1978). An individual and quantitative measure of stereotypes. *Journal of Personality and Social Psychology,* 39, 615–24.

McClintock, C. G. (1978). Social values: Their definition, measurement, and development. *Journal of Research and Development in Education,* 12, 121–37.

McConahay, J. B. (1986). Modern racism, ambivalence, and the modern racism scale. In J. F. Dovidio & S. L. Gaertner (eds), *Prejudice, Discrimination and Racism.* Orlando, FL: Academic Press.

McConnell, A. R., Sherman, S. J. & Hamilton, D. L. (1994). On-line and memory-based aspects of individual and group target judgements. *Journal of Personality and Social Psychology,* 67, 173–85.

McFarlin, D. B. & Blascovich. J. (1981). Effects of self-esteem and performance feedback on future affective preferences and cognitive expectations. *Journal of Personality and Social Psychology,* 40, 521–31.

McGarty, C., Turner, J. C., Hogg, M. A., David, B. & Wetherell, M. S. (1992). Group polarization as conformity to the prototypical group member. *British Journal of Social Psychology,* 31(1), 1–19.

McGrath, J. E. & Kravitz, D. A. (1982). Group research. *Annual Review of Psychology*, 33, 195–230.

McGuire, W. J. & Padawer-Singer, A. (1976). Trait salience in the spontaneous self-concept. *Journal of Personality and Social Psychology*, 33, 743–54.

McGuire, W. J., McGuire, C. V., Child, P. & Fujioka, T. (1978). Salience of ethnicity in the spontaneous self-concept as a function of one's ethnic distinctiveness in the social environment. *Journal of Personality and Social Psychology*, 36, 511–20.

McGuire, W. J., McGuire, C. V. & Winton, W. (1979). Effects of household sex composition on the salience of one's gender in the spontaneous self-concept. *Journal of Experimental Social Psychology*, 15, 77–90.

Meindl, J. R. & Lerner, M. J. (1984). Exacerbation of extreme responses to an outgroup. *Journal of Personality and Social Psychology*, 47, 71–84.

Melcher, W. (1996a). Impression management and ingroup favouritism. Paper presented in the symposium 'Identity, identifiability and self-presentation in group contexts' (R. Spears, T. Postmes, convenors). 11th General Meeting of the EAESP, Gmunden, July.

Melcher, W. (1996b). *Der Einfluß von Gruppendarstellung auf das Phaenomen der Ingruppenfavorisierung: Experimentelle Untersuchungen am Beispiel kategorialer Aggressionsurteile* [The influence of group composition on the phenomenon of ingroup favouritism: Experimental research on the case of group aggression judgements]. Muenster, Germany: Lit.

Messick, D. M. & Mackie, D. M. (1989). Intergroup relations. *Annual Review of Psychology*, 40, 45–81.

Meyer, J. P. & Allen, N. J. (1991). A three-component conceptualization of organizational commitment. *Human Resource Management Review*, 1, 61–89.

Meyer, J. P. & Allen, N. J. (1997). *Commitment in the workplace: Theory, Research, and Application*. London: SAGA Publications.

Meyer, J. P., Allen, N. J. & Smith, H. J. (1993). Commitment to organizations and occupations: Extension and test of a three-component conceptualization. *Journal of Applied Psychology*, 78, 538–51.

Meyer, J. P., Paunonen, S. V., Gellatly, I. H., Goffin, R. D. & Jackson, D. N. (1989). Organizational commitment and job performance: It's the nature of the commitment that counts. *Journal of Applied Psychology*, 74, 152–6.

Miller, A. G. (ed.) (1982). *In the Eye of the Beholder*. New York: Praeger Publishers.

Mischel, W. & Shoda, Y. (1995). A cognitive-affective system theory of personality: Reconceptualizing situations, dispositions, dynamics, and invariance in personality structure. *Psychological Review*, 102, 246–68.

Mlicki, P. & Ellemers, N., (1996). Being different or being better? National stereotypes and identifications of Polish and Dutch students. *European Journal of Social Psychology*, 26, 97–114.

Mobley, W. H., Griffeth, R. W., Hand, H. H. & Meglino, B. M. (1979). Review and conceptual analysis of the employee turnover process. *Psychological Bulletin*, 86, 493–522.

Moghaddam, F. M. & Stringer, P. (1988). Outgroup similarity and intergroup bias. *Journal of Social Psychology*, 128, 105–15.

Moreland, R. L. & Levine, J. M. (1982). Socialization in small groups: Temporal changes in individual-group relations. In L. Berkowitz (ed.), *Advances in Experimental Social Psychology* (vol. 15). New York: Academic Press.

Moreland, R., Hogg, M. & Hains, S. (1994). Back to the future: Social-psychological research on groups. *Journal of Experimental Social Psychology*, 30(6), 527–55.

Morrison, B. (1995a) Social cooperation and social dilemmas: The role of identity. Paper presented to the 1st Meeting of the Society of Australasian Social Psychologists, 24th Meeting of Australasian Social Psychologists, Hobart, Australia, 22–5 April.

Morrison, B. (1995b) Theories and paradigms: Understanding social cooperation. Paper presented to the Social Identity Symposium, University of Queensland, Brisbane, Australia, 25 August.

Morrison, B. E. (1998) Social cooperation: Redefining the self in self-interest. Unpublished PhD Thesis, ANU, Canberra, Australia.

Moscovici, S. (1981). On social representations. In J. Forgas (ed.), *Social Cognition*. London: Academic Press.

Motowidlo, S. J. & Van Scotter, J. R. (1994). Evidence that task performance should be distinguished from contextual performance. *Journal of Applied Psychology*, 79, 475–80.

Mowday, R. T., Steers, R. M. & Porter, L. W. (1979). The measurement of organizational commitment. *Journal of Vocational Behavior*, 14, 224–47.

Mudrack, P. E. (1989). Group cohesiveness and productivity: A closer look. *Human Relations*, 42, 771–85.

Mullen, B. (1991). Group composition, salience, and cognitive representation: The phenomenology of being in a group. *Journal of Experimental Social Psychology*, 27, 297–323.

Mullen, B. & Copper, C. (1994). The relation between group cohesiveness and performance: An integration. *Psychological Bulletin*, 115, 210–27.

Mullen, B., Brown, R. J. & Smith, C. (1992). Ingroup bias as a function of salience, relevance, and status: An integration. *European Journal of Social Psychology*, 22, 103–22.

Mullin, B. & Hogg, M. A. (1998). Dimensions of subjective uncertainty in social identification and minimal group discrimination. *British Journal of Social Psychology*, 37, 345–65.

Mummendey, A. & Otten, S. (in press) Positive-negative asymmetry in social discrimination. *European Review of Social Psychology*, 9.

Mummendey, A. & Schreiber, H. J. (1983). Better or different? Positive social identity by discrimination against or differentiation from outgroups. *European Journal of Social Psychology*, 13, 389–97.

Mummendey, A. & Schreiber, H. J. (1984a). Social comparison, similarity and ingroup favouritism: A replication. *European Journal of Social Psychology*, 14, 231–3.

Mummendey, A. & Schreiber, H. J. (1984b). 'Different' just means 'better': Some obvious and some hidden pathways to ingroup favoritism. *British Journal of Social Psychology*, 23, 363–8.

Mummendey, A. & Simon, B. (1989). Better or Different? III: The Impact of importance of comparison dimension and relative ingroup size upon intergroup discrimination. *British Journal of Social Psychology*, 28, 1–16.

Mummendey, A., Simon, B., Dietze, C., Grünert, M., Haeger, G., Kessler, S., Lettgen, S. & Schäferhoff, S. (1992). *Journal of Experimental Social Psychology*, 28, 125–44.

Myers, D. (1987). 'Anonymity is part of the magic': Individual manipulation of computer-mediated communication contexts. *Qualitative Sociology*, 10, 251–66.

Newport, E. L. (1976). Motherese: The speech of mothers to young children. In N. Castellan, D. Pisoni & G. Potts (eds), *Cognitive Theory* (vol. 2). Hillsdale, NJ: Lawrence Erlbaum.

Newston, D. & Czerlinsky, T. (1974). Adjustment of attitude communications for contrasts by extreme audiences. *Journal of Personality and Social Psychology*, 30, 829–37.

Nkomo, S. M. & Cox, T., jun. (1996). Diverse identities in organizations. In S. R. Clegg, C. Hardy & W. R. Nord (eds), *Handbook of Organization Studies*.

Noel, J. G., Wann, D. L. & Branscombe, N. R. (1995). Peripherical ingroup membership status and public negativity towards outgroups. *Journal of Personality and Social Psychology*, 68(1), 127–37.

Oaker, G. & Brown, R. J. (1986) Intergroup relations in a hospital setting: A further test of social identity theory. *Human Relations*, 39, 767–78.

Oakes, P. J. (1987). The salience of social categories. In J. C. Turner, M. A. Hogg, P. J. Oakes, S. D. Reicher and M. S. Wetherell (eds), *Rediscovering the Social Group: A Self-categorization Theory*. Oxford: Blackwell.

Oakes, P. J. (1996). Discussant: 'The social identity theory approach: promises, problems and perspectives'. XXVI International Congress of Psychology, Montreal, Canada, August.

Oakes, P. J. & Turner, J. C. (1980). Social categorization and intergroup behaviour: Does minimal intergroup discrimination make social identity more positive? *European Journal of Social Psychology*, 10, 295–301.

Oakes, P. J. & Turner, J. C. (1990) Is limited information processing capacity the cause of social stereotyping? *European Review of Social Psychology*, 1, 111–36.

Oakes, P. J., Haslam, S. A. & Turner, J. C. (1994). *Stereotyping and Social Reality*. Oxford: Blackwell.

Oakes, P. J., Reynolds, K. J., Haslam, S. A. & Turner, J. C. (in press) Part of life's rich tapestry: Stereotyping and the politics of intergroup relations. In E. Lawler & S. Thye (eds), *Advances in Group Processes* (vol. 7). Greenwich, CT: JAI Press.

Oakes, P. J., Turner, J. C. & Haslam, S. A. (1991). Perceiving people as group members: The role of fit in the salience of social categorizations. *British Journal of Social Psychology*, 30, 125–44.

Onorato, R. & Turner, J. C. (1996) Fluidity in the self-concept: A shift from personal to social identity. Paper presented to Symposium on 'Self, self-stereotyping and identity', 2nd Meeting of the Society of Australasian Social Psychologists, 25th Meeting of Australasian Social Psychologists, ANU, Canberra, Australia, 2–5 May.

Onorato, R. S. & Turner, J. C. (1997). Individual differences and social identity: A study of self-categorization processes in the Markus paradigm. Paper presented to 3rd Meeting of the Society of Australasian Social Psychologists, 26th Meeting of Australasian Social Psychologists, Wollongong, New South Wales, Australia.

Orbell, J. M., van de Kragt, A. J. C. & Dawes, R. M. (1988) Explaining discussion-induced cooperation. *Journal of Personality & Social Psychology*, 54, 811–19.

Organ, D. W. (1988). *Organizational Citizenship Behavior*. Lexington, MA: Lexington Books.

Organ, D. W. & Ryan, K. (1995). A meta-analytic review of attitudinal and dispositional predictors of organizational citizenship behavior. *Personnel Psychology*, 48, 775–802.

Ouwerkerk, J. W. & Ellemers, N. (1999). Being outperformed by an advantaged or disadvantaged group: Related attributes and consequences of intergroup comparisons. Manuscript under review.

Ouwerkerk, J. W., De Gilder, D. & De Vries, N. K. (1999). When the going gets tough the tough get going: Social identification and individual effort in intergroup competition. Manuscript under review.

Ouwerkerk, J. W., Ellemers, N., Smith, H. J. & Van Knippenberg, A. (1999). The swinging pendulum: Affective and motivational consequences of temporal intergroup comparisons. Manuscript under review.

Park, B. & Hastie, R. (1987). The perception of variability in category development: In-stance- versus abstraction-based stereotypes. *Journal of Personality and Social Psychology, 53*, 621–35.

Park, B. & Judd, C. M. (1990). Measures and models of perceived group variability. *Journal of Personality and Social Psychology, 59*, 173–91.

Park, B. & Rothbart, M. (1982). Perception of out-group homogeneity and levels of social categorization: Memory for the subordinate attributes of in-group and out-group members. *Journal of Personality and Social Psychology, 42*, 1051–68.

Park, B., Judd, C. M. & Ryan, C. (1991). Social categorization and the representation of variability information. *European Review of Social Psychology, 2*, 211–45.

Peabody, D. (1968). Group judgments in the Philippines: Evaluative and descriptive aspects. *Journal of Personality and Social Psychology, 10*, 290–300.

Pelham, B. W. (1991). On the benefits of misery: Self-serving biases in the depressive self-concept. *Journal of Personality and Social Psychology, 61*, 670–81.

Perreault, S. & Bourhis, R. Y. (1998) Social identification, interdependence and discrimination. *Group Processes & Intergroup Relations, 1*, 49–66.

Pettigrew, T. F. (1967). Social Evaluation Theory. In D. Levine (ed.), *Nebraska Symposium on Motivation*. Lincoln, Nebraska: University of Nebraska Press.

Pettigrew, T. F. (1979). The ultimate attribution error: Extending Allport's cognitive analysis of prejudice. *Personality and Social Psychology Bulletin, 5*, 461–76.

Pettigrew, T. F. (1985). Three issues in ethnicity: Boundaries, deprivations and perceptions. In J. M. Yinger & S. J. Cutler (eds), *Major Social Issues*. New York: Free Press.

Pillegge, A. J. & Holtz, R. (1997). The effects of social identity on the self-set goals and task performance of high and low self-esteem individuals. *Organizational Behavior and Human Decision Processes, 70*, 17–26.

Platow, M. J. (1998) Maintaining people In positions of distributive power: Fairness or social identity? Paper presented to Conference on the Social Psychology of Leadership, Melbourne, La Trobe University, Australia, 3–4 October.

Platow, M. J., Harley, K., Hunter, J. A., Hanning, P., Shave, R. & O'Connell, A. (1997). Interpreting in-group favouring allocations in the minimal group paradigm. *British Journal of Social Psychology, 36*, 107–17.

Platow, M. J., Hoar, S., Reid, S., Harley, K. & Morrison, D. (1997). Endorsement of distributive fair and unfair leaders in interpersonal and intergroup situations. *European Journal of Social Psychology, 27*, 465–94.

Podsakoff, P. M., Ahearne, M. & MacKenzie, S. B. (1997). Organizational citizenship behavior and the quantity and quality of work group performance. *Journal of Applied Psychology, 82*, 262–70.

Poppe, E. and Linssen, H. (in press). Ingroup favouritism and the reflection of realistic dimensions of difference between national states in Eastern European nationality stereotypes. *British Journal of Social Psychology*.

Postmes, T. (1995). Group polarization in computer-mediated communication. Paper presented at the 18th annual Nags Head Conference on Groups, Networks, and Organizations, Highland Beach, FL, June.

Postmes, T. (1997). Social influence in computer-mediated groups. Unpublished PhD thesis, University of Amsterdam.

Postmes, T. & Spears, R. (1997a). In pursuit of a virtually egalitarian world: Effects of anonymity, stereotype activation and discussion topic on gender differences in computer-mediated communication. Manuscript under review.

Postmes, T. & Spears, R. (1997b). Quality of decisions, group norms and social identity: Biased sampling or sampled biases. Paper presented at the Fifth Münster Workshop on the Social Identity Approach, Rothenberge, Germany, March.

Postmes, T. & Spears, R. (1998). Deindividuation and anti-normative behaviour: A meta-analysis. *Psychological Bulletin*, 123, 238–59.

Postmes, T., Branscombe, N. R., Spears, R. & Young, H. (1999). Comparative processes in personal and group judgments: Resolving the discrepancy. *Journal of Personality and Social Psychology*.

Postmes, T., Spears, R. & Lea, M. (1996). The effects of anonymity in intergroup discussion: Bipolarization in computer mediated groups. Manuscript under review.

Postmes, T., Spears, R. & Lea, M. (1998). Breaching or building social boundaries? SIDE-effects of computer-mediated communication. *Communication Research*, 25, 689–715.

Postmes, T., Spears, R., Sakhel, K. & de Groot, D. (1998). Social influence in computer-mediated groups: The effects of anonymity on group behavior. Manuscript under review.

Prentice-Dunn, S. & Rogers, R. W. (1989). Deindividuation and the self-regulation of behavior. In P. B. Paulus (ed.), *The psychology of Group Influence* (2nd edn). Hillsdale, NJ: Lawrence Erlbaum.

Rabbie, J. M. (1991) Determinants of instrumental intra-group cooperation. In R. A. Hinde & J. Groebel (eds), *Cooperation and Prosocial Behaviour*. Cambridge: Cambridge University Press.

Rabbie, J. M. & Horwitz, M. (1969) The arousal of ingroup–outgroup bias by a chance win or loss. *Journal of Personality and Social Psychology*, 13, 269–77.

Rabbie, J. M. & Horwitz, M. (1988) Categories versus groups as explanatory concepts in intergroup relations. *European Journal of Social Psychology*, 18, 117–23.

Rabbie, J. M., Schot, J. C. & Visser, L. (1989) Social identity theory: A conceptual and empirical critique from the perspective of a Behavioral Interaction Model. *European Journal of Social Psychology*, 19, 171–202.

Ralston, D. A., Cunniff, M. K. & Gustafson, D. J. (1995). Cultural accommodation: The effect of language on the responses of bilingual Hong-Kong Chinese managers. *Journal of Cross-Cultural Psychology*, 26, 6, 714–27.

Randall, D. M. (1990). The consequences of organizational commitment: Methodological investigation. *Journal of Organizational Behavior*, 11, 361–78.

Randall, D. M., Fedor, D. B. & Longenecker, C. O. (1990). The behavioral expression of organizational commitment. *Journal of Vocational Behavior*, 36, 210–24.

Raven, B. H. & Kruglanski, A. W. (1970). Conflict and power. In: P. Swingle (ed.), *The Structure of Conflict*. New York: Academic Press.

Reicher, S. D. (1982). The determination of collective behavior. In H. Tajfel (ed.), *Social Identity and Intergroup Relations*. Cambridge: Cambridge University Press.

Reicher, S. D. (1984). Social influence in the crowd: Attitudinal and behavioural effects of de-individuation in conditions of high and low group salience. Special Issue: Intergroup processes. *British Journal of Social Psychology*, 23(4), 341–50.

Reicher, S. D. (1987). Crowd behaviour as social action. In J. C. Turner, M. A. Hogg, P. J. Oakes, S. D. Reicher & M. S. Wetherell (eds), *Rediscovering the Social Group: A Self-categorization Theory*. Oxford: Blackwell.

Reicher, S. D. (1996a). 'The crowd' century: Reconciling practical success with theoretical failure. *British Journal of Social Psychology*, 35, 535–53.

Reicher, S.(1996b) Social identity and social change: Re-thinking the context of social psychology. In W. P. Robinson (ed.), *Social groups and identities: Developing the legacy of Henri Tajfel*. Oxford: Butterworth Heinemann.

Reicher, S. D. (1996c). 'The battle of Westminster': Developing the social identity model of crowd behaviour in order to explain the initiation and development of collective conflict. *European Journal of Social Psychology*, 26, 115–34.

Reicher, S. D. & Levine, M. (1994a). Deindividuation, power relations between groups and the expression of social identity: The effects of visibility to the out-group. *British Journal of Social Psychology*, 33, 145–63.

Reicher, S. D. & Levine, M. (1994b). On the consequences of deindividuation manipulations for the strategic considerations of self: Identifiability and the presentation of social identity. *European Journal of Social Psychology*, 24, 511–24.

Reicher, S. D., Levine, M. & Gordijn, E. (1998). More on deindividuation, power relations between groups and the expression of social identity: Three studies on the effects of visibility to the in-group. *British Journal of Social Psychology*, 37, 15–40.

Reicher, S. D., Spears, R. & Postmes, T. (1995). A social identity model of deindividuation phenomena. *European Review of Social Psychology*, 6, 161–98.

Reichheld, A. E. (1996). *The Loyalty Effect*. Boston: Harvard Business School Press.

Reichl, A. J. (1997). Ingroup favouritism and outgroup favouritism in low status minimal groups: Differential responses to status-related and status-unrelated measures. *European Journal of Social Psychology*, 27, 617–34.

Reynolds, K. J. (1996). Beyond the information given: Capacity, context and the categorization process in impression formation. Unpublished PhD thesis, Canberra, Australia.

Reynolds, K. J., Turner, J. C. & Haslam, S. A. (1998a) When are we better than them and they worse than us? A closer look at social discrimination in positive and negative domains. In submission.

Reynolds, K. J., Turner, J. C. & Haslam, S. A. (1998b) *Personality and prejudice*. Unpublished paper, ANU, Canberra, Australia.

Robinson, W. P. (1996) (Ed.), *Social Groups and Identities: Developing the Legacy of Henri Tajfel*. Oxford: Butterworth Heinemann.

Roccas, S. & Schwartz, S. H. (1993). Effects of intergroup similarity on intergroup relations. *European Journal of Social Psychology*, 23, 581–95.

Rojahn, K. (1996). Gender in the context of leadership. Unpublished PhD Thesis, University of Amsterdam.

Rokeach, M. (1960). *The Open and Closed Mind*. New York: Basic Books.

Rommetveit, R. (1974). *On Message Structure: A Framework for the Study of Language and Communication*. New York: John Wiley & Sons.

Rosch, E. (1978). Principles of categorization. In E. Rosch & B. Lloyd (eds), *Cognition and Categorization*. Hillsdale, NJ: Erlbaum.

Roseman, I., Wiest, C. & Swartz, T. (1994). Phenomenology, behaviors, and goals differentiate discrete emotions. *Journal of Personality and Social Psychology*, 67, 206–11.

Rosenberg, M. (1965). *Society and the Adolescent Self-Image*. Princeton, NJ: Princeton University Press.

Ross, L. & Nisbett, R. E. (1991) *The Person and the Situation: Perspectives of Social Psychology*. New York: McGraw-Hill.

Rothgerber, H. (1997). External intergroup threat as an antecedent to perceptions of in-group and out-group homogeneity. *Journal of Personality and Social Psychology*, 73, 1206–12.

Rothgerber, H. & Worchel, S. (1998). The view from below: Intergroup relations from the perspective of the disadvantaged group. *Journal of Personality and Social Psychology,* 73, 1191–205.

Rubin, M. & Hewstone, M. (1998). Social identity theory's self-esteem hypothesis: A review and some suggestions for clarification. *Personality and Social Psychology Review,* 2, 40–62.

Rubini, M. & Semin, G. R. (1994). Language use in the context of congruent and incongruent ingroup behaviors. *British Journal of Social Psychology,* 33, 355–62.

Ruggiero, K. & Taylor, D. (1995). Coping with discrimination: How disadvantaged group members perceive the discrimination that confronts them. *Journal of Personality and Social Psychology,* 68, 826–38.

Ruggiero, K. & Taylor, D. (1997). Why minority members perceive or do not perceive the discrimination that confronts them: The role of self-esteem and perceived control. *Journal of Personality and Social Psychology,* 72, 373–89.

Runciman, W. G. (1966). *Relative Deprivation and Social Justice: A Study of Attitudes to Social Inequality in Twentieth-century England.* Berkeley: University of California Press.

Sabini, J. (1995). *Social Psychology* (2nd edn). New York: Norton.

Sachdev, I. & Bourhis, R. Y. (1984). Minimal Majorities and Minorities. *European Journal of Social Psychology,* 14, 35–52.

Saks, A. M. (1995). Longitudinal field investigation of the moderating and mediating effects of self-efficacy on the relationship between training and newcomber adjustment. *Journal of Applied Psychology,* 80, 211–25.

Schaubroeck, J. & Ganster, D. C. (1991) Beyond the call of duty: A field study of extra-role behavior in voluntary organizations. *Human Relations,* 44, 569–82.

Schlenker, B. (1980). *Impression Management: The Self-concept, Social Identity, and Interpersonal Relations.* Monterey: Brooks/Cole.

Schmid, J. & Fiedler, K. (1996). The backbone of closing speeches: The impact of prosecution versus defense language on juridical attributes. Unpublished manuscript, University of Heidelberg, Germany.

Schmitt, M. & Branscombe, N. R. (1997). The good, the bad, and the manly: Effects of prototypicality and group identification on intragroup evaluations. Paper presented at the annual meeting of the Midwestern Psychological Association, Chicago, IL.

Schwartz, N. (1995). Judgement in a social context: Biases, shortcomings, and the logic of conversation. In M. P. Zanna (ed.), *Advances in Experimental Social Psychology,* (vol. 29). New York: Academic Press.

Searle, J. R. (1970). *Speech Acts: An Essay in the Philosophy of Language.* Cambridge: Cambridge University Press.

Sedikides, C. (1990). Effects of fortuitously activated constructs versus activated communication goals on person impressions. *Journal of Personality and Social Psychology,* 58, 397–408.

Semin G. R. & De Poot, C. J. de (1997). You might regret it if you don't notice how a question is worded! *Journal of Personality and Social Psychology,* 73, 472–80.

Semin, G. R. & Fiedler, K. (1988). The cognitive functions of linguistic categories in describing persons: Social cognition and language. *Journal of Personality and Social Psychology,* 54, 558–68.

Semin, G. R. & Fiedler, K. (1991). The linguistic category model, its bases, applications and range. In W. Stroebe & M. Hewstone (eds), *European Review of Social Psychology* (vol. 2). Chichester, England: Wiley.

Semin, G. R. & Fiedler, K. (1992). The inferential properties of interpersonal verbs. In G. Semin & K. Fiedler (eds), *Language, Interaction and Social Cognition*. Newbury Park, CA: Sage.

Sherif, M. (1966). *In Common Predicament: Social Psychology of Intergroup Conflict and Cooperation*. Boston: Houghton Mifflin.

Sherif, M. (1967) *Group Conflict and Co-operation: Their Social Psychology*. London: Routledge and Kegan Paul.

Short, J. A., Williams, E. & Christie, B. (1976). *The Social Psychology of Telecommunications*. Chichester: John Wiley.

Shrauger, J. S. (1975). Responses to evaluation as a function of initial self-perceptions. *Psychological Bulletin, 82*, 581–96.

Shute, H. B. (1987). Vocal pitch in motherese. *Educational Psychology, 7*, 187–205.

Siegel, J., Dubrovsky, V., Kiesler, S. & McGuire, T. W. (1986). Group processes in computer-mediated communication. *Organizational Behavior & Human Decision Processes, 37*, 157–187.

Simon, B. (1992a) The perception of ingroup and outgroup homogeneity: Reintroducing the intergroup context. *European Review of Social Psychology, 3*, 1–30.

Simon, B. (1992b). Intragroup differentiation in terms of ingroup and outgroup attributes. *European Journal of Social Psychology, 22*, 407–13.

Simon, B. (1993). On the asymmetry in the cognitive construal of ingroup and outgroup: A model of egocentric social categorization. *European Journal of Social Psychology, 23*, 131–47.

Simon, B. (1997). Self and group in modern society: Ten theses on the individual self and the collective self. In R. Spears, P. J. Oakes, N. Ellemers & S. A. Haslam (eds), *The Social Psychology of Stereotyping and Group Life* . Oxford: Blackwell.

Simon, B. (1998). Individuals, groups and social change: On the relationship between individual and collective self-interpretations and collective action. In C. Sedikides, J. Schopler & C. A. Insko (eds), *Intergroup Cognition and Intergroup Behavior*. Mahwah, NJ: Lawrence Erlbaum Associates.

Simon, B. & Brown, R. (1987). Perceived intragroup homogeneity in minority-majority contexts. *Journal of Personality and Social Psychology, 53*, 703–11.

Simon, B. & Hamilton, D. L. (1994). Self-stereotyping and social context: The effects of relative in-group size and in-group status. *Journal of Personality and Social Psychology, 66*, 699–711.

Simon, B., Kulla, C. & Zobel, M. (1995). On being more than just a part of the whole: Regional identity and social distinctiveness. *European Journal of Social Psychology, 25*, 325–40.

Simon, B., Loewy, M., Stürmer, S., Weber, U., Freytag, P., Habig, C., Kaupmeier, C. & Spahlinger, D. (1998). Collective identification and social movement participation. *Journal of Personality and Social Psychology, 74*, 646–58.

Simon, B., Pantaleo, G. & Mummendey, A. (1995). Unique individual or interchangeable group member? The accentuation of intragroup differences versus similarities as an indicator of the individual self versus the collective self. *Journal of Personality and Social Psychology, 69*, 106–19.

Smith, E. R. & Zarate, M. A. (1992). Exemplar-based model of social judgement. *Psychological Review, 99*, 3–21.

Smith, H. J. & Spears, R. (1996). Ability and outcome evaluations as a function of personal and collective (dis)advantage: A group escape from individual bias. *Personality and Social Psychology Bulletin, 22*, 690–704.

Smith, H. J. & Tyler, T. R. (1997). Choosing the right pond: The impact of group membership on self-esteem and group-oriented behavior. *Journal of Experimental Social Psychology, 33*, 146–70.

Smith, H. J., Spears, R. & Oyen, M. (1994). The influence of personal deprivation and salience of group membership on justice evaluations. *Journal of Experimental Social Psychology, 30*, 277–99.

Snyder, C. R. & Fromkin, H. L. (1980) *Uniqueness: The Human Pursuit of Difference.* New York: Plenum Press.

Snyder, C. R., Lassegard, M. A. & Ford, C. E. (1986). Distancing after group success and failure: Basking in reflected glory and cutting off reflected failure. *Journal of Personality and Social Psychology, 51*, 382–88.

Spears, R. (1995a). Isolating the collective self. In A. Oosterwegel & R. Wicklund (eds), *The Self in European and North American Culture: Development and Processes* (Nato ASI series, vol. 84). Amsterdam: Kluwer.

Spears, R. (1995b). Isolating the collective self: The content and context of identity, rationality and behaviour. Unpublished Pionier grant proposal, University of Amsterdam.

Spears, R. & Doosje, B. (1996). Categorization and individuation: The effect of group identification and encoding set. Unpublished manuscript, University of Amsterdam.

Spears, R. & Doosje, B. (in prep.). Salience, group valence and identification in the category confusion paradigm. Manuscript in preparation, University of Amsterdam.

Spears, R. & Haslam, S. A. (1997). Stereotyping and the burden of cognitive load. In R. Spears, P. J. Oakes, N. Ellemers, & S. A. Haslam (eds), *The Social Psychology of Stereotyping and Group Life.* Oxford: Blackwell.

Spears, R. & Jetten, J. (1998a). Social categorization, group distinctness and discrimination in the minimal group paradigm. Manuscript in preparation, University of Amsterdam.

Spears, R. & Jetten, J. (1998b). The moderating effect of group identification and perceived group permeability on the group distinctiveness – positive differentiation relation. Manuscript in preparation, University of Amsterdam.

Spears, R. & Lea, M. (1992). Social influence and the influence of the 'social' in computer-mediated communication. In M. Lea (ed.), *Contexts of Computer-Mediated Communication.* Hemel Hempstead: Harvester Wheatsheaf.

Spears, R. & Lea, M. (1994). Panacea or panopticon? The hidden power in computer-mediated communication. *Communication Research, 21*(4), 427–59.

Spears, R. & Manstead, A. S. R. (1989). The social context of stereotyping and differentiation. *European Journal of Social Psychology, 19*, 101–21.

Spears, R., Doosje, B. & Ellemers, N. (1997). Self-stereotyping in the face of threats to group status and distinctiveness: The role of group identification. *Personality and Social Psychology Bulletin, 23*, 538–53.

Spears, R., Doosje, B., Yzerbyt, V. Rocher, S., te Brake, H. & Haslam, S. A. (in prep.). Social categorization as a function of group identification, and cognitive load. Manuscript in preparation, University of Amsterdam.

Spears, R., Haslam, S. A. & Jansen, R. (in press). The effect of cognitive load on social categorization in the category confusion paradigm. *European Journal of Social Psychology.*

Spears, R., Jetten, J. & Van Harreveld, F. (1998). First among equals or worst among equals: Group identification as a fitting response to personal and collective self-esteem. Manuscript submitted for publication, University of Amsterdam.

Spears, R., Lea, M. & Lee, S. (1990). De-individuation and group polarization in computer-mediated communication. *British Journal of Social Psychology,* 29, 121–34.

Spears, R., Oakes, P. J., Ellemers, N., and Haslam, S. A. (eds) (1997). *The Social Psychology of Stereotyping and Group Life.* Oxford: Blackwell.

Spencer, S. J. & Quinn, D. M. (1995). Stereotype threat and women's math performance: The mediating role of anxiety. Paper presented at the annual meeting of the American Psychological Association. New York.

Stangor, C. & Ford, T. E. (1992). Accuracy and expectancy-confirming processing orientations and the development of stereotypes and prejudice. *European Review of Social Psychology,* 3, 56–89.

Stangor, C. & Lange, J. E. (1994). Mental representations of social groups: Advances in understanding stereotypes and stereotyping. In M. P. Zanna (ed.), *Advances in Experimental Social Psychology* (vol. 26). New York: Academic Press.

Stangor, C. & McMillan, D. (1992). Memory for expectancy-congruent and expectancy-incongruent information: A review of the social and social developmental literatures. *Psychological Bulletin,* 111, 42–61.

Stangor, C. & Schaller, M. (1996). Stereotypes as individual and collective representations. In C. N. Macrae, C. Stangor & M. Hewstone (eds), *Stereotypes and Stereotyping.* New York: Guilford.

Stangor, C., Lynch, L., Duan, C. & Glass, B. (1992). Categorization of individuals on the basis of multiple social features. *Journal of Personality and Social Psychology,* 62, 207–18.

Stasser, G. & Titus, W. (1985). Pooling of unshared information in group decision-making: Biased information sampling during discussions. *Journal of Personality and Social Psychology,* 48(6), 1467–78.

Staub, E. (1989). *The Roots of Evil: The Origins of Genocide and Other Group Violence.* New York: University Press.

Staub, E. (1996). Cultural-societal roots of violence: The examples of genocidal violence and of contemporary youth violence in the United States. *American Psychologist,* 51, 117–32.

Staub, E. & Rosenthal, L. H. (1994). Mob violence: Cultural-societal sources, instigators, group processes, and participants. In L. D. Eron, J. H. Gentry & P. Schlegel (eds), *Reason to Hope: A Psychosocial Perspective on Violence & Youth.* Washington, DC: American Psychological Association.

Steele, C. M. (1998). The psychology of self-affirmation: Sustaining the integrity of the self. In L. Berkowitz (ed.), *Advances in Experimental Social Psychology* (vol. 21). New York: Academic Press.

Steele, C. M. (1997). A threat in the air: How stereotypes shape intellectual identity and performance. *American Psychologist,* 52, 613–29.

Steele, C. M. & Aronson, J. (1995). Stereotype threat and the intellectual test performance of African Americans. *Journal of Personality and Social Psychology,* 69, 797–811.

Steele, S. (1990). White guilt. In S. Steele, *The Content of our Character: A New Vision of Race in America* . New York: Harper Collins.

Steil, J. (1983). The response to injustice: Effects of varying levels of social support and position of advantage or disadvantage. *Journal of Experimental Social Psychology,* 19, 239–53.

Stephan, W. G. & Stephan, C. W. (1984). The role of ignorance in intergroup relations. In N. Miller & M. B. Brewer (eds), *Groups in Contact: The Psychology of Desegregation.* Orlando, FL: Academic Press.

Stogdill, R. M. (1972). Group productivity, drive and cohesiveness. *Organizational Behavior and Human Performance, 6*, 26–53.

Strauss, S. G. (1996). Getting a clue: The effects of communication media and information distribution on participation and performance in computer-mediated and face-to-face groups. *Small Group Research*, 27, 115–42.

Struch, N. & Schwartz, S. H. (1989). Intergroup aggression: Its predictors and distinctness from ingroup bias. *Journal of Personality and Social Psychology, 56*, 364–73.

Swann, W. B., Griffin, J. J., Predmore, S. C. & Gaines B. (1987). The cognitive-affective crossfire: When self-consistency confronts self-enhancement. *Journal of Personality and Social Psychology, 52*, 881–9.

Tajfel, H. (1969). Cognitive aspects of prejudice. *Journal of Social Issues, 25*, 79–97.

Tajfel, H. (1972a) La catégorisation sociale [Social categorization]. In S. Moscovici (ed.), *Introduction à la psychologie sociale*. Paris: Larouse.

Tajfel, H. (1972b) Experiments in a vacuum. In J. Israel & H. Tajfel (eds), *The Context of Social Psychology*. London: Academic Press.

Tajfel, H. (1974).Social identity and intergroup behaviour. *Social Science Information*, 13, 65–93.

Tajfel, H. (1975). The exit of social mobility and the voice of social change. *Social Science Information*, 14, 101–18.

Tajfel, H. (ed.). (1978a). *Differentiation Between Social Groups: Studies in the Social Psychology of Intergroup Relations*. London: Academic Press.

Tajfel, H. (1978b). *The Social Psychology of the Minorities*. New York: Minority Rights Group.

Tajfel, H. (1979) Individuals and groups in social psychology. *British Journal of Social and Clinical Psychology*, 18, 183–90.

Tajfel, H. (1981a) *Human Groups and Social Categories*. Cambridge: Cambridge University Press.

Tajfel, H. (1981b). Social stereotypes and social groups. In J. C. Turner & H. Giles (eds), *Intergroup Behaviour* Oxford: Blackwell; Chicago: University of Chicago Press.

Tajfel, H. (1982a). *Human Groups and Social Categories*. New York: Cambridge University Press.

Tajfel, H. (1982b). Social psychology of intergroup relations. *Annual Review of Psychology*, 33, 1–39.

Tajfel, H. (ed.). (1982c). *Social Identity and Intergroup Relations*. Cambridge: Cambridge University Press.

Tajfel, H. (1984). Intergroup relations, social myths and social justice in social psychology. In H. Tajfel (ed.) *The Social Dimension: European Developments in Social Psychology*. Cambridge: Cambridge University Press.

Tajfel, H. & Turner, J. C. (1979). An integrative theory of intergroup conflict. In W. G. Austin & S. Worchel (eds), *The Social Psychology of Intergroup Relations*. Monterey, CA: Brooks/Cole.

Tajfel, H. & Turner J. C. (1986). The social identity theory of intergroup behavior. In S. Worchel & W. G. Austin (eds), *Psychology of Intergroup Relations*. Chicago: Nelson Hall.

Tajfel, H. & Wilkes, A. L. (1963). Classification and quantitative judgement. *British Journal of Social Psychology*, 54, 101–14.

Tajfel, H., Flament, C., Billig, M. G. & Bundy, R. F. (1971). Social categorization and intergroup behaviour. *European Journal of Social Psychology*, 1, 149–77.

Tangney, J. P. (1995). Shame and guilt in interpersonal relationships. In J. P. Tangney & K. W. Fischer (eds), *Self-conscious Emotions: The Psychology of Shame, Guilt, Embarrassment, and Pride*. New York: Guilford Press.

Tangney, J. P. & Fischer, K. W. (eds) (1995). *Self-conscious Emotions: The Psychology of Shame, Guilt, Embarrassment, and Pride*. New York: Guilford Press.

Tarde, G. (1921). *Les lois de l'imitation* [The laws of imitation]. Paris: Librairie Felix Alcan. (Original work published in 1890.)

Taylor, D. M. & McKirnan, D. J. (1984). A five-stage model of intergroup relations. *British Journal of Social Psychology*, 23, 291–300.

Taylor, D. M., Moghaddam, F. M., Gamble, I. & Zellerer, E. (1987). Disadvantaged group responses to perceived inequality: From passive acceptance to collective action. *Journal of Social Psychology*, 127, 259–72.

Taylor, D. M., Wright, S. C., Moghaddam, F. M. & Lalonde, R. N. (1990). The personal/group discrimination discrepancy: Perceiving my group, but not myself, to be a target for discrimination. Personality and Social Psychology Bulletin, 16, 254–62.

Taylor, S. E., Fiske, S. T., Etcoff, N. L. & Ruderman, A. J. (1978) Categorical and contextual bases of person memory and stereotyping. *Journal of Personality and Social Psychology*, 36, 778–93.

Taylor, S. E., Peplau, L. A. & Sears, D. O. (1994). *Social Psychology* (8th edn). Englewood Cliffs, NJ: Prentice-Hall.

Tedeschi, J. T. & Riess, M. (1981). Verbal strategies in impression management. In C. Antaki (ed.), *The Psychology of Ordinary Explanations of Social Behaviour*. London: Academic Press.

Ter Haar, W. (1997). The cognitive and strategic aspects of anonymity. Unpublished Master's thesis, University of Amsterdam.

Terry, D. J. & Hogg, M. A. (1996). Group norms and the attitude-behavior relationship: A role for group identification. *Personality and Social Psychology Bulletin*, 22, 776–93.

Tice, D. M. (1991). Esteem protection or enhancement? Self-handicapping motives and attributions differ by trait self-esteem. *Journal of Personality and Social Psychology*, 60, 711–25.

Trafimow, D., Silverman, E. S., Fan, R. M-T. & Law, J. S. F. (1997). The effects of language and priming on the relative accessibility of the private self and the collective self. *Journal of Cross-Cultural Psychology*, 28(1), 107–23.

Triandis, H. C. (1995). *Individualism and Collectivism*. Boulder, CO: Westview Press.

Triandis, H. C., McCusker, C. & Hui, C. H. (1990). Multimethod probes of individualism and collectivism. *Journal of Personality and Social Psychology*, 59, 1006–20.

Turkle, S. (1996). Parallel lives: Working on identity in virtual space. In D. Grodin & T. R. Lindlof (eds), *Constructing the Self in a Mediated World*. Thousand Oaks, CA: Sage.

Turner, J. C. (1975) Social comparison and social identity: Some prospects for intergroup behaviour. *European Journal of Social Psychology*, 5, 5–34.

Turner, J. C. (1978a) Towards a cognitive redefinition of the social group. Paper presented to the Research Conference on Social Identity, European Laboratory of Social Psychology (LEPS.), Université de Haute Bretagne (Rennes II), Rennes, France.

Turner, J. C. (1978b). Social comparison, similarity and ingroup-favoritism. In H. Tajfel (ed.), *Differentiation Between Social Groups: Studies in the Social Psychology of Intergroup Relations*. London: Academic Press.

Turner, J. C. (1981) The experimental social psychology of intergroup behaviour. In J. C.

Turner and H. Giles (eds), *Intergroup Behaviour*. Oxford: Blackwell; Chicago: University of Chicago Press.

Turner, J. C. (1982). Towards a cognitive redefinition of the group. In H. Tajfel (ed.), *Social Identity and Intergroup Relations*. Cambridge: Cambridge University Press.

Turner, J. C. (1984) Social identification and psychological group formation. In H. Tajfel (ed.), *The Social Dimension: European Developments in Social Psychology*. (vol. 2). Cambridge: Cambridge University Press; Paris: Editions de la Maison des Sciences de l'Homme.

Turner, J. C. (1985). Social categorization and the self-concept: A social cognitive theory of group behaviour. In E. J. Lawler (ed.), *Advances in Group Processes: Theory and Research* (vol. 2). Greenwich, CT: JAI.

Turner, J. C. (1987). A self-categorization theory. In J. C. Turner, M. A. Hogg, P. J. Oakes, S. D. Reicher and M. S. Wetherell, *Rediscovering the Social Group: A Self-categorization Theory*. Oxford: Blackwell.

Turner, J. C. (1991). *Social Influence*. Milton Keynes: Open University Press.

Turner, J. C. (1996a) Henri Tajfel: An introduction. In W. P. Robinson (ed.), *Social Groups and Identities: Developing the Legacy of Henri Tajfel*. Oxford: Butterworth Heinemann.

Turner, J. C. (1996b) Fifty years' research on intergroup relations: Advances and prospects. Invited plenary paper presented to Symposium on 'Social psychology over the last 50 years', at the 2nd Annual Meeting of the Society of Australasian Social Psychologists, Canberra, ACT, 2–5 May.

Turner, J. C. (1996c) Social identity theory and the concept of prejudice. Invited Keynote Lecture, 40th Kongress der Deutschen Gesellschaft fur Psychologie (40th Congress of the German Psychological Society), Ludwig-Maximilians-Universitat, Munich, Germany, 22–6 September.

Turner, J. C. (1998) Approaching leadership from the self-categorization analysis of social influence. Paper presented to Conference on the Social Psychology of Leadership, Melbourne, La Trobe University, Australia, 3–4 October.

Turner, J. C. & Bourhis, R. Y. (1996) Social identity, interdependence and the social group: A reply to Rabbie et al. In W. P. Robinson (ed.), *Social Groups and Identities: Developing the Legacy of Henri Tajfel*. Oxford: Butterworth Heinemann.

Turner, J. C. & Brown, R. (1978). Social status, cognitive alternatives and intergroup relations. In H. Tajfel (ed.), *Differentiation Between Social Groups: Studies in the Social Psychology of Intergroup Relations*. London: Academic Press.

Turner, J. C. & Haslam, S. A. (in press) Social identity, organizations and leadership. In M. E. Turner (ed.), *Groups at Work. Advances in Theory and Research*. Hillsdale, NJ: Lawrence Erlbaum.

Turner, J. C. & Oakes, P. J. (1986) The significance of the social identity concept for social psychology with reference to individualism, interactionism, and social influence. *British Journal of Social Psychology*, 25, 237–52.

Turner, J. C. & Oakes, P. J. (1989). Self-categorization theory and social influence. In P. B. Paulus (ed.), *Psychology of Group Influence* (2nd edn). Hillsdale, NJ: Lawrence Erlbaum.

Turner, J. C. & Oakes, P. J. (1997) The socially structured mind. In C. McGarty and S. A. Haslam (eds), *The Message of Social Psychology*. Oxford: Blackwell.

Turner, J. C., Hogg, M. A., Oakes, P. J., Reicher, S. D. & Wetherell, M. S. (1987). *Rediscovering the Social Group: A Self-categorization Theory*. Oxford: Blackwell.

Turner, J. C., Hogg, M. A., Oakes, P. J. & Smith, P. M. (1984). Failure and defeat as determinants of group cohesiveness. *British Journal of Social Psychology*, 23, 97–111.

Turner, J. C. & Onorato, R. (1999) Social identity, personality and the self-concept: A self-categorization perspective. In T. R. Tyler, R. Kramer & O. John (eds), *The Psychology of the Social Self*. Hillsdale, NJ: Lawrence Erlbaum.

Turner, J. C., Oakes, P. J., Haslam, S. A. & McGarty, C. (1994) Self and collective: Cognition and social context. *Personality and Social Psychology Bulletin*, 20, 454–63.

Turner, J. C., Sachdev, I. & Hogg, M. A. (1983) Social categorization, interpersonal attraction and group formation. *British Journal of Social Psychology*, 22, 227–39.

Turner, J. C., Wetherell, M. S. & Hogg, M. A. (1989). Referent informational influence and group polarization. *British Journal of Social Psychology*, 28(2), 135–47.

Tyler, T. R. (1997). The psychology of legitimacy. *Personality and Social Psychology Review*, 1, 323–44.

Tyler, T. R. & Dawes, R. M. (1993) Fairness in groups: Comparing the self-interest and social identity perspectives. In B. A. Mellers & J. Baron (eds), *Psychological Perspectives on Justice: Theory and Applications*. Cambridge, UK: Cambridge University Press.

Tyler, T. R. & Lind, E. A. (1992). A relational model of authority in groups. In M. Zanna (ed.), *Advances in Experimental Social Psychology* (vol. 25). New York: Academic Press.

Tyler, T. R. & Smith, H. J. (1998). Social justice and social movements. In D. Gilbert, S. T. Fiske & G. Lindzey, (eds), *Handbook of Social Psychology* (4th edn). New York: McGraw Hill.

Tyler, T. R., Boeckmann, R. J., Smith, H. J. & Huo, Y. J. (1977). *Social Justice in a Diverse Society*. Denver, Colorado: Westview Press.

Tyler, T. R., Kramer, R. & John, O. (eds) (1999) *The Psychology of the Social Self*. Hillsdale, NJ: Lawrence Erlbaum.

Vanbeselaere, N. (1991). The different effects of simple and crossed categorizations: A result of the category differentiation process or of differential category salience? *European Review of Social Psychology*, 2, 247–78.

Vanbeselaere, N. (1996). The impact of differentially valued overlapping categorizations upon the differentiation between positively, negatively, and neutrally evaluated social groups. *European Journal of Social Psychology*, 26, 75–96.

Van Dijk, J. A. G. M. (1997). The reality of virtual communities. *Trends in Communication*, 2, 39–63.

Van Dijk, T. A. (1984). *Prejudice and Discourse. An Analysis of Ethnic Prejudice in Cognition and Conversation*. Amsterdam: Benjamins.

Van Dijk, T. A. (1987). *Communicating Racism. Ethnic Prejudice in Thought and Talk*. Newbury Park, CA: Sage.

Van Knippenberg, A. (1978). Status differences, comparative relevance and intergroup differentiation. In H. Tajfel (ed.), *Differentiation Between Social Groups: Studies in the Social Psychology of Intergroup Relations*. London: Academic Press.

Van Knippenberg, A. (1984). Intergroup differences in group perceptions. In Tajfel, H. (ed.), *The Social Dimension: European Developments in Social Psychology*. Cambridge: Cambridge University Press.

Van Knippenberg, A. (1989). Strategies of identity management. In: J. P. Van Oudenhoven & T. M. Willemsen (eds), *Ethnic Minorities: Social Psychological Perspectives*. Amsterdam: Swets & Zeitlinger.

Van Knippenberg, A. & Ellemers, N. (1990). Social identity and intergroup differentiation processes. *European Review of Social Psychology*, 1, 137–69.

Van Knippenberg, A. & Van Oers, H. (1984). Social identity and equity concerns in intergroup perceptions. *British Journal of Social Psychology*, 23, 351–61.

Van Knippenberg, A. & Wilke, H. (1979). Perceptions of collegiens and apprentis re-analysed. *European Journal of Social Psychology,* 9, 427–34.

Van Knippenberg, A. & Wilke, H. (1988). Social categorization and attitude change. *European Journal of Social Psychology,* 18(5), 395–406.

Van Knippenberg, A., Van Twuyver, M. & Pepels, J. (1994). Factors affecting social categorization processes in memory. *British Journal of Social Psychology,* 33, 419–32.

Van Knippenberg, D., De Vries, N. & Van Knippenberg, A. (1990). Group status, group size and attitude polarization. *European Journal of Social Psychology,* 20(3), 253–57.

Vanneman, R. & Pettigrew, T. F. (1972). Race and relative deprivation in the urban United States, *Race,* 13, 461–86.

Van Rijswijk, W. & Ellemers, N. (1998). Emotionele reacties op feedback over de eigen groep. [Emotional responses to group-relevant feedback]. *Fundamentele Sociale Psychologie,* 12, 86–96.

Van Twuyver, M. & Van Knippenberg, A. (in press). Social categorization and group size. *British Journal of Psychology.*

Verkuyten, M. (1997). Discourses of ethnic minority identity. *British Journal of Social Psychology,* 36, 565–86.

Verkuyten, M. & Hagendoorn, L. (1988) Prejudice and self-categorization: The variable role of authoritarianism and ingroup stereotypes. *Personality and Social Psychology Bulletin,* 24, 99–110.

Von Hippel, W., Sekaquaptewa, D. & Vargas, P. (1997). The linguistic intergroup bias as an implicit indicator of prejudice. *Journal of Experimental Social Psychology,* 33, 490–509.

Vonk, R. (1998). The slime effect: Suspicion and dislike of likeable behavior towards superiors. *Journal of Personality and Social Psychology,* 74, 849–64.

Waldzus, S., Schubert, T. & Frindte, W. (1997). Ingroup-favouritism and ingroup-salience under computer mediated conditions: An extended replication of minimal group results. Manuscript under review.

Walker, I. & Mann, L. (1987). Unemployment, Relative Deprivation and Social Protest. *Personality and Social Psychology Bulletin,* 13, 275–83.

Walker , I. & Pettigrew, T. F. (1984). Relative Deprivation Theory: An Overview and Conceptual Critique. *British Journal of Social Psychology,* 23, 301–10.

Walsh, W. A. & Banaji, M. R. (1997) The collective self. In J. G. Snodgrass & R. L. Thompson (eds), *The Self Across Psychology: Self-recognition, Self-awareness, and the Self-concept.* New York, NY: Annals of the New York Academy of Sciences.

Walster, E., Walster, G. W., and Berscheid, E. (1978). *Equity: Theory and Research.* Boston: Allyn and Bacon.

Walther, J. B. (1996). Computer-mediated communication: Impersonal, interpersonal and hyperpersonal interaction. *Communication Research,* 23, 1–43.

Walther, J. B. (1997). Group and interpersonal effects in interpersonal computer-mediated communication. *Human Communication Research,* 23, 342–69.

Wann, D. L. & Branscombe, N. R. (1990). Die-hard and fair-weather fans: Effects of identification on BIRGing and CORFing tendencies. *Journal of Sport and Social Issues,* 14, 103–17.

Wann, D. L. & Branscombe, N. R. (1993). Sports fans: Measuring degree of identification with their team. *International Journal of Sport Psychology,* 24, 1–17.

We, G. (1993). Cross-gender communication in cyberspace, *Electronic Journal on Virtual Culture* (vol. 2). E-mail: comserve@vm.Its.Rpi.edu Message: send we v2n3.

Weber, R. & Crocker, J. (1983). Cognitive processes in the revision of stereotypic beliefs. *Journal of Personality and Social Psychology*, 45, 961–77.

Webster, D. M., Kruglanski, A. W. & Pattison, D. A. (1997). Motivated language use in intergroup contexts: Need for closure effects on the linguistic intergroup bias. *Journal of Personality and Social Psychology*, 72, 1122–31.

Weisband, S. (1994). Overcoming social awareness in computer-supported groups: Does anonymity really help? *Computer-Supported Cooperative Work*, 2, 285–297.

Weisband, S. P., Schneider, S. K. & Connolly, T. (1995). Computer-mediated communication and social information: Status salience and status differences. *Academy of Management Journal*, 38, 1124–51.

Wellman, B. (1997). An electronic group is virtually a social network. In S. Kiesler (ed.), *Culture of the Internet*. Mahwah, NJ: Erlbaum.

Wetherell, M. (1987). Social identity and group polarization. In J. C. Turner, M. A. Hogg, P.J. Oakes, S. D. Reicher & M. S. Wetherell (eds), *Rediscovering the Social Group: A Self-categorization Theory*. Oxford: Blackwell.

Wicklund, R. A. (1990). *Zero-variable Theories and the Psychology of the Explainer*. New York: Springer-Verlag.

Wigboldus, D. H. J., Spears, R., Semin, G. R. & Ham, J. R. C. (1999). Stereotyping, communication and categorization: How recipient group status moderates linguistic intergroup bias. Manuscript under review.

Wilder, D. A. (1978). Reduction of intergroup discrimination through individuation of the out-group. *Journal of Personality and Social Psychology*, 36, 1361–74.

Wilder, D. A. (1986). Social categorization: Implications for creation and reduction of intergroup bias. In L. Berkowitz (ed.), *Advances in Experimental Social Psychology*. New York: Academic Press.

Wilder, D. A. & Thompson, J. E. (1988). Assimilation and contrast effects in the judgment of groups. *Journal of Personality and Social Psychology*, 54, 62–73.

Williams, K. D., Karau, S. J. & Bourgeois, M. (1993). Working on collective tasks: Social loafing and social compensation. In M. A. Hogg & D. Abrams (eds), *Group Motivation: Social Psychological Perspectives*. New York: Harvester Wheatsheaf.

Williams, K. D. & Sommer, K. L. (1997). Social ostracism by coworkers: Does rejection lead to loafing or compensation? *Personality and Social Psychology Bulletin*, 23, 693–706.

Williams, R. M. (1956). Religion, value-orientations, and intergroup conflict. *Journal of Social Issues*, 12, 12–20.

Wood, W. (1987). Meta-analytic review of sex differences in group performance. *Psychological Bulletin*, 102, 53–71.

Worchel, S., Coutant-Sassic, D. & Grossman, M. (1992). A developmental approach to group dynamics: A model and illustrative research. In S. Worchel, W. Wood & J. A. Simpson (eds), *Group Process and Group Productivity*. Newbury Park: Sage.

Worchel, S., Morales, J. F., Paez, D. & Deschamps, J.-C. (eds) (1998). *Social Identity: International Perspectives*. London, UK & Newbury Park, USA: Sage.

Worchel, S., Rothgerber, H., Day, E. A., Hart, D. & Butemeyer, J. (1998). Social identity and individual productivity within groups. *British Journal of Social Psychology*, 37, 389–413.

Wright, S. C. (1997). Ambiguity, social influence, and collective action: Generating collective protest in response to tokenism. *Personality and Social Psychology Bulletin*, 23, 1277–90.

Wright, S. S. & Forsyth, D. R. (1997). Group membership and collective identity: Consequences for self-esteem. *Journal of Social and Clinical Psychology,* 16, 43–56.

Wright, S. C., Taylor, D. M. & Moghaddam, F. M. (1990). Responding to membership in a disadvantaged group: From acceptance to collective protest. *Journal of Personality and Social Psychology,* 58, 994–1003.

Yang, K.-S. & Bond, M. H. (1980). Ethnic affirmation by Chinese bilinguals. *Journal of Cross-Cultural Psychology,* 11(4), 411–25.

Young, H. (1997). Social context and the processing of ingroup and outgroup information. Unpublished PhD dissertation, University of Nijmegen, The Netherlands.

Young, H., Van Knippenberg, A., Ellemers, N. & De Vries, N. K. (1997). The effects of group membership and social context on information organization. *European Journal of Social Psychology,* 27, 523–37.

Zander, A. & Armstrong, W. (1972). Working for group pride in a slipper factory. *Journal of Applied Social Psychology,* 2, 293–307.

Zimbardo, P. G. (1969). The human choice: Individuation, reason, and order vs. deindividuation, impulse and chaos. In W. J. Arnold & D. Levine (eds), *Nebraska Symposium on Motivation* (vol. 17). Lincoln: University of Nebraska Press.

Index